THEORIES OF SURPLUS VALUE

THEORIES OF
SURPLUS VALUE

By
KARL MARX

Selections

Translated from the German by
G. A. BONNER and EMILE BURNS

INTERNATIONAL PUBLISHERS
NEW YORK

CONTENTS

FOREWORD 9

A. THE PHYSIOCRATS AND SOME OF THEIR PREDECESSORS AND CONTEMPORARIES

1. SIR WILLIAM PETTY 15
2. CHARLES D'AVENANT 24
3. SIR DUDLEY NORTH AND JOHN LOCKE . . . 26
4. DAVID HUME AND JOHN MASSIE 34
5. SIR JAMES STEUART 40
6. THE GENERAL CHARACTER OF THE PHYSIOCRATIC SYSTEM 44
7. TURGOT 58
8. THE REPRODUCTION AND CIRCULATION OF THE TOTAL SOCIAL CAPITAL ACCORDING TO QUESNAY'S *TABLEAU ECONOMIQUE* 67

APPENDIX TO THE *TABLEAU ECONOMIQUE* . . 73
  (1) The First Two Circulation Movements of the *Tableau* 73
  (2) The Circulation between Landowner and Farmer 74
  (3) The Final Movements of Circulation . . 78
  (4) The Circulation between Capitalist and Worker 81
  (5) The Quantity of Money required for Circulation 87
  (6) Explanation of the Profit on Capital on the Ground that the Worker's Wage is advanced before the Commodity is sold . . . 97

B. ADAM SMITH AND THE CONCEPT OF PRODUCTIVE LABOUR

1. His Determination of Value by Labour . . 107

2. The Origin of Surplus Value 117
   (a) Profit 117
   (b) Land Rent 121
   (c) Interest on Capital 122
   (d) Taxes 124
   (e) Adam Smith's Advance beyond the Physio-
       crats 124
   (f) The Exchange of More Labour for Less
       Labour 126
   (g) Confusion of Surplus Value with Profit . 129

3. Capital and Landed Property as Sources of Value 134

4. The Analysis of Price into Wages, Profit and
   Rent 140

5. Productive and Unproductive Labour . . 148
   (a) Definition of Productive Labour as Labour
       which produces Capital 148
   (b) Definition of Productive Labour as Labour
       which produces Commodities . . . 154
   (c) The Polemic against Adam Smith's Definition 175
   (d) Appendix: The Concept of Productive Labour 177

C. DAVID RICARDO

I. Surplus Value and Profit

1. The Structure of Ricardo's Work . . . 201

2. Ricardo's Theory of Profit 208
   (a) Ricardo's Conception of Value . . . 208
   (b) Ricardo's Conception of Profit, Rate of
       Profit, Prices of Production, etc. . . . 211
   (c) Prices of Production and Market Prices . 245
       (i) Ricardo's Views 245
       (ii) Adam Smith's Views . . . 260

3. RICARDO'S CONCEPTION OF SURPLUS VALUE

   (a) Surplus Value and Profit 283
   (b) Quantity of Labour and Value of Labour . 295
   (c) Value of Labour Power and Value of Labour 301
   (d) Surplus Value 305
   (e) Relative Surplus Value 318

4. THE RATE OF PROFIT

   (a) Amount of Profit and Rate of Profit . . 329
   (b) Formation of the General Rate of Profit . 336

II. Accumulation of Capital and Crises

1. SIMPLE REPRODUCTION 343

2. TRANSFORMATION OF REVENUE INTO CAPITAL . . 351

3. TRANSFORMATION OF ACCUMULATED SURPLUS VALUE
   INTO VARIABLE AND CONSTANT CAPITAL . . 361

4. CRISES

   (a) Causes of Crises 368
   (b) Overproduction of Commodities and Over-
      abundance of Capital 373
   (c) Unity of Purchase and Sale, of the Process of
      Production and the Process of Circulation . 376
   (d) General and Partial Overproduction . . 391
   (e) Expansion of Production and Expansion of
      the Market 402

5. ACCUMULATION AND CONSUMPTION 415

INDEX 429

FOREWORD

In the preface to Volume I of *Capital* published in 1867, Marx speaks of projected further volumes, including a Book IV, "the history of the theory." After Marx's death, Engels prepared, from manuscripts left by Marx, Volumes II and III of *Capital* (published in 1885 and 1894). In his preface to Volume II, Engels notes that a considerable section of a manuscript written by Marx between 1861 and 1863 is entitled "Theories of Surplus Value," and continues: "This section contains an exhaustive critical history of the main point of political economy, the theory of surplus value. . . . I reserve for myself the privilege of publishing the critical part of the manuscript, after the elimination of the numerous parts covered by Volumes II and III [of *Capital*], in the form of Volume IV."

Engels was however unable to begin the preparation of this Volume IV before his death in 1895, and the task was undertaken by Karl Kautsky, who completed it between 1905 and 1910. But it was published as a separate work under the title of *Theorien über den Mehrwert* ("Theories of Surplus Value"), not as Volume IV of *Capital*.

It consists of a series of studies of economists who preceded Marx, with some essays on particular themes, and in the German edition runs to over 1,750 pages, arranged in three books as under:

I. Early Theories of Surplus Value up to Adam Smith.
II. David Ricardo.
III. From Ricardo to Vulgar Economics.

Kautsky's editing of Marx's manuscript has been criticised both for its arrangement of the various sections, which differs considerably from that of the manuscript, and for the omission of important passages. A new edition of the German text is therefore being prepared by the Marx-Engels-Lenin Institute in Moscow. Meanwhile it is desirable to make available to English readers a selection of those sections of the manuscript which are of most immediate interest and importance to us.

In the present volume, which is the first translation to appear in English, it has not been possible to publish more than the major part of Book I, covering mainly the Physiocrats and Adam Smith, and those parts of Book II which deal with Ricardo's views on surplus value and profit, and accumulation and crises, but omitting the treatment of rent (which is dealt with at some length in Volume III of *Capital*).

These sections are of special interest to British readers because of the detailed studies of Adam Smith and David Ricardo. Moreover, as in everything that Marx wrote, the subject directly handled is illuminated by comments showing the relation between the ideas which he is examining and the economic conditions of the period that gave birth to these ideas. In this sense these economic studies help to an understanding also of historical materialism.

Many of the still current arguments which seek to justify capitalist profits are merely refurbished versions of the old views critically examined by Marx in this work. And these old theories are not only examined and criticised. Marx shows the conditions in which they arose and which gave them some historical justification in the period of transition from the feudal to the capitalist order and in the early stages of capitalism. The repetition of these views to-day has no historical justification.

Marx notes that the "classical" economists, especially Adam Smith and Ricardo, attempted a scientific examination of the underlying laws of capitalist production, in contrast to the later, the "vulgar" economists, who are still with us today. It was of these that he wrote, in his preface to the second edition of Volume I of *Capital* (1873): "In place of disinterested enquirers, there were hired prize-fighters; in place of genuine scientific research, the bad conscience and the evil intent of apologetic."

Those who have already read *Capital* will find in these selections from *Theories of Surplus Value* new material of exceptional interest, both elaborating the ideas in *Capital* and showing how they were developed historically. Those who have not read *Capital* will find in them some of the principal points in Marx's economic theory, made all the easier to understand because of the criticism of the closely-related but inadequate views of the earlier economists.

An attempt has been made in the translation to adhere as closely as possible to the German original while making it readable in English. The difficulties are all the greater because the manuscript was never worked up by Marx for publication, and some passages are little more than notes for further elaboration. Passages and words interpolated in Marx's text by Kautsky for the sake of clarity are enclosed in square brackets; these are also used for interpolations by Marx in quotations from other writers.

Where Marx has quoted from other writers, the text has been taken from the editions to which he refers (or contemporary English translations). In the case of Adam Smith's *Wealth of Nations* and Ricardo's *The Principles of Political Economy and Taxation*, however, the current Everyman Library edition has been used as the most easily available to readers.

I have to thank Bertha Clark, W. N. Clark and P. Dance for their help at various stages, and Maurice Dobb for reading the proofs and making invaluable suggestions.

EMILE BURNS.

A. THE PHYSIOCRATS AND SOME OF THEIR PREDECESSORS AND CONTEMPORARIES

1. SIR WILLIAM PETTY

THE founder of modern political economy is Sir William Petty, one of the most gifted and original economic investigators. In his *Treatise of Taxes and Contributions*, London, 1662 (the edition here quoted is that of 1679), there are numerous passages dealing with the origin and determination of surplus value. They are somewhat confused and disconnected, but it is possible to sort out the leading ideas which run through all these scattered observations.

Petty distinguished between natural price and political price, "the true price Currant" (p. 66–7). By natural price he means in fact *value*, and it is only this that concerns us here, since it is on the determination of value that the determination of surplus value depends.

In this treatise he in fact determines the value of commodities by the comparative quantity of labour they contain.

> "But before we talk too much of Rents, we should endeavour to explain the mysterious nature of them, with reference as well to Money the rent of which we call Usury; as to that of Lands and Houses aforementioned" (p. 23).

What is at issue here is what causes the phenomena, not the phenomena themselves.

> "This, I say to be the foundation of equallising and ballancing of values; yet in the superstructures and practices hereupon, I confess there is much variety and intricacy" (p. 25).

The first question is: what is the value of a commodity?

> "If a man can bring to *London* an ounce of Silver out of the Earth in *Peru*, in the same time that he can produce a bushel of Corn, then one is the natural price of the other; now if by reason of new and more easie Mines a man can get two ounces of Silver as easily as formerly he did one, then Corn will be as cheap at ten shillings the bushel, as it was before at five shillings, *cæteris paribus*" (p. 31).

> "And let the production of a Bushel of this Corn be

supposed of equal labour to that of producing an ounce of Silver" (p. 66).

This is, to begin with, the "real and not an imaginary way of computing the prices of Commodities" (p. 66).[1]

The second point which has now to be examined is the value of labour:

"for then the Law that appoints such Wages were ill made, but which would allow the Labourer but just wherewithal to live; for if you allow double, then he works but half so much as he could have done, and otherwise would; which is a loss to the Publick of the fruit of so much labour" (page 64).

This passage is to be understood as follows: If the worker were to get for six hours' labour the value of six hours, he would get twice as much as he now gets when he is given the value of six hours' labour (for twelve hours' labour). He will then work only six hours.

The value of labour is therefore determined by the necessary means of subsistence. The worker is impelled to produce surplus value and to perform surplus labour only by the fact that he is forced to use the whole of the labour power within his capacity in order to get for himself just as much as he needs to live. The cheapness or dearness of his labour, however, is determined by two factors: natural productivity, and the standard of expenditure (needs) conditioned by the climate:

"Natural dearness and cheapness depends upon the few or more hands requisite to necessaries of Nature: As Corn is cheaper where one man produces Corn for ten, then where he can do the like but for six; and withal, according as the

---

[1] In Petty's *Political Anatomy of Ireland*, London, 1672 (the edition here quoted is that of 1682), he says however:

"Wherefore the days food of an adult Man, at a Medium, and not the days labour, is the common measure of Value, and seems to be as regular and constant as the value of fine Silver. . . . Wherefore I valued an *Irish* Cabbin at the number of days food, which the Maker spent in building of it" (p. 65).

This has quite a Physiocratic ring.

"That some Men will eat more than others, is not material, since by a days food we understand 1/100 part of what 100 of all Sorts and Sizes will eat, so as to Live, Labour, and Generate" (p. 64).

But what Petty seeks here in the Irish statistics is not the immanent measure of values, but the measure of values in the sense that money is a measure of values.

Climate disposes men to a necessity of spending more or less" (p. 67).

For Petty surplus value exists only in two forms: rent of land and rent of money (interest). He derives the latter from the former. For him, as later for the Physiocrats, the first form is the true form of surplus value. In his detailed presentation he describes rent (surplus) not only as the excess resulting from the amount of labour applied above the necessary labour, but also as the excess of the surplus labour of the producer himself over his wage and the replacement of his capital:

"Suppose a man could with his own hands plant a certain scope of Land with Corn, that is, could Digg, or Plough; Harrow, Weed, Reap, Carry home, Thresh, and Winnow so much as the Husbandry of this Land requires; and had withal Seed wherewith to sow the same. I say, that when this man hath subducted his seed out of the proceed of his Harvest,[1] and also what himself hath both eaten and given to others in exchange for Clothes, and other Natural necessaries; that the Remainder of Corn is the natural and true Rent of the Land for that year; and the *medium* of seven years, or rather of so many years as makes up the Cycle, within which Dearths and Plenties make their revolution, doth give the ordinary Rent of the Land in Corn" (pp. 23-4).

With Petty, therefore, since the value of the corn is determined by the labour time contained in it, and the rent is equal to the total product minus the wages and the seed, rent is in fact equal to the surplus product in which the surplus labour is materialised. Rent therefore includes profit; the latter is not yet separated from rent.

In the same ingenious way Petty goes on to ask:

"But a further, though collateral question may be, how much *English* money this Corn or Rent is worth; I answer so much as the money, which another single man can save, within the same time, over and above his expence, if he imployed himself wholly to produce and make it; *viz.* Let another man go travel into a Countrey where is Silver, there Dig it, Refine it, bring it to the same place where the other man planted his Corn; Coyne it, &c. the same person,

---

[1] That is, an equivalent for the constant capital.

all the while of his working for Silver, gathering also food for his necessary livelihood, and procuring himself covering, &c. I say, the Silver of the one must be esteemed of equal value with the Corn of the other: The one being perhaps twenty Ounces and the other twenty Bushels. From whence it follows that the price of a Bushel of this Corn to be an Ounce of Silver" (p. 24).

The difference in the kind of labour, Petty expressly notes, is here quite immaterial; all that matters is the labour time:

"And forasmuch as possibly there may be more Art and Hazard in working about the Silver, then about the Corn, yet all comes to the same pass; for let a hundred men work ten years upon Corn, and the same number of men the same time, upon Silver; I say, that the neat proceed of the Silver is the price of the whole neat proceed of the Corn, and like parts of the one, the price of like parts of the other" (p. 24).

After Petty has thus explained rent—which is here equivalent to the total surplus value including profit—and its expression in money, he then sets to work again very ably, on how the money value of land is determined:

"Wherefore we would be glad to find the natural values of the Fee simple of Land, though but no better then we have done that of the *usus fructus* above-mentioned, which we attempt as followeth.

"Having found the Rent or value of the *usus fructus per annum*, the question is, how many years purchase (as we usually say) is the Fee simple naturally worth? If we say an infinite number, then an acre of Land would be equal in value to a thousand acres of the same Land; which is absurd, an infinite of Unites being equal to an infinity of Thousands: wherefore we must pitch upon some limited number, and that I ap-prehend to be the number of years, which I conceive one man of fifty years old, another of twenty eight, and another of seven years old, all being alive together may be thought to live; that is to say, of a Grandfather, Father and Child, few men having reason to take care of more remote Posterity: for if a man be a great Grandfather, he himself is so much the nearer his end, so as there are but three in a continual line of descent usually co-existing together: and as some are Grandfathers at forty years, yet as many are not till above sixty, and *sic de cæteris*.

"Wherefore I pitch the number of years purchase, that any Land is naturally worth, to be the ordinary extent of three such persons their lives. Now in *England* we esteem three lives equal to one and twenty years, and consequently the value of Land, to be about the same number of years purchase" (pp. 26–7).

Having resolved rent into surplus labour and therefore surplus value, Petty explains that the value of land is nothing but the capitalised rent—that is, a certain sum of yearly rentals or the sum of rents during a certain number of years.

In fact, rent is capitalised and reckoned as the value of the land in the following way:

Let 1 acre yield an annual rent of £10. If the rate of interest is 5 per cent., then £10 represents the interest on a capital of £200, and since at 5 per cent. the interest replaces the capital in twenty years the value of the acre would be equal to £200 (20×10). The capitalisation of the rent therefore depends on the rate of interest. If the rate of interest is 10 per cent., then the rent represents the interest on a capital of £100 or the sum of ten years' rentals. Since however Petty starts with land-rent as the general form of surplus value and includes profit therein, he cannot take interest on capital for granted, but must rather arrive at it as a special form of rent. Petty handles this just as Turgot—consistently from his own standpoint—also does. In what way then is he to determine the sum of the yearly rentals, which constitutes the value of the land? A man has an interest in buying as many yearly rentals as he reckons years of life for himself and his immediate successors—that is, as long as an average man, grandfather, father and child live. This is about 21 years according to the "English" computation. Therefore, whatever lies beyond the 21 years *usus fructus* has no value for him. He therefore pays for the usufruct for 21 years, and this constitutes the value of the land. In this subtle way he gets himself out of the difficulty; but he has not got rid of the important facts:—

Firstly, that rent, as the expression of the total agricultural surplus value, is derived not from land but from labour, and is the excess of labour over and above what is necessary for the subsistence of the worker.

Secondly, that the value of the land is nothing but the rent purchased in advance for a certain number of years—a transmuted form of rent itself, in which, for example, 21 years' surplus value (or surplus labour) appears as the value of the land; in short, that the value of land is nothing but capitalised rent.

Such is Petty's deep insight into the matter.

From the point of view of the purchaser of rent (that is, of land) rent appears merely as the interest on his capital, and in this form rent has become completely unrecognisable and seems to be interest on capital.

After Petty has thus determined the value of land and the value of the yearly rental, he is able to derive from the rent of land money rent or usury as a secondary form:

> "As for Usury, the least that can be, is the Rent of so much Land as the Money lent will buy, where the Security is undoubted" (p. 28).

Here interest appears to be determined by the price of rent, while conversely the price of rent or the purchase-value of the land is determined by interest. But this is quite consistent, since rent is presented as the general form of surplus value, and interest on money must therefore be derived from it as a secondary form.[1]

*   *   *

[With the extracts from the *Treatise of Taxes and Contributions* quoted above should be compared certain passages from Petty's *Political Arithmetick*, London, 1690 (the edition here quoted is that of 1699) which also show an appreciation of surplus value, although admittedly here also it is treated only in the form of land-rent.]

These passages are as follows:

> "As Trades and curious Arts increase; so the Trade of Husbandry will decrease, or else the Wages of Husbandmen

---

[1] Petty says of the fixing by Law of the rate of interest: "But of the vanity and fruitlessness of making Civil Positive Laws against the Laws of Nature" (that is, against the laws corresponding to the nature of bourgeois society) "I have spoken elsewhere" (p. 29).

must rise, and consequently the Rents of Land must fall."

"If Trade and Manufacture have increased in *England* (that is to say) if a greater part of the People, apply themselves to those Faculties, than there did heretofore, and if the price of Corn be no greater now, than when Husbandmen were more numerous, and Tradesmen fewer; it follows from that single reason . . . that the Rents of Land must fall; As for Example, suppose the price of Wheat be 5*s*. or 60*d*. the Bushel; now if the Rent of that Land whereon it grows be the third Sheaf; then of the 60*d*. 20*d*. is for the *Land*, and 40*d*. for the *Husbandman*; but if the Husbandman's Wages should rise one eighth part, or from 8*d*. to 9*d*. *per Diem*, then the Husbandman's share in the Bushel of Wheat, rises from 40*d*. to 45*d*. and consequently the Rent of the Land must fall from 20*d*. to 15*d*. for we suppose the price of the Wheat still remains the same; especially since we cannot raise it, for if we did attempt it, Corn would be brought in to us, (as into *Holland*) from Foreign Parts, where the State of Husbandry was not changed" (*Political Arithmetick*, London, 1699 (pp. 193–4).

*   *   *

In Petty is also to be found the first conception of differential rent. He derives it not from the different fertility of pieces of land of the same size, but from the different location, the different distance from the market of pieces of land of equal fertility, which, as is known, is one element in differential rent. He says:

"As great need of Money heightens Exchange [interest], so doth great need of Corn raise the price of that likewise, and consequently of the Rent of the Land that bears Corn,[1] and lastly of the Land it self; as for example, if the Corn which feedeth *London*, or an Army, be brought forty miles together, then the Corn growing within a mile of *London*, or the quarters of such Army, shall have added unto its natural price, so much as the charge of bringing it thirty nine miles doth amount unto: . . .

"Hence it comes to pass, that Lands intrinsically alike near populous places, such as were the Perimeter of the

---

[1] Here therefore he says explicitly that the price of corn determines rent, it being implicit in the earlier analysis that rent does not determine the value of corn.

Area that feeds them is great, will not only yield more Rent for these Reasons, but also more years purchase than in remote places, by reason of the pleasure and honour extraordinary of having Lands there" (p. 29).

Petty also makes mention of the second cause of differential rent—the differing fertility of land and therefore the differing productivity of labour on equal areas of land:

"The goodness or badness, or the value of Land depends upon the greater or lesser share of the product given for it in proportion to the simple labour bestowed to raise the said Product" (p. 67).

Petty's exposition of differential rent is therefore superior to that of Adam Smith.

In regard to land-rent the following passage, which treats surplus value as the consequence of greater productivity of labour, is also of importance:

"Or if the said Shires by greater labour than now is used, (as by Digging instead of Ploughing, Setting instead of Sowing, picking of choice Seed instead of taking it promiscuously, steeping it instead of using it wholly unprepared, and manuring the ground with Salt instead of rotten Straw, &c.) could be fertilized, then will the Rent be as much more advanced, as the excess of encrease exceeds that of the labour" (p. 32).

By increased labour is here meant the increased price or wages of labour. From the *Treatise of Taxes and Contributions* the following should also be noted:

1. Petty's idea of total production is shown in the passage:

"For if there be 1000 men in a Territory, and if 100 of these can raise necessary food and rayment for the whole 1000; if 200 more make as much Commodities as other Nations will give either their Commodities or Money for, and if 400 more be imployed in the Ornaments, pleasure, and magnificence of the whole? if there be 200 Governours, Divines, Lawyers, Physicians, Merchants, and Retailers, making in all 900, the question is, since there is food enough for this supernumary 100 also, how they should come by it? whether by begging, or by stealing" (p. 12).

2. Petty is much preoccupied with "the natural par" between land and labour:

"Our Silver and Gold we call by several names, as in *England* by Pounds, Shillings, and Pence; all which may be called and understood by either of the three. But that which I would say upon this matter is, that all things ought to be valued by two natural Denominations, which is Land and Labour; that is, we ought to say, a Ship or Garment is worth such a measure of Land, with such another measure of Labour; forasmuch as both Ships and Garments were the Creatures of Lands and mens Labours thereupon: This being true, we should be glad to find out a natural Par between Land and Labour, so as we might express the value by either of them alone, as well or better than by both, and reduce one into the other, as easily and certainly, as we reduce Pence into Pounds" (p. 25).[1]

For this reason Petty seeks the true value of land, after he has found its monetary expression in rent.

He uses three measures of value, which run confusedly through his writings:

(*a*) The magnitude of value, which is determined by equal labour time, labour being here regarded as the source of value.

(*b*) Value as the form of social labour. From this standpoint money appears as the true crystallisation of value, although in another passage Petty rejects all the illusions of the monetary system.

(*c*) Labour as the source of exchange value is confused with labour as the source of use value; labour here presupposes material provided by nature (land). In reality, he cuts across the "natural par" between land and labour by describing the price of land as capitalised rent—therefore not treating land as material provided by nature to which concrete labour is applied.

---

[1] So also he says in his *Political Anatomy of Ireland*: "And this brings me to the most important Consideration in Political Oeconomies *viz.* how to make a *Par* and Equation between Lands and Labour, so as to express the Value of any thing by either alone" (p. 63). In fact, the root problem here is only to reduce the value of land itself to labour.

2. CHARLES D'AVENANT

THE following passages from D'Avenant are not uncharacteristic of the ideas of surplus value put forward by the Mercantilists:

"For 'tis the Exportation of our own Product that must make *England* rich; to be Gainers in the Ballance of Trade, we must carry out of our own Product, what will purchase the Things of Foreign Growth that are needful for own Consumption, with some Overplus either in Bullion or Goods to be sold in other Countries; which Overplus is the Profit a Nation makes by Trade, and it is more or less according to the natural Frugality of the People that Export,[1] or as from the low Price of Labour and Manufacture they can afford the Commodity cheap, and at a rate not to be undersold in Foreign Markets" (D'Avenant, *An essay upon the probable methods of making a people gainers in the balance of trade etc.*, London, 1699, pp. 45–46).

"By what is Consum'd at Home, one loseth only what another gets, and the Nation in General is not at all the Richer; but all Foreign Consumption is a clear and certain Profit," says D'Avenant in his *Essay on the East India trade* (London, 1697, p. 31).[2]

This work, which was printed with D'Avenant's *Discourses on the Publick Revenues and on the Trade of England* (London, 1698), is not the same as the *Considerations on the East India Trade* (1701) quoted by McCulloch.

Incidentally, one must not think of these mercantilists as so stupid as they were subsequently made out to be by the vulgar free traders.

In the second volume of the *Discourses on the Publick Revenues* just mentioned, D'Avenant says *inter alia*:

[1] A frugality which the Dutch but not the English possess, as D'Avenant further explains in the work here quoted.

[2] [The same view is expressed in another work on the East India Trade:] "Trade confined amongst ourselves, procures little advantage to the Kingdom; no more than the buying and selling of Land, one hath more, and another hath less; the Owners are changed but the Land is still the same. It is Foreign Trade, that is the great Interest and Concern of the Kingdom" (*The East India Trade a Most Profitable Trade to the Kingdom etc.*, London, 1677).

"Gold and Silver are indeed the Measure of Trade, but the Spring and Original of it, in all Nations, is the Natural, or Artificial Product of the Country, that is to say, what their Land, or what their Labour and Industry produces. And this is so true, that a Nation may be suppos'd, by some Accident, quite without the Species of Money, and yet, if the People are numerous, industrous, vers'd in Traffick, skill'd in Sea-Affairs, and if they have good Ports, and a Soil fertile in variety of Commodities, such a People will have Trade, and gather Wealth, and, they shall quickly get among 'em, a plenty of Gold and Silver: So that the real and effective Riches of a Country, is its Native Product" (p. 15). "Gold and Silver are so far from being . . . *the only Things that deserve the Name of Treasure, or the Riches of a Nation*, that in truth, Money is at Bottom no more than the Counters with which Men in their dealings have been accustom'd to reckon" (p. 16). "We understand that to be Wealth, which maintains the Prince, and the general Body of his People, in Plenty, Ease and Safety. We esteem that to be Treasure which for the use of Man has been converted from Gold and Silver, into Buildings, and Improvements of the Country; As also other Things convertible into those Metals, as the Fruits of the Earth, Manufactures, or Foreign Commodities, and stock of Shipping . . . but even perishable Goods, may be held *the Riches of a Nation*, if they are convertible, *tho' not converted into Gold and Silver*; and this we believe does not only hold between *Man and Man*, as he talks of, but between one Country and another" (pp. 60–1). "And the Common People being the Stomach of the Body Politick." (In Spain this stomach did not accept the money in seemly fashion, and did not digest it.) "Trade and Manufactures are the only Mediums by which such a digestion and distribution of Gold and Silver can be made, as will be Nutritive to the Body Politick" (pp. 62, 63).

3. SIR DUDLEY NORTH AND JOHN LOCKE

COMPARISON of the works of North and Locke with Petty's *Quantulumcunque concerning money* (1682), *A Treatise of Taxes and Contributions* (1662) and *The Political Anatomy of Ireland* (1672) shows their indebtedness to Petty, especially his views on the regulation of the rate of interest and the debasement of money, etc. Their works are directly linked with Petty's writings and are based on them.

North and Locke wrote the works which we deal with here at the same time, and prompted by the same occasion. Locke's *Some considerations of the consequences of the lowering of interest, and raising the value of money* appeared in London in 1691, and in the same year North published his *Discourses upon Trade* (London). They represent however opposing standpoints. For Locke, the shortage of money is responsible for the high rate of interest. North shows on the contrary that it is not shortage of money but of capital or revenue [which keeps up the rate of interest]. A definite conception of "stock" or capital, or rather of money as a pure form of capital, in so far as it is not means of circulation, appears for the first time in his writings. And Sir Dudley North develops the first correct conception of interest, in opposition to Locke's.

*　　　*　　　*

Taking Locke's theory of labour together with his theory of the origin of interest and rent—for in his writings surplus value appears only in these specific forms—surplus value is nothing other than the labour of another person, surplus labour, which land and capital—the conditions of labour—enable their possessors to appropriate. And the ownership of a greater quantity of means of production than one person can put to use with his own labour is, according to Locke, a *political* device which contradicts the law of nature on which property or the right to private property is founded.

The relevant passages are as follows:

"Though the earth, and all inferior creatures, be common to all men, yet every man has a property in his own person: this no body has any right to but himself. The labour of his body, and the work of his hands, we may say, are properly his. Whatsoever then he removes out of the state that nature hath provided, and left it in, he hath mixed his labour with, and joined to it something that is his own, and thereby makes it his property" (*Of Civil Government*, Book II, ch. V, *Works*, ed. 1768, II, p. 229). "His labour hath taken it out of the hands of nature, where it was common and belonged equally to all her children, and hath thereby appropriated it to himself" (p. 230). "The same law of nature, that does by this means give us property, does also bound that property too. . . . As much as any one can make use of to any advantage of life before it spoils, so much he may by his labour fix a property in: whatever is beyond this, is more than his share, and belongs to others" (p. 230). "But the chief matter of property being now not the fruits of the earth, and the beasts that subsist on it, but the earth itself . . . I think it is plain, that property in that too is acquired as the former. As much land as a man tills, plants, improves, cultivates, and can use the product of, so much is his property. He by his labour does, as it were inclose it from the common" (p. 230). "And hence subduing or cultivating the earth, and having dominion, we see are joined together" (p. 231). "The measure of property nature has well set by the extent of men's labour and the conveniencies of life: no man's labour could subdue, or appropriate all; nor could his enjoyment consume more than a small part; so that it was impossible for any man, this way, to intrench upon the right of another, or acquire to himself a property, to the prejudice of his neighbour. . . . This measure did confine every man's possession to a very moderate proportion, and such as he might appropriate to himself, without injury to any body, in the first ages of the world. . . . And the same measure may be allowed still without prejudice to any body, as full as the world seems" (pp. 231–2).

Labour bestows on objects almost their whole value ("value" is here equivalent to use value, and labour is taken as concrete labour, not as a quantum; but the measuring of exchange value by labour is in reality based on the fact that labour creates use value). The remainder of the use value which cannot be resolved into labour is the gift of nature and hence in its essence common property. What Locke therefore seeks to prove is not the contrary, namely, that property can be acquired in other ways than by labour, but how, in spite of the common property provided by nature, individual property has been created by individual labour.

"For it is labour that puts the difference of value on every thing . . . of the products of the earth useful to the life of man, nine tenths are the effect of labour" (p. 234). "It is labour then which puts the greatest part of the value upon land" (p. 235). "Though the things of nature are given in common, yet man, by being master of himself, and proprietor of his own person, and the actions of labour of it, had still in himself the great foundation of property" (p. 235).

One limit to property is therefore the limit of personal labour; the other limit is that a man does not accumulate more things than he can use. The latter limit however is extended, apart from other exchanges, by the exchange of perishable products for [a less perishable product such as gold, silver, diamonds, etc., for] money.

"He might heap up as much of these durable things as he pleased; the exceeding of the bounds of his just property[1] not lying in the largeness of his possession, but the perishing of any thing uselessly in it. And thus came in the use of money, some lasting thing that men might keep without spoiling and that by mutual consent men would take in exchange for the truly useful, but perishable supports of life" (p. 236).

Thus arises the inequality of individual property, though the limit of personal labour remains.

"This partage of things in an inequality of private possessions, men have made practicable out of the bounds of society, and without compact; only by putting a value on gold and silver, and tacitly agreeing in the use of money" (p. 237).

[1] Apart from the limits set by his personal labour.

We must now compare with this the following passage from Locke's work on interest, not forgetting that according to him natural law makes personal labour the limit of property.

"Let us next see how it comes to be of the same nature with land, by yielding a certain yearly income, which we call use, or interest. For land produces naturally something new and profitable, and of value to mankind; but money is a barren thing, and produces nothing, but by compact transfers *that profit, that was the reward of one man's labour, into another man's pocket.* That, which occasions this, is the unequal distribution of money; which inequality has the same effect too upon land, that it has upon money. . . . For as the unequal distribution of land, (you having more than you can or will manure, and another less) brings you a tenant for your Land; and the same unequal distribution of money . . . brings me a tenant for my money: so my money is apt in trade, *by the industry of the borrower*, to produce more than six per cent to the borrower, as well as your land, *by the labour of the tenant*, is apt to produce more fruits, than his rent comes to" (*Some Considerations of the Consequences of the lowering of Interest, and raising the Value of Money*, Folio edn. of Locke's Works, 1740, Vol. II, p. 19).

In this passage Locke is partly concerned to polemise against landed property, by showing that rent differs in no way from usury. Both however "transfer that profit, that was the reward of one man's labour, into another man's pocket," through the unequal distribution of the means of production.

Locke's analysis is all the more important since he is the classical exponent of bourgeois society's ideas of right in opposition to the feudal, and his philosophy moreover served all subsequent English economists as the foundation for all their ideas.

*   *   *

In his *Discourses upon Trade etc.* Sir Dudley North is chiefly concerned with commercial capital; so far as this is so the work is not relevant here, though it shows masterly skill in the field with which it deals. It is particularly remarkable that from the time of the Restoration of Charles II up to the middle of the eighteenth century continual complaints were voiced by the landlords over the fall in rentals; following the steady decline from ?[1] onwards in the price of wheat. Although the industrial capitalist class was very much concerned in the compulsory reduction in the rate of interest (according to Culpepper and Sir J. Child), the real protagonists of these measures were the landowners. The value of land and how to raise it were made matters of national concern; just as on the other hand from about 1760 the rise in rents, in the value of land and in the price of corn and other means of subsistence, along with the complaints of the industrialists against these increases, form the basis of the economic investigations into this subject.

With few exceptions it is the struggle between "moneyed interest" and "landed interest" which fills the century from 1650 to 1750, as the nobility, who lived in the grand style, observed with disgust how the usurers were devouring them, and, with the building up of the modern credit system and the National Debt from the end of the seventeenth century, lording it over them in legislation, etc.

Already *Petty* speaks of the landowners' complaints over the fall in rents in spite of land improvements. He defends the usurer against the landlord, and puts money-rent and land-rent on the same footing.

Locke reduces both to the exploitation of labour. He takes the same standpoint as Petty. Both attack the compulsory regulation of interest. The landowners had noticed that when the rate of interest fell the value of land rose. At a given level of rents, the *capitalised expression* of this level, that is, the value of land, falls or rises in inverse relation to the rate of interest.

The third writer to follow this line of Petty's is *Sir Dudley North*, in the work referred to above.

This is the first form in which *capital* gets up on its hind legs against *landed property*, as in fact the *usurer* was a principal agent in the accumulation of capital, that is, through the share he took in the revenues of the landowners. But industrial and commercial capital go more or less hand in hand with the landowners against this antiquated form of capital.

---

[1] The question mark is in the original text. What is intended is probably the year 1662, when the quarter of wheat cost 74s., a price it never reached again for another hundred years.—*K.*

"But as the Landed Man letts his Land, so these still lett their Stock" (who possess stock in trade but lack the necessary skill, or shirk the trouble to employ it in trade) "this latter is call'd Interest, but is only Rent for Stock, as the other is for Land.[1] And in several Languages, hiring of Money, and Lands, are Terms of common use; and it is also in some Countries in *England*. Thus to be a Landlord, or a Stock-lord is the same thing; the Landlord hath the advantage only in this: That his Tenant cannot carry away the Land, as the Tenant of the other may the Stock; and therefore Land ought to yield less profit than Stock, which is let out at the greater hazard" (p. 4).

Interest: North seems to have been the first to get a correct notion of interest, since by stock, as will be seen from the passage about to be quoted, he means not only money but capital, while Petty also distinguishes between stock and money. According to Locke, interest is exclusively determined by the quantity of money; this is also Petty's view.

"So if there be more Lenders than Borrowers, Interest will also fall; wherefore it is not low Interest makes Trade, but Trade increasing, the Stock of the Nation makes Interest low" (p. 4).
"Gold and Silver, and, out of them, Money are nothing but the Weights and Measures, by which Traffick is more conveniently carried on, than could be done without them: and also a proper Fund for a surplusage of Stock to be deposited in" (p. 16).

Price and Money: Price is nothing but the equivalent of the commodity expressed in money—and, when it is a question of sale, realised in money—and thus the presentation of the commodity as an exchange-value, so that it can then be again transformed into a use-value. In this passage we have one of the earliest recognitions of the fact that in this connection what matters is gold and silver as a mere form of existence of the exchange-value of the commodity itself, a phase in its metamorphosis and not gold and silver as such. North puts this very felicitously for his time.

[1] Here, as also in Petty's writings, it can be seen that in the transition from the Middle Ages to modern times rent was regarded as the original form of surplus value.

"What do these People want, who cry out for Money? I will begin with the Beggar; he wants, and importunes for Money: What would he do with it if he had it? buy Bread etc. Then in truth it is not Money, but Bread, and other Necessaries for Life that he wants. Well then, the Farmer complains, for the Want of Money: surely it is not for the Beggar's Reason, to sustain Life, or pay Debts; but he thinks that were more Money in the Country, he should have a Price for his Goods. Then it seems Money is not his want, but a Price for his Corn, and Cattle, which he would sell but cannot" (pp. 11–12).

This lack of buyers can arise from three causes, either from an excessive production of corn and cattle, or from a disappearance of the usual outlets for exports, as in time of war, or finally from an insufficient consumption as a result of too great poverty on the part of the consumers.

The same holds good for merchants and retailers. "Money being thus the Common Measure of Buying and Selling, every body who hath any thing to sell, and cannot procure Chapmen for it, is presently apt to think, that want of Money in the Kingdom, or Country is the cause why his Goods do not go off: and so, want of Money, is the common cry; which is a great mistake" (p. 11).

Capital is self-expanding value, while in the formation of a hoard the aim is the crystallised form of exchange value as such. One of the earliest discoveries of the classical economists is therefore the antithesis between the *formation of a hoard* and *the utilisation of money to make profit*, that is, the exposition of *money as capital*.

"No man is richer for having his Estate all in Money, Plate, &c. lying by him, but on the contrary, he is for that reason the poorer. That man is richest, whose Estate is in a growing condition, either in Land at Farm, Money at Interest, or Goods in Trade" (p. 11).[1] "Altho every one desires to have it, yet none, or very few care for keeping it, but they are forthwith contriving to dispose it; knowing

[1] Similarly, John Bellers, in *Essays about the Poor, Manufactures, Trade Plantations, & Immorality etc.*, London, 1699, says: "Money neither increaseth, nor is useful, but when it's parted with, and as Money is unprofitable to a private Person but as he disposeth of it, for something more valuable, so what Money is more than of absolute necessity for a home Trade, is dead Stock to a Kingdom or Nation and brings no profit to that Country it's kept in" (p. 13).

that from all the Money that lies dead, no benefit is to be expected, but it is a certain loss" (p. 21).

Money as world money:

"A Nation in the World, as to Trade, is in all respects like a City in a Kingdom, or Family in a City" (p. 14). "In this course of Trade, Gold and Silver are in no sort different from other Commodities, but are taken from them who have Plenty, and carried to them who want, or desire them" (p. 13).

The quantity of money that can circulate is determined by the exchange of commodities.

"And if never so much be brought from abroad, or never so much coyned at home, all that is more than what the Commerce of the Nation requires, is but Bullion, and will be treated as such; and coyned Money, like wrought Plate at second hand, shall sell but for the Intrinsick" (pp. 17–18).

Landed Property and Trade:

"The Moneys imployed at Interest in this Nation, are not near the Tenth part, disposed to Trading People, wherewith to manage their Trades; but are for the most part lent for the supplying of Luxury, and to support the Expence of Persons, who though great Owners of Lands, yet spend faster than their Lands bring in; and being loath to sell, choose rather to mortgage their Estates" (pp. 6, 7).

4. DAVID HUME AND JOHN MASSIE

MASSIE's anonymous work, *An Essay on the governing causes of the natural rate of interest; wherein the sentiments of Sir William Petty and Mr. Locke, on that head, are considered*, appeared in 1750. The second part of Hume's *Essays*, in which the one "On Interest" occurs, appeared in 1752, two years later. Massie therefore has priority. Hume attacks Locke only, but Massie attacks both Petty and Locke, both of whom still held the view that the height of the rate of interest depends on the quantity of money, and that in fact what is really lent is money (not capital).

Massie, more decisively than Hume, laid down that interest is a mere part of profit.

Let us begin with the latter.

[In his *Essays*, with which we are dealing here, the following passage is noteworthy]: "Every thing in the world is purchased by labour" (*Essays*), 2nd edn., London, 1764, I, p. 289).

[Land rent also appears in Hume's work as the original form of surplus value, interest on capital as the second form. Land rent arises, in his view, through the exclusion of large sections of the population from the ownership of land.

"The political authorities and the population of a nation breed of necessity inequality in private property, because in every law-abiding and numerous community, a part of the inhabitants possess a large extent of the land, while others are owners of only very small portions, and others are deprived of any property at all. Those who possess more land than they can cultivate, share it with those who have none, on the condition that the cultivators give them a portion of the harvest. It is in this way that there is established what one can call interest on land, to contrast it with interest on money, and it exists in the case of even the least civilised of peoples."]

The height of the rate of interest depends on the demand on the part of the borrowers and the supply on the part of the lenders, or in other words on demand (for) and supply (of) money-capital. But essentially it depends on the level of profit "arising from commerce" (*Essays*, London, 1764, p. 329).

"The greater or less stock of labour and commodities must have a great influence; since we really and in effect borrow these, when we take money upon interest" (p. 337).

"No man will accept of low profits, where he can have high interest; and no man will accept of low interest, where he can have high profits" (p. 335).

A higher interest rate and a higher profit are both the expression of the slow progress of trade and industry, and not of the rarity of gold and silver; and a lower interest rate indicates the opposite, [for "High interest arises from three circumstances: a great demand for borrowing; little riches to supply that demand: and great profits arising from commerce"] (p. 329).

"In a state, therefore, where there is nothing but a landed interest" (or, as he later says, landed gentry and peasants) "the borrowers must be very numerous, and the rate of interest must hold proportion to it" (p. 330); because wealth which is only for enjoyment is driven by boredom to seek pleasures, while on the other hand production, except for agriculture, is very restricted. The opposite takes place as soon as trade has developed. The lust for gain entirely dominates the merchant. He "knows no such pleasure as that of seeing the daily increase of his fortune.[1] And this is the reason why trade increases frugality, and why, among merchants, there is the same overplus of misers above prodigals, as, among the possessors of land, there is the contrary" (p. 333).

"An increase of commerce, by a necessary consequence, raises a great number of lenders, and by that means produces a lowness of interest" (p. 334).

"Low interest and low profits of merchandize are two events, that mutually forward each other, and are both originally derived from that extensive commerce, which produces opulent merchants, and renders the monied interest considerable. Where merchants possess great stocks, whether represented by few or many pieces of metal, it

---

[1] The lust for exchange-value, abstract wealth, is here far greater than that for use-values.

must frequently happen, that when they either become tired of business, or have heirs unwilling or unfit to engage in commerce, a great deal of these riches naturally seeks an annual and secure revenue. The plenty diminishes the price, and makes the lenders accept of a low interest. This consideration obliges many to keep their stocks in trade, and rather be content with low profits than dispose of their money at an under value. On the other hand, when commerce has become very extensive, and employs very large stocks, there must arise rivalships among the merchants, which diminish the profits of trade, at the same time that they increase the trade itself. The low profits of merchandize induce the merchants to accept more willingly of a low interest, when they leave off business, and begin to indulge themselves in ease and indolence. It is needless, therefore, to enquire which of these circumstances, *viz. low interests or low profits*, is the cause, and which the effect? They both arise from an extensive commerce, and mutually forward each other. . . . An extensive commerce, by producing large stocks, diminishes both interests and profits; and is always assisted in its diminution of the one, by the proportional sinking of the other. I may add, that as low profits arise from the increase of commerce and industry, they serve in their turn to the further increase of commerce, by rendering the commodities cheaper, encouraging the consumption, and heightening the industry. And thus, if we consider the whole connection of causes and effects, interest is the true barometer of the state, and its lowness is a sign almost infallible of the flourishing of a people" (pp. 334-6).

*   *   *

[The following passages from his anonymous work mentioned above are typical of Massie's views:]

"It appears from these several Extracts, that Mr. *Locke* attributes the Government of the Natural Rate of Interest to the Proportion which the Quantity of Money in a Country bears to the Debts of its Inhabitants one amongst another, and to the Trade of it; and that Sir *William Petty* makes it depend on the Quantity of Money alone" (pp. 14-15). Rich People "instead of employing their Money themselves, must let it out to other People for them to make Profit of, reserving for the Owners a Proportion of the Profits so made:

But when the Riches of a Country are dispersed into so many Hands, and so equally divided, as not to leave many People enough to maintain two Families, by employing it in Trade, there can be little borrowing; for £20,000 when it belongs to one Man, may be lent, because the Interest of it will keep a Family, but if it belongs to ten Men, it cannot be lent, because the Interest of it will not keep ten Families" (pp. 23-4).

"All Reasoning about natural Interest from the Rate which the Government pays for Money, is, and unavoidably must be fallacious; Experience has shown us, they neither have agreed, nor preserved a Correspondence with each other; and Reason tells us they never can; for the one has its Foundation in Profit, and the other in Necessity, the former of which has Bounds, but the latter none: The Gentleman who borrows Money to improve his Land, and the Merchant or Tradesman who borrow to carry on Trade, have Limits beyond which they will not go; if they can get 10 *per Cent.* by Money, they may give 5 *per Cent.* for it; but they will not give 10; whereas he who borrows through Necessity, has nothing else to determine by, and this admits of no Rule at all; the Law cannot govern where it prevails; for if it could, the Government would never have gone beyond the Rule which is prescribed for private Men; but Necessity, whether publick or private, has no Law" (pp. 31-2).

"The Equitableness of taking Interest, depends not upon a Man's making or not making Profit by what he borrows, but upon its being capable of producing Profit if rightly employed" (p. 49).

"If that which Men pay as Interest for the Use of what they borrow, be a Part of the Profits it is capable of producing, this Interest must always be govern'd by those Profits" (p. 49).

"What Proportion of these Profits do of Right belong to the Borrower, and what to the Lender; and this there is no other Method of determining, then by the Opinions of Borrowers and Lenders in General; for Right and Wrong in this Respect, are only what common Consent makes so" (p. 49).

"This Rule of dividing Profits is not however to be apply'd particularly to every Lender and Borrower, but to Lenders and Borrowers in general . . . remarkably great and small Gains are the Rewards of Skill, and the Want of Understanding, which Lenders have nothing at all to do with; for as they will not suffer by the one, they ought not to benefit by the other. What has been said of particular Men in the same Business is applicable to particular Sorts of Business" (pp. 50-1).

"The natural Rate of Interest is governed by the Profits of Trade to Particulars" (p. 51).

Why then does the rate of interest in England to-day amount to only 4 per cent. instead of 8 per cent. as it was earlier? Because English merchants at that time "were making double the Profit that they are making now."

Why is the rate of interest 3 per cent. in Holland, 5 and 6 in France, Germany, Portugal, 9 per cent. in the West and the East Indies and 12 per cent. in Turkey?

"One general Answer will do for the whole, which is, that the Profits of Trade in these several Countries differ from the Profits of Trade here, and so much as to produce all these different Rates of Interest" (p. 51).

But whence comes the fall in profits? From competition, both abroad and at home.

"Owing either to an Increase of Traders or a Decrease of Trade,[1] or to People in Trade lowering the Prices of their Commodities upon each other; . . . whether it be through Necessity to get some Trade, or through Avarice to get most" (pp. 52-3).

"The Profits of Trade in general, are governed by the Proportion which the Number of Traders bears to the Quantity of Trade" (p. 55).

In Holland, where the "Number of People employ'd in Trade, bears the greatest Proportion to the whole number of Inhabitants, . . . Interest is the lowest." In France, where the greatest proportion is the opposite, the rate of interest is highest (pp. 55-6).

"What governs the Proportion between Trade and Traders?" (p. 57).

[1] As a result of foreign competition.

"The Causes which govern the Proportion between Trade and Traders.

I   Natural Necessity.
II   Liberty.
III The Preservation of Men's Private Rights.
IV   Publick Safety" (p. 58).

"There are no two Countries which furnish an equal Number of the Necessaries of Life in equal Plenty, and with the same Quantity of Labour; and that Mens Wants increase or diminish with the Severity or Temperateness of the Climate they live in; And consequently, the Proportion of Trade which the Inhabitants of different Countries are obliged to carry on through Necessity, cannot be the same, nor is it practicable to ascertain the Degree of Variation further than by the Degrees of Heat and Cold; from whence one may make this general Conclusion, that the Quantity of Labour required for the Maintenance of a certain Number of People is greatest in cold Climates, and least in hot Ones; for in the former, Men not only want more Cloaths, but the Earth more cultivating, than in the latter" (p. 59).

"One kind of Necessity" (of Trade) "which is peculiar to *Holland*, and this arises from the Country being over-peopled; which, with the great Labour required to fence and drain their Land, makes their Necessity to trade greater than it is in any other Part of the habitable World" (p. 60).

Even more definitely than Hume, Massie presents interest as a mere part of profit. Both attribute the fall in interest rates to the accumulation of capitals (Massie specially mentions saving), and the fall in profits resulting therefrom. Both say equally little about the origin of commercial profit itself.

5. SIR JAMES STEUART

ALL economists share the error of not considering surplus value as such in its pure form, but in the specific forms of profit and rent. The theoretical errors that must necessarily arise from this will be shown later, in the analysis of the great change in form assumed by surplus value as profit.

Before the Physiocrats, surplus value—that is, profit, in the form of profit—was explained purely by *exchange*, the sale of the commodity above its value. On the whole *Sir James Steuart* did not get beyond this shallow view; he must rather be regarded as the man who reproduced it in scientific form. I say "scientific", for Steuart does not share the illusion that the surplus value which accrues to the individual capitalist when he sells the commodity above its value is the creation of new wealth. He therefore distinguishes between *positive* profit and *relative* profit.

"*Positive profit*, implies no loss to anybody; it results from an augmentation of labour, industry, or ingenuity, and has the effect of swelling or augmenting the public good . . . *Relative profit*, is what implies a loss to somebody; it marks a vibration of the balance of wealth between parties, but implies no addition to the general stock. . . . The *compound* is easily understood; it is that species of profit and loss which is partly *relative* and partly *positive* . . . both sides may subsist inseparably in the same transaction" (*Principles of Political Economy, The Works of Sir James Steuart*. Ed. by General Sir James Steuart, his son etc. in 6 Volumes, London, 1805, I, pp. 275–6).

Positive profit arises out of the "augmentation of labour, industry, or ingenuity." Steuart does not attempt to give any account of *how* it arises out of this. The further statement that this profit has the effect of increasing and swelling "the public good" seems to indicate that Steuart means by it nothing more than the greater mass of use-values, which are created as a result of the development of the productive powers of labour, and that he conceives this positive profit as quite distinct from capitalists' profit, which always presupposes an increase of exchange value. This interpretation is completely confirmed by his further exposition. He says in particular:

"In the price of goods, I consider two things as really existing, and quite different from one another; to wit; the real value of the commodity, and the profit upon alienation" (p. 244).

The price of goods comprises therefore two elements which are quite different from each other: Firstly their *real value*, secondly, the "profit upon alienation", the profit which is realised through their being transferred to another, their sale. This "profit upon alienation" arises therefore out of the fact that the price of the goods is greater than their real value, or that the goods are sold *above* their value. Gain on the one side therefore always involves loss on the other. There is no addition to the general wealth. Profit, that is, surplus value, is relative and resolves itself into a vibration of the balance of wealth between the parties. Steuart himself rejects the idea that surplus value can be explained in this way. His theory of the "vibration of the balance of wealth between the parties", however little it concerns the nature and origin of surplus value itself, remains important in considering the distribution of surplus value among the different classes and the different categories of profit, interest and rent.

That Steuart limits all profit of individual capitalists to this "relative profit", the profit obtained through alienation, is shown by the following:

"The first thing to be known of any manufacture when it comes to be sold, is, by how much of it a person can perform, upon an average only, in a day, a week, a month. . . ."

"The second thing to be known, is the value of the workman's subsistence and necessary expence, both for supplying his personal wants, and providing the instruments belonging to his profession, which must be taken upon an average as above;"

"The third and last thing to be known, is the value of the materials" (pp. 244-5).

"These three articles being known, the price of manufacture is determined. It cannot be lower than the amount of all the three, that is, than the real value; whatever it is higher, is the manufacturer's profit. This will ever be in proportion to demand, and therefore will fluctuate according to circumstances."

"Hence appears the necessity of a great demand, in order to promote flourishing manufactures . . . the industrious, who regulate their living and expence according to their certain profit" (pp. 245–6).

From this it is clear that: The profit of the "manufacturers", of the individual capitalists, is always "relative profit", always "profit upon alienation", always derived from the excess of the price of the commodity over its real value, its sale above its value. If therefore all commodities were sold at their *value*, no profit would exist.

Steuart wrote a special chapter on this question, examining in detail "how profits consolidate into prime cost" (Vol. III, p. 11).

Steuart on the one hand rejects the concept of the Monetary and Mercantilist systems, according to which the sale of the commodity above its value, and the profit arising therefrom, created surplus value, a positive increase in wealth.[1] On the other hand he clings to their view that the profit of the individual capital is nothing but the excess of the price over the value, the "profit upon alienation", which however according to him is only *relative*, since the gain on the one side is compensated by the loss on the other, and its movement is, therefore, nothing but "a vibration of the balance of wealth between the parties".

In this respect Steuart is as it were the *rational* exponent of the Monetary and Mercantilist systems.

His service to the theory of capital is that he shows how the process of separation takes place between the conditions of production, as the property of definite classes, and labour-power. He gives a great deal of attention to this process of the birth of capital—without as yet having the direct concept of

[1] Even the Monetary system, however, does not assume that this profit arises within a country, but only in exchange with other countries. In the Mercantilist System it is further assumed that this value is represented in money (gold and silver), and the surplus value is therefore expressed in the balance of trade, which is settled with money.

it as capital, although he sees it as a condition for large-scale industry. He examines the process principally in agriculture; and he correctly presents the rise of manufacturing industry proper as dependent on this prior process of separation in agriculture. In Adam Smith's works this process of separation is assumed as already completed.

Steuart's book appeared in 1767 in London. Turgot's [*Réflexions sur la formation et la distribution des richesses*] in 1766 in Paris, Adam Smith's [*Inquiry into the nature and the causes of the wealth of Nations*] in 1776 in London.

6. THE GENERAL CHARACTER OF THE PHYSIOCRATIC SYSTEM

THE analysis of capital, within the bourgeois horizon, is essentially the work of the Physiocrats. It is this service which makes them the true fathers of modern economics. In the first place, their analysis of the various *material components* in which capital exists during the labour process, and into which it is divided. It is not a matter of reproach to the Physiocrats that, like all their successors, they conceived these material forms of existence, such as tools, raw materials, etc., in isolation from the social conditions in which they appear in capitalist production; in a word, in the form in which they are elements of the labour process in general, independently of their social form as capital—and thereby made of the capitalist form of production an eternal, natural form of production. To them the bourgeois forms of production necessarily appeared to be its natural forms. It was their great merit that they conceived these forms as physiological forms of society: as forms arising out of the natural necessity of production itself, forms independent of the will or of politics, etc. They are material laws. The error of the Physiocrats is only that they regard the material law of a definite historical stage of society as an abstract law governing equally all forms of society.

In addition to this analysis of the material elements of which capital consists during the labour process, the Physiocrats examined the forms which capital assumes in circulation (fixed capital, circulating capital, even though they give them other names), and in general the connection between the process of circulation and the process of reproduction of capital. We shall come back to this in the chapter on circulation.

In these two principal points Adam Smith inherited the legacy of the Physiocrats. His contribution—in this connection—is limited to defining the abstract categories and to bestowing more precise names on the different forms analysed by the Physiocrats.

The general condition for the development of capitalist

production is, as we saw, that *labour power*, as a *commodity* belonging to the workers, should confront the conditions of labour as commodities existing independently of it and maintained in the essential form of capital. As a commodity, it is essential to determine the *value* of labour power. This value is equal to the labour time required to produce the means of subsistence necessary for the reproduction of labour power, or to the price of the means of subsistence necessary for the existence of the worker as a worker. Only on this basis does the difference arise between the *value* of labour power and its *profitable utilisation*, a difference which exists with no other commodity, since there is no other commodity whose use value, and therefore also whose actual use, can raise its *exchange value* or the exchange value resulting from its use. The conception of the value of labour power as something fixed, as a given magnitude—as indeed it is in practice in each definite case—is therefore one of the foundations of modern political economy, whose business is the analysis of capitalist production. The minimum level of wages correctly, therefore, forms the pivotal point of physiocratic doctrine. They were able to establish this, although they had not yet recognised the nature of value itself, because this *value of labour power* reveals itself in the price of the necessary means of subsistence, and therefore in a sum of definite use-values. Consequently, without being in any way clear as to the nature of value, they could take the value of labour power, in so far as it was necessary for their investigations, as a definite magnitude. If they made the further mistake of conceiving the wage as an unchangeable amount, in their view entirely determined by nature—and not by the stage of historical development, a magnitude itself subject to fluctuations—this in no way affects the abstract correctness of their conclusions, since the difference between the value and the profitable use of labour power does not in any way depend on whether the value is assumed to be great or small.

The Physiocrats themselves transferred the investigation into the origin of surplus value from the sphere of circulation into the sphere of direct production, and thereby laid the foundation for the analysis of capitalist production.

Quite correctly they lay down the fundamental principle

that only that labour is *productive* which creates *surplus value*; in whose product therefore a higher value is contained than the sum of the values consumed during the production of this product. Since the value of raw and other materials is given, while the value of the labour power is equal to the wage, this surplus value can evidently only consist in the excess of labour which the worker gives back to the capitalist over and above the quantity of labour that he receives in his wage. It is true that it does not appear in this form in the Physiocrats, because they have not yet reduced value in general to its simple substance—the quantity of labour or labour time.

Their method of exposition is, of course, necessarily governed by their general view of the nature of value, which to them is not a definite social form of existence of human activity (labour), but consists of material things—land, nature, and the various modifications of these material things.

The difference between the *value* of labour power and the *value created by its use*—that is, the surplus value which the purchase of labour power secures for the person who sets it to work—appears most tangibly, most incontrovertibly, of all branches of production, in agriculture, primary production. The sum total of the means of subsistence which the worker consumes from one year to another, or the mass of material substance which he consumes, is smaller than the sum total of means of subsistence which he produces. In industry generally the worker is not found directly reproducing his means of subsistence, or directly producing the surplus over his means of subsistence. The process is mediated through purchase and sale, through the various acts of circulation, and the analysis of value in general is required for it to be understood. In agriculture it shows itself directly in the surplus of use values produced over use values consumed by the worker, and can therefore be grasped without an analysis of value in general, or a clear understanding of the nature of value. This is true even when value is reduced to use value, and this latter to material substance in general. Agricultural labour is therefore for the Physiocrats the only productive labour, because it is the only labour which creates a surplus value, and *land rent is the only form of surplus value* which they recognise.

The worker in industry, they find, does not increase the material substance; he only changes its form. The raw material—the mass of material substance—is given to him by agriculture. Admittedly he adds value to the material, not through his labour, but through the production costs of his labour; through the sum of means of subsistence which he consumes in the course of his labour, equivalent to the wage, which he receives from agriculture. Because agricultural labour is conceived as the only productive labour, the form of surplus value which distinguishes agricultural from industrial labour, land rent, is conceived as the only form of surplus value. Profit on capital in the true sense, of which land rent itself is only an offshoot, therefore does not exist for the Physiocrats. Profit appears to them only as a kind of superior wage, paid by the landowners, which the capitalists consume as revenue (and which, therefore, enters into their cost of production in the same way as the wages of ordinary workers), and which increases the value of the raw material, because it enters into the consumption costs which the industrialist (capitalist) consumes, while he is producing the product, transforming the raw material into a new product. Surplus value in the form of interest on money—another offshoot of profit—is therefore declared by one group of Physiocrats, such as the elder Mirabeau, to be usury and contrary to nature. Turgot on the other hand justifies it on the ground that the money capitalist could buy land, that is, rents, and that therefore his money capital must bring him as much surplus value as he would receive if he transformed it into landed property. On this basis, therefore, interest too is not a newly created value, is not surplus value: all that is done is to explain why a part of the surplus value won by the landowners finds its way to the money capitalists in the form of interest; just as other grounds are given to explain why a part of that surplus value accrues to the industrial capitalists in the form of profit. Because agricultural labour is the only productive labour, the only labour which creates surplus value, the *form* of surplus value which distinguishes agricultural from all other branches of labour, *land rent*, is *the general form of surplus value*. Industrial profit and interest on money are only different categories into which land rent is divided and, in definite portions, passes from the hands of the landowners into those of other classes. This is the direct opposite of how it is treated by the later economists since Adam Smith, as they correctly see *industrial profit* as the *form* in which surplus value is originally appropriated by capital, that is, as the primary general form of surplus value; so that interest and land rent represent only branches of industrial profit which are distributed by the industrial capitalists to various classes who are co-owners of surplus value.

In addition to the reason already given—that agricultural labour is labour in which the creation of surplus value appears in material and tangible form—and leaving out of account the processes of circulation, the Physiocrats had several other reasons which explain their view.

First, because in agriculture land rent appears as a third element, as a form of surplus value which does not occur in industry or only to a negligible degree. It was surplus value over and above surplus value (profit), and so the most palpable and striking form of surplus value, surplus value to the second power. As Karl Arnd, the home-bred economist, says:

> "By means of agriculture, a value is created—in land-rent—which does not occur in industry and trade: A value, which remains over, when the return to the labour and capital that have been employed, has been met" (*Die naturgemässe Volkswirthschaft, gegenüber dem Monopoliengeist und dem Kommunismus*, Hanau, 1845, pp. 461-2).

Secondly: If one ignores foreign trade—as the Physiocrats correctly did and had to do in an abstract study of bourgeois society—it is then clear that the number of workers employed in industry etc. and completely released from agriculture—the number of "free hands" as Steuart calls them—is fixed by the quantity of agricultural products which the agricultural workers produce over and above their own consumption.

> "It is obvious that the relative numbers of those persons who can be maintained without agricultural labour, must be measured wholly by the productive powers of the cultivators" (R. Jones, *An Essay on the Distribution of Wealth*, London, 1831, p. 159).

Since agricultural labour thus forms the natural basis not only for surplus labour in its own sphere but also for the independent existence of all other branches of labour, and therefore also for the surplus value created in them it is clear that it had to be conceived as the creator of surplus value, so long as definite, concrete labour, not abstract labour and its measure, labour time, was regarded as the substance of value.

Thirdly: All surplus value, not only relative but absolute, depends on a given productivity of labour. If the productivity of labour were only developed to such a degree that a man's labour time was only sufficient to keep him alive, to produce and reproduce his own means of subsistence, then there would be no surplus labour and no surplus value, and there would be absolutely no difference between the value of labour power and the value created by its use. The possibility of surplus labour and of surplus value is conditioned therefore by a certain degree of productivity, a productivity which enables labour power to reproduce more than its own value, to produce in excess of the necessities required by its life process. And indeed—as we saw in the second point above—this degree of productivity, which serves as a starting-point, must first be present in agricultural labour. It appears therefore as a *gift of nature*, a *productive power of nature*. Here, in agriculture, from the very beginning, co-operation with the powers of nature existed on a large scale, the increase of human labour power by the application and exploitation of natural forces which acted like an automatic machine. This extensive use of the forces of nature appears in industry only with the development of large-scale industry. A definite stage in the development of agriculture, whether in the country concerned or in other countries, is the basis for the development of capital. Up to this point absolute surplus value coincides with relative.

This is stressed by Buchanan—a great opponent of the Physiocrats—even against Adam Smith; he attempts to prove that such an agricultural development also preceded the rise of modern town industry.

Fourthly: Since it was the great and specific contribution of the Physiocrats to derive value and surplus value not from circulation but from production, in contrast to the monetary and mercantilist system they necessarily began with that branch of production which can be thought of as completely separate from and independent of circulation and exchange, and which presupposes exchange not between man and man but only between man and nature.

It is in fact the first system which analyses capitalist production, and it presents the conditions within which capital is produced, and within which capital produces, as eternal natural laws of production. On the other hand, this system has more the character of a bourgeois reproduction of the feudal system, the domination of landed property; and the industrial spheres, within which capital first develops independently, are depicted rather as "unproductive" branches of labour, mere appendages of agriculture. The first condition for the development of capital is the separation of ownership of land from labour—so that land, that primary condition of labour, emerges as an independent force in the hands of a separate class, over against the free labourer. In the Physiocrats' account, therefore, the owner of land appears as the true capitalist, that is, as the appropriator of surplus value. Feudalism is thus reproduced and explained in the guise of bourgeois production; agriculture becomes that branch of production in which capitalist production—that is, the production of surplus value—exclusively appears. While feudalism is thus made bourgeois, bourgeois society is given a semblance of feudalism. This semblance deceived Dr. Quesnay's followers among the nobility, including the crotchety and patriarchal Mirabeau the elder. Among the later leaders of the Physiocrats, especially Turgot, this semblance disappears completely, and the Physiocratic system is presented as the new capitalist society forcing its way through within the framework of feudal society. It corresponds therefore with bourgeois society in the period when the latter breaks its way out from the feudal order. The starting point is therefore in France, a predominantly agricultural country, not in England, a predominantly industrial, commercial and seafaring country. In the latter country attention was naturally focussed on circulation, on the fact that the product first receives value, becomes a commodity, as the embodiment of general social labour, through its transformation into money. In so far therefore as what is in question is not the form of value, but the amount of value and the increase of value, it is here that the "profit upon alienation"—that is, the relative profit described by Steuart—is to be found. But if the creation of surplus value in the sphere of production itself is to be established, it is necessary to go back in the first place to that branch of production in which it appears *independently* of circulation, that is, to agriculture. The initiative for this study therefore developed in a predominantly agricultural country. Ideas related to those of the Physiocrats are to be found here and there in the works of earlier writers, partly in France itself, Boisguillebert for example. But these ideas become an epoch-making system first with the Physiocrats.

The agricultural worker, assigned the minimum of wages, the *strict nécessaire*, reproduces more than this *strict nécessaire*, and this excess is land rent, the *surplus value* which is appropriated by the owner of the fundamental condition of labour—nature, the land. Thus the Physiocrats did not say: the worker works over and above the labour time necessary for the reproduction of his labour power; the value which he produces is therefore greater than the value of his labour power; or the labour which he gives is greater than the quantity of labour which he receives in the form of wages. What they say is: the sum of use values which he consumes during the period of production is smaller than the sum of use values which he creates, and so there remains a surplus of use values. If he worked only for the time required for the reproduction of his own labour power, no surplus would be left over. But [they did not carry their reasoning through to this conclusion]; they only got to the point of establishing that the productivity of the earth enables the worker in his day's work—which is taken as something fixed—to produce more than he needs to consume in order to continue to exist. This surplus value appears therefore as a *gift of Nature*, through whose joint action [on] a certain quantity of organic material—plant-seeds, and animals—labour is enabled to transform more inorganic material into organic. On the other hand, it is also taken for granted that the landowner confronts the worker as a capitalist.

He pays him for his labour power, which the worker offers him as a commodity, and in return not only receives an equivalent, but appropriates to himself the increased value arising from the use of this labour power. The mutual alienation of the material conditions of labour and of labour power itself are presupposed in this exchange. The feudal landowner is the starting point, but he makes his appearance as a capitalist, as a mere owner of commodities, who makes profitable use of the goods exchanged by him for labour, receiving in return not only their equivalent but a surplus in excess of this equivalent, because he pays for the labour power only as a commodity. He confronts the free labourer as the owner of commodities; or in other words, this landowner is in essence a capitalist. In this respect also the Physiocratic system hits the mark, in so far as the separation of the labourer from the land and from the ownership of land is a fundamental condition for capitalist production and the production of capital.

There are therefore contradictions in this system. While it was the first to explain *surplus value* by the appropriation of the labour of others, and even to base this appropriation on the exchange of commodities, it did not see that value in general is a form of social labour, and that surplus value is surplus labour. On the contrary, it conceived value merely as use value, merely as material substance, and surplus value merely as a gift of nature, which returns to labour, in place of a given quantity of organic matter, a greater quantity. On the one hand it stripped land rent—that is, the true economic form of landed property—from its feudal wrapping, and reduced it to pure surplus value in excess of the worker's wage. On the other hand, it explains this surplus value still as if it were feudal, derived from nature and not from society, from man's relation to the land and not from his social relations. Value itself is reduced to mere use value and consequently into something material. And yet again the only thing that matters in this material substance is its quantity—the excess of the use values produced over those consumed; that is, the purely quantitative relation of the use values to each other, and therefore once again, in the last resort, their mere exchange value, which resolves itself ultimately into labour time.

All these are the contradictions of capitalist production when it is working its way out of feudal society and only interprets feudal society itself in a rather more bourgeois way, without having yet discovered its own peculiar form—somewhat in the same way as philosophy first builds itself up out of the religious form of consciousness, and thereby on the one hand destroys religion as such, while on the other hand, in its positive content, it still moves only within this religious sphere, which is now idealised, reduced to terms of thought.

For this same reason, in the conclusions which the Physiocrats themselves draw, the ostensible veneration of landed property becomes transformed into the economic negation of it, and the affirmation of capitalist production. All taxes are transferred on to land rent, or, in other words, landed property is partially confiscated, which is what the legislation of the French Revolution, in spite of the protests of Roederer and others, sought to carry through; and which is also the final outcome of the modern, more fully developed economics of Ricardo. Taxes are entirely passed on to land rent, because it is the sole form of surplus value and therefore all taxation of other forms of income ultimately falls only on landed property— but indirectly, and therefore only in an economically harmful way, one which hinders production. With this exclusive taxation of landed property, taxes, and along with them all forms of State intervention, are removed from industry itself, and the latter is thus freed from all intervention by the State. This is ostensibly done for the benefit of landed property, not in the interests of industry.

Connected with this is *laissez-faire, laissez-aller*, unhampered free competition, the removal from industry of all interference by the State and monopolies, etc. Since industry, as the Physiocrats see it, creates nothing, but only changes the values given to it by agriculture into other forms; since it adds to these values no new value, but only returns in equivalent value though in altered form the value supplied to it, it is naturally desirable that this process of transformation should proceed without hindrances and in the cheapest way, and this will only be realised through free competition, in which capitalist production is left to itself. Thus the emancipation of bourgeois society from the absolute monarchy set up on the ruins of feudal society takes place only in the interests of a feudal landowner transformed into a capitalist and bent solely on enrichment. The capitalists are only capitalists in the interests of landed property, just as economics in its later development would have them be capitalists only in the interests of the working class.

It is therefore evident how little modern economists such as Eugen Daire (who published the works of the Physiocrats and wrote a prize essay on them), understood the Physiocrats, when they treated their specific theories—about agricultural labour as the sole productive labour, land rent as the only form of surplus value, and the landowner's outstanding role in the system of production—as if they had no connection with and were only fortuitously associated with their proclamation of free competition, with the principle of large-scale industry and capitalist production. It is also understandable that the feudal semblance of this Physiocratic system, with the aristocratic tone of its exposition, was bound to win a mass of feudal lords as enthusiastic supporters and exponents of a system which, in its essence, proclaimed the rise of the bourgeois system of production on the ruins of the feudal.

*   *   *

There were contradictions in this system taken as a whole. Among others, Quesnay was for the absolute monarchy.

"There can be only one supreme power. . . . The system of counter-balances in a government is ruinous. It indicates friction among the leaders and the suppression of the masses" ("Maximes Générales du gouvernement économique d'un Royaume Agricole," *Physiocrates*, ed. Daire, I, p. 81).

Mercier de la Rivière says:

"Because of the fact that man is intended to live in a community, he is intended to live under a despotism" (*Ordre naturel et essentiel des sociétés politiques*, 1767, I, p. 280).

And then the "Friend of the People", the Marquis de Mirabeau—Mirabeau the Elder! It was precisely this school, with its *laissez-faire, laissez-aller*, that overthrew Colbertism and all forms of government interference in the activities of bourgeois society. It allowed the State to live on only in the pores of this society, as Epicurus placed his Gods in the pores of the world!

Then Turgot himself, the radical bourgeois minister who prepared the way for the French Revolution. With all their false semblance of Feudalism, the Physiocrats worked hand-in-hand with the Encyclopaedists.

We shall come back later to the great service rendered by the Physiocrats in connection with the analysis of capital. However, for the history of the theory of surplus value the result is: According to the Physiocrats, surplus value is due to the productivity of a special form of labour, agriculture. And this special productivity is in its entirety attributable to nature herself.

*   *   *

In the Mercantile System surplus value is only relative; what one wins the other loses. "Profit upon alienation", "oscillation" or "vibration of the balance of wealth between different parties". In the interior of a country, therefore, considered in relation to the total capital, no creation of surplus value actually takes place. It can arise only in the relations of one nation to other nations. And the surplus, which one country realises over the other, manifests itself in money (balance of trade), simply because money is the direct and independent form of exchange value. As against this—since the Mercantile System denies in fact the creation of absolute surplus value—the Physiocrats attempt to explain this latter as net product—*produit net*. And since the surplus product is fixed in their minds as a use value, they see agriculture as the sole creator of it.

Jérôme A. Blanqui (*Histoire de l'Economie Politique*, Brussels, 1839, p. 139) says of the Physiocrats:

"Labour applied to the cultivation of the soil produced not only the wherewithal to maintain itself throughout the entire duration of the task, but also an excess of value which could be added to the mass of already existing wealth. They called this excess the *produit net*" (surplus product, thus conceiving surplus value in the form of the use values in which it reveals itself). "The 'produit net' ought necessarily to belong to the owner of the land and constituted in his hands a revenue fully at his disposal. What then was the *produit net* of the other industries? . . . manufacturers, merchants, workmen, all were the servants, the employees (*salariés*) of agriculture, sovereign creator and dispenser of all wealth. The products of the labour of these latter represented in the system of the *Economistes* only the equivalent of what they had consumed during the task, so that after their work was completed, the sum total of wealth was absolutely the same as before, unless the workmen or the masters had placed in reserve, that is to say saved, what they had the right to consume. Thus, then, labour applied to the soil was the only labour productive of wealth, and labour in other industries was regarded as sterile, because no increase in the general capital resulted from it."

Thus the Physiocrats see the production of surplus value as the essence of capitalist production. They were concerned to explain this phenomenon. And this *was* the problem, after they had rejected the profit arising on alienation (*profit d'expropriation*) of the Mercantile System.

"In order to acquire money, one must buy it, and, after this purchase, one is no richer than one was before; one has simply received in money the same value that one has given in commodities" (Mercier de la Rivière, *Ordre naturel et essentiel des sociétés politiques*, 1767, II, p. 338).

This holds good equally for purchase as for sale, as also for the outcome of the entire metamorphosis of the commodity, or for the result of the exchange of different commodities at their value, that is, the exchange of equivalents. Whence, therefore, comes surplus value, that is, whence comes capital? This is the problem for the Physiocrats. Their error flows from the fact that they confused the increase of *material substance*, which as a result of natural growth and reproduction distinguishes agriculture and stock-raising from manufacture, with the increase of *exchange value*. Use value was the basis from which they started out. And the use value of all commodities reduced to a universal commodity, as the scholastics say, was natural substance as such, whose increase in the same form occurs only in agriculture.

* * *

The rise of the Physiocrats was connected with both the opposition to Colbertism, and particularly also with the hullabaloo over John Law's system.

Among the direct historical circumstances which helped the spread of the Physiocratic system and even its rise, J. A. Blanqui mentioned in the work previously quoted:

"Of all the industrial values, which shot up in the fetid atmosphere of the system [Law's], nothing remained except ruin, desolation and bankruptcy. Landed property alone did not go under in the storm.[1] In fact it improved its position by changing hands and subdividing itself on a large scale, perhaps for the first time since feudalism" (p. 138). In particular: "The innumerable changes of ownership, which were effected under the influence of the system, began the process of division of property. . . . Landed property arose for the first time from the condition of torpor in which the feudal system had kept it for so long. This constituted a veritable renaissance for agriculture. . . . It [i.e., the land] passed now from out of a condition of mortmain and came again into circulation" (pp. 137–8).

[1] For this reason Mr. Proudhon in his *Philosophie de la Misère* makes "landed property" also come after "credit."

7. TURGOT

WE shall now examine a number of passages, partly for the sake of clarification, partly in proof of the statements made above.

According to Quesnay himself, in the *Analyse du Tableau Economique* (Versailles, 1758), the nation consists of three classes of citizens,

> "The productive class (agricultural workers), the class of landowners and the sterile class, or all citizens who are occupied with tasks and labour other than agriculture" (*Physiocrates, etc.*, ed. Daire, Paris, 1846, I, p. 58).

Only the agricultural workers, not the landowners, appear as the productive class and as the class which creates surplus value. The importance of the landowning class, which is not "sterile", since it represents surplus value, is not due to its being the creator of surplus value but solely to the fact that it appropriates this surplus value.

In Turgot we find the Physiocratic doctrine in its most developed form. With him for the first time the product, the "pure gift of nature", is presented in occasional passages as surplus value, while on the other hand the necessity for the worker to give up that part of his product which is over and above his wage is explained by the divorce of the worker from the conditions of his labour, and then by these confronting him as the private property of a class which uses this property as a means to a profitable deal.

The first reason why agricultural labour alone is productive lies in the fact that it forms the natural basis and necessary condition for the independent functioning of all other forms of labour.

> "His (i.e. the Husbandman's) labour, in the sequence of the labours divided among the different members of the society retains the same primacy, the same pre-eminence, as the labour which provided his own food had among the

different kinds of labour which, when he worked alone, he was obliged to devote to his different kinds of wants. We have here neither a primacy of honour nor of dignity; it is one of physical necessity. . . . What his labour causes the land to produce beyond his personal wants is the only fund for the wages which all the other members of the society receive in exchange for their labour. The latter, in making use of the price of this exchange to buy in their turn the products of the Husbandman, only return to him exactly what they have received from him. We have here a very essential difference between these two kinds of labour" (*Réflexions sur la Formation et la Distribution des Richesses*, 1766, Turgot, ed. Daire, Paris, 1844, I, pp. 9, 10).

How then does surplus value arise? It does not arise in circulation, but is realised there. The product is sold for its value, not *above* its value. There is no excess of price over value. But because it is sold for its value, the seller realises a surplus value. This is only possible because he has not himself paid the full value for which he sells it, or because the product contains a portion of value which the seller has not paid for or replaced by an equivalent value. And this is the case with agricultural labour. The seller sells what he has not bought. This unbought element Turgot describes as the "pure gift of Nature." We shall however see that in Turgot's writings this "pure gift of Nature" is surreptitiously transformed into the surplus labour of the agricultural labourer which has not been paid for by the landowner, and which the latter sells in the form of agricultural products.

"As soon as the labour of the Husbandman produces more than his wants, he can, with this superfluity that nature accords him as a pure gift, over and above the wages of his toil, buy the labour of the other members of the society. The latter, in selling to him gain only their livelihood; but the Husbandman gathers, beyond his subsistence, a wealth which is independent and disposable, which he has not bought and which he sells. He is therefore, the sole source of the riches, which, by their circulation, animate all the labours of the society; because he is the only one whose labour produces over and above the wages of the labour" (p. 11).

In this first conception we have, to begin with, the essence of
surplus value, that it is value realised in sale, without the
seller having given an equivalent for it or bought it. It is
unpaid value. Secondly, however, this surplus over the "wage"
is conceived as a "pure gift of Nature"; inasmuch as it is,
when all is said and done, a gift of Nature, dependent on the
productivity of Nature, that the worker is capable of producing
in his working day more than is necessary for the reproduction
of his labour power, more than his wage. In this first conception
the total product is still appropriated by the worker himself.
And this total product falls into two parts. The first forms his
wage; he is presented as his own hired labourer, who pays
himself that part of the product which is necessary for the
reproduction of his labour power, for his subsistence. The
second part, which is the excess over the first, is the *gift of
Nature* and forms surplus value. The nature of this surplus
value, of this "pure gift of Nature", assumes clearer shape,
however, as soon as the premise of a peasant working his own
land (*propriétaire cultivateur*) ceases to apply, and the two parts
of the product, the wage and the surplus value, fall to different
classes, the one to the wage labourer, the other to the landowner.

The formation of a class of wage labourers, whether in
industry or in agriculture itself—for all industrial workers first
appear only as *stipendiés*, wage-workers of the *cultivateur-
propriétaire*—requires the separation of the conditions necessary
for labour from labour power, and the basis of this separation
is the land itself becoming the private property of one section
of society, so that the other section is shut off from this objective
condition for making use of its labour.

> "In the first ages the Proprietor cannot have been distin-
> guished from the Cultivator. . . . Moreover, in this early
> time, as every industrious man would find as much land as
> he wished, he could not be tempted to till the soil for
> others. . . . But in the end all land found its master, and
> those who could not have properties had at first no other
> resource than that of exchanging the labour of their arms,
> in the employments of the stipendiary class (i.e. the
> industrial class, all non-agricultural workers), for the

superfluous portion of the crops of the cultivating Proprietor" (p. 12).

The *propriétaire cultivateur*, with the considerable surplus which the earth gave to his labour, could—

"pay men to cultivate his land; and for men who live on wages, it was as good to earn them in this business as in any other. Thus ownership could be separated from the labour of cultivation; and soon it was. The landowners began to be able to shift the labour of cultivating the soil on to the wage-labourers" (p. 13).

In this way, therefore, the relationship between capital and wage labour arises in agriculture itself. It first arises when a number of persons find themselves cut off from ownership of the conditions necessary for their labour—above all, from the land—and have nothing to sell but their labour power itself.

For the wage labourer, however, who can no longer produce commodities but must sell his labour power itself, the value of this labour power, the equivalent to the necessary means of subsistence, necessarily becomes the law which governs his exchange with the owner of the conditions necessary for his labour.

"The mere Workman who has only his arms and his Industry, has nothing except insofar as he succeeds in selling his toil to others. . . . In every kind of work it cannot fail to happen, and as a matter of fact it does happen, that the wages of the workman are limited to what is necessary to procure him his subsistence" (p. 10).

As soon as wage-labour has arisen,

"the produce of land is divided into two parts. The one includes the subsistence and the profits of the Husbandman, which are the reward of his labour and the condition upon which he undertakes to cultivate the field of the Proprietor. What remains is that independent and disposable part which the land gives as pure gift to him who cultivates it, over and above his advances and the wages of his trouble; and this is the portion of the Proprietor, or the revenue with which the latter can live without labour and which he carries where he will" (p. 14).

This "pure gift of Nature" is now, however, already defined as a gift which she makes "to him who cultivates it", and therefore as a gift which she makes to *labour*; as the productive power of labour, applied to the land, a productive power which labour possesses through using the productive power of Nature, and thus which labour creates out of the land, but only creates out of the land *as labour*. In the hand of the land-owner, therefore, the surplus no longer appears as a "gift of Nature", but as an appropriation—without an equivalent in exchange—of another's labour, which through the productivity of Nature is enabled to produce more than its own needs, more than its own means of subsistence, but which, because of its being wage-labour, is restricted to appropriating for itself, out of the product of the labour, only "what is necessary to procure him his subsistence".

"The labour of the Cultivator produces his own wages, and, in addition, the revenue which serves to pay the whole class of Artisans and other stipendiaries. . . . The Proprietor has nothing except through the labour of the Cultivator;[1] he receives from him his subsistence and that wherewith he pays the labours of the other stipendiaries . . . the Cultivator has need of the Proprietor only by virtue of the human conventions and the civil laws" (pp. 15, 16).

In this passage, therefore, surplus value is plainly described as that part of the agricultural worker's labour which the landowner appropriates to himself without giving any equivalent in return, and the product of which therefore he sells though he has not bought. Only what Turgot has in mind is not the exchange value as such, the labour time itself, but the surplus of products which the labour of the agricultural worker provides to the landowner in excess of his own wage. This surplus of products, however, is only the embodiment of the amount of time which he works gratis for the landowner, in addition to the time which he works for the reproduction of his own wage.

Thus we see how, *in the framework of agricultural labour*, the Physiocrats correctly grasp surplus value, how they conceive it as the product of the labour of the wage worker, although they

[1] Not, therefore, as a pure gift of Nature.

then conceive this labour itself in the concrete form in which it appears as use values.

We may note in passing that Turgot describes the *capitalist* exploitation of agriculture—the leasing or letting of land (large-scale agriculture, dependent on the modern system of leases)—as "the most advantageous of all; but it presupposes a land that is already rich" (p. 21).

Quesnay and his other disciples were also of the same opinion. In his *Maximes Générales* Quesnay says:

"The pieces of land which are employed in growing grain should as far as possible, be joined together in large-scale farms which can be managed by rich farmers [*laboureurs*— here capitalists] since the expenses for the maintenance and repair of the buildings are smaller and therefore the costs are correspondingly lower and the *produit net* greater in the case of large agricultural undertakings than in the case of small" (*Physiocrates*, ed. Daire, I, p. 96).

Moreover, in the same passage, Quesnay admits that the increase in the productivity of agricultural labour accrues to the net income, *revenu net*; in the first place, therefore, to the landowner, that is, the owner of the surplus value; and that the relative increase of the latter arises not from the land but from the social and other arrangements which increase the productivity of labour. For he says:

"Every advantageous economy [advantageous, that is, for the *produit net*] in labour which can be accomplished with the aid of animals, machines, water-power, etc., will be of benefit to the community."

At the same time Mercier de la Rivière has a suspicion that surplus value in industry (Turgot extends this to all production) has at least something to do with the industrial workers themselves. In the work already quoted (II, p. 407) he exclaims:

"Moderate your enthusiasm, ye blind admirers of the false products of industry. Before ye extol your wonder, open your eyes and see, how many live in poverty or at least in need among those producers who understand the art of converting twenty sous into the value of a thousand thalers. To whom then does this enormous increase in value fall?

What do you say! Those through whose hands it is accomplished reap no benefit therefrom. Take warning then by this contrast."

In the Physiocratic system the *propriétaires*, the landowners, are the *salariants*, the wage-payers. The workers and the *manufacturiers* in all other branches of industry are *salariés* or *stipendiés*—paid people. Hence also *gouvernants* and *gouvernés*—the governors and the governed.

Turgot analyses the conditions necessary for labour as follows:

"In every craft, it is necessary that the Workman should have tools in advance, that he should have a sufficient quantity of the materials upon which he has to labour; it is necessary that he should subsist while waiting for the sale of his finished goods" (p. 34).

All these advances, these conditions upon which alone labour can be carried on, and which are, therefore, *preconditions* of the labour process, are originally provided *gratis* by the land: "It is the land which has provided the first fund of advances prior to all cultivation", in fruits, fish, game, etc., in tools such as branches of trees and stones, in domestic animals, which multiply themselves by the procreative process, and in addition give each year products such as "milk, fleeces, hides and other materials, which, with the wood obtained in the forests, have formed the first fund for the works of industry" (p. 34).

These conditions of labour, these advances made to labour, become *capital* when they have to be advanced to the worker by a third person, and this is the case from the moment when the worker owns nothing but his labour power itself.

"When a large part of the Society had only their arms to maintain them, it was necessary that those who thus lived on wages should begin by having something in advance, either to procure the materials upon which to labour, or to maintain them while waiting for the payment of their wages" (pp. 37–8).

Turgot explains capital as "movable accumulated values" (*Valeurs mobilières accumulées*). Originally (pp. 38–9) the landowner or farmer pays the wage directly each day and provides the material, e.g., flax, to the spinner. When industry is developed, larger advances and continuity in the process of production become necessary. That is then undertaken by the owner of capital (*possesseur des capitaux*). In the price of his products he must recover all his advances and a profit equal to "what his money would have been worth to him if he had employed it in the purchase of an estate," as well as his wage, "For doubtless, if the profit were the same, he would have preferred to live without any exertion on the revenue of the land he could have acquired with the same capital" (pp. 38–9).

The class of paid industrialists (*classe stipendiée industrieuse*) is itself again divided into "Undertakers, possessed of large capitals, and simple Artisans" (p. 39). Agricultural undertakers (*entrepreneurs fermiers*) are in the same position as these industrial undertakers. They must similarly get all their advances replaced in addition to profit, as shown above.

"All this must first be deducted from the price of the products of the earth; the surplus serves the Cultivator for paying the Proprietor for the permission he has given him to make use of his field for setting his enterprise on foot. This is the price of the lease, the revenue of the Proprietor, the net produce; for all the land produces, up to the exact amount of the advances of every kind and of the profits of every kind due to him who has made the advances, cannot be regarded as a revenue, but only as the return of the expenses of cultivation; when one considers that, if the Cultivator did not get them back, he would take care not to employ his riches and his toil in cultivating the field of another" (p. 40).

Finally:

"Although capitals are partly formed by saving from the profits of the working classes, yet, as these profits always come from the earth—inasmuch as they are all paid either from the revenue, or as part of the expenditure which serves to produce the revenue—it is evident that capitals come from the land just as much as the revenue does; or, rather, that they are nothing but the accumulation of the part of the values produced by the land that the proprietors of the revenue, or those who share it with them, can lay by every year without using it for the satisfaction of their wants" (p. 66).

Only land rent constitutes surplus value. Already on p. 11 Turgot says, "He" (that is, the Husbandman) "is the only one whose labour produces over and above the wages of the labour" and on p. 20 "the Cultivator causes, over and above that recompense, the revenue of the Proprietor to come into existence; and the Artisan causes no revenue to come into existence either for himself or for others."

It is quite consistent, since land rent alone forms surplus value, that accumulation takes place out of it alone. What the capitalists accumulate apart from this, they pinch themselves of out of their pay, *salaire*, their revenue, which is destined for their consumption—for that is how profit is conceived.

While profit, like wages, is reckoned in with the costs of cultivating the land and only the surplus forms the revenue of the landowner, the latter revenue is actually excluded from the costs of cultivation—and therefore, in spite of the honoured place given to it, does not count as an agent in production. The same view was held by Ricardo's followers.

*   *   *

Turgot attempted to anticipate the measures of the French Revolution. In the edict of February, 1776, he abolished the guilds; this edict was revoked three months after its publication. Similarly, he abolished the roadmaking *corvée* (compulsory labour service) of the peasants and attempted to introduce the *impot unique*; the single tax on land rent to replace all previous taxes.

8. THE REPRODUCTION AND CIRCULATION OF THE TOTAL SOCIAL CAPITAL ACCORDING TO QUESNAY'S *TABLEAU ECONOMIQUE*

QUESNAY's *Tableau Economique* portrays in a few bold strokes how the yearly output of the national production, determined according to its value, is distributed in the process of circulation in such a way that, all other conditions remaining unchanged, the simple reproduction of itself can proceed, that is, reproduction on the same scale. The appropriate starting point for the period of production is the harvest of the preceding year. The countless individual acts of circulation are from the outset taken as aggregates in the social mass movement which characterises them—their circulation between great economic classes of society defined by their function.

Quesnay starts by assuming a large State, whose soil yields annually a total product with an average value of five milliards of livres—prices remaining the same. The nation consists of three classes: The productive class (engaged in agriculture), the sterile class (all engaged in work outside agriculture), and the landowners (comprising the actual owners of land, the Sovereign and the receivers of tithe).

The annual advances of working capital (*avances annuelles*), which the productive class has to lay out for the production of the five milliards, amount to two milliards. Two milliards are *produit net*, the revenue of the landowners. The sterile class finally makes a capital advance of one milliard for raw materials, and consumes means of subsistence amounting to one milliard during the process of production in order to make an industrial product of two milliards.

In addition to the total product valued at five milliards, the productive class also possesses at the beginning of the process of circulation a stock of money of two milliards.

The process of circulation between the various classes now shapes itself as follows, according to the *Tableau*:

Total newly created value, 5 milliards

Annual Working Capital of the productive class.		Revenue of the landowner.	Annual Working Capital of the sterile class.
	2 Milliards	2 Milliards	*1 Milliard*
Sums used for paying the revenue of the landowner and the interest on fixed capital (*avances primitives*)	1 Milliard 1 Milliard 1 Milliard		1 Milliard 1 Milliard
Replacement of the annual working-capital	2 Milliards		
Total	5 Milliards	Total	2 Milliards of which half is put back as working capital for the following year.

The first point to note in this *Tableau*, the point which must have impressed his contemporaries, is the way in which the circulation of money appears to be determined purely by the circulation and reproduction of commodities—in fact, by the circulation process of capital.

The farming class F (*fermier*) pays, directly in money, two milliard francs to the landowning class P (*propriétaire*). With this amount the latter buys from F means of subsistence to the value of one milliard. One milliard in money therefore flows back to F, while a fifth of the gross product is disposed of, passing out of circulation into consumption.

Next, P buys, with one milliard of money, a milliard of industrial commodities from the sterile class S. This milliard of money is now in the hands of the sterile class, who buys with it means of subsistence from F. In this way the second thousand million which F has paid to P flows back to F. On the other hand, the second fifth of F's product has gone out of circulation into consumption. At the end of this movement therefore we have the two thousand million of money again in the hands of F.

To replace one half of his annual capital advances, in so far as they consist partly of implements and partly of manufactured goods consumed by F during the process of production, F now buys, with a thousand millions of money, manufactured goods from S. In this way the second half of S's product is disposed of.

S once again employs the thousand millions of money, which he has received for the second half of his goods, to buy the second half of his means of production, raw materials, etc., and so the milliard of money flows back to F.

[Thus two thousand millions of industrial goods and three thousand millions of agricultural products have been circulated.]

Two fifths of these latter products now remain over.

[On the other hand, however, half of the annual working capital and interest on the fixed capital in agriculture remain to be replaced. Quesnay starts, as we have seen, with the assumption that the circulating capital (*avances annuelles*) of agriculture amounts to two milliards. Besides that, however, fixed capital has to be considered—buildings, livestock, and the like. Quesnay assumes the value of these, in his example, as ten milliards, and his annual interest (*intérêts*) at 10 per cent. is therefore one milliard. By this interest, however, he does not mean surplus value but the cost of repairing and maintaining the buildings and renewing the stock, as well as the accumulation of a fund for equalising out losses, which might occur through bad harvests, cattle diseases, floods and the like, and where possible for improving the soil and for extending operations.

This third milliard corresponds therefore, broadly speaking, to that part of the value of the fixed capital which is equal to its annual wear and tear and which reappears in the value of the annual product. It is moreover for the most part consumed within agriculture, which has produced it (means of subsistence for those working on the buildings, cattle for replacement, stocks for emergencies which may arise, and so on). The sum-total of the circulating, annually consumed capital, and of the fund which is produced for replacing the amount of fixed capital used up annually, amounts to three milliards. Of the part of the gross product which corresponds to this consumed capital, only one milliard is sold and industrial products bought in exchange; two milliards represent products which agriculture itself consumes. These therefore do not circulate.

At the end of the whole process, therefore, we find in the hands of agriculture industrial products to the value of one milliard, and agricultural products to the value of two milliards, which represent the elements of their circulating capital as well as the renewal of the fixed capital used up in the previous year. In the hands of industry we find one milliard of raw materials, as well as another milliard in means of subsistence, to enable industrial production to continue. Reproduction on the same scale is therefore assured up to the coming harvest.]

*   *   *

Even from Quesnay's standpoint—that the whole sterile class are in fact only wage earners—the *Tableau* makes it clear that his assumptions are false.

The *avances primitives* (the fixed capital) made by the productive class are assumed to be five times the amount of the *avances annuelles* (the circulating capital). In the case of the sterile class, however, this item is not mentioned at all—which of course does not prevent it from existing.

Furthermore it is not correct that reproduction is equal to five milliards. The *Tableau* itself shows that it is equal to seven millions: five for the productive class, and two for the sterile class.

The product of the sterile class is equal to two milliards. This product is composed of one milliard of raw materials—which therefore partly enters into the product, and partly replaces the depreciation of the machinery which has entered into the value of the product—and one milliard of means of subsistence, consumed during the period of production.

They sell this entire product to the landowner and the productive class in order firstly to replace the advances (in raw materials) and secondly to obtain agricultural means of subsistence. There remains therefore not a scrap of the manufactured products for their own consumption, and still less for interest and profit. This was noticed by Baudeau (or Letrosne). His explanation is that the sterile class sell their product for more than its value, and so what they sell for two milliards is equal to two milliards minus x.

Their profit, and even their consumption of necessary means of subsistence in the form of manufactured goods, are thus explained only by *the raising of the price of the commodities above their value.* At this point, therefore, the Physiocrats inevitably fall back upon the concept of the mercantilist system, "profit upon alienation". It is this that makes free competition among the industrialists so very essential, so that they may not cheat the productive cultivators too much. This free competition is also necessary in order that agricultural products may be sold at a "good price", and through sale abroad may rise above their domestic price—for a country which exports wheat, etc., is assumed.

[Nevertheless, the *Tableau* was an extremely brilliant conception.] It was an attempt to present the whole productive process of capital as a *process of reproduction*, with circulation merely as the form through which this reproduction took place; and the circulation of money only as a phase in the circulation of capital. The *Tableau* at the same time attempted to show the origin of revenue in this process of reproduction, the exchange between capital and revenue, the relation between productive and final consumption, and to include in the circulation of capital the circulation between producers and consumers (in reality, between capital and revenue), and finally, to show the circulation between the two great divisions of productive labour—raw materials production and industry— as a phase in this process of reproduction. All this was done in a *Tableau* actually consisting of only five lines linking together six points of departure and return; and this was in the first third of the eighteenth century, when political economy was in its infancy. It was incontestably the most brilliant idea for which political economy had up to then been responsible.

The hyperbolical declaration made by the Marquis de Mirabeau, and quoted by Adam Smith with a certain irony, is therefore understandable—"Since the beginning of the world there have been three great discoveries. The first was the birth of writing . . . the second the invention (!) of money . . . the third is the *Tableau economique*, the outcome and the completion of the two others".

As regards the circulation of capital—its reproduction

process—the various forms which it assumes in this process of reproduction—the connection between the circulation of capital and circulation in general (that is, not only the exchange of capital for capital, but of capital for revenue)—Adam Smith in fact only took over the inheritance of the Physiocrats and classified and specified more precisely the separate items in the inventory. But his exposition and interpretation of the movement as a whole was hardly as correct as its outline presentation in the *Tableau economique*, in spite of Quesnay's false assumptions. When moreover Adam Smith says of the Physiocrats: "their labours were certainly of some use to their country", this is an immoderately moderate statement of the significance for example of Turgot, one of the immediate fathers of the French Revolution.

APPENDIX TO THE *TABLEAU ECONOMIQUE*

(1) *The First Two Circulation Movements of the Tableau*

[THE circulation of money starts from the farming class, who, after nature has replaced their working capital, have at their disposal three milliards of agricultural produce and two milliards of money. It is assumed that all purchases and sales which take place between class and class in the course of the working year are aggregated together into one single sum.

The farmers F pay two milliards rent to the landowners P. These in turn purchase means of subsistence from F for one milliard and manufactured goods from S for the other milliard. From there the money returns to F in the purchase of means of subsistence. The farmers are once again in possession of their two milliards of money, but now of only one milliard of produce.]

The two milliards of money have performed *four* processes of circulation.

First, they served as a *means of payment* of rent. In this capacity they do not circulate any part of the annual produce, but are only circulated as an assignment of that part of the total produce which is equal to rent.

Secondly, with one half of the 2,000 millions P buys means of subsistence from F. The latter actually receives back, in the 1,000 millions of money, only half the assignment made to the landowner (in payment of rent) amounting to two-fifths of his product. These 1,000 million serve now as means of purchase, and circulate goods to this amount which go into final consumption.

If we consider only the isolated act, in this transaction the money fulfils for the farmer only the role which, as means of purchase, it always fulfils for the seller—namely that of being the changed form of his commodity. But if we consider this act in conjunction with the previous act of circulation, the money is not merely another form of the farmer's commodity, it is not a golden equivalent for his goods. True, for 1,000 millions in commodities he receives 1,000 millions in money, but in fact he is only buying back the money which he paid as rent to the landowner. The latter pays the farmer with money which he has received from him without giving any equivalent.

This flowing back of the money to the farmer, taken in conjunction with the first act—the payment of rent—does not make it possible for him to regard the money as mere means of circulation. For the return of the money is essentially different from the flowing back of money to its starting point, when this movement is the expression of a process of reproduction.

(2) *The Circulation between Landowner and Farmer*

Let us take an example: The capitalist, or, to leave out of account entirely the characteristics of capitalist reproduction, a producer, lays out £100 for raw materials, work-tools and means of subsistence for the period during which he works. We will assume that he adds no more labour to the means of production than he has laid out in the means of subsistence, the wage which he pays to himself. If the raw materials, etc., equal £60, the consumed means of subsistence £20, and the labour added similarly £20, then the product is equal to £100. If he sells it, then the £100 flows back to him in money, and so on. This flowing back of money to its point of departure expresses here nothing but the regular process of reproduction. The simple metamorphosis M-C-M, the transformation of money into commodities and the retransformation of commodities into money—this mere change of form into commodities and money represents at the same time the process of reproduction. We have at the same time the transformation of money into commodities—means of production and means of subsistence—furthermore the entering of these commodities as elements into the labour process and their emergence from it as a finished product. Thus we see the commodity once more as the result of the process—as soon, that is, as the finished product enters again into the process of circulation, and thereby once again confronts money as a commodity, and finally its retransformation into money, since the finished commodity can only be exchanged again for its production elements after it has first been transformed into money. The constant flowing back of the money to its point of departure expresses here not only the formal transformation of money into commodity and commodity into money—as in the simple process of circulation or the mere exchange of goods—but at the same time the continuous reproduction of the commodity on the part of the same producer. The exchange value (money) is transformed into commodities which enter into consumption and are consumed as use values, but they enter into reproductive or industrial consumption, and therefore recreate their original value, and hence reappear in the same sum of money (as in the above example in which the producer works only for his own subsistence). M-C-M here indicates that M is not only formally transformed into C, but that C is actually consumed as a use value and falls out of circulation into consumption—into industrial consumption, however, so that its value is maintained and reproduced in consumption, and M therefore reappears at the end of the process, and maintains itself in the movement M-C-M.

On the other hand, in the case given above, when money flows back from the landowner to the farmer, no reproduction process takes place. It is as if the farmer had given the landowner tokens or certificates for 1,000 millions of products. As soon as the landowner spends these certificates, they flow back to the farmer, who redeems them. If the landowner had had half the rent paid at once in kind, no circulation of money would have taken place. The whole circulation would have been limited to a simple change of hands, the transfer of the product from the hand of the farmer to that of the landowner. First the farmer gives the landowner the money instead of the commodity, and then the latter returns the money to the farmer in order to take the commodity itself. The money serves the farmer as a *means of payment* to the landowner; it serves the latter as a *means of purchase* in relation to the farmer. In the first function it leaves the farmer, in the second it returns to him. This type of flowing back of money to the producer must take place every time he pays to his creditors, instead of a part of his product, the value of this product in money; and everyone who is a joint owner of his surplus is in this connection a creditor.

For example, all taxes are paid by the producers in money. Here the money is a means of payment to the State. With this money the State buys goods from the producers. In its hands the money becomes a means of purchase and it flows back to the producers in the same measure as their goods leave their hands.

This type of return flow—this peculiar flowing back of money which is not determined by reproduction—must take place in all cases where revenue is exchanged against capital. What makes the money flow back in this case is not reproduction but consumption. The revenue is paid in money; but it can only be consumed in commodities. The money which is received from the producers as revenue must therefore be handed back to them in order to receive the same amount of value in commodities, that is, in order to consume the revenue. The money in which revenue is paid—rent, for example, or interest or taxes (the industrial capitalist pays himself his revenue either in the product itself, or that part of the proceeds of selling the product which forms his revenue)—has the general form of a means of payment. That part of the farmer's product, therefore, which constitutes his rent requires for its circulation between farmer and landowner only a sum of money equal to the value of the product, although this value circulates twice. First the farmer pays the rent in money; then the landowner buys the product with the same money. On the first occasion there is a simple transfer of money, since the money functions only as a means of payment. The second time, however, it acts as a means of purchase, a means for the circulation of commodities. It is as if the farmer had used the money with which he pays his rent to buy from the landowner the latter's share in the product. The latter then, with the same money that he has thus received from the farmer, buys the product back again from the farmer.

The same sum of money, therefore, which is handed over by the producers to the owners of revenue in the form of means of payment, serves the owners of revenue as a means of purchase for the producers' commodities. This twofold change of place

of the money—from the hands of the producer into the hands
of the owner of revenue, and from the hands of the latter back
into the hands of the producer—thus expresses only a single
transfer of the commodity, from the hands of the producer into
those of the owner of revenue. Since the producer, as it were,
owes the owner of revenue a share of his product, the money
rent is in fact only a subsequent payment to the latter of the
value of commodities which have already passed into his
ownership. The commodities are in the hands of the farmer,
but they do not belong to him. With the money which he pays
in the form of revenue, he therefore makes them his own
property. In this transaction the commodities do not change
hands. When the money changes hands, this represents only
the transfer of ownership of the commodities, which remain as
before in the hands of the producer. Hence this twofold change
of place of the money with only a single change of hands for
the commodities. The money circulates twice in order to make
the goods circulate once. But it too circulates only once as
means of circulation (means of purchase), while it circulated
the other time as means of payment, in which type of circulation, as I have shown above, a simultaneous transfer of
commodities and money does not take place.

In fact when the farmer, apart from his product, has no
money, he can only buy his product after he first sells his
commodities, that is, he has to put them through their first
metamorphosis before he can pay them out as money to the landowner. Even taking this into account, there are more changes
of place on the part of the money than of the commodities.
First we have C-M. The commodity is sold and transformed
into money. Here there is a simultaneous exchange of commodity and money. Then however the same money, without
the commodity changing place, passes from the farmer's hand
into the hand of the landowner. Here is a change of place of
the money without the commodity changing place. It is as if
the farmer had had a partner. He has taken the money, but
he must share it with his partner. Or rather, in the case of the
two milliards, it is as if a servant of the landowner had taken
the money. This servant must give it to the landowner; he
cannot keep it in his own pocket. The passing of the money

from one hand into another indicates here no metamorphosis of the commodity, but purely a transfer of money from the hand of its immediate possessor into the hand of its owner. This can happen if the first receiver of the money is merely a carrier of money for his master, etc. Then also the money is not a means of payment, but there is a simple passing over from the hand of the receiver, to whom it does not belong, into the hand of the owner.

This change of place of money has absolutely nothing to do with the metamorphosis of the commodity, any more than the transfer which arises out of mere exchange of one kind of money for another. A means of payment however always implies that the person making the payment has received commodities for which he subsequently pays. As far as the farmer, etc., is concerned, he has not *received* this commodity; it is in his hands before it comes into the hands of the land-owner, and it is a part of his *product*. *Legally*, however, he only gets the ownership of it when he gives up to the landowner the money which he has received for it. His legal title to the commodity changes; the latter, both before and after, is in his hands. But at first it was in his hands as something *in his possession*, but the owner of which was the landowner. Now it is in his hands as his own property. The change in the legal form by which the commodity finds itself in the same hands, has of course not caused the commodity itself to change hands.

(3) *The Final Movements of Circulation*

Let us now turn to the third circulation movement. For the second milliard received as rent P buys manufactured goods from S. Goods to the value of 1,000 millions now pass from S to P, against which money to the value of 1,000 millions passes from P to S. This is simple circulation. Money and commodities merely change hands in reverse directions. Manufactured goods for 1,000 millions, which S sells to P, pass into consumption.

Finally the fourth circulation movement: S on his part now buys, with the 1,000 millions of money, means of subsistence from F, which likewise pass into consumption. These 1,000 millions of money function between S and F as a means of circulation. At the same time, however, two things happen here which do not occur in the circulation process between S and P. In the latter process S had once again transformed a part of his product into money. But in the exchange with F he again transforms the money into means of subsistence, which according to Quesnay are the equivalent of wages; and thereby he replaces his capital which had been laid out in wages and consumed. This retransformation of the 1,000 millions of money into commodities represents in the case of P mere consumption, but in the case of S *industrial* consumption or *reproduction*, since he transforms a part of his commodities once again into one of their elements of production—means of subsistence. The one metamorphosis of the commodity, its retransformation from money into commodities, therefore represents here at the same time the beginning of its *real* and not merely of its *formal* metamorphosis—the beginning of its reproduction—the beginning of its retransformation into the elements of its own production. It is here at the same time the metamorphosis of capital. As against this, for P revenue is only transformed from the form of money into that of commodities. This represents merely consumption.

Secondly, however, when S buys means of subsistence from F for 1,000 millions, the second 1,000 millions of money which F paid to P as land rent return to him. But they return to him only because he withdraws them from circulation again, buys them back with commodities equivalent to 1,000 millions. It is the same as if the landowner had made the farmer pay him the 1,000 millions of means of subsistence, in addition to the first 1,000 millions—that is to say, the second part of his money-rent—in commodities, and had now exchanged these commodities for S's commodities. S merely lifts on behalf of P the second part of the 2,000 millions in commodities, which F has paid to P in money. If payment in kind had taken place F would have given to P means of subsistence to the value of 2,000 millions; P would have consumed 1,000 millions of these himself and exchanged the other 1,000 millions of means of subsistence with S for the latter's manufactured goods.

In this case only the following transactions would have taken place: (1) transfer of the 2,000 millions of means of subsistence from F to P; (2) barter between P and S, in which the former would exchange 1,000 millions worth of means of subsistence for 1,000 millions worth of manufactured goods, and *vice versa*. Instead of these, four circulation movements have occurred: (1) the transfer of 2,000 millions in money from F to P; (2) P buys, for 1,000 millions in money, means of subsistence from F, the money flowing back to F and serving as means of circulation; (3) P buys manufactured goods from S for 1,000 millions of money, the money functioning as means of circulation, changing hands in the reverse direction to the commodity; (4) with the 1,000 millions of money, S buys means of subsistence from F, the money functioning as means of circulation, but for S it circulates at the same time as capital. It flows back to F, because now the second 1,000 millions for which the landowner has a claim on him has been settled. The money does not however flow back directly to him from the landowner, but only after it has served as means of circulation between P and S and has collected on its way (before it takes up the 1,000 millions of means of subsistence) the 1,000 millions of manufactured goods and has transferred them from the manufacturer to the landowner. The transformation of these goods into money (in the exchange with the landowner), like the subsequent transformation of money into means of subsistence (in the exchange with the farmer) as far as S is concerned represent the metamorphosis of his capital, first into the form of money and then into the form of the constituent elements necessary for the reproduction of the capital.

In the hands of F there are now once again 2,000 millions in money and 1,000 millions in goods. To replace his capital F now buys, with the 1,000 millions of money, 1,000 millions of manufactured goods from S. This is a simple process of circulation. On both sides a metamorphosis of capital takes place. The farmer's 1,000 millions of money are transformed back again into productive elements for its own reproduction process. The finished commodity of S is transformed back again into money, making the formal metamorphosis of commodity into money without which the capital cannot retransform itself into its productive elements.

This constitutes the fifth movement of circulation. 1,000 millions of manufactured goods fall out of circulation into reproductive consumption.

Finally, S transforms the 1,000 millions of money, in which form half of his goods now exist, back into the other half of his means of production [purchasing the last 1,000 millions which F has in the form of commodities] in the form of raw materials. This is simple circulation, which is simultaneously for S a metamorphosis of his capital into a form in which it can be reproduced, and for F a retransformation of his product into money. At this point the last fifth of the gross product falls out of circulation into consumption.

F therefore is once again in possession of the 2,000 millions of money, which is logical, since Quesnay conceives the farmer as the capitalist, with P related to him merely as a receiver of revenue and S merely as a wage-worker. If he paid them directly in his products, he would not hand out any money. If therefore he does pay out money, they use it to buy his product, and the money flows back to him. This is the formal flowing back of money to the industrial capitalist, who as a purchaser opens and closes the whole undertaking.

(4) *The Circulation between Capitalist and Worker*

In that part of capital which circulates between the industrial capitalist and the worker, that is, the portion of the circulating capital equal to the variable capital, there is also a flowing back of the money to its point of departure. The capitalist pays the worker his wage in money; with it the worker buys goods from the capitalist, and so the money flows back to the latter—in practice, to the capitalist's banker. Actually, however, the bankers represent the aggregate capital of individual capitalists, the total capital in so far as this takes the form of *money*. This flowing back of the money does not in itself mark any process of reproduction. The capitalist buys labour from the worker with money, and the worker buys commodities from the capitalist with the same money. The same money

appears first as means of purchase for labour, later as means
of purchase for commodities. That it flows back to the capitalist
therefore depends on the fact that he first appears as a buyer
and then again as a seller in relation to the same person. It
leaves him as a buyer and returns to him as a seller. The
worker on the other hand appears first as a seller and then as
a buyer, and consequently he first receives the money and then
he pays it out, while the capitalist, in relation to him, first
pays it out and then receives it. In the case of the capitalist
there takes place here the movement M-C-M. He buys with
money a commodity (labour power); with the product of this
commodity, labour power, he buys money, or in other words
he sells this product once again to the former buyer of money,
the worker.

The worker on the other hand represents the circulation
C-M-C. He sells his commodity, labour power, and with the
money for which he has sold it he buys back a part of his
own product, his own commodity. It could indeed be said
that the worker sells his commodity, labour power, for money,
spends this money on commodities and then sells his labour
power again, so that he likewise represents the movement
M-C-M; and as the money is constantly fluctuating between
him and the capitalist, it could equally be said, according to
whether one looks at it from the standpoint of one side or the
other, that he as well as the capitalist represents the movement
M-C-M. The capitalist however is the buyer. The renewal of
the process starts with him and not with the worker, while
the flowing back of the money is necessary, since the worker
must buy means of subsistence. In this, as in all movements in
which M-C-M is the form of circulation on the one side and
C-M-C the form of circulation on the other, it is apparent
that the aim of the labour process is on the one side exchange
value, money, and therefore its increase, and on the other side
use value, consumption. This takes place also when money
flows back as in the example first considered, where the
movement M-C-M is on the side of the farmer and C-M-C on
the side of the landowner, in as much as the M with which
he buys from the farmer is the money form of land rent, and
therefore already the result of C-M, the changed form of that

part of the product which belongs to the landowner already in the land, in kind.

The same applies, for example, in the exchange of constant capital. The machine maker buys iron from the ironmaster and sells a machine to him. In this case the money flows back. It was expended as a means of purchase for the iron. It then serves the producer of iron as a means of purchase for the machine and so flows back to the maker of the machine. In return for the money that he paid out, the maker of the machine has received the iron, and in return for the money that he has received he has given the machine. The same money has here circulated against double its value. For example, with £1,000 the machine maker bought iron. With the same £1,000 the ironmaster buys machines. The values of the iron and of the machinery amount together to £2,000. But in the process £3,000 must be set in motion: £1,000 in money, £1,000 in machines and £1,000 in iron. If the capitalists exchanged in kind, then the goods would change hands without a farthing being circulated. The same thing happens when they have an account with one another, and money serves them as means of payment. Should it be paper money or credit money (bank notes) that circulates, this makes no difference. Then there is still £1,000 circulating in bank notes, though they have no real value. However that may be, in this case also there is £3,000: £1,000 in iron, £1,000 in machines, and £1,000 in bank notes. But these £3,000 exist only, as in the first case, because the machine maker had £2,000, machines worth £1,000 and £1,000 in money—in gold and silver or bank notes. In both cases the iron master returns to him only the money, which he receives because the machine maker did not pay for the first commodity, the iron, with a commodity (a machine), and therefore paid for it in money. As soon as he pays for it with a commodity, that is, sells the commodity to the iron master, the latter gives him the money back, since it is not paid for twice over, once in money and then in goods.

In both cases the money or the bank note represents the changed form of a commodity previously purchased from the machine maker, or commodity transformed into money, even though not sold (as in the case of revenue). Here the flowing back of the money therefore expresses only the fact that the man who has handed out the money for a commodity, has thrown the money into circulation, draws the money back again from circulation by the sale of another commodity which he throws into circulation. This same £1,000 could pass through thirty hands among capitalists in one day, and it would only transfer capital from the one to the other. The machine would go to the ironmaster, iron to the peasant, corn to the starch-maker or the distiller and so on. Finally, the £1,000 could fall once again into the hands of the machine maker, and go on from him to the iron master, and so on. And so over £40,000 of goods could circulate with £1,000 of money, in such a way that this could always flow back again to the man who laid it out.

A part of the profit made with this £40,000 forms interest, which is paid by various capitalists—for example, by the machine maker to the man who lends him £1,000, by the iron master to the man who lends him £1,000, which he has long ago spent on coal or wages, etc.

From this fact Proudhon concludes that this £1,000 in money brings in the *entire interest* received from the £40,000. If therefore this were 5 per cent., it would yield £2,000 interest. Hence he logically gets the result that the £1,000 has produced interest at 200 per cent. And here we have the critic *par excellence* of political economy!

Although however M-C-M, representing the money circulation between capitalist and worker, in itself does not signify any act of reproduction, it nevertheless expresses the continuous repetition of this act, the continuity of the flowing back of money. No buyer can continually come forward as a seller without the reproduction of the commodity which he sells. This in fact holds good for all who do not live on rent, interest or taxes. For one section, however, if the act is completed, the flowing back process M-C-M continually takes place—as in the case of the capitalist in relation to the worker or landowner or rentier (on this side there is purely a flowing back process). For the other section, as in the case of the worker, the act is completed when he buys the commodity and so has completed the process C-M-C. It is this act which he continuously renews. His initiative is constantly as a seller and not as a buyer. This holds good for the entire circulation of money which represents simply the expenditure of revenue.

The capitalist himself, for example, consumes a certain amount each year. He has transformed his commodity into money in order to spend this money on commodities, which he will finally consume. Here it is C-M-C, and there is no flowing back of the money to him. The flowing back takes place, however, in relation to the seller, for example the shop-keeper, for whom the expenditure of revenue brings the replacement of his capital.

In such cases there can be an exchange, a circulation of revenue against revenue. The butcher buys bread from the baker; the baker meat from the butcher; both consume their revenue. That meat which the butcher and the bread that the baker themselves eat, they do not pay for. This part of their revenue is consumed in kind by each of them. It is however possible that the meat which the baker buys from the butcher replaces for the latter not capital but revenue—that part of the meat he has sold which represents not only his profit but the part of his profit which he wishes to consume himself as revenue. The bread which the butcher buys from the baker is also an expenditure of his revenue. If they have an account with each other, then one or the other has only the balance to pay out. There is no circulation of money so far as concerns that part of their mutual purchases and sales which has been set off against each other. But supposing that the baker has to pay the balance, and this balance represents revenue for the butcher. Then he spends the baker's money, for other articles of consumption. Let us assume that this amounts to £10, which he spends at the tailor's. If this £10 represents revenue for the tailor, then he spends it in a similar way. He in turn buys bread, etc., with it. In this way money flows back to the baker, no longer however to replace his revenue, but his capital.

Yet another example. The flowing back of bank notes to a bank which discounts a bill or makes advances in notes, is a phenomenon quite different from the return movements of money considered hitherto. In this case the transformation of the commodity into money is anticipated. The commodity receives the form of money before it is sold, perhaps before it is produced. Or it may have been already sold, for bills of exchange. *In any case* it has not yet been *paid for*, not yet transformed back again into money. In each case, therefore, this transformation is anticipated. As soon as it is sold, or due to be sold, the money flows back to the bank, either in gold and silver or in its own notes, which then return from circulation, or else in notes of some other bank which are then exchanged for their own between bank and bank, so that then both notes are withdrawn from circulation and return to their point of issue. If gold and silver is demanded in exchange for the bank's notes which are in the hands of some third party, then the notes return. If they are not converted, then there will be in circulation so much the less gold and silver which now lies in the bank's vaults instead of notes. In all these cases the process is: the existence of the money, the transformation of the commodity into money, was anticipated. When then it is really transformed into money, it is transformed into money for the second time. This its second existence as money, however, brings the money back, dissolving and replacing its first existence as money, returning it to the bank from circulation. It may be *the same identical* bundle of notes which expressed its first existence as money that also expresses the second. In return for a bill of exchange, for example, bank notes have been advanced to a spinner; he has received the bill of exchange from the weaver. He pays out the notes which he has received for coal, cotton, etc. The various people into whose hands these notes come when their commodities are paid for finally spend them on linen, and so they reach the weaver, who on the day when the bill matures pays the identical notes to the spinner, who returns them to the bank. It is not at all necessary that the second, posthumous, transformation of the commodity into money—after its first transformation in anticipation—should be in different money from the first. And so it seems as if the spinner has in fact got nothing out of it, for he has borrowed notes, and the end of the process is that he gets them back and returns them to the bank that issued them. In fact, however, during the period one and the same note has served as means of circulation and as means of payment, and with it the spinner has in part paid his debts and in part bought the commodities necessary for the reproduction of the yarn; and in this way he has realised surplus value (which means, exploitation of the workers) out of which he can now pay back a part to the bank, also paid in money—since more money has flowed back to him than he had expended, advanced or laid out.

(5) *The Quantity of Money required for Circulation*

S buys from F means of subsistence for 1,000 millions, and raw materials for 1,000 millions; and F in turn buys from him only 1,000 millions of commodities to replace his *avances*. Therefore S has a balance of 1,000 millions to settle, which in the final instance he pays with the 1,000 millions he has received from P. Quesnay seems to have confused this *payment* of 1,000 millions to F with the *buying* of F's product to an amount of 1,000 millions.

In fact, according to our reckoning, the 2,000 millions of money had only served:

(1) to pay rent to an amount of 2,000 millions in money;

(2) to circulate 3,000 millions of the farmer's gross product (of which 1,000 millions are P's means of subsistence, and 2,000 millions means of subsistence and raw materials for S), and to circulate 2,000 millions of S's gross product (of which 1,000 millions are for P, who consumes them, and 1,000 millions for F, who consumes them for reproduction). The final purchase, in which S buys raw materials from F, S settles with F in money.

[Two alternatives are possible:]

S has received 1,000 millions of money from P. With these 1,000 millions of money he buys from F means of subsistence for 1,000 millions. With the same 1,000 millions of money, F buys from S manufactured goods. With the same 1,000 millions of money, S buys from F raw materials.

Or, S buys from F raw materials for 1,000 millions of money and means of subsistence for 1,000 millions in money. F buys commodities from S for 1,000 millions of money. In this case, 1,000 millions flowed back to S, but only because it was assumed that, in addition to the 1,000 millions of money which he receives from P and the 1,000 millions of commodities which he has for sale, he had over and above these sums another 1,000 millions of money, which he himself threw into circulation. Instead of 1,000 millions of money circulating the goods between him and the farmer, on this assumption 2,000 millions would be used for this purpose. Then 1,000 millions returns to S. For he buys from the farmer to an amount of 2,000 millions of money. The latter buys commodities from S to an amount of 1,000 millions, for which F would have to pay back half of the money received from him.

In the first case S buys in two stages. First, he spends 1,000 millions; this flows back to him from F, and then once again he pays them out finally and nothing flows back.

In the second case, on the other hand, S makes a single purchase for 2,000 millions. If F now buys back commodities from S for 1,000 millions, this money will remain with S. The circulation would have used 2,000 millions instead of 1,000. While in the first case 1,000 millions of money realised 2,000 millions of commodities in two rotations, in the second case these commodities were realised by a simple rotation of 2,000 millions of money. If the farmer now pays back 1,000 millions to S, the latter then has no more than in the first case. For in addition to the 1,000 millions of commodities he has thrown into circulation 1,000 millions of money from funds of his own which existed before the circulation process began. He laid them out for circulation, and they therefore flow back to him.

In the first case, the aggregate value in circulation (if the money is real money) amounts to 4,000 millions, 3,000 in commodities, and 1,000 in money. The amount of money circulating and (from F's standpoint) originally thrown into circulation was never more than 1,000 millions, that is, never more than the balance which S had to pay to F. Inasmuch as F buys from S to the value of 1,000 millions, S can settle his balance with this 1,000 millions.

In the second case, S throws 2,000 millions into circulation. It is true that with it he buys commodities from F for 2,000 millions. In this case 2,000 millions is needed as means of circulation and is paid out against an equivalent in commodities. But F buys back from S to an amount of 1,000 millions. 1,000 millions therefore returns to S, since the balance which he has to pay to F only amounts to 1,000 millions and not 2,000 millions. He has now reimbursed F with 1,000 millions in commodities, and so F must pay back to him the 1,000 millions which it *now* appears S had paid him in money to no purpose. This case is interesting enough to dwell on for a moment.

In the circulation assumed above of 3,000 millions of commodities, of which 2,000 millions are means of subsistence and 1,000 millions industrial goods, there are various possible alternatives; but we must consider, first, the case as advanced by Quesnay, presupposing 1,000 millions of money in the hands of S and 1,000 millions of money in the hands of F at the moment when the circulation between the two begins; secondly, let us assume for the sake of illustration that S, in addition to the 1,000 millions of money which he receives from P, has a further 1,000 millions of money in his safe.

I. First, the case as put by Quesnay. With 1,000 of money, S buys 1,000 of commodities from F. With the 1,000 of money thus received from S, F buys 1,000 of commodities from S. Finally S, with the 1,000 of money he has thus got back, buys 1,000 of commodities from F. The 1,000 of money remains therefore with F, and represents for him capital (in fact, together with the other 1,000 of money, which he has received back from P, and which constitutes revenue, with which in the following year he once again pays the rent in money, namely 2,000 of money). Here 1,000 of money has circulated three times, from S to F, from F to S, from S to F, and each time for 1,000 of commodities, therefore for a total of 3,000. If the money itself has value, then values totalling 4,000 are in circulation. Money functions here only as means of circulation; but it is transformed into money, and, what is more essential, into capital, for F, whose hand it reaches last, where it remains.

II. Second: The money functions purely as means of payment. In this case S, who buys commodities from F for 2,000, and F, who buys commodities from S for 1,000, come to a settlement with each other. S has to pay, at the end of the transaction, a balance of 1,000 in money. As before, 1,000 of money find their way into F's cash-box, but without having served as means of circulation. For him the money is a change-over of capital, since it only replaces for him a capital of 1,000 in commodities. Total values of 4,000 have therefore been in circulation as before. However, instead of the 3 movements of 1,000 in money, only one has taken place, and the money has paid for a total value of commodities equal only to itself. Previously it was three times as much. What would be saved as compared with the first case would be the two superfluous movements of circulation.

III. Third: F, with the 1,000 in money (received from P) appears first as a purchaser, and buys commodities from S for 1,000. Instead of lying fallow with him as a reserve for paying the next rent, the 1,000 of money now circulates. S has now 2,000 in money (1,000 from P and 1,000 from F). With this 2,000 in money he buys 2,000 commodities from F. A value of 5,000 has now therefore been in circulation (3,000 in commodities and 2,000 in money). A circulation of 1,000 in money and 1,000 in commodities, and a circulation of 2,000 in money and 2,000 in commodities has taken place. Of this 2,000 in money, the 1,000 originating from the farmer circu-lates twice, that originating from S only once. Now 2,000 in money returns to F, of which however only 1,000 settles his balance; the other 1,000 in money, which he himself threw into circulation by taking the initiative as buyer, flows back to him in the course of circulation.

IV. Fourth: With 2,000 in money (1,000 from P and 1,000 which he himself throws into circulation from his own resources) S buys 2,000 in commodities from F in one transac-tion. F buys back 1,000 of commodities from S, and so returns to him 1,000 in money. He retains as before 1,000 in money for settling the balance between himself and S. Now total values of 5,000 have circulated, in two movements of circulation.

In this case 1,000 in money returns to S, but this is the 1,000 in money which he threw into circulation himself, out of his own resources and not from the sale of his commodities to P.

If in case I, as indeed in case II, never more than 1,000 millions circulates in money, but changes hands three times, while in case II it circulates only once, this is simply due to the fact that case II assumes a development of credit, and so an economy in payments, while in case I a rapid movement takes place; but each time the money comes in as means of circulation, so each time the value must seem to be doubled at the two poles, once in money and once in commodities. If, in cases III and IV, 2,000 in money circulates instead of 1,000 as in I and II, this is because once in both cases (in case III by S as buyer, who closes the process of circulation, and in case IV by S as buyer, who opens the process of circulation), 2,000 of commodities enter circulation together, and indeed on the presupposition that payment for them is not to be made in the balance of an account, but that they are to be bought outright.

The most interesting thing in the movement is in every case the 1,000 in money which, in case III F, and in case IV S, leave behind, although in both cases the balance of 1,000 in money is paid to F, and he receives in case III not a farthing more and in case IV not a farthing less. Naturally, what are here exchanged are always equivalents, and when we speak of a balance, we mean no more than the equivalent value which is paid in money instead of in commodities.

In case III, F throws 1,000 in money into circulation and receives from S its equivalent in commodities or 1,000 in commodities. S, however, now buys commodities from him for 2,000 in money. The first 1,000 in money, which F has thrown in, thus returns to him, because 1,000 in commodities is taken from him in exchange. With the money laid out by him, he gets paid for the 1,000 of commodities. The second 1,000 in money he receives in payment for the second 1,000 in commodities. This balance of money is due to him, because he buys commodities for a total of only 1,000 in money, and commodities to the amount of 2,000 are bought from him.

In case IV, S puts into circulation in a single payment 2,000 in money for which he takes 2,000 in commodities from F. F in turn buys from him 1,000 in commodities with the money spent by S himself, and so 1,000 in money return to F.

In case IV, S in fact gives F 1,000 in commodities, the equivalent of 1,000 money; and 2,000 money in cash; that is,

3,000 money. He receives from him, however, only 2,000 in commodities. Therefore F has to return to him 1,000 money.

In case III, F gives S in commodities 2,000, the equivalent of 2,000 money, and 1,000 money in cash. This makes therefore 3,000 money; but he receives from him only 1,000 in commodities, the equivalent of 1,000 money. Therefore S has to return to him 2,000 money. He pays back 1,000 in the money which F himself has put into circulation, and he himself puts 1,000 into circulation.

In both cases S receives 2,000 commodities, and F 1,000 commodities plus 1,000 money, that is, the money balance. If in case III a further 1,000 money flows to F, it is only the money which he has thrown into circulation in excess of the commodities which he has drawn out of circulation. It is the same with S in case IV.

In both cases S has to pay a balance of 1,000 money in cash, because he withdraws from circulation 2,000 in commodities, and puts into circulation commodities to the amount of only 1,000. In both cases F has to receive a balance of 1,000 money in cash, because he puts into circulation 2,000 in commodities, and draws out of it commodities to the amount of only 1,000; the second 1,000 commodities must therefore be paid to him in money. In both cases it is only this 1,000 in money which in the last resort can change hands. Since however 2,000 in money are in circulation, 1,000 money must flow back to the one who put it into circulation. This may be F, who receives a balance of 1,000 money from circulation, but in addition to that has put into circulation another 1,000 in money; or it may be S, who has to pay on balance only 1,000 money, but has in addition put 1,000 money into circulation.

In case III, it is possible for 1,000 money to come into circulation [over and above the sum of money which in the given circumstances is needed for the circulation of the quantity of commodities], because F appears first as a purchaser and therefore must put money into circulation, whatever his ultimate relationship may turn out to be. In case IV similarly 2,000 money come into circulation, instead of only 1,000 as in II, because firstly S appears first as buyer and secondly because he buys the 2,000 commodities in one lump.

In both cases the money circulating between these buyers and sellers can ultimately only equal the balance which one has to pay to the other. For the money laid out by either S or F in excess of this amount is paid back to him.

Assuming that F buys commodities from S for 2,000 in money; then the transaction would be as follows. First, F gives 1,000 in money to S for commodities. S buys commodities from F for 2,000 in money; hence the first 1,000 returns to F, and also a further 1,000. F again buys commodities from S for 1,000 money; so that this 1,000 now returns to S. At the end of the process, F would have commodities equal to 2,000 money, and the 1,000 money which he had originally, before the process of circulation began; and S would have commodities to the amount of 2,000 and the 1,000 money which he similarly had originally. F's 1,000 money and S's 1,000 money would have changed places only as means of circulation, in order then to return as money—and in this case also as capital—to the two persons who had laid them out. If they had both used money only as means of payment, they would have set off 2,000 commodities against 2,000 commodities; their accounts would have cancelled out, and not a penny would have circulated between them.

The money, therefore, which as means of circulation passes between two parties who face each other in the twofold capacity of buyer and seller, returns to each, and can circulate in three cases.

First: The values of commodities supplied are equal. In this case the money returns to the one who has advanced it for circulation and so has met the costs of circulation out of his capital. For example, if F and S each buy commodities from the other for 2,000, and S commences the process, then he buys commodities from F for 2,000 in money. F returns to him the 2,000 money, buying with it from him 2,000 commodities. Thus after the transaction, just as before, S has 2,000 commodities and 2,000 money. Or if, as in the case previously taken, both advance the means of circulation in equal proportions, then the amount advanced by each for circulation returns to him; as above, 1,000 money to F and 1,000 money to S.

Second: The commodity values exchanged between the two parties are not equal. There is a balance to be paid in money.

If now the circulation of commodities has taken place as in case I above, so that no more money entered *into circulation* than was necessary for the paying of this balance, always only this sum being transferred backwards and forwards between the two parties, then it falls finally into the hands of the last seller who keeps the balance for himself.

Third: The commodity values exchanged on both sides are not equal. There is a balance to pay; but the circulation of commodities takes such a form that more money circulates than is necessary for paying the balance. In this case the superfluous money, in excess of the balance, returns to the party that advanced it. In case III, to the man who receives the balance, in case IV to the one who has to pay for it.

In the second case the money only *returns* if the receiver of the balance is the first purchaser, as for example with the worker and the capitalist. It changes hands when the other one first appears as a purchaser.

All this, of course, is on the assumption that the amounts of commodities in question are bought and sold by the same person, so that the relation of each to the other is alternately buyer and seller. Suppose, on the other hand, that the 3,000 commodities are equally divided among the commodity-owners A, A', and A", the sellers, and that the transactions are with the buyers B, B', and B". If the three purchases take place simultaneously, and therefore at different points in space, then 3,000 money must circulate, so that as the outcome each A is in possession of 1,000 money and each B in possession of 1,000 commodities. If the sales follow each other at successive times, the same 1,000 money can set several 1,000's of commodities in circulation, if the commodity metamorphoses are interlinked, so that some of the persons are both buyers and sellers, even if they are not, as in the above case, dealing with the same persons, but with one person as buyer and the other as seller. For example:

(1) A sells commodities to B for 1,000 money.
(2) A buys from B' with the 1,000 money.
(3) B' buys from A' with the 1,000 money.
(4) A' from B" with the 1,000 money.
(5) B" from A" with the 1,000 money.

The money would have changed hands five times among the six persons, and commodities also would have been circulated therefore for 5,000 money. If commodities for only 3,000 are to be circulated then we have: (1) A buys commodities from B for 1,000 money. (2) B buys from A' for 1,000 money. (3) A' buys from B' for 1,000 money. Three changes of position among four persons. And so on.

The examples outlined above do not contradict the law expounded earlier: "That with a given rapidity of circulation of money, and a given total price of commodities, the quantity of the circulating medium is determined" (*Critique of Political Economy*, Kerr edition, p. 137).

In example 1 above, 1,000 money circulates three times, and so commodities circulate to the amount of 3,000 money. The quantity of money in circulation is therefore

$$\frac{3,000 \text{ (the price-total)}}{3 \text{ circulations}} = 1,000 \text{ money.}$$

In example III or IV the total price of the commodities in circulation is indeed the same—equivalent to 3,000 money; but the rapidity of circulation is different. 2,000 money circulates once; that is, 1,000 money plus 1,000 money. Of the 2,000 money, however, 1,000 circulates once more. 2,000 money circulates two-thirds of the 3,000 commodities, and half of that amount will circulate 1,000 commodities, or one-third. The one 1,000 money circulates twice, but the other 1,000 money circulates only once. The twofold circulation of 1,000 money realises an aggregate commodity price equal to 2,000 money; and the single circulation of 1,000 money realises an aggregate commodity price equal to 1,000 money; both together=3,000 commodities. What then is the rapidity of circulation of the money in relation to the commodities which in this case it circulates? The 2,000 money makes $1\frac{1}{2}$ circulations (it is the same as if the total sum first completed one circulation, and then half of it completed another circulation)=3/2. And in fact,

$$\frac{3,000 \text{ (the price total)}}{3/2 \text{ circulations}} = 2,000 \text{ money.}$$

But how is the *varying rapidity* of the money circulation determined in this case?

Both in III and in IV the difference arises in contrast to I from the fact that in I the aggregate price of the commodities circulating at each moment is never greater and never smaller than one-third of the price of the total amount of commodities circulating. Commodities circulate in each transaction only to the amount of 1,000 money. In III and IV, on the other hand, commodities circulate once to the amount of 2,000 and once to the amount of 1,000; that is, once two-thirds of the existing stock of commodities, and once one-third. This is the reason why in wholesale trade larger currency denominations are required for circulation than in retail trade.

As I have already said, in the circulation of money the flowing back of the money shows in the first place that *the buyer has again become a seller*, so that it is in fact immaterial whether he sells to the same persons from whom he bought, or not. If this however takes place between the same persons, then the phenomena occur which have occasioned so many mistakes (Destutt de Tracy). The buyer becoming a seller shows that new commodities are for sale. It is continuity in the circulation of commodities—which is the same thing as their continual renewal; that is, reproduction. The buyer can again become a seller—as for example the manufacturer in relation to the worker—without this expressing an act of reproduction. It is only the continuous repetition in the flowing back of the money that can be said to show reproduction.

The flowing back of money, in as much as it represents the retransformation of capital into its money form, necessarily indicates the end of a cycle, and the start of a new reproductive process if the capital continues to function as such. Here also the capitalist, as in all other cases, was a seller, C-M, and then a buyer, M-C, but it is only in M that his capital once again has the form in which it can exchange for its reproductive elements, and the C here represents these productive elements. M-C here represents the transformation of money capital into productive or industrial capital.

Furthermore, as we have seen, the flowing back of the money to its point of departure may indicate that the money balance in a series of purchases and sales is in favour of the buyer with whom this series of transactions began.

The first buyer F buys from S for 1,000 money. S buys from F for 2,000 money. Here 1,000 money flows back to F. In the case of the other 1,000, what takes place is only a simple transfer of money from S to F.

Finally, however, the money may return to its point of departure without this representing the payment of a balance, both (1) when the balance of payments cancels out, so that there is no balance to be paid in money; (2) when the balances do not cancel out, and therefore a balance has to be settled in money. See the cases explained above. In all these cases it is immaterial whether for example F's transactions are with the same S. For S here represents, as opposed to F, and F as opposed to S, the total number of those who sell to him and those who buy from him (just as in the example where the payment of a balance accounts for the return of the money). In all these cases the money flows back to the person who has, so to speak, financed the circulation. It has performed its function in circulation, just as bank notes do, and returns to the person who issued it. *In this case it is only a means of circulation. The capitalists in question pay each other, and so it returns to the person who disbursed it.*

(6) *Explanation of Profit on Capital by the Fact that the Worker's Wage is advanced Before the Commodity is Sold*

It can be seen from the foregoing how preposterous is the suggestion that "explains" the capitalist's profit from the fact that he advances money to the worker before he has transformed the commodity into money. Firstly: when I buy goods for my own consumption I do not receive any profit, in spite of the fact that I am the buyer and the owner of the commodity is the "seller", and that my commodity has the form of money while his has first to be transformed into money. The capitalist however only pays for the labour after he has consumed it, while other commodities are paid for before they are consumed. This corresponds with the peculiar nature of the commodity which is sold, and which in fact is only delivered in so far as it is consumed. In this transaction money is a means of payment.

The capitalist has always appropriated the commodity labour *before* he pays for it. The fact, however, that he only buys it in order to make a profit out of the re-sale of its product is not a *reason* for his making this profit. It is a motive. And it only amounts to saying that he makes a profit on the purchase of wage labour, *because* he wants to make a profit out of its re-sale.

Secondly: But he does nevertheless advance to the worker, in the form of money, that part of the product which belongs to him as wages, thus saving him the trouble and the risk and the time involved if he had himself to transform into money that part of the commodity which belongs to him as wages. Is the worker not to pay him for this trouble, this risk and this time? Then he must on this account receive less from the product than he would otherwise get! This upsets the whole relationship between wage labour and capital and destroys the economic justification of surplus value. The result of the process is in fact that the fund out of which the capitalist pays the wage earner is nothing but the latter's own product, and that therefore capitalist and worker *actually* share the product in definite parts. But this actual result has nothing whatever to do with the transaction between capital and wages (on which rests the economic justification of surplus value, the justification founded on the laws of commodity exchange itself). What the capitalist buys is the temporary right to dispose of labour power; he only pays for it when this labour power has worked, embodied itself in a product. Here, as in all cases where money serves as a means of payment, purchase and sale precede the real transfer of the money by the buyer. After that transaction, however, is completed, and before the real process of production begins, the labour *belongs* to the capitalist. The commodity, which comes from this process as its product, belongs wholly to him. He has produced it with means of production which he owns and with labour which he has bought and which therefore, although not yet paid for, belongs to him. It is the same as if he had not consumed another person's labour in its production. The profit which the capitalist makes, the surplus value which he realises, originates precisely from the fact that what the worker sells to him is not labour realised in a commodity, but his labour power itself as a commodity. If he had confronted him in the first form—as owner of commodities—the capitalist would not have been able to make any profit, to realise any surplus value, since according to the law of value equivalents are exchanged, an equal quantity of labour for an equal quantity of labour. The surplus value of the capitalist originates precisely from the fact that he buys from the worker not commodities but his labour power itself, and this has less value than its product, or—what is the same thing—realises itself in more embodied labour than is realised in itself. But now, in order to justify profit, its very source is covered up and the whole transaction from which it springs is renounced. Because in fact—once the process is continuous—the capitalist pays the worker only out of his own product, the worker is paid only from a part of his own product, and the advance is therefore a mere illusion— now it is said that the worker has sold his share of the product to the capitalist *before it was transformed into money.* (Perhaps before it was capable of being transformed into money, for although the labour of the worker has materialised itself in a product, it may be that only an instalment of the saleable commodity is as yet realised, as for example parts of a house.) Thus the capitalist ceases to be the owner of the product, and thereby the whole process through which he has appropriated another's labour *gratis* is renounced. Now commodity owner confronts commodity owner. The capitalist has the money, and the worker sells to him not his labour power but commodities, namely the part of the product in which his own labour is realised.

The worker will then say to the capitalist: "Of this 5 lb. of yarn say three-fifths represent constant capital. They belong to you. Two-fifths, that is 2 lb., represent my newly added labour. You have therefore to pay me for two lb. So pay me the value of 2 lb." And therewith he would pocket not only the wages but also the profit, in short, a sum of money equal to the amount of the newly added, materialised labour in the form of the 2 lb.

"But," the capitalist says, "have I not advanced the constant capital?"

"That's right," says the worker, "so you deduct 3 lb., and pay me only 2."

"But," the capitalist goes on, "you couldn't materialise your labour, you couldn't spin, without my cotton and my machine! You must pay extra for them."

"Oh," says the worker, "the cotton would have rotted and the spindles rusted if I hadn't used them for spinning. The 3 lb. of yarn which you are deducting do represent, it is true, only the value of your cotton and the spindles used up in the 5 lb. of yarn and so contained. in them. But it is only my labour that has maintained the value of the cotton and spindles by using these means of production as means of production. For this value-maintaining power of my labour I don't ask anything of you, because it hasn't cost me any extra labour time over and above the spinning, for which I get the 2 lb. This is a natural faculty of my labour, which costs me nothing, though it maintains the value of the constant capital. I don't ask anything of you for that, and just as little can you ask anything of me for not being able to spin *without* spindles and cotton. For without spinning the spindles and cotton would not be worth a straw."

Driven into a corner, the capitalist now says: "The 2 lb. of yarn are in fact worth 4s. They represent that much labour time of yours. But am I to pay you for them before I have sold them! Perhaps I may not sell them at all. That is risk No. 1. Secondly, perhaps I may sell them at less than their price. That is risk No. 2. And thirdly, in any case it takes time to sell them. Am I to incur both risks for you *for nothing* and lose my time into the bargain? You can't expect something for nothing!"

"Wait a moment," answers the worker. "What is our relationship? We face each other *as owners of commodities, you as buyer, I as seller*, for you want to buy from me the 2 lb., my share of the product, and in fact they contain nothing but my own labour time materialised. Now you assert that I must sell you my commodity *below* its value, so that as a result you may receive more value in commodity form than you now possess in money. The value of my commodity is 4s. You want to give for it only 2s., so that—since 2s. contains as much labour

time as 1 lb. of yarn—you get from the exchange twice as
much value as you give. I on the other hand get instead of an
equal value only half as much—instead of an equivalent for
2 lb. of yarn, an equivalent for only 1 lb. And on what do you
base this demand, which is contrary to the law of value and of
exchange of commodities in proportion to their value? On
what? On the fact that you are buyer and I am seller, that my
value is in the form of yarn, a commodity, and yours in the
form of money, that the same value in the form of yarn
confronts the same value in the form of money. Or do you
hold the childish view that every commodity must be sold
under its price—that is, for less than the sum of money which
represents its value—because it takes on a greater value in the
form of money? But no, my friend, it gets no greater value from
the exchange; the amount of value in it does not change, it
merely shows up as exchange value in pure form. Besides, my
friend, think of the troubles you are laying up for yourself if
you adopt this standpoint. Your assertion amounts to saying
that the seller must always sell his commodity to the buyer
below its value. Certainly this was so when we workers sold
you, not at that time our goods, but our labour power itself.
True, you bought it at its value, but you bought our labour
itself for less than the value in which it makes itself manifest.
But let us say no more of that unpleasant memory. We've got
beyond that, thank goodness, since—by your own decision—
we are no longer to sell you our labour power as a commodity,
but the commodity itself which is the product of our labour.
Now we come back to the troubles you laid up for yourself.
The law you now set up, that the seller pays for the transformation of his commodity into money not only with his commodity,
through the exchange of his commodity for money, but that in
addition he pays by selling the commodity under its price—
this law, according to which the buyer always cheats and gets
the better of the seller, must hold good in like measure for
every buyer and seller. That granted, we'll agree to your
proposition, but on condition that you submit yourself to the
law you have just created, namely the law that the seller must
present the buyer with a part of his commodity *for nothing* in
return for the buyer transforming it for him into money. So

you buy my 2 lb., which are worth 4s., for 2s., thus making a
profit of 2s. or 100 per cent. But now you have 5 lb. of yarn,
of a value of 10s., after buying from me the 2 lb. belonging to
me. Now you think you're going to make a deal. The 5 lb.
cost you only 8s., and you want to sell them at 10s. Stop!—
says the buyer. Your 5 lb. of yarn are a commodity, and you
are a seller. I have the same value in money, I am buyer.
So, in accordance with the law which you acknowledge, I
must make 100 per cent. profit out of you. You must therefore
sell me the yarn at 50 per cent. of its value, for 5s. I'll give
you then 5s., and get in exchange commodities to the value
of 10s., and make a hundred per cent. profit out of you, for
what's sauce for the goose is sauce for the gander. So you see,
my friend, where you get with your new law; you would only
have overreached yourself—at one moment, true, you are a
buyer, but after that you are again a seller. In this particular
case you would lose more as a seller than you gain as a buyer.
And don't forget this—Before the 2 lb. of yarn which you want
to buy from us was in existence, didn't you make other purchases in advance, but for which the 5 lb. of yarn would never
have been there at all? Didn't you buy cotton and spindles,
which are now represented in 3 lb. of yarn? At that time the
cotton jobber in Liverpool and the spindle manufacturer in
Oldham faced you as sellers, and you faced them as buyer;
they represented commodities, you money—exactly the same
relationship as we at the moment have the honour, or the
misfortune, to have to each other. Wouldn't the cunning cotton
jobber and your jovial colleague from Oldham have had a
good laugh at you, if you had demanded that they should
hand over to you for nothing a part of the cotton and spindles,
or, what is the same thing, sell you these commodities below
their price (and their value), because you transformed their
commodities into money, while they transformed money into
commodities for you—because they were sellers, you buyer?
They risked nothing, for they got ready money, exchange value
in the pure, independent form. You on the other hand, what
a risk you were taking! First to make spindles and cotton into
yarn, taking all the risks of the production process, and then
finally the risk of selling the yarn again, of transforming it into

money! The risk whether it would sell at its value, over, or under its value? The risk of not selling it at all, of not transforming it back into money. The yarn as such hasn't the slightest interest for you. You don't eat yarn, you don't drink it, you have no use for it at all except to sell it. And do you think that you must anyhow be paid for the loss of time wasted in transforming the yarn back again into money, that is, in essence, in transforming the spindles and cotton into money? Old boy, your colleagues will reply, don't make an ass of yourself, and don't talk nonsense. What the devil do we care what you mean to do with our cotton and our spindles? Burn them, chuck them away, do what you like with them, but pay for them! What an idea! We are to make you a present of our goods, because you've set yourself up as a spinner and don't seem much at home in business, inasmuch as you make such a song about its risks and dangers. Give up your spinning mill, or don't come to market with such preposterous ideas!"

The capitalist, with a supercilious smile, replies to this tirade from the workers: "Evidently you people are a bit out of your depth. You're talking about things you don't understand. Do you imagine that I've paid ready money to the Liverpool fellow and the chap in Oldham? Not a brass farthing! I've paid them in bills of exchange, and the Liverpool fellow's cotton was in fact spun and sold before his bill fell due. With you it's another affair altogether. You want to get ready money."

"Very well," say the workers, "and what did the Liverpool fellow and the chap from Oldham do with your bills of exchange?"

"What did they do with them?" rejoins the capitalist. "That's a stupid question. They deposited them with their bankers and got them cashed then and there."

"How much do they pay the banker for that?"

"How much? Money is very cheap just now. I imagine they paid about 3 per cent. discount—that is to say, not 3 per cent. of the sum involved, but an amount for the term of the bill corresponding to a 3 per cent. rate for the whole year."

"So much the better," say the workers. "Pay us 4s., which is the price of our commodity—or pay us 24s., as we'd like to reckon it weekly. But take from it 14 days' interest at the rate of 3 per cent. per annum."

"But," says the capitalist, "this bill of exchange is too small. No banker would discount it."

"Very well," the workers reply. "There are a hundred of us, so you have to pay us 2,400s. Give us a bill of exchange for this amount. £120—that's not too small a sum to be discounted. In fact you can discount it yourself, and then the amount can't be too small for you, as it's the same as the amount from which, you allege, you draw your profit from us. The amount deducted wouldn't be worth mentioning. And since in this way we would get the major part of our product in its entirety, we would soon reach the point at which we no longer needed you to discount for us. Naturally we shall not give you longer credit than the fourteen days the stockjobber gives you."

If—completely reversing the actual relationship—wages are to be derived from the discount on the part of the value of the total product which belongs to the worker, from the fact that the capitalist pays the worker this part in advance in *cash*, the capitalist would have to give the worker very short term bills of exchange, such as for example he himself pays to the cotton jobber and others. The worker would receive most of his product, and the capitalist would soon give up being a capitalist. Instead of being the owner of the product he would have become only the workers' banker. Incidentally, just as the capitalist runs the risk of selling the commodities below their value, he equally has the chance of selling them above their value. If the product cannot be sold, then the worker is thrown on to the street. If for a long period it falls below the market price, his wages will be reduced below the average and short time will be worked. He therefore runs the greatest risk.

Finally, it never enters anyone's mind that the farmer, who has to pay his rent in money, or the industrial capitalist, who has to pay interest in money, is entitled to deduct a part of his rent or of his interest, simply on the ground that before he could pay he must first have transformed his product into money.

B. ADAM SMITH AND THE CONCEPT OF PRODUCTIVE LABOUR

1. HIS DETERMINATION OF VALUE BY LABOUR

ADAM SMITH, like all economists worth mentioning, takes over from the Physiocrats the conception of the average wage, which he calls the natural price of wages.

"A man must always live by his work, and his wages must at least be sufficient to maintain him. They must even upon most occasions be somewhat more; otherwise it would be impossible for him to bring up a family, and the race of such workmen could not last beyond the first generation" (*Wealth of Nations*, Book I, Chapter VIII, p. 60).

Adam Smith expressly states that the development of the productive power of labour does not benefit the worker himself. He says:

"The produce of labour constitutes the natural recompense or wages of labour. In that original state of things, which precedes both the appropriation of land and the accumulation of stock, the whole produce of labour belongs to the labourer. He has neither landlord nor master to share with him. Had this state continued, the wages of labour would have augmented with all those improvements in its productive powers, to which the division of labour gives occasion. All things would gradually have become cheaper.[1] They would have been produced by a smaller quantity of labour; and as the commodities produced by equal quantities of labour would naturally in this state of things be exchanged for one another, they would have been purchased likewise with the produce of a smaller quantity. . . . But this original state of things, in which the labourer enjoyed the whole produce of his own labour, could not last beyond the first introduction of the appropriation of land and the accumulation of stock. It was at an end, therefore, long before the most considerable improvements were made in the productive powers of labour, and it would be to no purpose to trace further what might have been its effects upon the recompense or wages of labour" (pp. 57–8).

[1] At any rate, all those things which required a smaller quantity of labour for their reproduction. But they not only "would have" become cheaper; they did in fact become cheaper.

Here Adam Smith very acutely notes that the really great development of the productive power of labour starts only from the moment when it is transformed into wage labour, and the conditions of labour confront it on the one hand as landed property and on the other hand as capital. The development of the productive power of labour, therefore, begins only under conditions in which the worker himself can no longer appropriate its result. It is, therefore, quite futile to go into the question of how this growth of productive powers might have influenced wages, taken here as still equal to the product of labour, or would have affected wages on the hypothesis that the product of labour (or the value of this product) belonged to the worker himself.

Adam Smith is very heavily infected with the conceptions of the Physiocrats, and often whole strata run through his writings which belong to the Physiocrats and are in complete contradiction with the views specifically elaborated by himself. This is so, for example, in the treatment of land rent, etc. Those passages in his writings which are not characteristic of him, but in which he is a mere Physiocrat, can be completely disregarded for our present purpose.

I have already, in the first part of this work,[1] when dealing with the analysis of the commodity, pointed out Adam Smith's inconsistency in his account of how exchange value is determined. In particular I have shown how he sometimes confuses, and at other times substitutes, the determination of the value of *commodities* by the quantity of labour required for their production, with the quantity of commodities required to buy a definite quantity of human labour—or, what is the same thing, the quantity of living labour required to buy a definite quantity of commodities. Here he makes the *exchange value* of labour the measure for the value of commodities. In fact he makes wages the measure, for wages are equal to the quantity of commodities bought with a definite quantity of living labour, or are equal to the quantity of labour that can be bought by a definite quantity of commodities. The value of labour, or rather of labour power, changes, like that of any other commodity, and in no way differs specifically from the value of

---

[1] *The Critique of Political Economy*, Kerr edition, p. 68.

other commodities. Here value is made the measuring rod and the basis for the explanation of value—so we have *cercle vicieux*, a vicious circle.

From the exposition that follows, however, it will be seen that this instability and this jumbling up of completely hetero- geneous determinations of value do not affect Smith's investiga- tions into the nature and origin of surplus value, because in fact, without even being aware of it, whenever he touches this question he keeps firmly to the correct determination of the exchange value of commodities, that is, its determination by the quantity of labour or the labour time expended on them.

Secondly, however, this contradiction in Adam Smith and his passing over from one kind of explanation to another is based upon something deeper, which Ricardo, in exposing this contradiction, overlooked, did not rightly appreciate, and therefore also did not solve. Let us assume that all workers are producers of commodities, and not only produce their commodities but also sell them. The value of these commodities is determined by the necessary labour time contained in them. If therefore the commodities are sold at their value, the worker buys with one commodity, which is a product of 12 hours' labour time, again 12 hours' labour time in the form of another commodity, that is to say, 12 hours' labour time which is embodied in another use value. The value of his labour is, therefore, equal to the value of his commodity, that is to say, equal to the product of 12 hours' labour time. The selling and buying again, in short the whole process of exchange, the metamorphosis of the commodity, does not in any way alter this. It changes only the form of the use value in which this 12 hours' labour time appears. The "value of labour", there- fore, is equal to the value of the product of labour. In the first place, in the commodities—so far as they are exchanged at their value—equal quantities of materialised labour are exchanged. Secondly, however, there is an exchange of a definite quantity of living labour for an equal quantity of materialised labour, because, firstly, the living labour is materialised in a product, a commodity, which belongs to the worker, and secondly, this commodity is in turn exchanged for another commodity which contains an equally large quantity of labour. In fact, therefore, a definite quantity of living labour is exchanged for an equally large quantity of materialised labour. Thus, it is not only commodity which exchanges for commodity in the proportion in which they represent an equal quantity of materialised labour time, but a quantity of living labour exchanges for a commodity which represents the same quantity of materialised labour. On this assumption the "value of labour" (the quantity of a commodity which can be bought with a given quantity of labour, or the quantity of labour which can be bought with a given quantity of a commodity) could serve as the measure of its value just as well as the quantity of labour contained in the commodity; for the "value of labour" always represents the same quantity of materialised labour as the living labour requires for the production of this commodity, or a definite quantity of living labour time always commands a quantity of commodities representing the same quantity of materialised labour time. But in all modes of production—and particularly also in the capitalist mode of production—in which the material conditions of labour belong to one or several classes, while on the other hand nothing but labour power belongs to another class, the working class, the contrary takes place. The product, or the value of the product of labour, does not belong to the worker. A definite quantity of living labour does not command the same quantity of materialised labour, or a definite quantity of labour materialised in a commodity commands a greater quantity of living labour than is contained in the commodity itself.

As Adam Smith quite correctly starts out from the commodity and the exchange of commodities, and therefore the producers originally confront each other only as possessors of commodities, sellers of commodities and buyers of commodities, he thus discovers (so it seems to him) that in the exchange between capital and wage labour—materialised labour and living labour—the general law is immediately set aside, and commodities (for labour also is a commodity, so far as it is bought and sold) do not exchange in proportion to the quantities of labour they represent. *Hence* he concludes that labour time is no longer the immanent measure which regulates the exchange value of commodities, from the moment when the conditions of labour confront the worker in the form of landed property and capital. He should on the contrary, as Ricardo rightly pointed out, have concluded that the expression "quantity of labour" and "value of labour" are then no longer identical, and therefore the relative value of commodities, although determined by the labour time contained in them, is not determined by the "value of labour", as the latter expression was only correct so long as it remained identical with the first. Later on, when we come to deal with Malthus, we shall show how wrong and absurd it would be, even when the worker himself appropriates his own product, that is the value of his own product, to make this value or the value of labour the measure of value, in the same sense in which labour time or labour itself is the measure of value and the value-creating element. For even in the case we have assumed, the labour which can be bought with a commodity cannot serve as a measure in the same sense as the labour which is contained in it. One would be merely an index to the other.

In any case, Adam Smith feels the difficulty of deducing the exchange between capital and labour from the law which determines the exchange of commodities, since the former apparently rests upon opposite and quite contradictory principles. And the contradiction was incapable of solution so long as capital was set directly against labour instead of against labour power. Adam Smith was well aware that the labour time which the labour power costs for its production and maintenance is very different from the labour which it itself can perform. Thus he himself quotes from Cantillon: *Essai sur la nature du commerce*:

"The labour of an able-bodied slave, the same author adds, is computed to be worth double his maintenance; and that of the meanest labourer, he thinks, cannot be worth less than that of an able-bodied slave" (*Wealth of Nations*, Book I, Chapter VIII, p. 60).

On the other hand it is strange that Adam Smith did not grasp how little connection the objection he raises has with the law which regulates the exchange of commodities among themselves. That commodities A and B exchange in proportion to the labour time contained in them is in no way upset by the proportions in which the producers of A or of B divide the products A and B, or rather their value, among themselves. If a part of A goes to the landowner, another to the capitalist, and a third part to the worker, no matter what the share of each may be, this does not alter the fact that A itself exchanges with B according to its value. The mutual relation of the labour time contained in each of the two commodities A and B is in no way affected by how the labour time contained in A and B is appropriated by different persons.

"When the exchange of the cloth for the linen has been accomplished, the producers of the cloth will share in the linen in precisely the same proportions as they before shared in the cloth" (Karl Marx, *The Poverty of Philosophy*, Kerr edition, p. 56).

It is this, too, that later the Ricardians rightly drove home against Adam Smith. Thus the Malthusian John Cazenove says that "Interchange of commodities"—exchange of commodities—must not be confused with "Distribution"—the distribution of them:

"The circumstances which affect the one do not always affect the other. For instance, a reduction in the cost of producing any particular commodity will alter its relation to all others; but it will not necessarily alter its own distribution, nor will it in any way influence that of the others. Again, a general reduction of commodities affecting them all alike will not alter their relation to each other. It might or might not affect their distribution" (John Cazenove: Preface to T. R. Malthus, *Definition in Political Economy*, London, 1853).

But the "distribution" of the value of the product between capitalist and worker is itself based on an "interchange" between commodities—commodities and labour power—and therefore this is the cause of some confusion in Adam Smith's investigation. The fact that he incidentally made "the value of labour" or the extent to which one commodity (money) can purchase labour, the measure of value, has a disturbing effect on the development of Adam Smith's argument when he comes to the theory of prices, develops the influence of competition on the rate of profit, etc.; it deprives his work in general of all unity, and even excludes a mass of essential questions from his investigation. As we shall soon see, however, it remains without influence on his exposition of *surplus value in general*, inasmuch as here he consistently keeps to the correct determination of value by the labour time expended in different commodities.

Before we proceed to his presentation of surplus value one other fact must be mentioned. Adam Smith mixes up different things. First, he states in Book I, Chapter V:

"Every man is rich or poor according to the degree in which he can afford to enjoy the necessaries, conveniences, and amusements of human life. But after the division of labour has once thoroughly taken place, it is but a very small part of these with which a man's own labour can supply him. The far greater part of them he must derive from the labour of other people, and he must be rich or poor according to the quantity of that labour which he can command, or which he can afford to purchase. The value of any commodity, therefore, to the person who possesses it, and who means not to use or consume it himself, but to exchange it for other commodities, is equal to the quantity of labour which it enables him to purchase or command. Labour, therefore, is the real measure of the exchangeable value of all commodities" (p. 26).

Further:

"They [the goods] contain the value of a certain quantity of labour which we exchange for what is supposed at the time to contain the value of an equal quantity. . . . It was not by gold or by silver, but by labour, that all the wealth of the world was originally purchased; and its value, to those who possess it, and who want to exchange it for some new productions, is precisely equal to the quantity of labour which it can enable them to purchase or command" (p. 26).

Finally:

"Wealth, as Mr. Hobbes says, is power. But the person who either acquires, or succeeds to a great fortune, does not necessarily acquire or succeed to any political power, either civil or military. . . . The power which that possession immediately and directly conveys to him, is the power of purchasing; a certain command over all the labour, or over all the produce of labour, which is then in the market" (pp. 26–7).

We see that in all these passages Adam Smith mixes up "the labour of others" and "the product of this labour". The exchange value of the commodity which anyone possesses consists, after the introduction of the division of labour, in the commodities of other persons which he can purchase, that is to say, in the quantity of other persons' labour contained in them, the quantity of materialised labour of others. And this quantity of the labour of others is equal to the quantity of labour contained in his own commodity. As he expressly says: "They [the goods] contain the value of a certain quantity of labour, which we exchange for what is supposed at the time to contain the value of an equal quantity . . .", in which last sentence the word "value" is superfluous and meaningless.

The emphasis here is on the change brought about by *the division of labour*: that is to say, wealth consists no longer in the product of *one's own* labour but in the quantity of the labour *of others* which this product commands, the quantity of social labour it can purchase, which quantity is determined by the quantity of labour contained in one's own product. In fact, only the concept of exchange value is here involved—that my labour counts only as social labour, and consequently its product determines my wealth by its command over an equal quantity of social labour. My commodity, which contains a definite quantity of necessary labour time, gives me command of all other commodities of equal value, that is, of an equal quantity of the labour of others realised in other use values. The emphasis here lies on the equalisation, brought about by the division of labour and exchange value, of *my* labour with the labour of others, in other words, on social labour (the fact that *my* labour too or the labour contained in my commodity is already *socially* determined, and has essentially changed its character, escapes Adam) and not at all on the difference between *materialised* labour and *living* labour and the specific laws of their exchange. In fact, Adam Smith says nothing more than that the value of commodities is determined by the labour time contained in them, and the wealth of the owner of commodities consists in the quantity of social labour at his disposal. The incidental equating of *labour* with *the product of labour* provides here, however, the first occasion for the confusion between the determination of the value of commodities by the quantity of labour contained in them, and the determination of their value by the quantity of living labour which they can buy, that is to say, their determination by the "value of labour."

When Adam Smith says further on: "his fortune is greater or less precisely in proportion to the extent of this power [the right to dispose of labour or to buy the products of labour]; or to the quantity of other men's labour, or, what is the same thing [here is the false identification], of the produce of other men's labour which it enables him to purchase or command" (p. 38), he might just as well have said: His fortune is large or small in proportion to the quantity of social labour contained in it.

The false conclusion already emerges in this same fifth chapter, when, for example, it is stated that:

> "Labour alone, therefore, never varying in its own value, is alone the ultimate and real standard by which the value of all commodities can at all times and places be estimated and compared" (Book I, Chapter V, p. 29).

What is true of labour itself and consequently of its measure, labour time, that the value of commodities is always proportionate to the labour time realised in them, no matter how the "*value of labour*" may change, is here claimed for this changing value of labour itself.

Here Adam Smith for the first time explained the exchange of commodities as such: the nature of exchange value, of the division of labour and of money. The parties to the exchange still confront each other only as owners of commodities. They purchase the labour of others in the form of commodities, just as their own labour appears in the form of commodities. The amount of social labour which they command is, therefore, equal to the quantity of labour contained in the commodity which they themselves buy. But when in the following chapters he comes to the exchange between materialised labour and living labour, between capitalist and worker, and then *stresses* that the value of the commodity is now no longer determined by the quantity of labour it itself contains, but by the quantity

—which differs from this—of the living labour of others which this commodity can command (that is, can buy), he thereby in fact does not say that the commodities themselves no longer exchange in proportion to the labour time contained in them. What he does say is that the *increase of wealth*, the profitable use of the value contained in the commodity, and the extent of this profitable utilisation, depends upon the greater or less quantity of living labour which the materialised labour sets in motion. Put this way it is correct. But Adam Smith remains unclear.

*   *   *

How often in the course of his work, when he is explaining actual facts, Adam Smith conceives the amount of labour contained in the product as value and as determining value, can be shown by many examples. Some of these examples are dealt with by Ricardo. His whole doctrine of the influence of the division of labour and improved machinery on the prices of commodities is based on this. Here it is enough to quote one passage. In Book I, Chapter XI, Adam Smith speaks of the cheapening of many manufactured goods in his time as compared with former centuries, and then remarks: "It cost a greater quantity of labour to bring the goods to the market. When they were brought thither, therefore, they must have purchased or exchanged for the price of a greater quantity" (p. 211).

In addition to the points here discussed it must be said that among his inconsistencies in defining value—apart from the apparent contradiction in regard to wages—there is a further confusion: the measure of value as an immanent measure, which at the same time forms the substance of value, is confused with the measure of value in the sense that money is spoken of as the measure of value. With this then comes the attempt to square the circle—to find a commodity of unchanging value which would serve as a constant measure for others. As to the relation between the measurement of value by money and the determination of value by labour time, see the first part of my work.[1] This confusion can also be found in certain passages of Ricardo.

[1] *Critique of Political Economy*, Kerr edition, p. 75.

2. THE ORIGIN OF SURPLUS VALUE

(a) Profit

IN Chapter VI of Book I Adam Smith passes on from those relations in which it is assumed the producers confront each other only as sellers and owners of commodities, to the relations of exchange between the owners of the conditions of labour and those who own only labour power.

"In that early and rude state of society which precedes both the accumulation of stock and the appropriation of land, the proportion between the quantities of labour necessary for acquiring different objects seems to be the only circumstance which can afford any rule for exchanging them for one another. . . . It is natural that what is usually the produce of two days' or two hours' labour, should be worth double of what is usually the produce of one day's or one hour's labour" (Book I, Chapter VI, pp. 41–2).

That is to say, the labour time necessary to produce different goods determines the proportion in which they exchange for one another, or their *exchange value*.

"In this state of things, the whole produce of labour belongs to the labourer; and the quantity of labour commonly employed in acquiring or producing any commodity, is the only circumstance which can regulate the quantity of labour which it ought commonly to purchase, command, or exchange for" (Book I, Chapter VI, p. 42).

Consequently, on this assumption the worker is a mere seller of commodities, and one commands the labour of the other only in so far as he buys the commodities of the other with his commodities. He thus commands with his commodities only so much of the other's labour as is contained in his own commodities, since both exchange only commodities against each other, and the exchange value of the commodities is determined by the labour time or quantity of labour contained in them.

But, continues Adam Smith, "as soon as stock has accumulated in the hands of particular persons, some of them will naturally employ it in setting to work industrious people, whom they will supply with materials and subsistence, in order to make a profit by the sale of their work, or by what their labour adds to the value of the materials" (p. 42).

Stop a moment, before we follow the passage further. In the first place, whence come the "industrious people" who possess neither means of subsistence nor materials of labour, who are hanging in the empty air? If we strip Smith's statement of its naïve phrasing, it means nothing more than that capitalist production begins at the moment when the conditions of labour belong to one class, and another class has at its disposal nothing but labour power. This separation of labour from the conditions of labour is the precondition of capitalist production.

Secondly, however, what does Adam Smith mean when he says that the owners of capital employ "industrious people in order to make a profit by the sale of their work, or by what their labour adds to the value of the materials"? Does he mean by this that the profit comes from the *sale*, that the commodities are sold *above* their value—that is, what Steuart calls profit upon alienation—which is nothing but a changed distribution of already existing wealth? Let him answer for himself:

"In exchanging the complete manufacture either for money, for labour,[1] or for other goods, over and above what may be sufficient to pay the price of the materials, and the wages of the workmen, something must be given for the profits of the undertaker of the work who hazards his stock in this adventure" (Book I, Chapter VI, p. 42).

This "something" which must be given "for the profits of the undertaker" in the exchange of the completed commodity, does it come from the sale of the goods above their value, is it Steuart's profit upon alienation?

"The value", says Adam Smith immediately afterwards, "which the workmen add to the material, therefore, resolves itself in this case[2] into two parts, of which the one pays their wages, the other the profits of their employer upon the whole stock of materials and wages which he advanced."

Here therefore Adam Smith explicitly states: the profit which is made on the sale of the completed commodity origin-

---

[1] Here again is a source of new error.

[2] When capitalist production has appeared.

ates not from the *sale* itself, not from the sale of the commodity *above* its value, is not profit upon alienation. The value, that is to say, the quantity of labour which the workers add to the material, falls rather into two parts. One pays their wages and is paid through their wages. The workers therewith give back only as much labour as they have received in the form of wages. The other part forms the profit of the capitalist, that is, it is a quantity of labour which he sells without having paid for it. Thus if he sells the commodity at its value, that is, according to the amount of labour time contained in it, in other words, if he exchanges it for other commodities according to the law of value, then his profit originates from the fact that he has not *paid for* one part of the labour contained in the goods, but has nevertheless *sold* it. Adam Smith has thereby himself refuted the idea that the circumstance which results in the whole product of his labour no longer belonging to the worker, but it or its value having to be shared with the owner of capital—that this circumstance invalidates the law according to which the relation in which commodities exchange one with another, or their exchange value, is determined by the quantity of labour time materialised in them. Indeed, on the contrary, he traces the profit of the capitalist to the fact that this capitalist has not paid for a part of the labour added to the commodity, and thence comes his profit on the sale of the commodity. We shall see how Adam Smith further on even more explicitly derives profit from the labour which the worker performs beyond the quantity of labour with which he pays for the wages, that is, with which he replaces the wages by an equivalent. Adam Smith has thereby recognised the true origin of surplus value. He has at the same time expressly stated that it does not arise from funds advanced whose value—no matter how useful they may be in the actual labour process—merely reappears in the product, but that it arises exclusively from the new labour which the "workers add to the raw material" in the new process of production, in which those funds figure as means of labour or instruments of labour.

On the other hand the phrase "in exchanging the complete manufacture either for money, for *labour*, or for other goods" is wrong (and arises from the confusion mentioned earlier).

If he exchanges the goods for money or other goods, his profit comes from his selling more labour than he has paid for; from the fact that he does not exchange an equal quantity of materialised labour for an equal quantity of living labour. Therefore, Adam Smith must not put on the same par "exchange for money or other goods" and "exchange of the complete manufacture for labour". For in the first exchange the surplus value originates from the fact that the goods are exchanged at their value, at the labour time contained in them, which, however, is partly *unpaid*. Here it is assumed that the capitalist does not exchange an equal quantity of past labour for an equal quantity of living labour; that the quantity of living labour appropriated by him is greater than the living labour paid for by him. Otherwise the wage of the worker would be equal to the value of his product. The profit on the exchange of the complete manufacture for money or other goods, if they are exchanged at their value, therefore arises from the fact that the exchange between the finished commodity and the living labour is subject to other laws: that here equivalents are not exchanged. These cases, therefore, must not be lumped together. Therefore profit is nothing but a deduction from the value which the workers have added to the material of labour. They add to the material, however, nothing but a new quantity of labour. The labour time of the worker, therefore, resolves itself into two parts: the one, for which he has received from the capitalist an equivalent, his wages; the other, which he gives to him gratis and which constitutes the *profit*. Adam Smith rightly points out that only the part of the labour (value) which the worker adds to the material, resolves itself into wages and profit, that is to say, the newly created surplus value in itself has nothing to do with the part of capital which has been advanced (as material and instruments of labour).

Adam Smith, who has thus reduced profit to the appropriation of the unpaid labour of others, at once goes on to say:

"The profits of stock, it may perhaps be thought, are only a different name for the wages of a particular sort of labour, the labour of inspection and direction" (Book I, Chapter VI, p. 43).

And he refutes this false idea of wages for the labour of inspection and direction. We shall come back to this in another chapter. Here it is only important to stress that Adam Smith very well knows and expressly emphasises the contrast between his view of the origin of profit and this apologist view.

After dealing with this contrast in greater detail, he continues:

> "In this state of things, the whole produce of labour does not always belong to the labourer. He must in most cases share it with the owner of the stock which employs him. Neither is the quantity of labour commonly employed in acquiring or producing any commodity, the only circumstance which can regulate the quantity which it ought commonly to purchase, command, or exchange for. An additional quantity, it is evident, must be due for the profits of the stock which advanced the wages and furnished the materials of that labour" (Book I, Chapter VI, pp. 43-4).

This is quite correct. Given capitalist production, materialised labour—in the form of money or goods—always purchases, in addition to the amount of labour contained in it itself, an "additional quantity" of living labour for the "profit of the stock", which, however, in other words, means nothing but that it appropriates for nothing, appropriates without paying for it, a part of living labour. Adam Smith is superior to Ricardo in that he so strongly emphasises that this changed relationship makes its appearance *with capitalist production*. On the other hand, Adam Smith is inferior to Ricardo in that he is never able to free himself from the viewpoint—though it is one refuted by his own analysis—that through this changed relation between materialised labour and living labour a change also takes place in the determination of the relative value of commodities, although in their reciprocal relations these represent nothing but different, though definite, given quantities of realised, materialised labour.

(b) Land Rent

After having thus presented surplus value in one form, the form of profit, as part of the labour which the worker performs over and above the part of the labour which replaces his wages,

Adam Smith does the same with the other form of surplus value, land rent. One of the objective conditions of labour alienated from labour, and therefore confronting it as the property of others, is *capital*. The other is the *land* itself, the land as *landed property*. Therefore after having dealt with the owner of capital, Adam Smith continues:

"As soon as the land of any country has all become private property, the landlords, like all other men, love to reap where they never sowed, and demand a rent even for its natural produce. . . . He [the labourer] must then pay for the licence to gather them; and must give up to the landlord a portion of what his labour either collects or produces. This portion, or, what comes to the same thing, the price of this portion, constitutes the rent of land" (Book I, Chapter VI, p. 44).

Like industrial profit proper, land rent too is only a part of the labour which the worker has added to the raw materials and which he hands over to the owner of the land without being paid for it: that is to say, only a part of the surplus labour performed by him over and above the part of the labour time which he works in order to replace his wages, or in order to give back an equivalent for the labour time contained in the wages.

Thus Adam Smith regards *surplus value*, that is, surplus labour, the excess of the labour performed and realised in the commodity *above* the paid labour—above the labour which has received its equivalent in the wages—as the *general category*, of which profit in the strict sense and land rent are merely branches. Nevertheless, he does not distinguish surplus value as such as a category distinct from the specific forms which it takes in profit and rent. This is the source of many errors and shortcomings in his investigations, and of even more in the work of Ricardo.

(c) *Interest on Capital*

Another form in which surplus value appears is interest, "the interest or the use of money". But this "interest of money is always", says Adam Smith later in the same chapter (Chapter VI of Book I), "a derivative revenue which, if it is not paid from the profit which is made by the use of the money, must be paid from some other source of revenue,[1] unless perhaps the borrower is a spendthrift, who contracts a second debt in order to pay the interest of the first" (p. 46).

Interest is, therefore, either a part of the *profit* made by loan capital; in which case it is a secondary form of profit itself, a branch of profit, or merely a further division between different persons of the surplus value appropriated in the form of profit. Or it is paid out of rent. In which case the same holds good. Or the borrower pays the interest out of his own or someone else's capital. In which case it in no way constitutes surplus value, but is merely a different distribution of existing wealth—"vibration of the balance of wealth between parties", as in "profit upon alienation". Excluding the latter case, when interest is in no way a form of surplus value (and excluding the case where it is a deduction from wages or is itself a form of profit; Adam Smith does not mention this latter case) interest is, therefore, merely a secondary form of surplus value, a mere part of profit or of rent (affecting merely the distribution of these) and constitutes, therefore, nothing but a part of unpaid surplus labour.

A separate chapter (the fourth) of Book II deals with loan capital. It begins with the following propositions:

"The stock which is lent at interest is always considered as a capital by the lender. He expects that in due time it is to be restored to him, and that in the meantime the borrower is to pay him a certain annual rent for the use of it. The borrower may use it either as a capital, or as a stock reserved for immediate consumption. If he uses it as a capital, he employs it in the maintenance of productive labourers, who reproduce the value with a profit. He can, in this case, both restore the capital and pay the interest without alienating or encroaching upon any other source of revenue. If he uses it as a stock reserved for immediate consumption, he acts the part of a prodigal, and dissipates in the maintenance of the idle what was destined for the support of the industrious. He can, in this case, neither restore the capital nor pay the interest without either alienating or encroaching upon

---

[1] That is to say, either land rent or wages. In the latter case, taking the average wage, interest is not derived from surplus value but is a deduction from wages themselves, or—and in this form, as we shall have occasion to see later, it appears in undeveloped capitalist production—it represents a special form of profit.

some other source of revenue, such as the property or the rent of land" (Book II, Chapter IV, p. 313).

Thus, whoever borrows money, which is here called stock, either applies it himself as capital and makes a profit with it. In this case, the interest which he pays to the lender is nothing but a part of the profit under a special name. Or he consumes the money he borrowed. Then he is increasing the wealth of the lender by reducing his own. What takes place is only a different distribution of the wealth, which passes from the hand of the spendthrift into that of the lender, but there is no creation of surplus value. In so far therefore as interest in any way represents surplus value, it is nothing but a part of profit, which itself is nothing but a definite form of surplus value, that is, of unpaid labour.

(d) Taxes

Finally, Adam Smith observes that in the same way all incomes of persons who live on the proceeds of taxation are paid either out of wages, and are thus a deduction from wages themselves; or have their source in profit and land rent, being thus only legal titles under which various strata participate in profit and land rent, which themselves are nothing but different forms of surplus value.

"All taxes, and all the revenue which is founded upon them, all salaries, pensions, and annuities of every kind, are ultimately derived from some one or other of those three original sources of revenue, and are paid either immediately or mediately from the wages of labour, the profits of stock, or the rent of land" (Book I, Chapter VI, pp. 46–7).

Thus interest, along with taxes or revenues derived from taxes—in so far as they are not deductions from wages themselves—are merely shares in profit and land rent, which are themselves in turn reducible to surplus value, that is, unpaid labour time.

(e) Adam Smith's Advance beyond the Physiocrats

We now come to Adam Smith's general theory of surplus value.

In yet another passage Adam Smith sums up the whole of his views on surplus value. This for the first time makes it quite clear how far he is from in any way even attempting to prove that the value added by the worker to the product (after deduction of the value of the raw material and wear and tear of the instruments of labour) is no longer determined by the labour time contained in the product, on the ground that the worker does not appropriate this value in full for himself but has to share it with the capitalist and the landowner. The way in which the value of a commodity is distributed among the producers of this commodity naturally does not in any way alter the nature of this value or the relative value of this commodity to other commodities.

"As soon as land becomes private property, the landlord demands a share of almost all the produce which the labourer can either raise, or collect from it. His rent makes the first deduction from the produce of the labour which is employed upon land.

"It seldom happens that the person who tills the ground has wherewithal to maintain himself till he reaps the harvest. His maintenance is generally advanced to him from the stock of a master, the farmer who employs him, and who would have no interest to employ him, unless he was to share in the produce of his labour, or unless his stock was to be replaced to him with a profit. This profit makes a second deduction from the produce of the labour which is employed upon land.

"The produce of almost all other labour is liable to the like deduction of profit. In all arts and manufactures the greater part of the workmen stand in need of a master to advance them the materials of their work, and their wages and maintenance till it be completed. He shares in the produce of their labour, or in the value which it adds to the materials upon which it is bestowed; and in this share consists his profit" (Book I, Chapter VIII, p. 58).

Here, therefore, Adam Smith in plain terms characterises rent on land and profit on capital as mere *deductions* from the worker's product or from the value of his product, which is equal to the quantity of labour added by him to the material. This deduction, however, as Adam Smith himself shows at an earlier point, can only consist of that part of the labour which the worker adds to the raw materials, over and above the quantity of labour which only pays his wages, or which produces only an equivalent for his wages; that is to say, the surplus labour, the unpaid portion of his labour. (Therefore, incidentally, capital and landed property can never be sources of value.)

We see the great advance made by Adam Smith as compared with the Physiocrats, in the analysis of surplus value and hence of capital. In their view, only one definite kind of concrete labour—agricultural labour—creates surplus value. Thus what they examine is the use value of labour, not labour time, general social labour, which is the sole source of value. In this particular kind of labour, however, it is *nature*, the land, which in fact creates the surplus value, consisting in an increase of (organic) matter, the excess of the organic matter produced over the organic matter consumed. They grasp the subject, however, still in a very limited form and hence distorted by fanciful conceptions. But to Adam Smith it is general social labour, no matter in what use values it appears, the mere quantity of necessary labour, which creates value. Surplus value, whether in the form of profit or rent, or in the secondary form of interest, is nothing but a part of this labour, which the owners of the material conditions of labour appropriate in the exchange with living labour. The Physiocrats consequently also see surplus value only in the form of land rent. To Adam Smith, rent, profit and interest are only different forms of surplus value.

When I speak of surplus value, in so far as it relates to the total capital advanced, as *profit on capital*, this is because the capitalist directly engaged in production *directly* appropriates the surplus labour, no matter among what categories he has subsequently to share this surplus value—whether with the landowner or with the lender of capital. Thus the farmer pays the landowner. So also the manufacturer pays, out of the surplus value appropriated by him, rent to the owner of the land on which the factory stands, and interest to the capitalist who has made an advance of capital to him.

(f) *The Exchange of More Labour for Less Labour*

Wages, or the equivalent with which the capitalist buys the temporary disposal of labour power, are not a commodity in its direct form, but the metamorphosised commodity, money, the commodity in its independent form as exchange value, as the direct materialisation of social labour, of general labour time. With this money the worker naturally buys commodities at the same price as any other possessor of money (leaving out of account such details as for example that he buys on less favourable conditions and in worse circumstances, etc.). He faces the seller of commodities as does every other possessor of money—as a buyer. He enters into the circulation of commodities itself not as a worker, but as pole Money confronting pole Commodity, as possessor of the commodity in its generalised, always exchangeable form. His money is once more transformed into commodities which are to serve him as use values, and in this process he buys the commodities at the price they fetch in the market normally, or speaking generally, at their value. In this transaction he carries through the act M-C, which indicates a change of form, but, as a general rule, not in any way a change in magnitude of value. Inasmuch as the worker, by his labour materialised in the product, has added not only the quantity of labour time contained in the money he has received, has paid not only an equivalent, but has given surplus labour *gratis*, which is precisely the source of profit, so he has *in fact* (the mediating process—the sale of his labour power—has no bearing on the result) given a higher value than the value of the money he has received as wages. He has bought in kind with more labour time the quantity of labour which is materialised in the money which comes to him as wages. It can therefore be said that in the same way he has bought indirectly all the commodities on which the money (which after all is only the independent expression of a definite quantity of social labour time) he has bought is spent, for more labour time than is contained in them, although he buys them at the same price as any other buyer or owner of a commodity in its first transformation. Conversely, the money with which the capitalist buys labour contains a smaller quantity of labour, a smaller labour time, than the quantity of labour or labour time of the worker contained in the commodity he produces. In addition to the quantity of labour contained in this sum of money, which constitutes the wage, the capitalist buys an additional sum of labour for which he does not pay, an excess over the quantity of labour contained in the money paid out by him. And this additional quantity of labour constitutes in fact the surplus value created by capital. But as the money with which the capitalist buys the labour power, and therewith, in the actual result, a definite quantity of labour—as this money is nothing but the altered form of *all other commodities*, their independent existence as exchange value, it can equally well be said that all commodities, in exchange with living labour, buy more labour than they contain. This excess constitutes precisely surplus value. It is greatly to Adam Smith's credit that in Book I (Chapters VI, VII and VIII)—just where he passes from simple commodity exchange and its law of value to exchange between materialised and living labour, to an examination of profit and land rent in general, in short, to the origin of surplus value—that here he feels that at this point some flaw has emerged. He senses that, however it may have come about—and this he does not grasp— the law is in fact suspended in the result: more labour is exchanged for less labour (from the standpoint of the worker); less labour is exchanged for more labour (from the standpoint of the capitalist). He emphasises (and this he evidently finds disconcerting) that with the accumulation of capital and with property in land—that is, when the conditions necessary for labour assume an independent existence over against labour itself—a new development occurs, which is apparently (and actually, in the result) a reversal of the law of value into its opposite. It is his theoretical strength that he feels and stresses this contradiction, just as it is his theoretical weakness that this contradiction shakes his confidence in the general law even for simple commodity exchange. He does not see how this contradiction arises through labour power itself becoming a commodity, and that in the case of this specific commodity its use value, which is quite a different thing from its exchange value, is precisely the energy which creates exchange value. Ricardo is ahead of Adam Smith in that these apparent contradictions, which in their result are real contradictions, cause him no trouble. But he is inferior to Adam Smith in that he does not even suspect that this presents a problem;

the specific development which the law of value undergoes when capital develops does not for a moment puzzle him or even attract his attention. The point in which Adam Smith revealed his genius was used by Malthus as a reactionary argument against Ricardo.

Naturally, however, it is also this deep insight which makes Adam Smith irresolute and uncertain, cuts the firm ground from under his feet, and prevents him—in contrast to Ricardo—from reaching a unified and comprehensive theoretical view of the abstract, general foundations of the capitalist system.

This view expressed by Adam Smith—that the commodity buys more labour than it contains, or that the worker pays for the commodity a higher value than is contained in it—is thus formulated by Hodgskin:

"Natural or necessary price means, on the contrary, the whole quantity of labour nature requires from man, that he may produce any commodity . . . labour was the original, is now, and ever will be the only purchase money in dealing with nature. . . . Whatever quantity of labour may be requisite to produce any commodity, the labourer must always, in the present state of society, give a great deal more labour to acquire and possess it, than is requisite to buy from nature. Natural price thus increased to the labourer is *social price*." These two prices must always be distinguished. (Thomas Hodgskin, *Popular Political Economy, etc.*, London, 1827, pp. 219, 220.)

In this presentation Hodgskin repeats both what is correct in Adam Smith's ideas and what is confused and confusing.

(g) Confusion of Surplus Value with Profit

We have seen how Adam Smith explains surplus value in general, of which land rent and profit are only different forms and constituent parts. As he presents it, that part of the capital which consists of raw materials and instruments of labour has nothing directly to do with the creation of surplus value. The latter arises exclusively from the additional quantity of labour which the worker performs, in excess of that portion of his labour which constitutes only the equivalent of his wages. Therefore, also, it is only that part of the capital advanced which consists of wages from which surplus value directly arises; for it is the only part of the capital that not only reproduces itself but produces a surplus in product and value.

In profit, on the other hand, the surplus value is calculated on the total sum of capital advanced, and besides this modification other new ones appear as a result of the equalisation of profits in the various spheres of production of capital. Although Adam Smith explains the essence of surplus value, he does not explicitly present it in the form of a definite category distinct from its specific forms, and because of this in his later treatment he directly confuses it with the further developed forms of profit. This error persists with Ricardo and all his disciples. Hence arise (and with Ricardo all the more strikingly because he works out the fundamental law of value with greater systematic unity and consistency, so that the inconsistencies and contradictions are more strikingly apparent) a series of inconsistencies, unresolved contradictions and fatuities, which the Ricardians (as we shall see later in the section dealing with Profit) try to solve with scholastic phraseology. Crass empiricism is transformed into false metaphysics, scholasticism, which toils painfully to deduce undeniably empirical phenomena by simple formal analysis from the general law, or to reason out a justification for them on the basis of that law. We will give an example at this point from Adam Smith, because the confusion creeps in not where he is dealing as an expert with profit or land rent, those particular forms of surplus value, but where he is thinking of them only as forms of surplus value in general, as "deductions from the labour which the workmen have expended on the material".

We have already quoted the passage:

> "The value which the workmen add to the materials, therefore, resolves itself in this case into two parts, of which the one pays their wages, the other the profits of their employer upon the whole stock of materials and wages which he advanced" (Book I, Chapter VI, p. 42).

Adam Smith continues:

> "He [the employer] could have no interest to employ them [the workers], unless he expected from the sale of their work something more than what was sufficient to replace his stock to him; and he could have no interest to

employ a great stock rather than a small one, unless his profits were to bear some proportion to the extent of his stock."

We note in the first place that Adam Smith at the start reduces the surplus value—the excess which the employer makes over and above the quantity of value necessary to replace his capital—to the portion of the labour which the workers add to the raw material in excess of the quantity that replaces their wages. After he has thus made this surplus arise purely from that portion of the capital which is laid out in wages, he then immediately conceives this same surplus in the form of profit—that is to say, not in relation to that part of the capital from which it arises, but as a surplus over the *total value* of the capital advanced, "upon the whole stock of the materials and wages which he advanced".[1] He therefore conceives surplus value directly in the form of profit. Hence the difficulties that soon appear. The capitalist, Adam Smith says, "could have no interest to employ them [the workers], unless he expected from the sale of their work something more than was sufficient to replace his stock to him".

Once capitalist relations are taken for granted, this is quite correct. The capitalist does not produce in order to satisfy his needs with the product; he produces as a rule with no immediate regard to consumption. He produces in order to produce surplus value. Adam Smith, however, does not *explain surplus value*—as some of his stupid disciples later did—by this assumption, which means nothing more than that, assuming capitalist production, the capitalist produces for the sake of surplus value; that is to say, he does not explain the existence of surplus value by the interests of the capitalist, by his *desire* for surplus value. On the contrary, he has already derived this surplus value from the value which the workers add to the raw materials in excess of the value added in exchange for the wages they receive.

But he then immediately goes on to say: the capitalist could have no interest in employing a larger instead of a smaller capital, unless his profits bore a definite relation to the magnitude of the capital advanced. Here profit is no longer explained by the nature of surplus value, but by the "interest" of the

[1] It is an oversight that he here leaves out of account the instruments of labour.

capitalist. Which is just silly. Adam Smith is not aware that, by lumping together in this direct way surplus value with profit and profit with surplus value, he is upsetting the law as to the origin of surplus value which he has just established. If surplus value is only the part of value (or of the quantity of labour) added by the worker to the raw material, in excess of that part of the value added to replace the wage, why should that second part grow as the direct result of the value of the advanced capital being greater in one case than in another? The contradiction is even more evident in the example which Adam Smith himself gives immediately following this passage, in order to refute the view according to which profit is a wage paid for the so-called "labour of inspection and direction". He says:

"They [the profits of stock] are, however, altogether different [from wages], are regulated by quite different principles, and bear no proportion to the quantity, the hardship, or the ingenuity of this supposed labour of inspection and direction. They are regulated altogether by the value of the stock employed, and are greater or smaller in proportion to the extent of this stock. Let us suppose, for example, that in some particular place, where the common annual profits of manufacturing stock are ten per cent., there are two different manufactures, in each of which twenty workmen are employed at the rate of £15 a year each, or at the expense of 300 a year in each manufactory. Let us suppose, too, that the coarse materials annually wrought up in the one cost only £700, while the finer materials in the other cost £7,000. The capital annually employed in the one will in this case amount only to £1,000; whereas that employed in the other will amount to £7,300. At the rate of 10 per cent., therefore, the undertaker of the one will expect a yearly profit of about £100 only, while that of the other will expect about £730. But though their profits are so very different, their labour of inspection and direction may be either altogether or very nearly the same" (Book I, Chapter VI, p. 43).

From surplus value in its general form we come straight to a common rate of profit, which has nothing directly to do with it. But let that be! In both of the factories twenty workers are employed; in both their wages are the same—£300: proof therefore that this is not a case of a higher kind of labour being employed in one factory as against the other, so that an hour of labour, and so therefore an hour of surplus labour, in one factory might be equal to several hours of surplus labour in the other. On the contrary, it is the same average labour that is assumed in both cases, as the equality of their wages shows. How then can the surplus labour added by the workers in excess of their wages be worth seven times as much in one factory as in the other? Or why should the workers in one factory, because the material they work up in it is seven times more costly than in the other, hand over seven times as much surplus labour as in the other, although they get the same wages in both factories, and therefore work the same time to reproduce their wages? The seven times greater profit in the one factory as compared with the other—or in general the law of profit that it is in proportion to the magnitude of the capital advanced—therefore contradicts *prima facie* the law of surplus value, or of profit (since Adam Smith treats the two as identical), according to which it consists simply in the unpaid surplus labour of the worker. Adam Smith puts this down with quite naïve thoughtlessness, without the faintest suspicion of the contradiction it presents. All his disciples faithfully followed him in this—since not one of them examined surplus value in general as distinct from its determinate forms. In the case of Ricardo, as already noted, it assumes an even cruder form.

As Adam Smith resolves surplus value not only into profit but also into rent—two distinct species of surplus value, whose motion is determined by quite different laws—he should certainly have seen that he ought not to confuse the general abstract form with any of its specific forms. With all later bourgeois economists, as with Adam Smith, the lack of a theoretical bent of mind for grasping the distinctive forms of economic relations constantly leads them to snatch clumsily at the empirical material before them and concentrate their interest on it. Hence also their incapacity to get a correct understanding of money, in which the issue is only various transformations in the form of exchange value while the magnitude of value remains unchanged.

3. CAPITAL AND LANDED PROPERTY AS SOURCES OF VALUE

In *An Inquiry into the Nature and Origin of public Wealth* (Edinburgh, 1804) Lauderdale raises the objection to Adam Smith's explanation of surplus value—which he says is in accord with the views already advanced by Locke—that capital is not an original source of wealth as Smith makes out, but only a derivative source. The relevant passage runs:

> "More than 100 years ago Locke expressed almost the same opinion as Adam Smith. 'Money', he said, 'is a barren thing and does not produce anything, but as a result of agreement carries in its pocket something which was the reward for the labour of somebody else.'[1] If that point of view regarding the profits of capital would be quite true, it would result that profits would serve not the primary but the producing source of wealth, and capital would therefore not be considered as the source of wealth, as profit from it merely transfers the money from the pocket of the worker to that of the capitalist" (pp. 157–8).

In so far as the value of the capital reappears in the product, it cannot be called "the source of wealth". In this case it is only as accumulated labour, as a definite quantity of materialised labour, that it passes its own value over into the product.

Capital is productive of value only as *a relation*, in so far as it is a coercive force on wage labour compelling it to perform surplus labour, spurring on the productive power of labour to create relative surplus value. In both cases it only produces value as the power, alienated from labour, of labour's own material conditions over labour, only as one of the forms of wage labour itself; as a condition of wage labour. But in the sense commonly used by the economists, as stored-up labour existing in the form of money or commodities, capital functions productively in the labour process like all other conditions of

---

[1] Locke, *Some Considerations of the Consequences of the Lowering of Interest and Raising the Value of Money*, 1692, p. 53.

labour, including the unpaid natural forces, in the production of use values; but it is never the source of value. It creates no new value, and only adds exchange value to the product at all in so far as it has exchange value—that is to say, in so far as it itself consists in materialised labour time, so that labour is the source of its value.

Lauderdale is right in this respect—that Adam Smith, after explaining the nature of surplus value and of value, is wrong in presenting capital and landed property as independent sources of exchange value. They are sources of revenue for their owner, in so far as they are the title to a certain quantity of surplus labour, which the worker has to perform over and above the labour time required to replace his wages. Thus Adam Smith says for example:

"Wages, profit and rent, are the three original sources of all revenue as well as of all exchangeable value" (Book I, Chapter VI, p. 46).

Just as it is true to say that they are the "three original sources of all revenue", it is equally false to say that they are also "the three original sources of all exchangeable value", since the value of a commodity is determined exclusively by the labour time contained in it. How can Adam Smith, immediately after presenting rent and profit as mere *deductions*, deductions from the value or the labour added by the worker to the raw material, call them "original sources of exchangeable value"? (They can be so described only in the sense that they set the "original sources" in motion, that is, compel the workers to perform surplus labour.) In so far as they are titles (conditions) for the appropriation of a part of the value, that is, of the labour materialised in the commodity, they are sources of income for their owner. But the distribution or appropriation of value is certainly not the source of the value that is appropriated. If this appropriation did not take place, and the worker received as wages the whole product of his labour, the value of the commodities produced would be just the same as before, although it was not shared with the land-owner and the capitalist. Landed property and capital, which constitute sources of revenue for their owners—that is to say, give them the power to appropriate a part of the value created by labour—do not thereby become sources of the value which they appropriate. It is equally wrong, however, to say that wages are an "original source of exchange value", although wages—or rather, the continuous sale of labour power—constitute a source of income for the worker. It is the *labour* and not the wages of the worker that creates value. Wages are only value that already exists, or if we are considering the whole of production, that part of the value created by the worker which he himself appropriates; but this appropriation does not create value. His wages can therefore rise or fall without this affecting the value of the commodities produced by him.

Adam Smith's erroneous conception, which he develops in spite of his original correct exposition, is revealed also in the following passage:

"Rent . . . enters into the composition of the price of commodities in a different way from wages and profit. High or low wages and profit are the causes of high or low price; high or low rent is the effect of it" (*Wealth of Nations*, Book I, Chapter XI, p. 132).

For the moment we will take no account of how far Adam Smith regards rent as a constituent element in the price of commodities. This question is all the more irrelevant at this point in our enquiry because he conceives rent equally with profit as a mere portion of the surplus value—"a deduction from the labour, which the worker has employed on the raw materials"—and therefore in fact also as a deduction from profit, inasmuch as the total unpaid surplus labour, so far as the worker is concerned, is *directly* appropriated by the capitalist. It makes no difference among what categories the capitalist may later have to share this surplus value with other owners of the means of production, owners of land or lenders of capital. To simplify the presentation, therefore, we shall speak only of wages and profit as the two categories into which the newly created value is divided.

Let us assume that twelve hours of labour time are materialised in a commodity (apart from the value of the raw materials and means of production used up in it). Its value as such can only be expressed in *money*. Let us assume therefore that twelve hours of labour time are likewise materialised in five shillings. Thus the value of the commodity is five shillings. By the natural price of commodities Adam Smith understands nothing more than their value expressed in money (the market price of the commodity being of course above or below its value. Indeed, as I shall show later, even the average price of commodities is *always* different from their value. But Adam Smith, in his investigation into natural price, does not touch on this. However, neither the market price, nor still less the fluctuations in the average price of commodities, can be grasped except on the basis of an understanding of the nature of value).

If the amount of the surplus value contained in the commodity is 20 per cent. of its total value, or what amounts to the same thing, 25 per cent. of the necessary labour contained in it, then this value of 5s., the natural price of the commodity, can be resolved into 4s. wages and 1s. surplus value (which we will here call profit, following Adam Smith). It would be correct to say that the magnitude of value of the commodity determined independently of wages and profit, or its natural price, is divisible into 4s. wages (the price of labour) and 1s. profit (the price of profit). But it would be wrong to say that the value of the commodity arises from the adding together or combining of the price of the wages, which is regulated quite independently of the value of the commodity, and the price of the profit. If this were so there would be absolutely no reason why the total value of the commodity should not be 8s. or 10s. or more, according as it is assumed that the wages are 5s., the profit 3s., and so on. When Adam Smith is examining the "natural rate" of wages or the "natural price" of wages, what guides his investigation? The "natural price" of the means of subsistence required for the reproduction of labour power. But by what does he determine the natural price of these means of subsistence? In so far as he determines it at all, he comes back to the correct determination of value, namely, the labour time required for the production of these means of subsistence. But when he abandons this correct course, he falls into a vicious circle. What is it that determines the natural price of the means of subsistence, which determine the natural price of wages? The natural price of "wages", of "profit", of "rent", which constitute the natural price of all means of subsistence as of all commodities. And so *in infinitum.* The twaddle about the law of demand and supply of course cannot help us out of this vicious circle. For the "natural price" or the price which corresponds to the value of the commodity is supposed to become effective at the moment when demand and supply are equal, that is, when the price of the commodity does not, as a result of fluctuations of demand and supply, stand above or below its value; when, in other words, the price of production of the commodity (or the value of the commodity supplied by the seller) is equal to the price which the demand is paying.

But as we have said: in investigating the natural price of wages Adam Smith in fact falls back—at least in some passages —on the correct determination of the value of commodities. On the other hand, in the chapter which deals with the natural rate or the natural price of profit he loses himself, when he comes up against the real problem, in meaningless commonplaces and tautologies. At the outset it was in fact the value of the commodity which he saw as regulating wages and profit and rent. Then however he sets to work the other way round (which is closer to empirical semblance and to everyday conceptions), and now the natural price of commodities is supposed to be discovered and calculated by adding together the natural price of wages, profit and rent. It is one of Ricardo's chief merits that he put an end to this confusion. We shall touch on this point again when we are dealing with him.

There is only this further point to be noted here: the given magnitude of value of the commodity, serving as a fund out of which wages and profit are to be paid, appears empirically to the industrialist in the form of the fact that a definite market price for the commodity holds good for a shorter or longer period, in spite of all fluctuations in wages.

In regard to this peculiar train of thought in Adam Smith's book we should therefore note: at first the value of the commodity is examined and in some passages correctly determined, so correctly that in general Adam Smith discovers the origin of surplus value and its specific forms, and consequently deduces from this value wages and profit. Then, however, he takes the opposite course, and seeks to deduce the value of commodities (from which he has just deduced wages and profit) by adding together the natural prices of wages, profit and rent. It is this latter procedure that is responsible for the fact that he nowhere correctly explains the influence of fluctuations of wages, profit, etc., on the price of commodities, as he lacks the basis for such an explanation.

4. THE ANALYSIS OF PRICE INTO WAGES, PROFIT AND RENT

(a) *Adam Smith on this*

WE come now to another point, which is linked with the analysis of the price or value (since the two are here still assumed to be identical) of the commodity. We assume that Adam Smith has reckoned correctly in that, given the value of the commodity, he has analysed it into the constituent parts in which this value is distributed among the various agents of production—but not where he attempts the converse, to deduce the value from the price of these constituent parts. We therefore take no account of this latter view in what follows. We also leave out of account the one-sided way in which wages and profit are presented only as forms of distribution, and hence as both in the same sense revenues which their owners can consume. Leaving all this out of account, Adam Smith himself raises a difficulty—and this once more shows his superiority over Ricardo; not because he finds the correct answer to the question he raises, but in that he raises it at all.

What Adam Smith says is:

"These three parts [wages, profit and rent] seem either immediately or ultimately to make up the whole price of corn.[1] A fourth part, it may perhaps be thought, is necessary for replacing the stock of the farmer, or for compensating the wear and tear of his labouring cattle, and other instruments of husbandry. But it must be considered that the price of any instrument of husbandry, such as a labouring horse, is itself made up of the same three parts; the rent of the land upon which he is reared, the labour of tending and rearing him, and the profits of the farmer who advances both the rent of this land, and the wages of this labour.[2] Though the price of the corn, therefore, may pay the price as well as the maintenance of the horse, the whole price

[1] Of commodities in general. Adam Smith here takes corn, because in many commodities rent is not a constituent part of the price.

[2] Here profit appears as the most primary form, which also includes rent.

still resolves itself either immediately or ultimately into the same three parts of rent, labour and profit"[1] (Book I, Chapter VI, pp. 44–5).

But was it not equally obviously necessary to take into consideration the fact that just as the farmer included the price of the horse or the plough in the price of the corn, so also the breeder of horses or the maker of ploughs from whom the farmer bought the horse or the plough also included in the price of the horse or plough the price of the instruments of labour (in the first case perhaps another horse) and raw materials, fodder and iron; while the fund out of which horse-breeder and plough-maker *pay* wages and profit (including rent) consists only of the new labour which, in their sphere of production, they *add* to the amount of value present in their constant capital? Since therefore Adam Smith admits, in relation to the farmer, that besides the wages, profit and rent paid by himself and others, there enters into the price of his corn also a *fourth* and different additional *constituent*—the value of the constant capital, such as horses, agricultural implements, etc., used up by him—this must apply equally in the case of the horse-breeder and the maker of agricultural implements, and it is of no avail for Adam Smith to send us from pillar to post. Incidentally, the example of the farmer is particularly unhappily chosen for sending us from pillar to post, for among the separate posts of the constant capital there is in this case one which does not at all need to be bought from a third person, namely the seed; and is this constituent of value divided for anyone into wages, profit and rent?

But let us now proceed, and see whether Adam Smith sticks to his view that the value of every commodity can be analysed into one or all of the sources of revenue: wages, profit and rent; and so whether, being destined for consumption, it can be devoured or in any case applied in one way or another for personal use (not productive, industrial consumption).

First another preliminary point. In the case of the gathering of berries and such like it can be assumed that their value consists entirely of wages, although here also as a rule some

---

[1] Here it is perfectly preposterous that all of a sudden he says labour instead of wages, while he does not put landed property or capital for rent and profit.

appliances, such as baskets and so on, are required as instruments of labour. But examples of this kind are quite irrelevant here, where what is being considered is capitalist production.

We have first the repetition of the view expressed in Book I, Chapter VI.

In Book II, Chapter II, which deals with "Money considered as a particular Branch of the general stock of the Society", the following statement comes right at the beginning:

> "It has been shown in the first Book, that the price of the greater part of commodities resolves itself into three parts, of which one pays the wages of the labour, another the profits of the stock, and a third the rent of the land."

According to this, the whole value of every commodity resolves itself into revenue, and therefore falls to the share of one or another of the classes which live on this revenue, as a fund for consumption. Now as the total production of a country, each year for example, consists merely of the sum of values of the commodities produced, and as the value of each one of these commodities resolves itself into revenue, so also must their sum, the annual product of the labour, the gross revenue, be consumable annually in this form. And so immediately after this passage Smith himself raises the point:

> "Since this is the case, it has been observed, with regard to every particular commodity, taken separately: it must be so with regard to all the commodities which compose the whole annual produce of the land and labour of every country, taken complexly. The whole price or exchangeable value of that annual produce, must resolve itself into the same three parts, and be parcelled out among the different inhabitants of the country, either as the wages of their labour, the profits of their stock, or the rent of their land."

This is in fact the necessary consequence. What is true of the individual commodity is necessarily true of the total sum of commodities.

But *quod non*, says Adam. He continues:

> "But though the whole value of the annual produce of the land and labour of every country is thus divided among and constitutes a revenue to its different inhabitants, yet as in the rent of a private estate we distinguish between the

gross rent and the nett rent, so may we likewise in the
revenue of all the inhabitants of a great country."

But stop! Above he told us exactly the opposite: In the case
of the individual farmer we can distinguish a fourth part into
which the value for example of his corn resolves itself, namely,
the part which merely replaces the constant capital used up.
This, Adam Smith continues, is *directly* true for the individual
farmer. But when we go further into it, what for him is constant
capital resolves itself, at an earlier point, in the hand of another
person before it became capital in his, into wages, profit, etc.,
in short, into revenue. So although it is true that commodities,
considered in the hand of the individual producer, resolve
themselves into portions of value of which one does not
constitute revenue, yet it is false for "all the inhabitants of a
great country", since that which in one man's hand is constant
capital always draws its value from the fact that it came from
another person's hand as the aggregate price of wages, profit
and rent.

Now Adam says the direct opposite.

He continues:

"The gross rent of a private estate comprehends whatever
is paid by the farmer; the nett rent, what remains free to the
landlord, after deducting the expense of management, of
repairs, and all other necessary charges; or what, without
hurting his estate, he can afford to place in his stock reserved
for immediate consumption, or to spend upon his table, etc.
His real wealth is in proportion, not to his gross, but to his
nett rent."

In the first place, Adam Smith is here confusing different
things. What the farmer pays as rent to the landowner, just as
what he pays as wages to the worker, and just as his own
profit, is a part of the value or of the price of the commodities,
which resolves itself into revenue. The question is, however,
whether the commodity contains yet another constituent part
of value. Here he admits that it does, as he admitted it in the
case of the farmer, though this is supposed not to prevent the
latter's corn (that is to say, its price or exchange value) from
resolving itself merely into revenue.

Secondly, a note in passing. For the individual farmer,

considered as a farmer, the real wealth of which he can dispose depends on his profit. But on the other hand, as owner of commodities, he can sell the whole farm, or if the land does not belong to him, all the constant capital on it, such as draught cattle, agricultural implements, etc. The value which he can realise in this way, that is, the wealth of which he can dispose, is conditioned by the value and therefore the size of the constant capital which belongs to him. He can however only sell this to another farmer, in whose hands it is not disposable wealth but constant capital.

So we are still just where we were.

"The gross revenue of all the inhabitants of a great country, comprehends the whole annual produce of their land and labour;[1] the nett revenue, what remains free to them after deducting the expense of maintaining, first, their fixed, and, secondly, their circulating capital;[2] or what, without encroaching upon their capital, they can place in their stock reserved for immediate consumption.[3]

"The whole expense of maintaining the fixed capital must evidently be excluded from the nett revenue of the society. Neither the materials necessary for supporting their useful machines and instruments of trade, their profitable buildings etc., nor the produce of the labour necessary for fashioning those materials into the proper form, can ever make any part of it. The price of that labour may indeed make a part of it; as the workmen so employed may place the whole value of their wages in their stock reserved for immediate consumption. But in other sorts of labour, both the price and the produce go to this stock, the price to that of the workmen, the produce to that of other people, whose subsistence, conveniences, and amusements are augmented by the labour of those workmen" (pp. 251–2).

Here Adam Smith comes closer to the correct standpoint, but again he jumps away from the question which he has to answer—the question about the fourth portion of the total

---

[1] We were told previously that this total aggregate, that is, its value, resolves itself into wages, profits and rents, pure forms of nett revenue.

[2] Adam Smith therefore first deducts instruments of labour and raw materials.

[3] So now we learn that the price or exchange value of the total sum of commodities, as with individual capitalists so also for the whole country, resolves itself into a fourth part, which is not a revenue for anyone, and is not resolvable into either wages, profit or rent.

price of the commodity, which is not resolved into either wages or profit or rent.

First something that is quite wrong. In the case of makers of machinery, as of all other industrial capitalists, the labour which works up the raw material of the machines, etc., into the correct form in fact resolves itself into necessary and surplus labour; therefore not only into wages, but also into the capitalist's profit. But the value of the materials and the value of the instruments used by the workers to give them the right form cannot be resolved into either the one or the other. That products which by their nature are destined not for individual but for industrial consumption do not enter into the consumption fund, has nothing at all to do with it. Seed, for example (that portion of the wheat which is used for sowing), by its nature could also enter into the consumption fund; but by its economic function it must go into the production fund.

Further, however, it is quite untrue that so far as concerns products destined for individual consumption, their whole price, along with the product itself, enters into the consumption fund. Linen, for example, when not used for sail cloth or other productive purposes, is entirely used up as a product in consumption. But not its price, for one part of this price replaces the linen yarn, another part looms, and so on, and only a part of the price of the linen is converted into revenue of any kind.

Adam just now told us that the raw materials necessary for machines, buildings for exploitation, etc., can never make a part of the nett revenue, any more than the machines, etc., made from them can do so. Hence, presumably, they form a part of the gross revenue. Shortly afterwards, in the same Chapter II of Book II, he says on the other hand:

> "The machines and instruments of trade, etc., which compose the fixed capital either of an individual or of a society, make no part either of the gross or of the nett revenue of either; so money . . ." (p. 254).

Adam's twistings and turnings, his contradictions and digressions from the point, prove that once he had made wages, profit and rent the elemental constituent parts of exchange value or of the total price of the product, he had got himself stuck in the mud and could only flounder.

*   *   *

Adam Smith's contradictions are of significance because they contain problems which it is true he does not solve, but which he reveals by contradicting himself. His correct instinct in this connection is best proved by the fact that his successors take opposing stands based on one aspect of his teaching or on the other.

*   *   *

In Book II, Chapter II, when dealing with the circulation of money and the credit system, Adam Smith expresses the same view—that the annual product of a country is divisible into wages and profits (the latter including rent, interest, etc.); he says:

> "The circulation of every country may be considered as divided into two different branches: the circulation of the dealers with one another, and the circulation between the dealers and the consumers.[1] Though the same pieces of money, whether paper or metal, may be employed sometimes in the one circulation and sometimes in the other; yet as both are constantly going on at the same time, each requires a certain stock of money of one kind or another, to carry it on. The value of the goods circulated between the different dealers, never can exceed the value of those circulated between the dealers and the consumers; whatever is bought by the dealers, being ultimately destined to be sold to the consumers" (pp. 286-7).

[This passage is incorrect. Let us take two peasants. The harvest of each amounts to 120 quarters of corn, of which each has to use 12 quarters again as seed.]

The peasant may sell his whole crop of 120 quarters; but then he must buy 12 quarters of seed from another peasant. As the latter must also use 12 quarters as seed, he has left only 96 quarters for sale for individual consumption. In either case,

---

[1] By dealers Adam Smith means all capitalists engaged in the production process and the circulation process; by consumers, the workers and the capitalists, landowners, etc., and their dependants, in so far as they expend revenue.

out of the 240 quarters 24 are returned to the land as seed.

In circulation, however, this makes a difference. In the first case, in which each deducts a tenth, 216 quarters come into circulation. In the second case 120 quarters pass into circulation from the first farmer, and 108 from the second, in total therefore 228 quarters. In either case only 216 quarters pass to actual consumers. Thus we have here already one example of the fact that the aggregate of values exchanged between dealers and dealers is greater than the aggregate of values exchanged between dealers and consumers.

Moreover, this difference is to be found in all cases where a part of the profits is transformed into capital; also where transactions between dealers and dealers extend over many years.

5. PRODUCTIVE AND UNPRODUCTIVE LABOUR

(a) *Definition of Productive Labour as Labour which produces Capital*

[WE come now to the last point which we have to examine in Adam Smith's theories, the distinction between productive and unproductive labour.]

In Adam Smith's definition of what he calls *productive labour* in contradistinction to *unproductive labour*, we find the same two-sided approach as we have found on every question up to now. We find jumbled together in his presentation two conceptions of what he calls productive labour, and to begin with we will examine the first, the correct conception.

Productive labour, in its significance for capitalist production, is wage labour which, exchanged against the variable part of capital, not only reproduces this part of the capital (or the value of its own labour power), but in addition produces surplus value for the capitalist. It is only through it that commodity or money is transformed into capital, produces as capital. Only that wage labour is productive which produces capital. This means that it reproduces in expanded form the sum of value laid out on it, or that it gives back more labour than it receives in the form of wages. Thus it is only that labour power whose utilisation produces a value greater than its own. The existence of a capitalist class, and therefore of capital, is founded on the productivity of labour; not however on its absolute, but on its relative productivity. For example, if a working day only sufficed to maintain the worker in existence, that is, to reproduce his labour power, then, speaking in an absolute sense, the labour would be productive, because it was reproductive—that is to say, it constantly replaced the values (equal to the value of its own labour power) which it consumed. But it would not be productive in the capitalist sense, because it produced no surplus value. It produced in fact no new value, but only replaced the old; it would have consumed the value in one form in order to reproduce it in another. And in this sense it has been said that a worker is productive whose production is equal to his own consumption, and that a worker is unproductive who consumes more than he reproduces.

The productivity of labour in the capitalist sense is based on relative productivity—that the worker not only replaces an old value but creates a new one; that he materialises more labour time in his product than is materialised in the product that maintains his existence as a worker. The existence of capital is founded on this type of productive wage labour.

This conception of productive labour follows naturally from Adam Smith's conception of the source of surplus value, that is, of the nature of capital. In so far as he holds to this conception he is following a course opened up by the Physiocrats and even by the Mercantilists; he only rids it of false notions, thus bringing out its inner kernel. The Physiocrats, though wrong in thinking that only agricultural labour is productive, maintained the correct view, from the capitalist standpoint, that only that labour is productive which creates a surplus value; and in fact a surplus value not for itself, but for the owner of the means of production; labour which creates a *produit net*, not for itself but for the landowner. For the surplus value or the surplus labour time is materialised in a surplus product or *produit net*.

But here again they have a false notion of it; they see it for example where there is a surplus of wheat beyond what the workers and farmers consume; but there is also a surplus of cloth beyond what the clothmakers (workers and employers) need for their own clothing.

Surplus value itself is wrongly conceived, because they have false ideas of value, reducing it to the use value of the labour, not to the labour time, to social, homogeneous labour. Nevertheless, there remains the correct proposition that only that wage labour is productive which creates more value than it costs. Adam Smith frees this from the false notion with which it was linked among the Physiocrats.

Let us go back beyond the Physiocrats to the Mercantilists. In their case also there is one aspect of their theory which, though they were not conscious of it, contains the same view of productive labour. Their theory was based on the idea that labour is only productive in those branches of production whose products, when sent abroad, bring back more money than they have cost (or than had to be disbursed for them); that is, which enabled a country to participate to a special degree in the products of newly opened gold and silver mines. They saw that there was a rapid growth of wealth and of the middle class in these countries. What in fact was the source of this influence exerted by gold? Wages did not rise in proportion to commodity prices; that is, wages fell, and hence the relative surplus labour was increased, the rate of profit rose— not because the workers had become more productive, but because the absolute wage (that is, the sum of the means of subsistence received by the worker) was forced down; in a word, the condition of the workers grew worse. Labour in these countries was therefore in fact more productive for those who employed it. This fact was linked with the inflow of the precious metals, and it was this, though they had only a dim awareness of it, that prompted the Mercantilists to declare that labour employed in such branches of production was alone productive.

"The remarkable increase of population which has taken place, not only in England, but in almost every European state, has perhaps proceeded chiefly from the increased productiveness of the American mines. An increased abundance of the precious metals raises the price of commodities in a greater proportion than the price of labour; it depresses the condition of the labourer, and at the same time increases the gains of his employer, who is thus induced to enlarge his circulating capital to the utmost of his ability, to hire as many hands as he has the means to pay;—and it has been seen that this is precisely the state of things most favourable to the increase of people. Mr. Malthus observes, that 'the discovery of the mines of America, during the time that it raised the price of corn between three and four times, did not nearly so much as double the price of labour'. The price of commodities intended for home consumption, (of corn for instance,) does not immediately rise in consequence of an influx of money; but as the rate of profit in agricultural employments is thus depressed below the rate of profit in manufactures, capital will gradually be withdrawn from the former to the latter: thus all capital comes to yield higher profits than formerly, and a rise of profits is always equivalent to a fall of wages" (John Barton, *Observations on the Circumstances which influence the Condition of the Labouring Classes of Society*, London, 1817, pp. 29 *ff*.).

So, firstly, according to Barton there was a repetition in the second half of the eighteenth century of the same phenomenon as that which gave the impulse to the Mercantile System in the last third of the sixteenth and in the seventeenth century. Secondly, as only exported goods were measured against gold and silver on the basis of its fallen value, while goods destined for consumption internally continued to be measured in gold and silver according to its old value (until competition among the capitalists put an end to this measurement by two different standards), labour in the former branches of production appeared to be directly productive—that is, creating surplus value—because of the fact that wages were depressed below their former level.

The second, wrong conception of productive labour which Adam Smith develops is so interwoven with the correct one that the two conceptions follow each other step by step in the same passage. To illustrate the first conception it is therefore necessary to tear the quotations apart and deal with them piecemeal.

Chapter III of Book II of *The Wealth of Nations* opens with the words:

"There is one sort of labour which adds to the value of the subject upon which it is bestowed: there is another which has no such effect. The former, as it produces a value, may be called productive; the latter, unproductive labour. Thus the labour of a manufacturer adds, generally, to the value of the materials which he works upon, that of his own maintenance, and of his master's profit. The labour of a menial servant, on the contrary, adds to the value of nothing. Though the manufacturer has his wages advanced to him by his master, he, in reality, costs him no expense, the value of those wages being generally restored, together with a profit, in the improved value of the subject upon which his labour is bestowed. But the maintenance of a menial servant never is restored. A man grows rich by employing a multitude of manufacturers: he grows poor by maintaining a multitude of menial servants" (pp. 294-5).

In this passage—and the contradictory statements jostle each other even more closely in the passages that follow, which we shall quote later—what is in the main treated as productive labour is labour which produces a surplus value—"his master's profit"—in addition to reproducing the value "of his (the worker's) own maintenance". Also, the industrialist could not "grow rich by employing a multitude of manufacturers" unless the latter, in addition to the value which their own maintenance costs, added also a surplus value.

Secondly, however, in this passage Adam Smith treats as productive labour that which "creates a value" in general. But leaving this latter statement out of account for the moment, we will first cite other passages in which the first view is partly repeated, partly formulated more sharply, but particularly also further developed.

"But if the quantity of food and clothing, which were thus consumed by unproductive, had been distributed among productive hands, they would have reproduced, together with a profit, the full value of their consumption".

Here a productive worker is stated quite explicitly to be one who not only reproduces for the capitalist the full value of the means of subsistence contained in the wages, but reproduces it for him with a profit.

Only labour which produces capital is productive labour. Commodities or money, however, become capital through being directly exchanged for labour power, and exchanged only in order to be replaced by more labour than they themselves contain. For the use value of the labour power to the capitalist as a capitalist does not consist in its *actual* use value, in the usefulness of this particular concrete labour—that it is spinning labour, weaving labour, and so on. He is no more concerned with this than he is concerned with the use value of the product of this labour in itself; inasmuch as for the capitalist the product is a commodity, and in fact before its first metamorphosis is not an article of consumption. What interests him in the commodity is that it possesses more exchange value than he paid for it; and so the use value of the labour consists for him in the fact that he gets back a greater quantity of labour time than he paid out in the form of the wages. Included among productive workers are of course all those who contribute to the production of the commodity in one way or another, from the actual operative to the manager or engineer (as distinct from the capitalist). And so even the latest English official Report on the Factories *explicitly* includes in the category of employed wage workers all persons employed in the factories and in the offices attached to them, with the exception of the manufacturers themselves. The productive worker is here defined from the standpoint of capitalist production, and Adam Smith got to the very essence of the concept, hit the nail on the head. This is one of his greatest scientific merits (as Malthus rightly observed, this critical differentiation between productive and unproductive labour remains the foundation of all bourgeois political economy)—that he defined productive labour as labour *which is exchanged directly with capital*; that is, an exchange through which the means of production required for labour, and value in general—money or commodities—are first transformed into capital and labour into wage labour in its scientific meaning. Thereby also what is *unproductive labour* is absolutely defined. It is labour which is not exchanged against capital, but *directly* against revenue, that is, against wages or profit, including of course the various categories of those who share in the profit of the capitalist, as interest and rent. Where all labour in part still pays itself, as for example the agricultural labour of the serfs, and in part is directly exchanged against revenue, as in the case of manufacturing labour in the cities of Asia, there exists no capital and no wage labour in the sense of bourgeois political economy. These definitions are therefore not derived from the material processes of labour—neither from the nature of its product nor from the work performed as concrete labour—but from the definite social forms, the social relations of production, within which these processes are realised.

An actor, for example, or even a clown, according to this definition is a productive worker, if he works in the employ of a capitalist (an *entrepreneur*) to whom he returns more labour than he receives from him in the form of wages; while a jobbing tailor who comes to the capitalist's house and patches his trousers for him, producing a mere use value for him, is an unproductive worker. The labour of the former is exchanged against capital, that of the latter against revenue. The former produces a surplus value; in the latter, revenue is consumed.

The distinction between productive and unproductive labour is here only conceived from the standpoint of the possessor of money, of the capitalist, not from that of the *worker*; and hence the stupidity of Ganilh etc., who have so little understanding of the matter that they raise the question whether the labour or function of the prostitute, or Latin and so on, produces money.

A writer is a productive worker not because he produces ideas, but in so far as he enriches the publisher who publishes his works, or if he is a wage worker for a capitalist.

(b) Definition of Productive Labour as Labour which produces Commodities

The use value of the commodity in which the labour of a productive worker is embodied may be of the most trivial kind. This material product is not at all bound up with this its peculiar property [as embodiment of productive labour], which is rather the expression of a definite social relation of production. This property does not arise from the content or the result of labour, but from its definite social form.

On the other hand, on the assumption that capital has conquered the whole of production—and therefore that *commodities* (as distinct from mere use values) are no longer produced by any worker who himself owns the means of production for producing these commodities; that therefore now only the capitalist is the producer of *commodities* (the sole commodity excepted being labour power)—then revenues must be exchanged either against commodities which capital alone produces and sells, or against labour, which just like those commodities is bought in order to be consumed; that is, only for its definite material form, for its use value, for the sake of the *services* which, in its definite material form, it renders to its buyer and consumer. For the provider of these services the acts performed are commodities. They have a definite use value (imaginary or real) and a definite exchange value. For the buyer, however, these services are merely use values, objects in which he consumes his revenue. These unproductive workers do not receive their share of the revenue (wages and profits), their share of the commodities produced by productive labour, *gratis* and for nothing: they have to buy it, but they have nothing to do with its production.

In any case it is however clear: the greater the part of the revenue (wages and profit) spent on commodities produced by capital, the less the part that can be spent on the services of unproductive workers, and *vice versa*.

The determinate material form of the labour, and consequently of its product, in itself has nothing whatever to do with this distinction between productive and unproductive labour. For example, the cooks and waiters in a public hotel are productive workers, in so far as their labour is transformed into capital for the proprietor of the hotel. These same persons are unproductive workers as "menial servants", in so far as I do not make capital out of their services, but spend revenue on them. In fact, therefore, these same persons also are for me, the consumer, unproductive workers in the hotel.

"That part of the annual produce of the land and labour of any country which replaces a capital never is immediately employed to maintain any but productive hands. It pays the wages of productive labour only. That which is immediately destined for constituting a revenue, either as profit or as rent, may maintain indifferently either productive or unproductive hands.

"Whatever part of his stock a man employs as a capital, he always expects it to be replaced to him with a profit. He employs it, therefore, in maintaining productive hands only; and after having served in the function of a capital to him, it constitutes a revenue to them. Whenever he employs any part of it in maintaining unproductive hands of any kind, that part is, from that moment, withdrawn from his capital, and placed in his stock reserved for immediate consumption" (Book II, Chapter III, pp. 296-7).

To the extent that capital conquers the whole of production, and therefore the home and petty form of industry producing non-commodities, use values for personal consumption, disappears, it is clear that the unproductive workers—those whose services are exchanged directly against revenue—perform for the most part only *personal* services, and only an infinitesimal part of them (like cooks, seamstresses, jobbing tailors and so on) will produce material use values. That they produce no *commodities* follows from the nature of the case. For the commodity as such is never a direct object of consumption, but a bearer of exchange value. Consequently only a quite insignificant part of these unproductive workers can play a direct part in material production once the capitalist mode of production has developed. It is only by the exchange of [their] services against revenue that they participate in the latter. This does not prevent, as Adam Smith notes, the value of the services of these unproductive workers being determined and determinable in the same (or an analogous) way as that of the productive workers: namely, by the production costs involved in their maintenance or production of their maintenance. Other factors also have importance in this connection, but they are not relevant here.

The labour power of the productive worker is a commodity for the worker himself. So is that of the unproductive worker. But the productive worker produces commodities for the buyer of his labour power. The unproductive worker produces for him a mere use value, not a commodity; an imaginary or a real use value. It is characteristic for the unproductive worker that he produces no commodities for his buyer, but indeed receives commodities from him.

> "The labour of some of the most respectable orders in the society is, like that of menial servants, unproductive of any value. . . . The sovereign, for example, with all the officers both of justice and war who serve under him, the whole army and navy, are unproductive labourers. They are the servants of the public, and are maintained by a part of the annual produce of the industry of other people. . . . In the same class must be ranked . . . : churchmen, lawyers, physicians, men of letters of all kinds; players, buffoons, musicians, opera-singers, opera-dancers, etc." (p. 295).

In itself, as has been said, this distinction between productive and unproductive labour has nothing to do either with the particular speciality of the labour or with the particular use value in which this special labour incorporates itself. In the one case the labour is exchanged against capital, in the other against revenue. In the one case the labour is transformed into capital and produces a profit for the capitalist; in the other case it is an expenditure, one of the articles in which revenue is consumed. For example, the worker employed by a piano maker is a productive worker. His labour replaces not only the wage which he consumes; but in the product, the piano, the commodity which the piano maker sells, is contained a surplus value over and above the value of the wage. If on the other hand I buy all the materials required for a piano (or for all it matters the worker himself may possess them) and, instead of buying the piano in a shop, have it made in my home— then the worker who makes the piano is an unproductive worker, because his labour is exchanged directly against my revenue.

Hence it is clear that in the same proportion as capital subjugates to itself the whole of production—that is, all commodities are produced for the market and not for direct consumption—and the productivity of labour rises to the same degree, a material difference between productive and unproductive labour will more and more develop, inasmuch as the former, with minor exceptions, will exclusively produce commodities, while the latter, with minor exceptions, will perform only personal services. The former class will consequently produce the immediate, material wealth consisting in *commodities*, all commodities except that which consists of labour power itself. This is one of the considerations which prompt Adam Smith to add other points of difference, in addition to this first *differentia specifica* by which they are defined in principle.

Thus, following through various associations of ideas, he says:

"The labour of a menial servant,[1] on the contrary, adds to the value of nothing . . . the maintenance of a menial servant never is restored. A man grows rich by employing a

[1] As distinct from that of the "manufacturer".

multitude of manufacturers: he grows poor by maintaining a multitude of menial servants. The labour of the latter, however, has its value, and deserves its reward as well as that of the former. But the labour of the manufacturer fixes and realises itself in some particular subject or vendible commodity, which lasts for some time at least after that labour is past. It is, as it were, a certain quantity of labour stocked and stored up to be employed, if necessary, upon some other occasion. That subject, or what is the same thing, the price of that subject, can afterwards, if necessary, put into motion a quantity of labour equal to that which had originally produced it. The labour of the menial servant, on the contrary, does not fix or realise itself in any particular subject or vendible commodity. His services generally perish in the very instant of their performance, and seldom leave any trace or value behind them for which an equal quantity of service could afterwards be procured.

"The labour of some of the most respectable orders in the society is, like that of menial servants, unproductive of any value, and does not fix or realise itself in any permanent subject, or vendible commodity . . ." (Book II, Chapter III, pp. 294–5).

For the definition of the unproductive worker we here have the following determinants, which at the same time form the links in Adam Smith's train of thought:

The labour of the unproductive worker "produces no value", "adds to the value of nothing", "the maintenance (of the unproductive worker) never is restored", "his labour does not fix or realise itself in any particular subject or vendible commodity". On the contrary, "his services generally perish in the very instant of their performance, and seldom leave any trace or value behind them for which an equal quantity of service could afterwards be procured". Finally, "his labour does not fix or realise itself in any permanent subject or vendible commodity".

In this presentation productive or unproductive is used in a sense different from its original use. It no longer refers to production of a surplus value, which by its nature includes reproduction of an equivalent for the value consumed. But according to this presentation, the labour of a worker is called productive in so far as he replaces the consumed value by an equivalent, by adding to any material, through his labour, a quantity of labour equal to that which was contained in his wage. Here the formal determination, the determination of productive and unproductive workers by their relation to capitalist production, is abandoned. From Book IV, Chapter IX, where Adam Smith criticises the teaching of the Physiocrats, it can be seen that Adam Smith came to make this aberration partly in opposition to the Physiocrats and partly under their influence. If a worker merely replaces each year the equivalent of his wages, then he is not a productive worker for the capitalist. He does indeed replace the wage, the purchase price of his labour. But it is absolutely the same transaction as if the capitalist had bought the commodity which this worker produced. He pays for the labour contained in the constant capital and in the wage. He possesses the same quantity of labour in the form of the commodity which he previously possessed in the form of money. His money is not thereby transformed into capital. In this case it is the same as if the worker himself were the owner of his means of production. He must each year deduct the value of the means of production from the value of his annual product, in order to replace them. What he consumes or could consume annually would be that portion of the value of his product which is equal to the new labour added in the year to his constant capital. In this case, therefore, there would be no capitalist production.

The first reason why Adam Smith calls this kind of labour "productive" is that the Physiocrats call it "sterile" and "non-productive".

Thus Adam Smith tells us in the Chapter referred to:

> "First, this class [namely the industrial classes, who do not carry on agriculture,] it is acknowledged [by the Physiocrats], reproduces annually the value of its own annual consumption, and continues, at least, the existence of the stock or capital which maintains and employs it. . . . Farmers and country labourers, indeed, over and above the stock which maintains and employs them, reproduce annually a net produce, a free rent to the landlord . . . the labour of farmers and country labourers is certainly more productive

than that of merchants, artificers and manufacturers. The superior produce of the one class, however, does not render the other barren or unproductive" (Book IV, Chapter IX, Vol. 2, pp. 168–9).

Here therefore Adam Smith falls back to the standpoint of the Physiocrats. The real "productive labour", which produces a surplus value and because of that a *produit net*, is agricultural labour. He abandons his own view of surplus value and accepts that of the Physiocrats. At the same time, he asserts, in opposition to that view, that industrial (and according to him also commercial) labour is nevertheless also productive, even if not in the same full sense of the word. He therefore drops the formal definition—the determination of what is a "productive worker" from the standpoint of capitalist production—and asserts, as against the Physiocrats, that the industrial class not engaged in agriculture reproduces its own wages— that is, it does after all produce a value equal to that which it consumes, and thereby "continues, at least, the existence of the stock or capital which maintains and employs it." Hence arises, under the influence of and in contradiction to the Physiocrats, his second definition of what is "productive labour".

"Secondly", says Adam Smith, "it seems, upon this account, altogether improper to consider artificers, manufacturers, and merchants in the same light as menial servants. The labour of menial servants does not continue the existence of the fund which maintains and employs them. Their maintenance and employment is altogether at the expense of their masters, and the work which they perform is not of a nature to repay that expense. That work consists in services which perish generally in the very instant of their performance, and does not fix or realise itself in any vendible commodity which can replace the value of their wages and maintenance. The labour, on the contrary, of artificers, manufacturers, and merchants naturally does fix and realise itself in some such vendible commodity. It is upon this account that, in the chapter in which I treat of productive and unproductive labour, I have classed artificers, manufacturers, and merchants among the productive labourers, and menial servants among the barren or unproductive" (Book IV, Chapter IX, Vol. 2, p. 169).

As soon as capital has conquered the whole of production, revenue, in so far as it is exchanged at all against labour, will not be directly exchanged against labour which produces *commodities*, but against mere *services*. It is exchanged partly against *commodities* which are to serve as use values, and partly against services, which by their nature are consumed as use values.

A commodity—as distinguished from labour power itself—is a material thing confronting man, a thing of a certain utility to him, in which a definite quantity of labour is fixed or realised.

We come therefore to the definition which in its essence was already contained in the first paragraph above. Productive workers are those whose labour *produces commodities*, and who in fact do not consume more commodities than they produce, than. their labour costs. Their labour fixes and realises itself "in any vendible commodity which can replace the value of their wages and maintenance". Through the production of commodities the productive worker constantly reproduces the variable capital which he constantly consumes in the form of wages. He constantly produces the fund which pays him, "which maintains and employs him".

In the first place, Adam Smith naturally includes in the labour which fixes or realises itself in a vendible commodity all intellectual activities which are directly consumed in material production. Not only the direct worker by hand or machine, but foreman, engineer, manager, clerk, etc.; in a word, the labour of the whole personnel required in a particular sphere of material production in order to produce a particular commodity, who must necessarily work together (co-operate) in the making of the commodities. In fact they add their aggregate labour to the constant capital and raise the value of the products by this amount. (How far is this true of bankers, etc.?)

Secondly, Adam Smith says that on the whole, as a rule, "generally", this is not the case with the labour of unproductive workers. Even when capital has conquered material production, and so, taken by and large, home industry has disappeared, or the industry of the petty craftsman who makes use values directly for the consumer at his home—even then, Adam Smith knows quite well, the seamstress whom I bring to my house to sew shirts for me, or the workers who repair furniture, or the servant who scrubs and cleans the house and so on, or the cook who gives meat and other things their palatable form, fix their labour in a thing and in fact increase the value of that thing, in exactly the same way as the seamstress who sews in a factory, the machine operative who repairs the machine, the workers who clean the machine, the cook who cooks in a hotel as a wage-worker for a capitalist. These use values can also, potentially, be commodities; the shirts may be sent to the pawnshop, the house sold again, the furniture sold by auction, and so on. Thus it is possible that these persons also have produced commodities and added value to the objects on which they have worked. This however is a very small category among unproductive workers. And it does not hold good of the mass of servants, parsons, Government officials, soldiers, musicians, etc.

But however large or small the number of these "unproductive workers" may be, at any rate what this makes clear and is admitted by the limiting word "in services which perish *generally* in the very instant of their performance", is that it is neither necessarily the special type of labour nor the outward form of its product that make it "productive" or "unproductive". The same labour can be productive, when I buy it as a capitalist, as a producer, in order to make a profit out of it, and unproductive, when I buy it as a consumer, a spender of revenue, in order to consume its use value, no matter whether this use value perishes with the activity of this labour power itself, or realises, fixes itself in an object. The cook in the hotel produces a commodity for the person who has bought her labour as a capitalist, the hotel proprietor. The consumer of the lamb cutlet has to pay for her labour, and this replaces for the hotel proprietor (apart from profit) the fund out of which he continues to pay the cook. But if on the other hand I buy the labour of a cook so that she may cook meat etc. for me, not to make a profit out of it as labour in general but to enjoy it, to use it as that particular concrete labour, then her labour is unproductive; although this labour fixes itself in a material product and could just as well (in its result) be a vendible commodity as it in fact is for the proprietor of the hotel.

The great difference remains however: the cook does not replace for me (the private person) the fund out of which I pay her. For I buy her labour not as a value-creating element, but merely for the sake of its use value. Her labour as little replaces for me the fund with which I pay for it, that is, her wage, as the dinner that I eat in the hotel in itself enables me to buy and eat the same dinner a second time. This distinction however is also to be found between commodities. The commodity which the capitalist buys in order to replace his constant capital (for example, cotton material, if he is a cotton-printer) replaces its value in the printed cotton. But if on the other hand he buys the cotton in order to consume it himself, this commodity does not replace his outlay. The largest proportion of society, that is to say the working class, must, for that matter, perform this kind of labour for itself; but it can only perform it when it has worked "productively". It can only cook meat for itself when it has produced a wage with which it can pay for the meat; and it can only keep its furniture and dwellings clean, or clean its boots, when it has produced the value of furniture, house rent and boots. For this class of productive workers itself, therefore, what appears as unproductive labour is labour which they perform for themselves. This unproductive labour never enables them to repeat the same unproductive labour a second time unless they have previously worked productively.

Thirdly. On the other hand: an *entrepreneur* of theatres, concerts, brothels, etc., buys the temporary disposal over the labour power of the actors, musicians, prostitutes, etc.—in reality in a roundabout way that is only of formal economic interest: in its result the movement is the same. He buys this so-called "unproductive labour", whose "services perish in the very instant of their performance" and do not fix or realise themselves in "any permanent (particular is also used) subject or vendible commodity" (other than themselves). The sale of these to the public provides him with wages and profit. And these services, which he has bought in this way, enable

him to repeat them: that is, they themselves renew the fund
out of which they are paid. The same is true for example of
the labour of a clerk employed by a lawyer in his office—
except for the fact that these services as a rule materialise
themselves in very comprehensive "particular subjects" in
the form of immense bundles of deeds. It is true that these
services are paid back to the *entrepreneur* from the revenue of
the public. But it is no less true that this holds good of all
products, in so far as they enter into individual consumption.
It is true that the country cannot export these services as
such; but it can export those who perform the services. Thus
France exports dancing masters, cooks, etc., and Germany
schoolmasters. With the export of the dancing master and the
schoolmaster, however, his revenue is also exported, whereas
the export of dancing shoes and books brings a reciprocal
value into the country.

If therefore on the one hand a part of the so-called unproductive labour embodies itself in material use values which
might just as well be commodities (vendible commodities), so
on the other hand a part of the services which assume no
objective form—have no existence as an object separated from
those performing the services, and do not enter into a commodity as a constituent part of value—may be bought with
capital (by the *direct* purchaser of the labour), replace their
own wage and yield a profit. In short, the production of these
services can be in part subordinated to capital, just as a part
of the labour which embodies itself in useful things is bought
directly from revenue and is not subordinated to capitalist
production.

Fourthly. The whole world of commodities can be divided
into two great parts. First, labour power; second, commodities
as distinct from labour power itself. And the purchase takes
place of such services as train, maintain, modify, etc., labour
power—in a word, give it a specialised form or even only
maintain it, as for example the service of the schoolmaster in
so far as it is "industrially necessary" or useful, the service of
the doctor in so far as he maintains health and thus preserves
the source of all value, labour power itself. These are therefore
services which put in their place "a vendible commodity", etc.,

namely, labour power itself, into whose costs of production and reproduction these services enter. However, Adam Smith knew how little "education" enters into the costs of production of the mass of the workers. And in any case the doctor's services belong to the *faux frais* of production. They can be counted as the costs of repair for labour power. Let us assume that wages and profit simultaneously decline in total value, whatever the cause—for example, because the nation has become lazier—and at the same time fall as measured in use value, because labour has become less productive owing to a bad harvest, etc.; in short, that the part of the product whose value is equivalent to revenue declines, because less new labour has been applied in the past year and because the labour that was applied has been less productive. If then capitalists and workers want to consume the same sum of value in material things as they did before, they would be able to buy less of the services of the doctor, schoolmaster, etc. And if they were compelled to continue the same outlay on both, then they would have to restrict their consumption of other things. It is therefore clear that the labours of the doctor and schoolmaster do not directly create the fund out of which they are paid, although their labours enter into the costs of production of the fund which creates all values whatsoever—the costs of production of labour power.

Adam Smith continues:

"Thirdly, it seems upon every supposition improper to say that the labour of artificers, manufacturers and merchants does not increase the real revenue of the society. Though we should suppose, for example, as it seems to be supposed in this system, that the value of the daily, monthly, and yearly consumption of this class was exactly equal to that of its daily, monthly, and yearly production, yet it would not from thence follow that its labour added nothing to the real revenue, to the real value of the annual produce of the land and labour of the society. An artificer, for example, who, in the first six months after harvest, executes ten pounds' worth of work, though he should in the same time consume ten pounds' worth of corn and other necessaries, yet really adds the value of ten pounds to the annual produce of the land and labour of the society. While he has been consuming a half-yearly revenue of ten pounds' worth of corn and other necessaries, he has produced an equal value of work capable of purchasing, either to himself or to some other person, an equal half-yearly revenue. The value, therefore, of what has been consumed and produced during these six months is equal, not to ten, but to twenty pounds. It is possible, indeed, that no more than ten pounds' worth of this value may ever have existed at any one moment of time. But if the ten pounds' worth of corn and other necessaries, which were consumed by the artificer, had been consumed by a soldier or by a menial servant, the value of that part of the annual produce which existed at the end of the six months would have been ten pounds less than it actually is in consequence of the labour of the artificer. Though the value of what the artificer produces, therefore, should not at any one moment of time be supposed greater than the value he consumes, yet at every moment of time the actually existing value of goods in the market is, in consequence of what he produces, greater than it otherwise would be" (Book IV, Chapter IX, Vol. 2, pp. 169–70).

Is not the value of the commodities to be found at any time on the market greater as a result of the "unproductive labour" than it would be without this labour? Are there not at every moment on the market, alongside wheat and meat and so on, also prostitutes, lawyers, sermons, concerts, theatrical performances, soldiers, politicians, etc.? These lads and wenches do not get the "corn and other necessaries" for nothing. In return they give or pester us with their services, which as such services have a use value, and because of their production costs have also an exchange value. Reckoned as consumable articles, at every moment, alongside the consumable articles in the form of commodities, there is a quantity of articles consumable as services. The total amount of consumable articles is thus at every moment greater than it would be without the consumable services. Secondly, however, the value also is greater; for it is equal to the value of the commodities which are paid for these services, and the latter is equal to the value of the services themselves. Inasmuch as in this case as in every exchange of commodities against commodities equal value is given for equal value, the same value is there in duplicate, once on the buyer's side and once on the seller's. Adam Smith goes on to say, in reference to the Physiocrats:

"When the patrons of this system assert that the consumption of artificers, manufacturers and merchants is equal to the value of what they produce, they probably mean no more than that their revenue, or the fund destined for their consumption, is equal to it" (Book IV, Chapter IX, Vol. 2, p. 170).

In this statement the Physiocrats were right in relation to workers and employers taken together, rent forming only a special category of the profits of the latter.[1]

---

[1] Adam Smith notes on the same occasion in criticising the Physiocrats (Book IV, Chapter IX):

"The annual produce of the land and labour of any society can be augmented only in two ways; either, first, by some improvement in the productive powers of the useful labour actually maintained within it, or, secondly, by some increase in the quantity of that labour.

"The improvement in the productive powers of useful labour depend, first, upon the improvement in the ability of the workman; and, secondly, upon that of the machinery with which he works.

". . . The increase in the quantity of useful labour actually employed within any society must depend altogether upon the increase of the capital which employs it; and the increase of that capital again must be exactly equal to the amount of the savings from the revenue, either of the particular persons who manage and direct the employment of that capital, or of some other persons who lend it to them" (Vol. 2, pp. 170-1).

In these passages there is a double vicious circle:

First: the annual product is increased by greater productivity of labour. All means to augment this productivity—in so far as it is not the result of accidents of nature such as a specially favourable season, etc.—require an increase of capital. But in order to increase the capital, the annual product of labour must be increased. First circle.

Second: The annual product can be increased by an increase in the quantity of labour employed. The quantity of labour employed, however, can only be increased if the capital that employs the labour is first increased. Adam Smith helps himself out of both vicious circles by "savings": by this he means in fact the transformation of revenue into capital. In itself it is already an error to present the whole of profit as the revenue of the capitalist. The law of capitalist production requires on the contrary that a part of the surplus labour, of the unpaid labour which the worker performs, is transformed into capital. When the individual capitalist is functioning as a capitalist—that is, as a functionary of capital—this may appear to him himself as savings; but he regards it as a necessary reserve fund. The increase of the quantity of labour does not however depend only on the number of workers, but also on the length of the working day. The quantity of labour can therefore be increased without an increase in that part of the capital which is used as wages. Similarly, on this assumption there need not be more machinery, etc. (though it will depreciate more rapidly; but this makes no difference here). All that would have to be increased is that part of the raw materials which consists in seeds, etc. And it remains true that, taking a single country (excluding foreign trade), surplus labour must first be applied to agriculture before it becomes possible in the industries which get their raw materials

Smith's second view of productive and unproductive labour —or rather the view that is interwoven with his other view— therefore amounts to this: that the former is labour which produces *commodities*, and the latter such as produces no commodities. He does not deny that the one kind of labour is just as much as the other *a commodity*. See the passage quoted above:

"The labour of the latter . . . has its value, and deserves a reward as well as that of the former" (Book II, Chapter III).

That is, from the economic standpoint. Neither in the one nor in the other kind of labour is there any question of moral or other standpoints.

The concept of a commodity, however, implies that labour embodies, materialises, realises itself in its product. Labour itself in its immediate being, in its living existence, cannot be directly conceived as a commodity, but only labour power, of which labour itself is the transient manifestation. Just as actual wage labour can only be explained in this way, so it is also with "unproductive labour", which Adam Smith throughout defines by the costs of production required to produce the "unproductive labourer". A *commodity* must therefore be conceived as having an existence distinct from the labour itself. Then, however, the world of commodities fall into two great categories:

On the one hand, labour power.

On the other, commodities themselves.

The materialisation, etc., of the labour is nevertheless not to be taken in such a Scottish sense as Adam Smith conceives it. When we speak of the commodity as a materialisation of labour—in the sense of its exchange value—this itself is only an imaginary, that is, a merely social mode of existence for the commodity, which has nothing to do with its corporeal reality; it is conceived as a definite quantity of social labour

from agriculture. A part of their raw materials, such as coal, iron, timber, fish, etc. (the last named for example as manure), can be procured merely through an increase of labour time (the number of workers remaining the same). There can therefore be no lack of these. On the other hand it has been shown above that the increase of productivity in its origin always presupposes merely the concentration of capital, not the accumulation of capital. Later however each process supplements the other.

or money. The concrete labour whose result it is may leave no trace in it. In manufactured commodities this trace remains in the outward form given to the raw material. Although on the other hand in agriculture, etc., the form given to the commodities—for example, wheat, oxen, etc.—is also the product of human labour, and indeed of labour transmitted and accumulated from generation to generation, nevertheless this cannot be seen in the product. In other forms of industrial labour it is in no way the purpose of the labour to alter the form of the thing, but only its position. For example when a commodity is brought from China to England, no trace of this labour is to be seen in the thing itself—except by those people who call to mind that the object is not an English product. Therefore the materialisation of labour in the commodity must not be understood in this way.[1] The mystification here arises from the fact that a social relation appears in the form of a thing. It may well be correct however that the commodity appears as past, objectivised labour, and therefore, when not in the form of a thing, can appear only in the form of labour power itself; though never directly as living labour itself, but in a roundabout way which in practice seems the same but is nevertheless not the same—in the determination of various wages. Productive labour would therefore be such labour as produces commodities or directly produces, trains, develops, maintains and reproduces labour power itself. Adam Smith excludes the latter from his category of productive labour; arbitrarily, but with a certain correct instinct: that if he included it, he would open the floodgates for false notions of productive labour.

In so far therefore as we leave out of account labour power

[1] That Adam Smith regards the fixation of labour as not something entirely extrinsic is shown by the following quotation, which enumerates among the various constituents of the fixed capital:

"4. . . . the acquired and useful abilities of all the inhabitants or members of the society. The acquisition of such talents, by the maintenance of the acquirer during his education, study, or apprenticeship, always costs a real expense, which is a capital fixed and realised, as it were, in his person. Those talents, as they make a part of his fortune, so do they likewise of that of the society to which he belongs. The improved dexterity of a workman may be considered in the same light as a machine or instrument of trade which facilitates and abridges labour, and which, though it costs a certain expense, repays that expense with a profit" (Book II, Chapter I).

itself, productive labour is that which produces commodities, material products, whose production has cost a definite quantity of labour or labour time. Among these material products are included all products of art and science, books, paintings, statues, etc., in so far as they take the form of things. In addition, however, the product of labour must be a *commodity* in the sense that it is a "vendible commodity", that is, a commodity in its first form, which has still to pass through its metamorphosis.

A manufacturer may himself construct a machine, when he cannot get it built anywhere else, not to sell it but to make use of it as a use value. But he then makes use of it as part of his constant capital, and thus sells it in instalments in the form of the product which it has helped to make.

Certain labours of "menial servants" may equally well take the form of (potential) commodities, and even of the same use values, considered as material objects. But they are not productive workers, because in fact they produce not commodities but immediate "use values". As for labours which are productive for their buyers or users themselves—as for example the labour of the actor for a theatrical *entrepreneur*—they are shown to be unproductive labours by the fact that their buyer cannot sell them to the public in the form of commodities, but only in the form of the action itself.

Apart from such cases, *productive* labour is that which produces commodities, and *unproductive* labour is that which produces personal services. The former labour is represented by a vendible thing; the latter must be consumed while it is being performed. The former (except for that labour which creates labour power itself) comprises all material and intellectual wealth—meat as well as books—that exists in the form of things; the latter covers all labours which satisfy any imaginary or real need of the individual—or even those which are forced upon the individual against his will.

The *commodity* is the most elementary form of bourgeois wealth. The explanation of "productive labour" as labour which produces " commodities" corresponds therefore to a far more elementary point of view than that which explains productive labour as labour which produces capital.

The opponents of Adam Smith have left out of account his first and pertinent definition, and have concentrated on the second, pointing out the unavoidable contradictions and inconsistencies to which it gives rise. Their attacks were made all the easier for them by their insistence on the material content of the labour, and particularly on the condition that the labour must be fixed in a more or less *durable* product. We shall see soon what it was that particularly gave rise to the polemics.

But first another point. Adam Smith says of the Physiocratic system that its great merit is its recognition of the fact that the wealth of nations consists "not in the unconsumable riches of money, but in the consumable goods annually produced by the labour of the society" (Book IV, Chapter IX).

Here we have the application of his second definition of productive labour.

The determination of surplus value naturally depended on the form in which value itself was conceived. In the Monetary and Mercantile system it is therefore presented as *money*; by the Physiocrats as the product of the land, as agricultural product; finally by Adam Smith simply as *commodity*. In so far as the Physiocrats touch on the substance of value, they resolve it into pure use value (matter, corporeal object), just as the Mercantilists resolve it into the pure form of value, the form in which the product *makes itself manifest* as general social labour: money. With Adam Smith, both properties of the commodity are grasped—use value and exchange value—and so all labour is productive which manifests itself in any use value, any useful product. The fact that it is labour that manifests itself in the product implies that the product is also equal to a definite quantity of general social labour. Adam Smith, in contrast to the Physiocrats, restores to its place the value of the product as the essential thing for bourgeois wealth; but on the other hand he strips off from value the purely fantastic form—that of gold and silver—in which it appeared to the Mercantilists. Every commodity is *in itself* money. It must be recognised that Adam Smith at the same time also falls back into the Mercantilist conception of "durability", in fact of "imperishability". We can recall the passage in Petty[1] where wealth is valued according to the degree to which it is more or less durable without perishing, and finally gold and silver are placed at the top as wealth that is "not perishable".

A. Blanqui says of Adam Smith: "In restricting the sphere of wealth exclusively to those values which are embodied in material substances, he erased from the book of production the whole boundless mass of immaterial values, daughters of the moral capital of civilised nations, etc." (*Histoire de l'Economie Politique*, Brussels, 1842, p. 152).

* * *

In Chapter I of Book IV Adam Smith himself says:

"Mr. Locke remarks a distinction between money and other movable goods. All other movable goods, he says, are of so consumable a nature that the wealth which consists in them cannot be much depended on. . . . Money, on the contrary, is a steady friend" (p. 376).

And further on in the same chapter:

"Consumable commodities, it is said, are soon destroyed; whereas gold and silver are of a more durable nature, and, were it not for this continual exportation, might be accumulated for ages together, to the incredible augmentation of the real wealth of the country" (p. 385).

The man of the Monetary System hankers after gold and silver because they are money, the independently existing, tangible substantiation of exchange value, its indestructible, eternally enduring substantiation—so long as it is not allowed to become means of circulation, the merely transient form of the exchange value of commodities. The accumulation of it, the amassing of it, the formation of a hoard is consequently his way of enriching himself. And, as I showed in the quotation from Petty, other commodities are themselves valued in the degree to which they are more or less durable, that is, remain exchange value.

Now in the first place Adam Smith repeats this same view—

[1] See *The Critique of Political Economy*, pp. 172–3 (Kerr edition), quoting Petty, *Political Arithmetick*, p. 196.

of the relatively greater or less durability of commodities—in the passage where he speaks of consumption which is more or less useful to the creation of wealth, in the measure that it creates more or less perishable articles of consumption. Thus here the Monetary System peeps through—and necessarily so, since even in direct consumption there is the reservation that the article of consumption is still wealth, a commodity—that is, a unity of use value and exchange value; and the latter depends on the degree to which the use value is durable, so that the article of consumption only slowly loses the possibility of being a commodity or bearer of exchange value.

Secondly, in his second distinction between productive and unproductive labour Adam Smith completely returns—in a broader form—to the distinction made in the Monetary System.

Productive labour "fixes and realises itself in some particular subject or vendible commodity, which lasts for some time at least after that labour is past. It is, as it were, a certain quantity of labour stocked and stored up to be employed, if necessary, upon some other occasion." As against this, the results of unproductive labour or services "generally perish in the very instant of their performance, and seldom leave any trace or value behind them for which an equal quantity of service could afterwards be procured" (Book II, Chapter III).

Thus Adam Smith makes the same distinction between commodities and services as the Monetary System did between gold and silver and other commodities. Here too the difference arises from accumulation, no longer however in the form of building up a hoard but in the real form of reproduction. The commodity perishes in consumption, but then it reproduces commodities of higher value, or if it is not so applied, it is itself value with which other commodities can be bought. It is the peculiarity of the product of labour that it exists in a more or less durable and therefore again alienable use value—in a use value in which it is the bearer of exchange value, is itself a commodity—or, in fact, in which it is money. Services, unproductive labours do not again become money. I cannot pay debts, nor buy commodities, nor buy labour that produces surplus value, with the services for which I pay the lawyer, doctor, priest, musician, statesman, soldier, etc. They have perished, like perishable articles of consumption.

So at bottom Adam Smith says the same thing as the Monetary System. For the latter, only that labour is productive which produces money, gold and silver. For Adam Smith, only that labour is productive which produces money for its buyer—though he sees the money character in all commodities in spite of its being covered over, while the Monetary System saw it only in the commodity which is the independent substantiation of exchange value. This distinction is· based on the nature of bourgeois production itself, since wealth is not equivalent to use value, but only the commodity is wealth—the use value as bearer of exchange value, as money. What the Monetary System did not understand was how this money is made and increased through the consumption of commodities—not through their transformation into gold and silver, for in this form they are crystallised as independent exchange value and not only lose their use value, but do not alter the magnitude of their value.

*　　　*　　　*

Had Adam Smith adhered with full consciousness to the analysis of surplus value which in substance is to be found in his work—that it is created only in the exchange of capital against wage labour—it would have followed that productive labour is only that which is exchanged against capital: never labour which is exchanged with revenue as such. In order that revenue may be exchanged against productive labour, it must first be transformed into capital.

But taking as his starting point on the one hand the traditional view—that productive labour is labour which produces directly any form of material wealth—and combining with this the distinction he made between the exchange of capital against labour and that of revenue against labour, Adam Smith drew the conclusion: The kind of labour for which capital is exchanged is always productive, it always creates material wealth, etc. The kind of labour for which revenue is exchanged may or may not be productive; but the spender of revenue far prefers to set in motion labour that is directly unproductive rather than productive labour. It can be seen that Adam Smith, by thus mixing together the two distinctions he draws, very much weakens and blunts the principal distinction.

(c) The Polemic against Adam Smith's Definition

The polemic against Adam Smith's differentiation between productive and unproductive labour was for the most part confined to the *dii minorum gentium*,[1] among whom moreover Storch was the most important; it is not to be found in the work of any outstanding economist—of any economist of whom it can be said that he made some discovery in political economy. On the contrary, it is the hobby-horse of the second-rate, and especially of the school-masterish compilers and writers of compendia, as well as of dilettanti with facile pens and vulgarisers in this field. What particularly gave rise to this polemic against Adam Smith was the following:

First: the great mass of the so-called "higher-grade" workers —such as State officials, military people, professional workers, doctors, priests, judges, lawyers, etc., some of whom are not only not productive but essentially destructive, but know how to appropriate to themselves a very great part of the "material" wealth partly through the sale of their "immaterial" commodities and partly by force and compulsion—found it not at all pleasant to be relegated *from the economic standpoint* to the same class as clowns and servants, to appear merely as consumers along with these, parasites on the actual producers (or rather agents of production). This classification was a particular profanation of precisely those functions which had formerly been surrounded with a halo, had enjoyed superstitious veneration. Political economy in its classical period, like the bourgeoisie itself in its *parvenu* period, adopted a severely critical attitude to the machinery of the State, etc. At a later stage it saw—practice also made it manifest—and learnt from experience, that the necessity for all these classes, in part completely unproductive, arose from its own organisation. In so far as those "unproductive workers" did not produce entertainment, so that their purchase entirely depended on the way in which the agent of production cared to spend his

[1] Gods of the lesser tribes.

wages or profit—in so far as on the contrary they were necessary or made themselves necessary because of bodily infirmities (like doctors) or spiritual weaknesses (like parsons), or because of the conflict between private interests and national interests (like State employees, all legal people, police, soldiers), they were regarded by Adam Smith, as by the industrial capitalists themselves and the working class, as *faux frais* of production, which are therefore to be cut down to the most indispensable minimum and to be provided as cheaply as possible. Bourgeois society reproduces in its own form everything against which it had fought in feudal or absolutist form. Hence it becomes a principal task for the sycophants of this society, especially of the upper classes, to restore theoretically the prestige of even the purely parasitic sections of these "unproductive workers", or to justify even the exaggerated claims of the section which is indispensable. The *dependence* of the ideological etc. class on the *capitalists* was in fact proclaimed.

Secondly, however, a part of the agents of production (of material production itself) were declared by one group or another of economists to be "unproductive". For example, the landowner, by the section of economists who represented industrial capital (Ricardo). Others (for example Carey) declared that the merchant was an "unproductive" worker. Then even a third group came along, who declared that the "capitalists" themselves were unproductive, or at least tried to reduce their claims to material wealth to "wages", that is, to the wages of a "productive worker". Many intellectual workers seemed also open to this doubt. It was therefore advisable to make a compromise and recognise the productivity of all classes not directly included among the agents of material production. One good turn deserves another; and, as in the fable of the bees, it had to be established that even from the "productive", economic standpoint the bourgeois world with all the "unproductive workers" is the best of all worlds. This was all the more timely because the "unproductive workers" on their part were making critical observations in regard to the productivity of the classes which when all is said and done were *"fruges consumere nati"* [1]—or even in regard to those agents

[1] Born to consume the fruits.

of production, such as landowners, who do nothing at all, etc. Both the *do-nothings* and the *parasites* on them had to be found a place in this best possible order of things.

Thirdly: As the dominion of capital extended, and in fact even those spheres of production not directly related to the production of material wealth became more and more dependent on it—and especially the positive sciences (natural sciences) were subordinated to it as means towards material production—second-rate sycophants of political economy thought it their duty to glorify and justify every sphere of activity by demonstrating that it was "linked" with the production of material wealth, that it was a means towards it; and they honoured everyone by making him a "productive worker" in the "narrowest" sense—that is, a worker who works in the service of capital, is useful in one way or another to its increase, etc.

There are also such people as Malthus to get honourable mention, who directly defend the necessity and usefulness of "unproductive workers" and pure parasites.

(d) Appendix: The Concept of Productive Labour

Capital is productive: (1) as a *force compelling* surplus labour; (2) as in itself the absorber and appropriator, as well as the personification, of the productive forces of social labour and of the general social productive forces, such as science.

The question arises as to how or for what reason labour as opposed to capital appears productive, or as *productive labour*, since the productive forces of labour are transferred to capital and the same productive force cannot be counted twice, once as the productive force of labour and the second time as the productive force of capital?

The answer to this question must follow from the preceding analysis.

Only bourgeois thick-headedness, which regards the capitalist forms of production as its absolute forms—hence as eternal, natural forms of production—can confuse the question as to what is *productive labour* from the standpoint of *capital* with the question as to what labour is productive in general, or what is productive labour in general; and consequently fancy itself very wise in giving the answer that all labour which produces anything at all, which has any kind of result, is *eo ipso*[1] productive labour.

Only labour *which is directly transformed into capital is productive*; that is, only labour which gives to variable capital its variable character. [If we denote by Δv the increment, the accretion, by which labour increases the variable capital v, then] labour which transforms v into $v + \Delta v$ is productive labour. This is the one point which has to be elucidated. Labour which creates surplus value or serves capital as a means to the creation of surplus value, and hence as a means through which capital becomes capital, value which produces more value.

Secondly: the social and general productive forces of labour are productive forces of capital; but these productive forces relate only to the labour process, or affect only the use value. They represent properties belonging to capital as a thing, as use value. They do not directly affect *exchange value*. Whether [in the making of a product under the socially necessary conditions of production] a hundred workers work together, or each of the hundred works by himself, the value of this product is equal to a hundred days of labour, whether this amount of labour is represented in a large or small number of products; that is to say, the productivity of the labour makes no difference to the value.

The varying productivity of labour only affects exchange value in one way.

If for example the productivity of labour is increased in a single branch of labour—for instance, if weaving with power-looms instead of hand-looms becomes no longer merely exceptional, and if the weaving of a yard with the power-loom requires only half the time taken with the hand-loom, then twelve hours' labour of a hand-weaver is no longer represented by a value of twelve hours, but by a value of six, since the necessary labour time has now become six hours. Although the hand-weaver works twelve hours as he did before, these twelve hours now represent only six hours of social labour time. But this is not what we are dealing with here. Take on the other hand another branch of production, for example type-setting,

---

[1] By that very fact.

in which up to the present no machines are used: twelve hours in this branch are productive of just as much value as twelve hours in the branches of production in which machinery etc. is developed to the utmost. Consequently labour, as productive of value, always remains the labour of the individual, only expressed in general terms. Hence productive labour—as labour producing value—in relation to capital, always presents itself as labour of an individual labour-power, as the labour of a separate worker, whatever social combinations these workers may enter into in the process of production. While therefore capital, in relation to the worker, presents itself as the social productive power of labour, the productive labour of the worker, in relation to capital, appears always only as the labour of an isolated worker.

Thirdly: Whereas it appears to be a natural property of capital—hence as a property deriving from its use value—to extort surplus labour and to appropriate to itself the social productive forces of labour, it appears on the other hand to be a natural property of labour to make its own social productive powers into productive powers of capital, and its own surplus product appears as surplus value, as the self-expansion of capital.

These three points must now be examined, and the distinction between productive and unproductive labour deduced from them.

(1) The productivity of capital consists in the fact that it confronts labour as wage labour; and the productivity of labour consists in the fact that it confronts the means of production as capital.

We have seen that money is transformed into capital—that is, a given exchange value is transformed into an exchange value that expands, into a value plus a surplus value—through one part of it being transformed into commodities which serve labour as means of production (raw materials, instruments, in a word, the material conditions of labour), and another part being used for the purchase of labour power. However, it is not this first exchange between money and labour power, or the mere purchase of the latter, which transforms the money into capital. This purchase incorporates in the capital the use of the labour power for a definite time, or makes a certain quantity of living labour one of the forms of existence, so to speak the entelechy, of the capital itself. In the actual process of production the living labour is transformed into capital in that on the one hand it reproduces the wage—that is, the value of the variable capital—and on the other hand it creates a surplus value; and through this transformation process the whole sum of money is transformed into capital, although the part of it which varies directly is only that part which is expended in wages. If the value was equal to $c + v$, now it is equal to $c + (v + \Delta v)$, which is the same as $(c + v) + \Delta v$; or the original sum of money, magnitude of value, has increased its value, has become a value which both maintains and increases itself.

This is what has to be grasped; and the circumstance that only the *variable part* of the capital produces its increment alters absolutely nothing in the fact that through this process the whole original value has added value to itself, has increased by a surplus value, and that therefore the whole original sum of money has been transformed into capital. For the original value is equal to $c + v$ (constant and variable capital). In the process it becomes $c + (v + \Delta v)$; the latter is the reproduced part, which has come into existence through the transformation of living labour into materialised labour, a transformation which is conditioned and initiated through the exchange of v against labour power, or its transformation into wages. But $c + (v + \Delta v)$ is equal to $c + v$ (the original capital) $+ \Delta v$. Moreover the transformation of v into $v + \Delta v$, and thus of $(c + v)$ into $(c + v) + \Delta v$, could only take place through a part of the money being transformed into c. The one part can only be transformed into *variable* capital through the other being transformed into constant capital.

In the actual production process labour is in reality transformed into capital, but this transformation is made possible by the original exchange between money and labour power. Through this *direct* transformation of labour into *materialised* labour belonging not to the worker but to the capitalist, the money is first transformed into capital, including that part of it which has taken the form of means of production, of the conditions necessary for labour. Up to this point the money is only in its nature capital, whether it exists in its own form or in the form of commodities (products of labour) of such a type as can serve as means of production of a commodity. This definite relation to labour first transforms money and commodities into capital, and that labour is productive labour which through this its relation to the means of production—to which corresponds a definite relation in the actual production process—transforms money or commodities into capital; that is to say, maintains and increases in its value the *materialised labour* which confronts labour power as something independent. Productive labour is only an abbreviated way of expressing the whole relationship and the form and manner in which labour power figures in the capitalist production process. But it is of the greatest importance to distinguish it from other kinds of labour, since this distinction expresses precisely the distinct form of that labour on which is based the whole capitalist mode of production and capital itself.

Productive labour is therefore—in the system of capitalist production—that which produces *surplus value* for its employer, or which transforms the objective conditions of labour into capital and their owner into a capitalist; and therefore labour which produces its own product as capital.

When therefore we speak of *productive labour*, we speak of *socially determined* labour, labour which implies a quite precise relation between the buyer and the seller of the labour.

But although the money which is in the hands of the buyer of labour power—or the supply of means of production and means of subsistence for the worker which he possesses in the form of commodities—first becomes capital through the process of production, is only in the process transformed into capital, and therefore these things are not capital before they enter into this process, but are only destined to be capital—nevertheless they are *in themselves* capital. They are in themselves capital because of the independent form in which they confront labour power and labour power confronts them; a relationship which the exchange with labour power and the subsequent process of the actual transformation of labour into capital conditions and consolidates. They have from the outset the *definite social relationship* to the workers which makes them into capital and gives them command over labour. They are therefore presupposed to be capital in relation to labour.

Productive labour, consequently, can be so described when it is directly exchanged with money *as capital*, or, what is only a shorter way of saying this, labour which is directly exchanged with capital—that is to say, with money which in itself is capital, which is destined to function as capital or confronts labour power as capital. The expression: labour which is directly exchanged with capital, implies that the labour is exchanged with money as capital, and thereby transforms it into capital. The significance of the *direct* exchange will be seen more clearly in a moment.

Productive labour is therefore labour which reproduces for the worker only the previously determined value of his labour power, but as a value-creating activity increases the value of the capital, or which confronts the worker himself with the values it creates as capital.

In the exchange between capital and labour, as we saw in examining the production process, two essentially different though interdependent aspects have to be distinguished.

First: The first exchange between capital and labour is a formal process, in which capital figures as money and labour power as commodity. The sale of the labour power takes place conventionally or legally in this first process, although the labour is paid for only after it has been applied, at the end of the day, the week, etc. This in no way alters the transaction in which the labour power is sold. What in this transaction is directly sold is not a commodity in which labour has already been realised, but the use of the labour power itself, and therefore in fact the labour itself, as the use of the labour power is its activity, labour. It is therefore not an exchange of labour mediated through an exchange of commodities. When A sells boots to B, both exchange labour, one labour realised in boots, the other labour realised in money. But in the case we are dealing with, on one side materialised labour in its general social form, that is, as money, is exchanged against labour that as yet exists only as a power, and what is bought and sold is the use of this power, that is, the labour itself; although the

value of the commodity sold is not the value of the labour
(a meaningless expression) but the value of the labour power.
A direct exchange therefore takes place between materialised
labour and labour power, which *de facto* resolves itself into
living labour; that is, between materialised labour and actual
labour. The wage—the value of the labour power—appears,
as explained above, in the form of direct purchase price, the
price of the labour.

In this first phase the relation between worker and capitalist
is that of seller and buyer of a commodity. The capitalist pays
the value of the labour power, that is, the value of the commodity which he buys.

At the same time, however, the labour power is only bought
because the labour which it can perform, and undertakes to
perform, is greater than the labour required for the reproduction of the labour power, and therefore expresses itself in a
value greater than the value of the labour power.

Secondly: The second phase of the *exchange* between capital
and labour has in fact nothing to do with the first, and strictly
speaking is not an exchange at all.

In the first phase there is an exchange of money and
commodity—of equivalents—and worker and capitalist confront each other simply as owners of commodities. Equivalents
are exchanged (that is to say, it makes no difference to the
transaction when they are exchanged and whether the price
of the labour is above or below the value of the labour power
or is equal to it. The transaction can therefore take place in
accordance with the general law of the exchange of commodities). In the second phase no exchange at all takes place.
The owner of money has ceased to be a buyer of commodities,
and the worker a seller of commodities. The owner of money
functions now as a capitalist. He consumes the commodity
which he has bought, and the worker supplies it, since the use
of his labour power is his labour itself. Through the earlier
transaction the labour itself has become part of materialised
wealth. The worker performs it, but it belongs to the capital
and is only just a function of the latter. It is performed therefore
directly under the control and direction of the capital, and the
product in which it is materialised is the new form in which

the capital appears, or in which rather it realises itself *actu* as capital. In this process, therefore, the labour materialises itself directly, is transformed directly into capital, after having already been formally incorporated in capital through the first transaction. And indeed more labour is here transformed into capital than capital was earlier expended in the purchase of labour power. In this process a part of unpaid labour is appropriated, and only through this is the money transformed into capital.

But although in this phase no exchange in fact takes place, the result, disregarding the intermediary stages, is that in the process—taking both phases together—a definite quantity of materialised labour has exchanged for a greater quantity of living labour. This finds expression in the result of the process in the fact that the labour materialised in its product is greater than the labour materialised in the labour power, and is consequently greater than the materialised labour paid to the worker; or that in the actual process the capitalist receives back not only the part of the capital which he expended in wages, but a surplus value which costs him nothing. The *direct* exchange of labour against capital here signifies (1) the direct transformation of the labour into capital, into a material constituent of capital in the production process; (2) the exchange of a definite quantity of materialised labour against the same quantity of living labour plus an additional quantity of living labour which is appropriated without an equivalent in exchange.

The statement that productive labour is labour which is directly exchanged with capital embraces all these phases, and is only a derivative formula signifying that it is labour which transforms money into capital, which is exchanged with the means of production as capital, and whose relation to them therefore is not at all a relation to simple means of production, nor in its relation to the means of production is it labour in general, without a specific social character.

This statement covers (1) the relation of money and labour power to each other as commodities, the purchase and sale between the owner of money and the owner of labour power; (2) the direct subsumption of labour under capital; (3) the

real transformation of labour into capital in the production
process, or what is the same thing, the creation of surplus
value for capital. Two kinds of exchange between labour and
capital take place. The first expresses simply the buying of the
labour power and hence *actu* of the labour and hence of its
product; the second, the direct transformation of living labour
into capital, or its materialisation as the embodiment of
capital.

The result of the capitalist production process is neither a
mere product (use value), nor a commodity, that is, a use
value which has a definite exchange value. Its result, its
product, is the creation of surplus value for capital, and hence
the actual transformation of money or commodity into capital.
Before the production process they were capital only in intention, in themselves, in their destiny. In the production process
more labour is absorbed than is bought. This absorption, the
appropriation of another's unpaid labour, which is consum-
mated in the production process, is the direct aim of the
capitalist production process; for what capital as capital
(hence the capitalist as capitalist) wants to produce is neither
an immediate use value for self-consumption, nor a commodity
to be turned first into money and then into a use value. Its
aim is *the accumulation, the expansion of value, its increase*; that is to
say, the maintenance of the old value and the creation of
surplus value. And it achieves this *specific product* of the capitalist
production process only in exchange with labour, which is
therefore called *productive labour*.

In order that it may produce a commodity, labour must be
useful labour; it must produce a use value, be manifested in a
use value. And consequently only labour which manifests
itself in commodities, that is, in use values, is labour with
which capital is exchanged. This is a self-evident premise.
But it is not this concrete character of labour, its use value as
such—that it is for example the labour of a blacksmith or a
cobbler, spinning, weaving, etc.—that constitutes its specific
use value for capital and hence stamps it as productive labour
in the system of capitalist production. What constitutes its
specific use value for capital is not its definite useful character,
any more than it is the particular useful properties of the

product in which it is materialised; but its character as the
creative element of exchange value, that it is abstract labour;
and not indeed that it represents simply a definite quantity
of this general labour, but a greater quantity than is contained
in its price, that is, in the value of the labour power.

The capitalist production process is therefore also not merely
the production of commodities. It is a process which absorbs
unpaid labour, which makes of the means of production means
for the absorption of unpaid labour.

It follows from what has been said that the designation of
labour as productive has absolutely nothing to do with the
definite content of the labour, with its special usefulness, or
with the particular use value in which it manifests itself.

The same kind of labour may be productive or unproductive.

For example, Milton, who wrote *Paradise Lost*, was an
unproductive worker. On the other hand, the writer who
turns out factory-made stuff for his publisher is a productive
worker. Milton produced *Paradise Lost* for the same reason
that a silk worm produces silk. It was an activity of his nature.
Later he sold the product for £5. But the literary proletarian
of Leipzig who fabricates books (for example, Compendia of
Economics) under the direction of his publisher is a productive
worker, for his production is subordinated to capital in advance
and takes place only because it increases that capital. A singer
who sells her song on her own is an unproductive worker.
But the same singer, commissioned by an *entrepreneur* to sing in
order to make money for him, is a productive worker. For she
produces capital.

Here there are various questions to be settled. Whether I
buy a pair of trousers or whether I buy the cloth and get a
journeyman tailor to come to my house to make up this cloth
into trousers for me, and pay him for his *service* (that is, his
tailoring labour), is a matter of absolute indifference to me, in
so far as what I am interested in is the pair of trousers. If I
buy the trousers from the capitalist tailor ("merchant tailor")
instead of taking the latter course, I do that because the
latter course is more expensive; and the trousers cost less
labour, and are cheaper in consequence, if the capitalist
tailor produces them than if I have them produced in the

latter way. But in both cases I transform the money with which I buy the trousers not into capital but into trousers; and in both cases what I am doing is using the money as mere means of circulation, that is to say, transforming it into this particular use value. Here therefore the money is not functioning as capital, although in one case it is exchanged for a commodity, and in the other it buys labour itself as a commodity. It functions only as money, and more precisely, as means of circulation. On the other hand the journeyman tailor (who works for me at home) is not a productive worker, although his labour provides me with the product, the trousers, and him with the price of his labour, the money. It is possible that the quantity of labour which the journeyman performs is greater than that contained in the price he receives from me. And this is even probable, since the price of his labour is determined by the price which the productive tailors receive. But it is a matter of absolute indifference to me. Whether, once the price is fixed, he works eight or ten hours, is of no interest at all to me. What I am concerned with is the *use value*, the trousers; and naturally, whatever way I buy them, I am interested in paying as little as possible for them—but in one case neither more nor less than in the other—or in paying for them only their normal price. This is an outlay for my consumption; there is no increase, but a diminution of my money. It is absolutely not a means to enrichment, any more that any other kind of outlay for my personal consumption is a means to enrichment. A disciple of Paul de Kock may tell me that without buying the trousers, as without buying bread, I cannot live and therefore also cannot enrich myself; that the trousers are therefore an indirect means or at least a condition for my enrichment. In the same way the circulation of my blood and my breathing would be conditions for my enrichment. But neither the circulation of my blood nor my breathing, in and by themselves, make me any the richer; on the contrary, both of them presuppose a costly assimilation of food, without which no poor devil could exist. Consequently, the mere direct exchange of money for labour does not transform the money into capital and the labour into productive labour.

What is it then that gives this exchange its special character? Wherein is it different from the exchange of money for productive labour? On the one hand, in that the money is spent as money, as the independent form of exchange value, which is to be transformed into a use value, a means of subsistence, an object of personal consumption. The money therefore does not become capital, but on the contrary, it loses its existence as exchange value in order to be dissipated and consumed as use value. On the other hand, the labour interests me only as use value, as service, through which cloth is transformed into trousers; as the service which its concrete useful character provides. In contrast to this, the service which the same journeyman employed by a master tailor provides for this capitalist does not consist in the transformation of cloth into trousers, but in the fact that the necessary labour time materialised in a pair of trousers is equal let us say to twelve hours, while the wage received by the journeyman is equal to six hours. The service with which he provides the capitalist consists therefore in the fact that he works six hours for nothing. That this takes place in the form of tailoring trousers only conceals the real relationship. As soon as he is able to, the capitalist tailor therefore tries to transform the trousers again into money, that is to say, into a form in which the concrete character of tailoring labour has completely disappeared, and in which the service performed expresses itself in the fact that instead of six hours of labour time, expressed in a definite sum of money, there is now twelve hours of labour time, expressed in double that sum of money. I buy the tailoring labour for the service it provides me with as tailoring labour, to satisfy my need for clothing, and therefore to serve one of my needs. The capitalist tailor buys the labour as a means to making two thalers out of one. I buy it because it produces a definite use value, provides me with a definite service. He buys it, because it produces more exchange value than it costs, as a mere means to exchanging less labour for more labour.

Where the direct exchange of money for labour takes place without the latter producing capital—that is, when it is not productive labour—it is bought as *service*; which in general is nothing but an expression for the particular use value which the labour, like any other commodity, provides. It is however a specific term for the particular use value of labour which provides this service in the form not of a *thing* but of an *activity*—which however in no way distinguishes it from a machine, for example a clock. *Do ut facias, facio ut facias, facio ut des, do ut des* (I give that you may make, I make that you may make, I make that you may give, I give that you may give) are here forms that can be used completely indifferently of the same relationship; while in capitalist production the *do ut facias* expresses a quite specific relation between the objective value which is given and the living activity which is accepted. For this reason, because the specific relation between labour and capital is in no way involved in these purchases of services, being either completely obliterated or altogether absent, they are naturally the favourite form used by Say, Bastiat and their consorts to express the relation between capital and labour.

The question how the value of these services is regulated and how this value is itself determined by the laws of wages is not relevant to the examination of the relation we are considering, and belongs to the treatment of wages.

It has been seen that the mere exchange of money for labour does not transform the latter into productive labour, and on the other hand that the content of this labour makes no difference at all.

The worker himself can buy labour, that is, commodities supplied in the form of services, and the expenditure of his wages on such services is an expenditure which is absolutely no different from the expenditure of his wages on any other kind of commodities. The services which he buys may be more or less necessary, for example the service of a doctor or of a parson, just as he may buy bread or schnaps. As buyer—that is, representative of money confronting commodities—the worker is absolutely in the same category as the capitalist where the latter appears only as buyer, that is to say, where there is no more in the transaction than the conversion of money into the form of a commodity. How the price of these services is determined and what relation it has to wages proper, how far it is regulated by the laws of the latter and how far it is not, must be considered in a treatment of wages, and are not relevant to our present enquiry.

If thus the mere exchange of money for labour does not transform the latter into productive labour, or what is the same thing, does not transform the former into capital, so also the *content*, the concrete character, the particular usefulness of the labour, makes absolutely no difference—as we have seen above, the same labour of the same journeyman tailor is in one case productive, in the other not.

The performance of certain services, or the use values resulting from certain activities or labours, are embodied in commodities; others on the contrary leave no tangible results separate from the persons themselves; or, their result is not a vendible commodity. For example, the service rendered to me by a singer satisfies my aesthetic need; but what I enjoy exists only in an action inseparable from the singer himself; and as soon as his labour, the singing, comes to an end my enjoyment is also over; I enjoy the activity itself—its reverberation on my ear. These services themselves, like the commodities which I buy, may be necessary or may only seem necessary—for example the service of a soldier, a doctor or a lawyer; or they may be services which only yield enjoyment. But this makes no difference to their economic character. If I am in good health and do not need a doctor, or have the good luck not to be involved in a lawsuit, I avoid paying out money for medical or legal services as I do the plague.

The services may also be forced on me: the services of officials, etc.

If I buy the service of a teacher not to develop my faculties but to acquire skills with which I can earn money—or when others buy this teacher for me—and if I really learn something, which in itself is quite independent of the payment for the service—these costs of education, like the costs of my maintenance, belong to the costs of production of my labour power. But the special usefulness of this service does not alter the economic relation; it is not a relation in which I transform money into capital, or whereby the supplier of the service, the teacher, transforms me into his capitalist, his master. Consequently it also does not affect the economic character of this relation whether the doctor cures me or the teacher makes a success of teaching me or the lawyer wins my lawsuit. What is paid for is the performance of the service as such, and by its very nature the result cannot be guaranteed by those who render the service. A great part of services belongs to the costs of consumption of commodities, such as those of a cook, maid, etc.

It is characteristic of all unproductive labours that they are at my disposal—as is the case in the purchase of all other commodities for consumption—in the same proportion as that in which I exploit productive workers. Of all persons, therefore, the productive worker has least command over the services of unproductive workers, although he has most to pay for the *involuntary* services (the State and taxes). *Vice versa*, however, my power to employ productive workers does not at all increase in proportion to the extent that I employ unproductive workers, but on the contrary falls in the same proportion.

Productive workers may, in relation to me, be unproductive workers. For example, if I have my house re-papered, and the paper-hangers are wage workers of an employer who sells me the job, it is just the same for me as if I had bought a house already papered: I would have expended money for a commodity for my consumption; but for the employer who gets these workers to hang the paper they are productive workers, for they produce surplus value for him.

What then is the position of independent handicraftsmen or peasants who employ no workers and therefore do not produce as capitalists? Either, as always in the case of the peasant (but not for example of a gardener whom I get to come to my house), they are commodity producers and I buy the commodity from them—in which case it makes no difference for example that the handicraftsman supplies it to order or the peasant brings to market what he can. In this relationship they meet me as sellers of commodities, not as sellers of labour, and this relation has therefore nothing at all to do with the exchange of capital, and therefore also nothing to do with the distinction between productive and unproductive labour, which is based purely on whether the labour is exchanged with money as money or with money as capital. They therefore belong neither to the category of productive nor to that of unproductive workers, although they are producers of commodities. But their production does not fall under the capitalist mode of production.

It is possible that these producers working with their own means of production not only reproduce their labour power but create surplus value, since their position makes it possible for them to appropriate their own surplus labour or a part of it (as one part is taken from them in the form of taxes, etc.). And here we come up against a peculiarity that is characteristic of a society in which one definite mode of production predominates, although all productive relations have not yet been subordinated to it. In feudal society, for example, as we can best observe in England because here the system of feudalism was introduced ready made from Normandy and its form was impressed on what was in many respects a different social foundation—even productive relations which were far removed from the nature of feudalism were given a feudal form; for example, simple money relations in which there was no trace of mutual personal service as between suzerain and vassal, for instance the fiction that the small peasant held his property as a fief. In just the same way in the capitalist mode of production the independent peasant or handicraftsman is sundered into two persons.[1] As owner of the means of production he is capitalist, as worker he is his own wage worker. As capitalist, he therefore pays himself his wages and draws his profit from his capital; that is to say, he exploits himself as wage worker and pays himself, with the surplus value, the tribute that labour owes to capital. Perhaps he also pays himself a third part as landowner (rent), in the same way, as we shall see later, that the industrial capitalist who works with his own capital pays himself interest and regards this as something which he owes to himself not as an industrial capitalist, but *qua* capitalist pure and simple. The social character of the means of production in capitalist production— the fact that they express a definite productive relation—has so grown together with, and in the mode of thought of bourgeois

[1] "In small enterprises the employer is often his own worker" (Storch, *Cours d'économie politique*, Paris, 1823, Vol. I, p. 242).

society is so inseparable from, the material existence of these means of production as means of production, that the same definition (definite category) is applied even where the relation is the very opposite. The means of production become capital only in so far as they have become an independent power confronting labour. In the case mentioned the producer—the worker—is the possessor, owner, of his means of production. They are therefore not capital, any more than in relation to them he is a wage worker. Nevertheless they are thought of as capital, and he himself is split in two, so that as capitalist he employs himself as wage worker. In fact this way of presenting it, however irrational it may seem at first sight, is nevertheless correct in so far as the producer in such a case actually creates his own surplus value (assuming that he sells his commodity at its value), or the whole product materialises only his own labour. That he is able to appropriate to himself the whole product of his own labour, and that the excess of the value of his product over the average price of his day's labour is not appropriated by someone else, he owes however not to his labour—which does not distinguish him from other workers—but to his ownership of the means of production. It is therefore only through his ownership of these that he takes possession of his own surplus labour, and thus arises his relation, as his own capitalist, to himself as wage worker. The separation between the two is the normal relation in this society. Where therefore it does not in fact exist, it is presumed, and, as shown above, up to a point with justice; for (as distinct for example from conditions in Ancient Rome or Norway or in the North-West of the United States) in this society the unity appears as accidental, the separation as normal, and consequently the separation is maintained as the relation, even when one person unites the different functions. Here emerges in a very striking way the fact that the capitalist as such is only a function of capital, the worker a function of labour power. For it is also a law that economic development divides out functions among different persons, and the artisan or peasant who produces with his own means of production will either gradually be transformed into a small capitalist who also exploits the labour of others, or he will suffer the loss of his means of production (this may happen to begin with although he remains their nominal owner, as in a mortgage) and be transformed into a wage worker. This is the tendency in the form of society in which the capitalist mode of production predominates. In examining the essential relations of capitalist production it can therefore be assumed that the whole world of commodities, all spheres of material production—the production of material wealth—are subordinated (formally or really) to the capitalist mode of production (since this is being continuously approximated to, is in principle the goal of capitalist production, and only if this is realised will the productive power of labour be developed to its highest point). On this premise, which expresses the goal (limit), and which therefore is constantly coming closer to exact truth, all workers engaged in the production of commodities are wage workers, and the means of production in all these spheres confront them as capital. It can then be said to be a characteristic of productive workers, that is, of capital-producing workers, that their labour is realised in commodities, in material wealth. And so productive labour, along with its determining characteristic—which takes no account of the content of the labour and is independent of that content—would be given a second, different and subsidiary definition.

The production of immaterial things, even when it is carried on purely for exchange, that is, when it produces commodities, may be of two kinds:

(1) Its result is commodities, use values, whose form is different from and independent of producer and consumer; they may therefore exist during an interval between production and consumption, and in this interval circulate as vendible commodities, as in the case of books, pictures, in a word all artistic products which are different from the artistic performance of the artist producing them. Here capitalist production is applicable only to a very limited extent: as for example when a writer of a joint work—say an encyclopaedia—exploits a number of others as hacks. In this sphere for the most part there is a survival of transitional forms to capitalist production, the various scientific or artistic producers, handicraftsmen or [intellectuals] working for the capital of a common buyer,

the publisher; a relation that has nothing to do with the capitalist mode of production proper, and even in form has not yet been brought under its sway. The fact that in these transitional forms the exploitation of labour is at its highest does not alter the case.

(2) The production cannot be separated from the act of its producer, as is the case with all performing artists, actors, teachers, doctors, parsons, etc. Here too the capitalist mode of production is met with only to a small extent, and from the nature of the case can only occur in a few spheres. For example the teachers in educational establishments may be mere wage workers for the *entrepreneur* of the establishment; many such educational factories exist in England. Although in relation to the pupils such teachers are not productive workers, they are productive workers in relation to their employer. He exchanges his capital for their labour power, and through this process enriches himself. It is the same with enterprises such as theatres and other places of entertainment. In such enterprises the relation of the actor to the public is that of an artist, but in relation to his employer he is a productive worker. All these manifestations of capitalist production in this sphere are so insignificant compared with total production that they can be left completely out of account.

With the development of the specific capitalist mode of production, in which many workers work together in the production of the same commodity, the direct relation which their labour bears to the object produced naturally varies greatly. For example the unskilled labourers in a factory have nothing directly to do with the working up of the raw material. The workers who function as overseers of those workers directly engaged in working up the raw material are one step further away; the works engineer is in yet another relation and in the main works only with his brain, and so on. But the totality of these workers, who possess labour powers of different value, produce the result, which, considered as the result of the labour process pure and simple, is expressed in commodities or in a material product; and all of them together, as workers, are the living production machines of these products, just as, taking the production process as a whole, they exchange their labour for capital and reproduce the capitalist's money as capital, that is, as value producing value, self-expanding value. It is indeed characteristic of the capitalist mode of production that it separates the various labours, and even labours by brain and labours by hand—or labours in which one or the other predominates—and divides them out among various persons. This however does not prevent the material product from being the common product of these persons, or their common product realised in material wealth; any more than on the other hand it prevents or in any way alters the relation of each one of these workers to capital from being that of a wage worker, and in this pre-eminent sense being that of a productive worker. All these persons are not only directly engaged in the production of material wealth, but they exchange their labour directly for money as capital, and therefore directly reproduce, in addition to their wage, a surplus value for the capitalists. Their labour consists of paid labour plus unpaid surplus labour.

In addition to extractive industry, agriculture and manufacturing industry, there exists yet a fourth sphere of material production, which also runs through the various stages of handicraft industry, manufacture and mechanical industry; this is the *transport industry*, transporting either people or commodities. The relation of the productive worker, that is, the wage worker, to the capitalist is here exactly the same as in the other spheres of material production. Moreover, in this sphere a material change in the object of labour is effected— a spatial change, a change of place. In relation to the transport of people this takes the form only of a service performed for them by the *entrepreneur*. But the relation between the buyer and seller of this service has nothing in common with the relation of the productive worker to capital, any more than the relation between the buyer and seller of yarn. If on the other hand we consider the transport of commodities, in this case there certainly takes place, in the labour process, a change in the object of labour, the commodity. Its spatial position is altered, and along with this goes a change in its use value, through the change in the location of this use value. Its exchange value increases in the same measure as this change in its use value requires labour—an amount of labour which is partly determined by the wear and tear of the constant capital, that is, the quantity of materialised labour which enters into it, and partly by the quantity of living labour—just as in the value-increasing process of all other commodities. When the commodity has arrived at its destination, this change which has taken place in its use value has vanished, and now finds expression only in its higher exchange value, in the enhanced price of the commodity. And although in this case the real labour has left no trace in the use value, it is nevertheless realised in the exchange value of this material product; and so it is true also of this industry, as of the other spheres of material production, that the labour is incorporated in the commodity, although it leaves no visible trace in the use value of the commodity.

Here we have still been dealing only with productive capital, that is, capital engaged in the direct process of production. We deal later with capital in the process of circulation, and only then, in considering the special form assumed by capital as merchant's capital, can the question be answered as to how far the workers employed by it are productive or not productive.

C. DAVID RICARDO

I. SURPLUS VALUE AND PROFIT

1. THE STRUCTURE OF RICARDO'S WORK

RICARDO starts from the determination of the relative value or exchange value of commodities by the quantity of labour[1] [necessary for their production]. The nature of this "labour" is not further examined. If two commodities are of equal value—or their values are in a definite ratio to each other, or what is the same thing, are of unequal magnitude according to the quantity of "labour" each contains—then however it is also clear that, in so far as they are exchange values, they are of the same *substance*. Their substance is labour. That is why they are "value". Their magnitude is different, according as each contains more or less of this substance. But Ricardo does not examine the type, the *character* of this labour—its special character as labour which creates exchange value or expresses itself in exchange values. He therefore does not grasp the connection of this labour with money, or the fact that it must assume the form of money. He therefore absolutely fails to grasp the connection between the determination of the exchange value of the commodity by labour time, and the necessity for commodities in their development to generate money. Hence his erroneous theory of money. From the outset he deals only with the *magnitude of value*—that is, with the fact that the quantities of value in commodities are to each other in proportion to the quantities of labour required for their production. He begins with this, and he expressly names Adam Smith as his source (*The Principles of Political Economy and Taxation*, Chapter I, Section I).

Ricardo's method is then as follows: starting with the determination of the magnitudes of value of commodities by labour time, he next examines whether the other economic relations or categories conflict with this definition of value, or how far they modify it. Both the historical justification for

[1] We can examine later the different senses in which Ricardo uses the word value. This ambiguity is the basis of Bailey's criticism, as also of Ricardo's shortcomings.

this mode of procedure—its scientific necessity in the history of economics—and at the same time its scientific inadequacy, can be seen at the first glance. It is an inadequacy which not only shows itself (from a formal standpoint) in the mode of presentation, but leads to erroneous results, because it skips necessary intermediate links and tries to establish *direct* proof of the consistency of economic categories with each other.

Historically this method of investigation was justified and necessary. With Adam Smith, political economy had developed into a single great aggregate, and to a certain extent the ground it covered had been delimited. It was this that made it possible for Say to make a superficial but systematic condensation of it in a textbook. The period between Adam Smith and Ricardo gave rise to only a few isolated investigations dealing with productive and unproductive labour, monetary theory, theory of population, landed property and taxation. Adam Smith himself moves with great *naïveté* in a continuous contradiction. On the one hand he traces the inner connection between the economic categories—or the hidden structure of the bourgeois economic system. On the other hand, alongside this inner connection he sets up also the connection as it is manifested in the phenomena of competition, and therefore as it presents itself to the unscientific observer as well as to the man who is preoccupied and interested from a practical standpoint in the process of bourgeois production. These two modes of approach in Adam Smith's work not only run unconstrainedly side by side, but are interwoven and continuously contradict each other: the one penetrating to the inner relations, the physiology as it were, of the bourgeois system; the other only describing, cataloguing, expounding and bringing under classifying definitions the external phenomena of the process of everyday life in their outward manifestation and appearance. He is justified in doing this because—if we except a few of his special enquiries such as that into money—his task was in fact a double one: on the one hand, to attempt to penetrate to the inner physiology of bourgeois society: on the other, partly for the first time to describe the living forms in which this inner physiology manifests itself outwardly, to show its relations as they appear on the surface, and partly also to find a nomenclature and the corresponding abstract ideas for these phenomena, and therefore partly also for the first time to reproduce them in language and in the process of thought. The one task interests him as much as the other, and as both proceed independently of the other, the result is a completely contradictory way of looking at things—one that more or less correctly expresses their intrinsic relations, the other with equal justice and without any internal relationship —with no connection at all with the other way of examining the subject—expressing the relations in their outward appearance. In these circumstances his successors—in so far as they do not express the resistance to his ideas of older ways of thought which he had overcome—are able tranquilly to proceed with their special enquiries and observations and always regard Adam Smith as their source, whether they link on to the esoteric or the exoteric part of his work—or whether, as is almost always the case, they jumble both together. At last, however, Ricardo comes on the stage, and calls to science: Halt!—The foundation, the starting point for the physiology of the bourgeois system—for the understanding of its internal organic coherence and life process—is the determination of *value by labour time*. Ricardo starts with this, and compels science to leave its old beaten track and render an account of how far the rest of the categories it has developed and described—the relations of production and commerce—correspond to or conflict with this foundation, with the starting point; how far in general the science that merely reflects and reproduces the phenomenal forms of the process—how far therefore also these phenomena themselves—correspond to the foundation on which the inner connections, the real physiology of bourgeois society, rests, or which forms its starting point; and what in general is the position with regard to this contradiction between the apparent and the actual movement of the system. This is therefore the great historical significance of Ricardo for the science; and it is why the inane Say, having had the ground taken from under his feet by Ricardo, vented his spleen in the remark that "under the pretext of extending it (the science), it had been pushed into a vacuum". With this service to economic science is closely linked the fact that

Ricardo discovers and proclaims the economic contradiction between the classes—as shown by the intrinsic relations—and hence the historical struggle and process of development is grasped at its roots and disclosed in economic science. Carey therefore denounces him as the father of communism:

> "Mr. Ricardo's system is one of discords...its whole tends to the production of hostility among classes and nations. .... His book is the true manual of the demagogue, who seeks power by means of agrarianism, war, and plunder" (H. Carey, *The Past, the Present, and the Future*, Philadelphia, 1848, pp. 74-5).

While therefore on the one hand the scientific importance and the great historical value of Ricardo's method of investigation is undoubted, yet on the other hand the scientific inadequacy of the way he sets about it is apparent, as will be shown in detail in what follows.

Hence arises also the extremely peculiar and inevitably faulty structure of his work. The whole work consists (in the third edition) of 32 chapters. Of these, eleven chapters deal with taxes, involving therefore only the application of the theoretical principles. Chapter XX, "Value and Riches, their Distinctive Properties", is nothing but an investigation of the difference between use value and exchange value, being thus supplemental to Chapter I, "On Value". Chapter XXIV, "Doctrine of Adam Smith concerning the Rent of Land", and similarly Chapter XXVIII, "On the Comparative Value of Gold, Corn, and Labour, in Rich and Poor Countries", and Chapter XXXII, "Mr. Malthus's Opinions on Rent" are mere supplements to and in part a vindication of Ricardo's theory of Rent, thus forming simply an appendix to Chapters II and III, which deal with Rent. Chapter XXX, "Of the Influence of Demand and Supply on Prices", is a mere appendix to Chapter IV, "On Natural and Market Price". Chapter XIX, "On Sudden Changes in the Channels of Trade", forms a second appendix to this chapter. Chapter XXXI, "On Machinery", is a mere appendix to Chapters V and VI, "On Wages" and "On Profits". Chapter VII, "On Foreign Trade", and Chapter XXV, "On Colonial Trade", are, like the chapters on taxes, merely the application of

principles already laid down. Chapters XXVI, "On Gross
and Net Revenue", and XXI, "Effects of Accumulation on
Profits and Interest", are an appendix to the chapters on
Rent, Profits, and Wages. Finally, Chapter XXVII, "On
Currency and Banks", stands quite by itself in the book, and
is merely a further exposition, and in part a modification, of
the views on money put forward in his earlier writings.

Ricardo's theory is thus contained exclusively in the first
six chapters of his work. When I speak of its faulty architecto-
nics, the reference is to this part of it. The rest of it consists
of applications, elucidations and addenda (apart from the
section on money) which in the nature of things are jumbled
together and lay no claim to a structure. The faulty structure
in the theoretical section, the first six chapters, is however not
accidental, but flows from Ricardo's very method of investigation and the definite task which he set for his enquiry. It
expresses the scientific shortcomings of this method of investigation itself.

Chapter I deals with value. It is subdivided into seven
sections. In the first section the actual question examined is:
do wages contradict the determination of the values of
commodities by the labour time contained in them? In the
third section it is shown that the entry of what I call constant
capital into the value of the commodity does not contradict
the determination of value, and that the value of commodities
is just as little affected by the rise and fall of wages. The
fourth section investigates to what extent the use of machinery
and other fixed and durable capital, in so far as it enters into
the total capital in varying proportions in the different spheres
of production, alters the determination of exchange value by
labour time. The fifth section investigates how far a rise or
fall in wages modifies the determination of value by labour
time, if capitals of unequal durabilty and with varying
periods of turnover are employed in different spheres of
production.

Thus it can be seen that in this first chapter not only
commodities are postulated—and nothing else has to be
postulated in considering value as such—but also wages,
capital, profit, and even the general rate of profit itself (as

we shall see); that is, the various forms of capital as they arise from the process of circulation; as also the distinction between "natural" and "market price", which latter moreover plays a decisive role in the following two chapters "On Rent" and "On the Rent of Mines".

This second chapter, "On Rent"—Chapter III, "On the Rent of Mines", is a mere supplement to it—fully in accordance with the flow of Ricardo's method of investigation, opens once more with the question: Does landed property, and rent, contradict the determination of the value of commodities by labour time?—

> "It remains however to be considered whether the appropriation of land, and the consequent creation of rent, will occasion any variation in the relative value of commodities, independently of the quantity of labour necessary to production" (p. 33).

Now in order to carry through this investigation, he not only introduces *en passant* the relation between "market price" and "real price" (which is the monetary expression of value), but also postulates the whole of capitalist production and his whole conception of the relation between wages and profit. Chapter IV, "On Natural and Market Price", Chapter V, "On Wages", and Chapter VI, "On Profits", are therefore not only taken for granted but fully developed in the two first chapters, "On Value" and "On Rent", and in the third chapter as an addendum to the second.

The second three chapters, in so far as they add new theoretical points, here and there fill in gaps or provide more precise definitions which for the most part should by rights have found their place in the first and second.

The whole of Ricardo's work is thus contained in its first two chapters. In these chapters the developed processes of bourgeois production, and therefore also the developed categories of political economy, are confronted with their basic principle—the determination of value—and called upon to answer how far they directly correspond to this principle, or what is the true state of affairs regarding the apparent discrepancies which they produce in the value relations of commodities. They contain his whole critique of previous political economy, making a categorical break with the contradiction between the esoteric and the exoteric mode of approach which runs through Adam Smith's writings, and through this critique achieves some altogether new and surprising results. Hence the high theoretical pleasure derived from these two first chapters, since they give with concise brevity a critique of the old diffuse and meandering political economy, and present the whole bourgeois system of economy as subject to one fundamental law, extracting the quintessence of the scattered and manifold phenomena. But the theoretical satisfaction given by these two first chapters because of their originality, unity of basic conception, simplicity, concentration, depth, novelty and comprehensive conciseness, is of necessity lost as the book proceeds. Even in later chapters certain passages fascinate us by the peculiar originality of the exposition. But as a whole it is boring and difficult to concentrate on. As it proceeds, there is no longer further development. When it is not the monotonous formal application of the same principles to different, extraneously introduced material, or polemical justification of these principles, there is only repetition or amplification, with at most in the final sections an occasional striking chain of reasoning.

In the critique of Ricardo we must therefore make a distinction which he himself did not make. There is first his theory of surplus value, which is certainly in his work, although he did not fix on surplus value as distinct from its particular form—profit, rent and interest; and secondly, his theory of profit. We shall begin with the latter.

2. RICARDO'S THEORY OF PROFIT

(a) Ricardo's Conception of Value

FIRST a few further observations on how Ricardo jumbles together different determinations of value. This is the ground for Bailey's polemic against him. It is therefore also important for us.

First he calls value exchange value ("value in exchange"), and defines it, following Adam Smith, as "the power of purchasing other goods" (p. 5). This is exchange value as in the first instance it *appears*. Then however he goes on to the real determination of value:

"It is the comparative quantity of commodities which labour will produce that determines their present or past relative value" (p. 9).

"Relative value" here means nothing other than exchange value determined by labour time. But *relative* value can also have another meaning; if for example I express the exchange value of one commodity in the use value of another—say the exchange value of sugar in the use value of coffee.

"Two commodities vary in relative value, and we wish to know in which the variation has really taken place" (p. 9).

What variation? Later on Ricardo calls this "relative value" also "comparative value" (Chapter XXVIII). We wish to know in which commodity "the variation" has taken place, that is, the variation of value, called "relative value" above. For example, if one pound of sugar is equal to two pounds of coffee, and is later equal to four pounds of coffee. The "variation" which we wish to know about is whether the "necessary labour time" for the sugar has changed, or that for the coffee; whether the sugar costs twice as much labour time as before, or the coffee half as much labour time as before; and which of these "variations" in the labour time necessary for the production of the commodities named has brought about the variation in their exchange relations. This "relative" or "comparative value" of sugar and coffee—the ratio in which they exchange—is therefore different from the relative value in the first sense. In its first meaning, the relative value of the sugar is determined by the quantity of sugar which can be produced in a definite labour time. In the second case, the relative value of sugar and coffee only expresses the ratio in which they are exchanged for each other, and the change in this ratio may be brought about by a change in the "relative value" in the first sense either in the coffee or in the sugar. The proportion in which they exchange for each other may remain the same, even though their "relative values" in the first sense have changed. One pound of sugar may still, as before, equal two pounds of coffee, even though the labour time necessary for the production of the sugar and of the coffee has risen to double or has fallen to half. *Variations* in their "comparative value"—that is, when the exchange value of sugar is expressed in coffee and *vice versa*—will only appear when their relative values in the first sense, that is, their values determined by the quantity of labour, have altered disproportionately and a change in their relation to each other has thus taken place. Absolute variations—if they do not alter the original proportion, that is, if they are of equal magnitude and in the same direction—will not cause any change in the comparative values; nor will they change the relation between the *money prices* of these commodities, since if the value of money should alter it changes simultaneously for both. Consequently, whether I express the value of two commodities in their own mutual use values, or in their money price— presenting both values in the use value of a third commodity— these *relative* or *comparative* values or prices are the same, and their variations must be distinguished from variations in their *relative value* in the first sense; that is, in so far as the variations express only a change in the labour time necessary for their *own* production and therefore *embodied in them themselves*. The latter *relative value* therefore appears as *"absolute value"* compared with relative values in the second sense, that is, in the sense of presenting the exchange value of one commodity in terms of the use value of the other or in money. Hence it comes that the expression *"absolute value"* is also to be found in Ricardo, in place of "relative value" in the first sense.

"The inquiry to which I wish to draw the reader's attention relates to the effect of the variations in the relative value of commodities, and not in their absolute value" (p. 12).

In other passages Ricardo calls this "absolute" value also "real value", or simply value (for example, p. 13).

See Bailey's polemic against Ricardo in *A Critical Dissertation on the Nature, Measures and Causes of Value; chiefly in reference to the writings of Mr. Ricardo and his followers*. By the Author of *Essays on the Formation and Publication of opinions*. London, 1825. (See also his *A Letter to a Polit. Economist; occasioned by an article in the Westminster Review*, etc. London, 1826.)

Bailey's whole polemic in part revolves around these different concepts in the definition of value, which are not developed by Ricardo but only presented in a factual way and confused with each other (Bailey only finds "contradictions" between them); and in part is directed against "absolute value" or "real value" as distinct from comparative value or relative value in the second sense. "Instead" says Bailey in the first work mentioned "of regarding value as a relation between two objects, they (Ricardo and his followers) seem to consider it as a positive result produced by a definite quantity of labour" (p. 30). They regard "value as something intrinsic and absolute" (p. 8). The latter reproach is the result of Ricardo's inadequate exposition, inasmuch as he does not examine value from the standpoint of the definite form assumed by labour as the substance of value, but is only concerned with magnitudes of value—the quantities of this abstract, general, and in this form social, labour, which result in differences in the *magnitudes of value* of commodities. But for this, Bailey would have seen that the relative nature of the concept of value is by no means negated by the fact that all commodities, in so far as they are exchange values, are only "*relative*" expressions of social labour time; and their relativity by no means consists only in the ratio in which they exchange for each other, but in the ratio of all of them to this social labour which is their substance.

As we shall see later, Ricardo is far more open to the opposite reproach: that he very often loses sight of this "real" or "absolute value" and keeps in mind only "relative" or comparative value.

(b) *Ricardo's Conception of Profit, Rate of Profit, Prices of Production, etc.*

In Section III of Chapter I Ricardo explains that when it is said that the value of commodities is determined by labour time, the latter includes both the labour directly expended on the commodity in the final labour process, and the labour time contained in the raw materials and instruments of labour required for the production of the commodity. That is to say, not only the labour time contained in the newly added labour that has been bought and paid for in the wages, but also the labour time contained in that portion of the commodity which I call constant capital.

The inadequacy of this third section of Chapter I is already obvious in the summary heading, which runs:

"Not only the labour applied immediately to commodities affect their value, but the labour also which is bestowed on the implements, tools, and buildings, with which such labour is assisted."

Here the raw materials are omitted, and yet the labour bestowed on the raw materials is just as different from "the labour applied immediately to a commodity" as the labour applied to the means of labour—"the implements, tools, and buildings". But Ricardo already has in mind his next section. In this section he assumes that the instruments of labour used enter into the production of the various commodities as equal constituent parts of their value. In the next section he examines the differences which arise through the incorporation in the commodities of fixed capital in *different proportions*. Hence Ricardo never arrives at the concept of *constant capital*, of which one part consists of fixed capital and the other part— raw materials and auxiliary materials—of *circulating capital*; just as *circulating capital* includes not only the variable capital but also raw materials, etc., and all the necessaries of life which enter into [industrial] consumption as a whole (not only those consumed by the workers).

The proportion in which constant capital enters into a commodity affects neither the *value* of the commodities nor the relative *quantities* of labour contained in the commodities, but it does directly affect the different quantities of *surplus value* or *surplus labour* contained in commodities which embody equal labour time. This different proportion consequently gives rise to average prices which are different from the values.

In regard to the fourth and fifth sections of Chapter I, it must in the first place be noted that instead of the highly complex difference in the proportion in which constant and variable capital form constituent elements in the same amount of capital engaged in different spheres of production (which directly affects the production of surplus value), Ricardo concerns himself exclusively with the differences in the form of the capital and with the different proportions in which the same capital assumes these various forms. These differences in form with which Ricardo deals arise from the process of circulation of capital—such as fixed and circulating capital, capital that is fixed to a greater or less degree (that is, fixed capital of different degrees of durability), and capital with different rates of circulation or turnover. The way in which Ricardo carries out this investigation is as follows. He assumes *a general rate of profit*, or *an average profit of equal magnitude* for different investments of capital of equal size, or for different spheres of production in which capitals of equal size are employed—or, what is the same thing, a profit proportionate to the amounts of capital employed in the various spheres of production. Instead of assuming this general rate of profit in advance, Ricardo should rather have investigated how far its existence is in any way consistent with the determination of value by labour time; and he would then have found that instead of being consistent with it, *prima facie* it contradicts it, and its existence has therefore to be explained through a number of intermediary stages—an explanation which is something very different from merely including it under the law of value. He would then have attained quite a different insight into the nature of profit, and would not have identified it directly with surplus value.

Having once made this assumption, Ricardo then asks himself: how will rises and falls in wages affect "relative values", if fixed and circulating capital are employed in different proportions? Or rather, he imagines that he is treating the question in this way. In fact, he deals with it in quite a different way. This is how he handles it: he poses the question, what will be the effect of rises or falls in wages in the case of capitals with varying periods of turnover and in which the different kinds of capital are contained in different proportions? And in this case he naturally finds that a rise or fall in wages has a very different effect on capitals according to whether they contain much or little fixed capital, according to whether a larger or smaller proportion of each capital consists of variable capital, that is, of capital which is expended directly in wages. In order therefore for profits in the various spheres of production to be equalised out again; in other words, in order to restore once more the general rate of profit, the prices of commodities—as distinct from their values—must be regulated in a different way. Hence, he further concludes, these differences affect the "relative values" when wages rise or fall. He should have said, on the contrary: that although these differences do not affect the value as such, they bring about, through their different effects on profits in the various spheres, average prices that differ from the values themselves— or, as we shall say henceforward, *prices of production,*[1] which are not directly determined by the values of the commodities, but by the capital advanced for their production plus the average profit. He should therefore have said: These average prices of production are different from the values of the commodities. Instead of this, he concludes that they are identical, and, on the basis of this erroneous premise, he proceeds to consider Rent. Ricardo is also making a mistake when he thinks that it is only in these cases which he examines that he comes up against variations in relative values which do not depend on

[1] In a later passage of the MS. Marx adds in a footnote, which can be brought in here: "These prices of production must be distinguished from *market prices*; they are the average market prices of commodities in the various spheres of production. The market price itself already implies an average, in so far as the prices of commodities in the same sphere are determined by the prices of the commodities which are produced under the mean, average conditions of production in this sphere. Certainly not under the worst conditions, as Ricardo assumes when dealing with rent; for the average demand depends on a certain price, even in the case of corn. A certain quantum of the supply is therefore not sold above this price; for then the demand would fall. Those producing under conditions that are below the average must therefore often sell their commodities not only below their value, but below their *price of production.*"—*K.*

the labour time contained in them—in fact, that is, the difference between prices of production and the values of commodities. He has already taken this difference for granted in postulating a general rate of profit, and hence in assuming that in spite of the different proportions of the organic constituents of a capital, it yields a profit proportionate to its size; although the surplus value yielded by capitals is absolutely determined by the quantity of unpaid labour time which they appropriate, and which, at a given rate of wages, depends entirely on the size of that part of the capital expended in wages, not on the absolute size of the capital. What in fact he examines is this: assuming prices of production different from the values of the commodities (and acceptance of a general rate of profit implies this difference), how are these prices of production—now called "relative values" for the sake of variety—themselves in turn reciprocally modified, proportionately modified, by rises and falls in wages, when the different proportions in the organic constituent parts of the capitals are also taken into account? Had he gone more deeply into the question, Ricardo would have found that because of the different organic composition of capitals—which first manifests itself in the immediate process of production as the difference between variable and constant capital, and is later further developed by differences arising from the process of circulation—the very existence of a general rate of profit involves prices of production that are different from values. This is so even if it is assumed that wages remain constant, and therefore the difference is quite independent of a rise or fall in wages, and prices of production are a new determinate form. He would also have seen how incomparably more important and decisive the understanding of this difference is for his whole theory than an examination of variations in the production prices of commodities caused by rises or falls in wages. The conclusion which satisfies him—and this satisfaction is typical of his whole method of investigation—is this: Once variations in the prices of production—or as he puts it, in "relative values"—are admitted and examined, to the extent that they are due to variations, rises or falls, in wages, when the organic composition of the capital invested in various

spheres is different, then the law holds good and is not contradicted—namely, the law that the "relative values" of commodities are determined by labour time; for all other changes
that are more than transitory in the production prices of
commodities remain explicable only by changes in the labour
time necessary for their respective production. On the other
hand, it must be recognised that Ricardo deserves great credit
for associating the difference between fixed and circulating
capital with the different periods of turnover of capital, and
deriving all these differences from the varying periods of
circulation, that is, in fact, from the periods within which
capital circulates or reproduces itself.

We will now consider these differences themselves, as
Ricardo first sets them out in the fourth section of Chapter I;
and then examine the way in which he sees them working or
bringing about variations in "relative values".

(1) ". . . in every state of society, the tools, implements,
buildings and machinery employed in different trades may
be of various degrees of durability, and may require different
portions of labour to produce them" (p. 18).

As for "different portions of labour required to produce
them", this may mean—and in this passage it seems to be
the only point Ricardo had in mind—that the less durable
require more labour—more frequently repeated, directly
applied labour, partly for their maintenance and partly for
their reproduction. Or also it may mean that machinery, etc.,
of the same durability may be more or less costly, the product
of more or less labour. This latter aspect, important as it is
for the proportion between variable and constant capital, is
not relevant to Ricardo's enquiry, and is therefore nowhere
taken up by him as a separate case.

(2) "The proportions, too, in which the capital that is to
support labour [the variable capital], and the capital that
is invested in tools, machinery, and buildings, may be
variously combined" (p. 18).

Thus we have a "difference in the degree of durability of
fixed capital", and a "variety in the proportions in which
the two sorts of capital may be combined" (p. 18). It can at

once be seen why it is that Ricardo is not interested in that part of constant capital which exists as raw materials. Raw materials are themselves part of the circulating capital. If wages rise, this does not cause an increased outlay for that part of the capital which consists of machinery and does not require replacement but remains available; though it probably does cause an increased outlay in the part which consists of raw materials, since this part has to be constantly restored and must therefore be constantly reproduced.

"The food and clothing consumed by the labourer, the buildings in which he works, the implements with which his labour is assisted, are all of a perishable nature. There is, however, a vast difference in the time for which these different capitals will endure. . . . According as capital is rapidly perishable, and requires to be frequently reproduced, or is of slow consumption, it is classed under the heads of circulating or of fixed capital" (pp. 18–19).

Here therefore the difference between fixed and circulating capital is reduced to the difference in the time of reproduction, which is the same as the time of circulation.

(3) "It is also to be observed that the circulating capital may circulate, or be returned to its employer, in very unequal times. The wheat bought by a farmer to sow is comparatively a fixed capital to the wheat purchased by a baker to make into loaves. One leaves it in the ground and can obtain no return for a year; the other can get it ground into flour, sell it as bread to his customers, and have his capital free to renew the same or commence any other employment in a week" (p. 19).

To what is *this* difference, in the time taken by various circulating capitals, due? To the fact that in one case the same capital remains for a longer time within the sphere of actual production, without a simultaneous extension of the labour process—as for example, wine that lies in the cellar to attain maturity, or certain chemical processes in tanning, dyeing, etc.

"Two trades then may employ the same amount of capital; but it may be very differently divided with respect to the portion which is fixed and that which is circulating" (p. 19).

(4) "Again, two manufacturers may employ the same amount of fixed and the same amount of circulating capital; but the durability of their fixed capitals[1] may be very unequal. One may have steam-engines of the value of £10,000, the other, ships of the same value" (p. 19).

"On account then of the different degrees of durability of their capitals, or, which is the same thing, on account of the time which must elapse before one set of commodities can be brought to market . . ." (p. 20).

(5) "It is hardly necessary to say that commodities which have the same quantity of labour bestowed on their production will differ in exchangeable value if they cannot be brought to market in the same time" (p. 23).

Hence we have: (1) A difference in the proportion of fixed and circulating capital. (2) A difference in the period of turnover of the circulating capital resulting from a break in the labour process while the productive process continues. (3) A difference in the durability of the fixed capital. (4) A difference in the relative time during which a commodity remains within the labour process as a whole—without any break in the labour period, without any difference between the production period and the labour period—before it can enter the actual process of circulation. Ricardo describes this latter case in the following terms:

"Suppose I employ twenty men at an expense of £1,000 for a year in the production of a commodity, and at the end of the year I employ twenty men again for another·year, at a further expense of £1,000 in finishing or perfecting the same commodity, and that I bring it to market at the end of two years, if profits be 10 per cent., my commodity must sell for £2,310; for I have employed £1,000 capital for one year, and £2,100 capital for one year more. Another man employs precisely the same quantity of labour, but he employs it all in the first year; he employs forty men at an expense of £2,000, and at the end of the first year he sells it with 10 per cent. profit, or for £2,200. Here, then, are two commodities having precisely the same quantity of labour bestowed on them, one of which sells for £2,310— the other for £2,200" (p. 23).

[1] Therefore also their period of reproduction.

But how then does this difference—either in the degree of durability of the fixed capital, or in the period of turnover of the circulating capital, or in the proportion in which the two kinds of capital are combined, or lastly in the time needed by different commodities on which the same quantity of labour has been bestowed to come on to the market—how does each of these differences bring about a change in the *relative* values of these commodities? Ricardo says in the first place it is because these differences and variations "introduce another cause, besides the greater or less quantity of labour necessary to produce commodities, for the variations in their relative value—this cause is *the rise or fall in the value of labour*" (p. 18. Marx's italics).

And how is this proved?

"A rise in the wages of labour cannot fail to affect unequally commodities produced under such different circumstances" (p. 19).

Namely, when capitals of equal size are employed in different branches of industry, and one consists mainly of fixed capital and only to a small degree of capital "employed in the support of labour", while in the other the proportions are exactly the reverse. To begin with, it is nonsense to speak of the commodities being affected. He means their values. But how far are their values affected by these circumstances? They are not even touched by them. What is affected in both cases is the profit. The man who, for example, lays out only a fifth of his capital in variable capital—assuming that wages and the rate of surplus value remain unaltered—can, if the rate of surplus value is 20 per cent., produce only a surplus value of 4 on every hundred. The other man, on the other hand, who laid out four-fifths in variable capital, would produce (at the same rate of surplus value) a surplus value of 16 on every hundred. The average profit for both would be $\frac{16+4}{2}$ or 10 per cent. This is actually the case to which Ricardo is referring. If therefore they both sold—and this is what Ricardo assumes--at prices of production, each would sell his commodities for 110. Suppose now that wages rose, for example by 20 per cent. of their former amount. Formerly one man cost £1.

Now he costs £1 4s. The first capitalist has still, as before, to lay out £80 in constant capital (as Ricardo here leaves raw materials out of account, we can do the same), and must, for the twenty workers he employs, lay out another £4 in addition to the £20. His capital therefore now amounts to £104. And out of the £110 he is left with only £6 profit, since his workmen produce a smaller surplus value instead of a greater. £6 on £104 is $5\frac{10}{13}$ per cent. On the other hand, the other man, who employs 80 workers, would have to pay them £16 more. He would therefore have to lay out £116. Consequently, if he were to sell for £110, instead of making a profit he would have a loss of £6. This however is only the case because the average profit has already modified the relation between the wages invested by the capitalist and the surplus value which he himself produces.

Instead therefore of investigating the important phenomenon—what are the changes that must take place so that the one capitalist, who lays out £80 of his £100 in wages, does not make four times the profit made by the other, who lays out only £20 of his £100 in wages—Ricardo investigates the subsidiary question of how it comes about that, after this great difference has been levelled out—i.e., with a given rate of profit—each change in this rate of profit, for example resulting from a rise in wages, affects the man who employs many workers with his £100 much more than the man who employs few workers with his £100; and that therefore—with an equal rate of profit—the prices or production prices of the first man's commodities would have to rise, and those of the second man's to fall, if the rate of profit is to continue to remain equal.

The first illustration which Ricardo gives has absolutely nothing to do with "a rise in the value of labour", although he originally informed us that the whole of the variation in relative values must arise from this cause. This illustration is as follows:

"Suppose two men employ one hundred men each for a year in the construction of two machines, and another man employs the same number of men in cultivating corn, each of the machines at the end of the year will be of the same value as the corn, for they will each be produced by the same quantity of labour. Suppose one of the owners of one of the machines to employ it, with the assistance of one hundred men, the following year in making cloth, and the owner of the other machine to employ his also, with the assistance likewise of one hundred men, in making cotton goods, while the farmer continues to employ one hundred men as before in the cultivation of corn. During the second year they will all have employed the same quantity of labour,[1] but the goods and machine together of the clothier, and also of the cotton manufacturer, will be the result of the labour of two hundred men employed for a year; or, rather, of the labour of one hundred men for two years, whereas the corn will be produced by the labour of one hundred men for one year, consequently if the corn be of the value of £500, the machine and cloth of the clothier together ought to be of the value of £1,000, and the machine and cotton goods of the cotton manufacturer ought to be also of twice the value of the corn. But they will be of more than twice the value of the corn, for the profit on the clothier's and cotton manufacturer's capital for the first year has been added to their capitals, while that of the farmer has been expended and enjoyed. On account then of the different degrees of durability of their capitals, or, which is the same thing, on account of the time which must elapse before one set of commodities can be brought to market, they will be valuable, not exactly in proportion to the quantity of labour bestowed on them—they will not be as two to one, but something more, to compensate for the greater length of time which must elapse before the most valuable can be brought to market.

"Suppose that for the labour of each workman £50 per annum were paid, or that £5,000 capital were employed and profits were 10 per cent., the value of each of the machines as well as of the corn, at the end of the first year, would be £5,500. The second year the manufacturers and farmers will again employ £5,000 each in the support of labour, and will therefore again sell their goods for £5,500; but the men using the machines, to be on a par with the farmer, must not only obtain £5,500 for the equal capitals of £5,000 employed on labour, but they must obtain a

[1] That is to say, they will have expended the same capital in wages, but they will by no means have employed the same quantity of labour.

further sum of £550 for the profit on £5,500, which they have invested in machinery, and consequently[1] their goods must sell for £6,050.[2] Here, then, are capitalists employing precisely the same quantity of labour annually on the production of their commodities, and yet the goods they produce differ in value on account of the different quantities of fixed capital, or accumulated labour, employed by each respectively.[3] The cloth and cotton goods are of the same value, because they are the produce of equal quantities of labour and equal quantities of fixed capital; but corn is not of the same value[4] as these commodities, because it is produced, as far as regards fixed capital, under different circumstances" (Chapter I, Section IV, pp. 20–1).

This exceedingly ponderous illustration of an exceedingly simple affair is built up in such a complicated way in order to avoid saying simply: Since capitals of equal size, whatever the relation between their organic constituent parts, or their periods of circulation, yield profits of equal size—which would be impossible if commodities were sold at their value, etc.— there exist prices of production which are different from the values of commodities. And this is in fact involved in the concept of a general rate of profit.

Let us go through this complicated example and reduce it to its very little "complicated" natural dimensions. For this purpose we begin at the end, and note at the outset, in order that it may be better understood, that Ricardo assumes that their raw material costs the farmer and the cotton manufacturer nothing; further, that the farmer does not expend any capital on the instruments of labour; and finally, that no part of the fixed capital expended by the cotton manufacturer enters into his product as wear and tear. All these assumptions are in fact absurd, but in themselves they do not affect the illustration.

[1] Because in fact an *equal annual rate of profit of 10 per cent. is assumed* as a necessary law.

[2] That is, as a result of the average profit—the general rate of profit presupposed by Ricardo—*prices of production* come into being which are *different* from the values of the commodities.

[3] Not for this reason, but because these fellows have the fixed idea that each of them ought to get the same spoils out of "the support they give to labour", in other words, that their commodities, whatever their values may be, must be sold at production prices which always yield the same rate of profit.

[4] This should read: production price.

On the basis of all these assumptions, Ricardo's example, starting from the end, is as follows: The farmer expends £5,000 in wages; the cotton manufacturer £5,000 in wages and £5,500 in machinery. The former therefore lays out £5,000 and the latter £10,500, that is to say, as much again as the former. If therefore they are both to make 10 per cent. profit, the farmer must sell his commodities for £5,500 and the cotton manufacturer his for £6,050—that is, on the assumption that no part of the £5,500 spent on machinery forms a constituent part of the value of the product as wear and tear. It is absolutely impossible to disregard the fact—as Ricardo made clear to himself in this example—that the production prices of commodities, in so far as they are determined by the value of the capitals contained in the commodities plus the same annual rate of profit, are different from the values of the commodities; and that this difference arises from the fact that commodities are sold at such prices that they yield the same rate of profit on the capital advanced; in a word, that this difference between production prices and values is identical with a general rate of profit. Even the difference between fixed and circulating capital which he brings in here is in this example sheer humbug. For if, for example, the additional £5,500 which the cotton manufacturer employs consisted of raw materials, while the farmer required no seed, etc., the result would be exactly the same. Nor does the example prove, as Ricardo asserts, that "the goods they produce differ in value on account of the different quantities of fixed capital, or accumulated labour, employed by each respectively". For according to his assumption the cotton manufacturer employs £5,500 fixed capital and the farmer *nil*; the former employs fixed capital and the latter does not. Therefore they certainly do not employ it "in different quantities", any more than it could be said that if one person eats meat and another eats no meat, they eat meat "in different quantities". On the other hand it is correct (though it is very incorrect to introduce the phrase with an "or") that they employ "accumulated labour", that is, materialised labour, in different quantities, namely, one to the extent of £10,500 and the other only £5,000. That they employ, however,

different quantities of accumulated labour means nothing
more than that they expend different quantities of capital in
their enterprises; that the amount of their profits is proportionate to this difference in size of the capitals employed,
because the same rate of profit is assumed; and that finally
this difference in the amount of profit, proportionate to the
size of the capitals, is expressed and revealed in the respective
production prices of the commodities.

But what clumsiness there is in Ricardo's illustration!

"Here, then, are capitalists employing precisely the same
quantity of labour annually on the production of their
commodities, and yet the goods they produce differ in
value. . . ."

This means that they do not employ the same quantity—
taking immediate and accumulated labour together—but that
they employ the same quantity of variable capital, capital
laid out in wages, the same quantity of living labour. And
since money exchanges for accumulated labour—i.e., existing
commodities in the form of machines, etc.—only according to
the law of commodities; since surplus value only arises from
the appropriation without payment of part of the living labour
employed—it is clear (since it is assumed that no part of the
machinery enters into the commodity as wear and tear) that
both could only make the same profit if profit and surplus
value were identical. The cotton manufacturer, like the farmer,
would have to sell his commodity for £5,500, even though he
advances more than twice as much capital. And even if the
whole of the machinery passed into the commodity, he could
still only sell his commodity for £11,000; that is to say, he
would not make 5 per cent. profit, while the farmer makes 10.
With these unequal profits, however, the farmer and the
manufacturer would have sold the commodities at their
values, on the assumption that the 10 per cent. which the
farmer makes represents actual unpaid labour embodied in
the commodity. If therefore they sell their goods with an
equal profit, this must be due to one of two things: either the
manufacturer arbitrarily claps 5 per cent. on to his commodities, and then the commodities of the manufacturer and the

farmer taken together are sold above their value; or the actual surplus value which the farmer makes is about 15 per cent.; and each of them adds the average, 10 per cent., on to their commodities. In this case, although the price of production of the respective commodity is either above or below its value, the aggregate of the two commodities is sold at its value, and the equalisation of the profits is itself determined by the total surplus value contained in them. Here, in this proposition put forward by Ricardo, when correctly modified, lies the truth: that the proportion between variable and constant capital, when the capitals advanced are of the same size, must result in commodities of unequal value which therefore yield a different profit; and that the levelling out of these profits must therefore bring about production prices which are different from the values of the commodities.

"Here, then, are capitalists employing precisely the same quantity of labour[1] annually on the production of their commodities, and yet the goods they produce differ in value[2] on account of the different quantities of fixed capital, or accumulated labour, employed by each respectively."

But Ricardo did not make explicit what he hints at in this passage. It only makes evident the meanderings and the patent falsity of the illustration, which up to this point had nothing to do with the different quantities of fixed capital employed.

Let us now go further back in the analysis. In the first year the manufacturer constructs a machine, with 100 men. Meanwhile the farmer produces corn, also with 100 men. In the second year the manufacturer takes the machine and with it makes cotton, for which he again employs 100 men. The farmer on the other hand employs his 100 men again on the cultivation of corn. Suppose, says Ricardo, that the value of the corn is £5,000 annually. Let us assume that the unpaid labour therein amounts to 25 per cent. [of the paid labour]. Then the value of the machine also at the end of the first year would be £5,000, of which £4,000 represents paid labour and £1,000 the value of the unpaid labour. We will assume that at the end of the second year the whole machine is used up and

---

[1] Immediate, living labour.

[2] That is, have production prices which differ from their value.

has entered into the value of the cotton. In fact Ricardo does assume this, as at the end of the second year he makes not only the value of the cotton but the value of the cotton and of the machine combined equal to the value of the corn.

Good. The value of the cotton at the end of the second year must then be equal to £10,000, namely £5,000 the value of the machine and £5,000 the value of the newly added labour. The value of the corn on the other hand is £5,000, namely £4,000 the value of the wages and £1,000 unpaid labour. So far there is nothing in this case which contradicts the law of value. The cotton manufacturer makes 25 per cent. profit, just as the corn grower does. But the former commodity is equal to £10,000 and the latter to £5,000, because in the commodity of the first the labour of 200 men is embodied, and in that of the second only the labour of 100 men each year. Moreover, the £1,000 profit (surplus value) which the cotton manufacturer has made on his machine in the first year, by absorbing into it a fifth of the labour time of the workmen constructing it without paying them for it, is realised by him only in the second year, since it is only then that he realises, in the value of the cotton, at the same time the value of the machine. But now comes the point. The cotton manufacturer sells for more than £10,000, that is, for a value higher than is contained in his commodity, while the farmer sells his corn for £5,000, that is, according to our assumption, at its value. If therefore there were only these two people to exchange with each other—the manufacturer buying corn from the farmer, and the farmer cotton from the manufacturer—the result would be the same as if the farmer sold his commodity for less than its value, and so made less than 25 per cent., and the manufacturer sold the cotton above its value. Let us drop the two capitalists, the clothier and the cotton manufacturer, whom Ricardo brings in here quite superfluously, and let us modify his example in such a way that it refers only to the cotton manufacturer. For the purpose of the illustration, in so far as it concerns us here, there is no point in the double calculation. We have therefore:

"But they [the cotton goods] will be of more than twice the value of the corn, for the profit on the . . . cotton manufacturer's capital for the first year has been added to his capital, while that of the farmer has been expended and enjoyed.[1] On account then of the different degrees of durability of their capitals, or, which is the same thing, on account of the time which must elapse before one set of commodities can be brought to market, they will be valuable, not exactly in proportion to the quantity of labour bestowed on them—they will not be as two to one, but something more, to compensate for the greater length of time which must elapse before the more valuable can be brought to market."

If the manufacturer sold the commodity at its value, he would sell it for £10,000—twice the price of the corn, because there is twice as much labour in it, £5,000 accumulated labour in the machine, £1,000 of which he has not paid for, and £5,000 in the labour on the cotton, £1,000 of which again he has not paid for. He, however, reckons as follows: The first year I laid out £4,000, and with it, by exploiting the workers, created a machine worth £5,000. I therefore made a profit of 25 per cent. The second year I lay out £9,000—namely, £5,000 in the said machine and again £4,000 in labour. [The surplus value comes to £1,000; the total value of the product is therefore £10,000.] If I am now again to make 25 per cent. profit, then I must sell the cotton for £11,250, that is, £1,250 more than its value—for this £1,250 does not represent labour contained in the cotton, neither labour accumulated in the first year nor labour added in the second. The aggregate amount of labour contained in it amounts to only £10,000.

On the other hand, let us assume that the two of them, the farmer and the cotton manufacturer, exchange with each other, or that half the capitalists find themselves in the position of the cotton manufacturer and the other half in the position of the farmer. From whom now are the first half to get paid their £1,250? From what fund? Obviously, only from the second half. But in this case it is clear that this second half does not make a profit of 25 per cent. The first half would

---

[1] This last bourgeois extenuating phrase is here quite meaningless from a theoretical standpoint. Moral considerations have nothing to do with the matter.

therefore cheat the second, using the pretext of a general rate of profit, while in reality the rate of profit for the manufacturer would be 25 per cent., and for the farmer less than 25 per cent. What takes place therefore must be something different from this.

In order to make the illustration more correct and clear, let us assume that the farmer uses £8,000 in the second year. With a 25 per cent. profit he has therefore made £1,000 on £4,000 in the first year, and £2,000 on £8,000 in the second, or £3,000 altogether. As against this, the manufacturer made £1,000 in the first year, or 25 per cent. on £4,000, but in the second year only £1,000 on £9,000, since no surplus value comes from the £5,000 laid out in machinery, but only from the £4,000 laid out in wages, and the profit is therefore only $11\frac{1}{9}$ per cent. In the two years together, his profit is £2,000 on an outlay of £13,000, or $15\frac{5}{13}$ per cent. [The average profit would therefore be 20 per cent. In order to obtain this, the manufacturer would have to add on 5 per cent., and the farmer to subtract the same amount.] This would result in a price of less than £5,000 for the farmer's commodity, and more than £10,000 for the manufacturer's.

If the manufacturer, instead of making cloth, had built a house—that is, if he had been a builder—then at the end of the first year there would be £5,000 in the unfinished house, and he would have had to spend £4,000 more in labour in order to complete it. The farmer, however, whose capital turned over within the year, can, out of his £1,000 profit, again capitalise a part—say, for example, £500—and lay it out again in labour, which the manufacturer in the case we have assumed cannot do. If the rate of profit is to be the same in both cases, then the commodity of the one must be sold above, and that of the other below, its value. Since competition strives to level out values into prices of production, this is what happens.

But it is incorrect to say, as Ricardo does, that in such a case a change in the relative values is brought about "on account of the different degrees of durability of their capitals" or "on account of the time which must elapse before one set of commodities can be brought to market". It is due rather to the acceptance of a general rate of profit, which in spite of the different values gives rise to prices of production which are equal and different from these values determined only by labour time.

Ricardo's illustration falls into two examples. In the latter the question of the *durability* of the capital or its character as fixed capital does not arise. It deals only with capitals which differ in size, but of which the same amount is laid out in wages, the same amount is expended as variable capital, and on which the profits have to be the same, although the surplus values and the values must be different.

In the first example also the durability has no bearing. It deals with a longer labour process—a longer period during which the commodity remains in the sphere of production before it can enter into circulation, before it is a finished commodity.

Here also, in Ricardo's example, in the second year the manufacturer employs a larger capital than the farmer does, although in both years he employs the same variable capital. The farmer, however, because of the shorter period his commodity remains in the labour process, its earlier transformation into money, could employ in the second year a larger variable capital. Moreover that part of the profit which is consumed as revenue can be consumed by the farmer at the end of the first year, but by the manufacturer not until the end of the second. He must therefore expend, advance to himself, a further amount of capital for his keep. Incidentally, it here depends entirely on how far the capitals which complete their turnover in a year again capitalise their profits—and therefore on the actual size of the profits produced—whether a compensation can take place in the second instance and the profits be equalised out. Where there is nothing, there is nothing to be equalised. Here the capitals again produce values, therefore surplus values, therefore profits, not in proportion to their size. If they are to produce profits proportionate to their size, there must be *prices of production* different from the values.

Ricardo gives a third illustration, which however is *exactly* the same as the first example in the first illustration and contains nothing new:

"Suppose I employ twenty men at an expense of £1,000 for a year in the production of a commodity, and at the end of the year I employ twenty men again for another year, at a further expense of £1,000 in finishing or perfecting the same commodity, and that I bring it to market at the end of two years, if profits be 10 per cent., my commodity must sell for £2,310; for I have employed £1,000 capital for one year, and £2,100 capital for one year more. Another man employs precisely the same quantity of labour, but he employs it all in the first year; he employs forty men at an expense of £2,000, and at the end of the first year he sells it with 10 per cent. profit, or for £2,200. Here, then, are two commodities having precisely the same quantity of labour bestowed on them, one of which sells for £2,310— the other for £2,200. This case appears to differ from the last, but is, in fact, the same" (p. 23).

It is the same not only "in fact" but also "in appearance", except that in the first case the commodity is called a "machine" while here it is called a "commodity" outright. In the first example the manufacturer laid out £4,000 in the first year and £9,000 in the second; this time £1,000 in the first and £2,100 in the second. The farmer laid out £4,000 in the first year and £4,000 in the second. This time the second man lays out £2,000 in the first year and nothing at all in the second. That is the whole difference. But in both cases the *fabula docet* refers to the fact that one of the men lays out in the second year the entire product of the first, including surplus value, plus an additional amount.

The clumsiness of these examples shows that Ricardo is wrestling with a difficulty which he does not clearly see and succeeds even less in overcoming. The clumsiness consists in the following: The first example of the first illustration is intended to bring in the *durability* of the capital; it does nothing of the sort. Ricardo himself made it impossible to do this, by allowing no part of the fixed capital to enter into the commodity as wear and tear, and therefore by omitting precisely that factor through which the special way in which fixed capital circulates is made evident. All he demonstrates is that as a result of the longer duration of the labour process, a greater capital is employed than when the labour process is shorter.

The third example is intended to illustrate something rather different, but it actually illustrates the same thing. The second example of the first illustration however is intended to show what differences arise as a result of different proportions of fixed capital. Instead of this, it shows only the difference arising from two capitals of unequal size, although both lay out the same part of the capital in wages. And moreover the manufacturer operates without cotton or yarn, and the farmer without seed or implements! The complete inconsistency, even absurdity, of this illustration necessarily arises from this underlying lack of clarity.

Finally, he states the moral to be drawn from all these illustrations as follows:

"The difference in value arises in both cases from the profits being accumulated as capital, and is only a *just compensation*[1] *for the time that the profits were withheld*" (p. 23. Marx's italics).

What does this mean other than that in a definite period of circulation, for example a year, a capital must yield ten per cent. whatever its specific period of circulation may be, and quite independently of the different surplus values which—irrespective of the process of circulation—capitals of equal size must produce in the various branches of production, according to the proportion between the organic constituent parts of each.

The conclusions that Ricardo should have drawn were the following:

First: Capitals of equal size produce commodities of unequal values, and consequently yield unequal surplus values or profits, because value is determined by labour time, and the amount of labour time which a capital realises depends not on its absolute size but on the size of the variable capital, of the capital laid out in wages.

Secondly: Granted even that capitals of equal size produce equal values, nevertheless the period within which they appropriate equal quantities of unpaid labour and can transform them into money, varies in accordance with their process of circulation. This therefore makes a second difference in the

[1] As if the question at issue were justice!

values, surplus values and profits which capitals of equal size in different branches of production must yield in a given period of time.

Consequently, if profits as a percentage of capital are to be equal, for example in a period of one year, so that capitals of equal size yield equal profits in the same period of time, then the prices of commodities must be different from their values. The sum total of the production prices of all the commodities taken together will be equal to their value. In the same way the total profit will be equal to the total surplus value which these capitals yield, during one year for example. The average profit, and therefore also the production prices, would be purely imaginary and without basis if we did not take the determined value as the foundation. The equalisation of the surplus values in different spheres of production makes no difference to the absolute magnitude of this total surplus value, but only alters its distribution among the different spheres of production. The determination of the surplus value itself however only arises from the determination of value by labour time. Without this, the average profit is an average of *nothing*, a mere figment of the imagination. And in that case it might just as well be 1,000 per cent. as 10 per cent.

All of Ricardo's illustrations serve merely to enable him to smuggle in the assumption of a general rate of profit. And this occurs in the first chapter, "On Value", although wages are supposed to be dealt with only in Chapter V and profit in Chapter VI. How from the mere determination of the value of commodities their surplus value, profit, and then even a general rate of profit are derived, remains shrouded in darkness for Ricardo. The only thing that he really proves in the above illustrations is that the prices of commodities, to the extent that they are determined by the general rate of profit, are completely different from their values. And he arrives at this difference by assuming the rate of profit as a law. We can see that while Ricardo is accused of being too abstract, the opposite accusation would be justified—i.e., lack of the power to abstract; inability, when dealing with the values of commodities, to keep out of his mind profit, a thing which confronts him as a result of competition.

Because Ricardo, instead of deriving the difference between production prices and values from the determination of value itself, admits that values are themselves determined by influences independent of labour time—here would have been the place for him to define the concept of "absolute" or "real" value, or "value" as such—and that the law of values is here and there abrogated by these influences, his opponents, such as Malthus, concentrate on this to attack his entire theory of value. Malthus remarked with justice that the differences between the organic constituents of capital and the turnover periods of capitals in different branches of production develop simultaneously with the advance in production, so that the conclusion would be what was Adam Smith's view—that the determination of value by labour time becomes progressively more inapplicable in "civilised" times (see also Torrens). On the other hand his disciples, in order to make these phenomena consistent with the fundamental principle (see Mill and the wretched McCulloch), have resorted to the most pitiful scholastic devices.

Ricardo does not dwell on the conclusion that follows from his own illustration—namely, that quite apart from rises or falls in wages, on the assumption that wages remain constant, the prices of production of commodities must differ from their values if production prices are determined by the same percentage of profit—but passes on in this section to the influence which rises or falls in wages exert on production prices in which values have already been levelled out.

This point is in itself extraordinarily simple.

The farmer advances a capital of £5,000 at 10 per cent. The value of his commodity is equal to £5,500. If the profit falls by 1 per cent., from 10 to 9 per cent., because wages have risen and the rise in wages has brought about this reduction, then he still sells as before for £5,500, as it is assumed that he advances his whole capital in wages. Let the manufacturer's capital again consist of £5,500 for machinery and £5,000 for wages. As before, the latter £5,000 of the capital is represented by £5,500 in the value of the product. On the other hand, on the fixed capital of £5,500 he can no longer reckon on 10 per cent. or £550, but only on 9 per cent.

or £495. He will therefore sell his commodity for £5,995 instead of for £6,050, and so, as a result of the rise in wages, the money price of the farmer's commodity has remained the same, while that of the manufacturer's commodity has fallen. The value of the farmer's commodity, therefore, compared with that of the manufacturer's, has risen (Ricardo, pp. 21, 22). The whole point of the example arises from the fact that if the manufacturer sold his commodity at the same price as before, he would make a profit higher than the average, because only that part of his capital which was laid out in wages would be directly affected by the rise in wages. In this illustration prices of production regulated by an average profit of 10 per cent., and different from the values of the commodities, are already assumed. The question is, what effect will rises or falls in profit have on these, according to the different proportions of their fixed and circulating capital. This illustration has no bearing on the essential question—the transformation of values into prices of production. But it is a nice point, because Ricardo here at any rate demonstrates that the raising of wages, which—contrary to the vulgar view—would produce only a fall in profit without affecting the values of commodities if the composition of the capitals was the same, would, if the organic composition of capitals is unequal, bring about only a fall in the prices of some commodities, instead of—as vulgar opinion believes—a rise in the price of all commodities. Here the fall in the prices of commodities is the result of a fall in the rate of profit or, which is the same thing, of a rise in wages. A large part of the production price of the commodity, in the case of the manufacturer, is due to the average profit which he calculates on the fixed capital. If therefore this rate of profit falls or rises as a result of the rise or fall in wages, the price of these commodities will fall or rise correspondingly, in proportion to that part of the price which originates from the profit calculated on the fixed capital. The same holds good for "circulating capitals returnable at distant periods and *vice versa*" (McCulloch). If the capitalists who employ less variable capital were to continue to chalk up their fixed capital at the same rate of profit and add it to the price of the commodity, then their rate of profit would rise, and it

would rise in the proportion in which they employ more fixed
capital, as compared with those whose capital consists to a
greater degree of variable capital. Competition would level
this out.

Ricardo, says McCulloch, was the first to investigate the
effects of fluctuations in wages on the value of commodities
when the capitals engaged in their production are not equally
durable. "Mr. Ricardo has not only shown that it is impossible
for any rise of wages to raise the price of all commodities, but
he has also shown that in most cases a rise of wages necessarily
leads to a fall in the price of some descriptions of commodities,
and a fall of wages to a rise in the price of others" (*The Principles
of Political Economy*, London, 1830, pp. 341–2).

Ricardo proves his point by first assuming that prices of
production are regulated by a general rate of profit; secondly
"There can be no rise in the value of labour without a fall of
profits" (p. 21).

Already in Chapter I, "On Value", we therefore find assumed
the laws which are dealt with in Chapters V and VI on Wages
and Profits and which are said to be derived from the chapter
on Value. We may note in passing that Ricardo concludes
quite erroneously that because "No rise in the value of labour
is possible without a fall in profits", therefore no rise in profits
is possible without a fall in the value of labour. The first law
refers to surplus value. But since the profit is equal to the
proportion between the surplus value and the total capital
advanced, the profit can rise though the value of labour
remains the same, if the value of the constant capital falls.

The general *fabula docet* of the last illustration is as follows:

"The degree of alteration in the relative value of goods,
on account of a rise or fall of labour,[1] would depend on the
proportion which the fixed capital bore to the whole capital
employed. All commodities which are produced by very
valuable machinery, or in very valuable buildings, or which
require a great length of time before they can be brought
to market, would fall in relative value, while all those which
were chiefly produced by labour, or which would be speedily
brought to market, would rise in relative value" (p. 22).

[1] Or, what is the same thing, a fall or rise in the rate of profit.

Ricardo again comes to the point with which alone he is really concerned in his investigation. These changes in the production prices of commodities which arise from the rise or fall of wages are of no significance compared with those changes in the same prices of production which are due to changes in the values of commodities (Ricardo is very far from stating this truth in this correct way)—changes in the quantities of labour required for their production. It is therefore possible by and large to abstract from the former changes, and the law of value consequently remains true also from a practical standpoint. (Ricardo should have added that the production prices themselves cannot be explained without values determined by labour time.) This is where his investigation really leads. In fact it is clear that, in spite of the transformation of the values of commodities into production prices, once the latter are assumed a change in them—in so far as it is not due to a permanent rise or fall in the rate of profit such as can only be established in the course of many years—has for its sole and only cause a *change* in their *values*, in the labour time necessary for their production.

"The reader however should remark that this cause of the variation of commodities[1] is comparatively slight in its effects. . . . Not so with the other great cause of the variation in the value of commodities, namely, the increase or diminution in the quantity of labour necessary to produce them. . . . An alteration in the permanent rate of profits, to any great amount, is the effect of causes which do not operate but in the course of years, whereas alterations in the quantity of labour necessary to produce commodities are of daily occurrence. Every improvement in machinery, in tools, in buildings, in raising the raw material, saves labour, and enables us to produce the commodity to which the improvement is applied with more facility, and consequently its value alters. In estimating, then, the causes of the variations in the value of commodities, although it would be wrong wholly to omit the consideration of the effect produced by a rise or fall of labour, it would be equally incorrect to attach much importance to it" (pp. 22–3).

[1] This should read "prices of production" or, as he calls them, the relative values of commodities.

He therefore takes no further account of it.

This whole fourth section of Chapter I, "On Value", is so extraordinarily confused that although Ricardo at the start announces his intention of investigating the influence of *variations* in value which the rise or fall in wages brings about as a result of the different composition of capitals, in fact he only does this incidentally. In reality the major part of the fourth section is on the contrary filled with illustrations which prove that, quite independently of rises or falls in wages—he himself makes the assumption that wages remain constant— the *hypothesis* of a general rate of profit must result in prices of production that differ from the values of commodities, and moreover do so independently even of differences [in the proportion of] fixed and circulating capital. He forgets this again at the end of the Section.

He announces the subject of his enquiry in the fourth section with the words:

"This difference in the degree of durability of fixed capital, and this variety in the proportions in which the two sorts of capital may be combined, introduce another cause, besides the greater or less quantity of labour necessary to produce commodities, for the variations in their relative value—*this cause is the rise or fall in the value of labour*" (p. 18. Marx's italics).

In reality he shows by his examples, in the first place, that it is the general rate of profit which first gives to the various combinations of kinds of capital—that is, variable and constant, etc.—this influence to differentiate the prices of commodities from their values. That therefore it, and not by any chance the value of labour (which is assumed to be constant), is the *cause* of these changes. Then, only in the second place, he assumes prices of production already differentiated from values as a result of the general rate of profit, and investigates how changes in the value of labour affect these. Number 1, the main point, he does not examine; he loses sight of it altogether, and closes the Section in the same way as he began it:

". . . it being shown in this section that, without any variation in the quantity of labour, the rise of its value merely will occasion a fall in the exchangeable value of those goods in the production of which fixed capital is employed; the larger the amount of fixed capital, the greater will be the fall" (p. 24).

And in the following section V of Chapter I Ricardo also proceeds in the same fashion; that is to say, he only investigates how the production prices of commodities can be varied by a *change in the value of labour or of wages*—not when the ratio between fixed and circulating capital is different in two capitals of equal size in different branches of production, but when there is "unequal durability of fixed capital" or "unequal rapidity with which the capital is returned to its employer". The correct surmise, which we meet in Section IV, of the difference between production prices and values resulting from the general rate of profit, here no longer comes to the surface. Only a secondary question—that of variations in the prices of production themselves—is considered. Hence this section has in fact hardly any theoretical interest, apart from the incidental introduction of the differences in the form of capitals which arise from the process of circulation.

"In proportion as fixed capital is less durable it approaches to the nature of circulating capital. It will be consumed and its value reproduced in a shorter time, in order to preserve the capital of the manufacturer" (p. 24).

Thus the lesser durability and the difference between fixed and circulating capital also are reduced to the difference in the period of reproduction. This is certainly the factor of decisive importance. But by no means the only one. The fixed capital in its entirety enters into the labour process, and only in successive stages and by instalments into the process of creating value. This is another main distinction in its form of circulation. Furthermore: for the most part the fixed capital enters into the circulation process only in the form of its *exchange value*, while its *use value* is consumed in the labour process and never goes outside it. This is another important distinction in the *form of circulation*. Both distinctions in the form of circulation also affect the period of circulation, but they are not identical with the degrees and differences of durability.

"If fixed capital be not of a durable nature it will require a great quantity of labour annually to keep it in its original state of efficiency; but the labour so bestowed may be considered as really expended on the commodity manufactured, which must bear a value in proportion to such labour" (p. 24).

"If the wear and tear of the machine were great, if the quantity of labour requisite to keep it in an efficient state were that of fifty men annually, I should require an additional price for my goods equal to that which would be obtained by any other manufacturer who employed fifty men in the production of other goods, and who used no machinery at all. But a rise in the wages of labour would not equally affect commodities produced with machinery quickly consumed, and commodities produced with machinery slowly consumed. In the production of the one, a great deal of labour would be continually transferred to the commodity produced[1]—in the other very little would be so transferred.[2] Every rise of wages, therefore, or, which is the same thing, every fall of profits, would lower the relative value of those commodities which were produced with a capital of a durable nature, and would proportionally elevate those which were produced with capital more perishable. A fall of wages would have precisely the contrary effect" (pp. 24–5).

In other words, the industrialist who employs fixed capital of less durability employs relatively less fixed capital and more capital expended in wages than the one who employs capital of greater durability. This case is therefore identical with the previous one, showing the effect of a change in wages on capitals, one of which employs relatively, proportionately, more fixed capital than the other. Here there is nothing new. What Ricardo further says of *machinery* (pp. 25–6) should be

---

[1] In the struggle with his general rate of profit Ricardo does not see that along with the labour a great quantity of surplus labour would also be transferred to the commodity.

[2] Hence also very little surplus labour and little surplus value—if the commodities are exchanged at their values.

held over until we come to Chapter XXXI, "On Machinery". It is curious how Ricardo in the end almost touches the truth in a *phrase* only to let it drop again, and how after hinting at it in the passages we are now going to quote he returns to his dominating idea of the effect of a change in the value of labour on prices of production, and finally concludes his investigation with this subsidiary point.

The passage in which the hint is contained is the following:

"It will be seen then, that in the early stages of society, before much machinery or durable capital is used, the commodities produced by equal capitals will be nearly of equal value, and will rise or fall only relatively to each other on account of more or less labour being required for their production;[1] but after the introduction of these expensive and durable instruments, the commodities produced by the employment of equal capitals will be of very unequal value, and although they will still be liable to rise or fall relatively to each other, as more or less labour becomes necessary to their production, they will be subject to another, though a minor variation, also from the rise or fall of wages and profits. Since goods which sell for £5,000 may be the produce of a capital equal in amount to that from which are produced other goods which sell for £10,000, *the profits on their manufacture will be the same;* but *those profits would be unequal if the prices of the goods did not vary with a rise or fall in the rate of profits*" (pp. 26–7. Marx's italics).

Capitals of equal size produce commodities of *equal values*, when the proportion between the organic constituents is *the same*, when equally large portions of them are expended in wages and in means of production. Then the same quantities of labour, therefore equal values, are embodied in their commodities—apart from any difference which might come in through the process of circulation. On the other hand, capitals *of equal size* produce commodities of very *unequal value*, if their organic composition is different, that is, when the difference between the portion existing as fixed capital and the portion

---

[1] This is badly put. It refers not to value, but to commodities. And it has no meaning unless what is referred to is their *prices*; for to say that *values* fall or rise in proportion to labour time means that values fall or rise in the measure that they fall or rise.

expended in wages is considerable. In the first place, only a part of the fixed capital enters into the commodity as a constituent part of its value, in consequence of which alone therefore the magnitude of their values would be very different, according as more or less fixed capital is employed in the production of the commodity. Secondly, the portion expended in wages—the percentage, calculated on an amount of capital of equal size—is much smaller, and so therefore is the total labour embodied in the commodity, therefore also the surplus labour (given a working day of equal length), which constitutes the surplus value. If therefore these capitals of equal size whose commodities are of unequal values—in which unequal values lie hidden unequal surplus values and consequently unequal profits—are to yield equal profits because they are of equal size, then the prices of the commodities, in so far as they are determined by the general rate of profit, must be very different from their values. It follows from this, not that the nature of the values has altered, but that the prices are different from the values. It is all the more surprising that Ricardo did not reach this conclusion since he certainly sees that even prices of production—which are determined by the general rate of profit—must change if there is a change in the rate of profit or of wages, in order that the rate of profit in the various branches of production may remain the same. How much more, therefore, must the emergence of a general rate of profit change unequal values, as indeed this *general rate of profit* is in any case nothing but the levelling out of the different rates of surplus value in the different commodities produced by equal capitals.

After Ricardo has thus, if not developed and understood, at any rate stated as a matter of fact the difference between costs and value, production prices and values of commodities, he concludes by saying:

> "Mr. Malthus appears to think that it is a part of my doctrine that the cost and value of a thing should be the same; it is, if he means by cost, 'cost of production' including profits"[1] (p. 30, footnote).

[1] That is, outlays plus the profit determined by the general rate of profit.

With this erroneous confusion of price of production with value, which he has himself refuted, he then proceeds to consider Rent.

But before he does so Ricardo states in Section VI of Chapter I, in regard to the influence of variations in the value of labour on the price of production of gold:

> "May not gold be considered as a commodity produced with such proportions of the two kinds of capital as approach nearest to the average quantity employed in the production of most commodities? May not these proportions be so nearly equally distant from the two extremes, the one where little fixed capital is used, the other where little labour is employed, as to form a just mean between them?" (pp. 28–9).

What Ricardo here says is much more applicable to those commodities into whose composition the various organic constituents enter in the average proportion, and whose circulation and reproduction period is average. For these commodities, price of production and value are identical, because in their case the average profit is identical with their actual surplus value; but also it is only in their case that this is so.

However inadequate Sections IV and V of Chapter I may seem, in treating the influence of changes in the value of labour on "relative values" as (from a theoretical standpoint) a secondary question compared with the transformation of values into production prices through the rate of profit, Ricardo draws from this an important conclusion, demolishing one of the errors that had kept recurring since Adam Smith— that the raising of wages, instead of reducing profit, increases the price of commodities. It is true that this conclusion is already implicit in the mere concept of *value*, and is in no way modified by the transformation of value into price of production, since this does nothing but affect the distribution of the surplus value made by the total capital among the various branches of production or capitals in various spheres of production. But it was important that Ricardo should bring this out strongly and even prove the opposite of the accepted view. He therefore says with justice in Section VI of Chapter I:

"Before I quit this subject, it may be proper to observe that Adam Smith, and all the writers who have followed him, have, without one exception that I know of, maintained that a rise in the price of labour would be uniformly followed by a rise in the price of all commodities.[1] I hope I have succeeded in showing that there are no grounds for such an opinion, and that only those commodities would rise which had less fixed capital employed upon them than the medium in which price was estimated,[2] and that all those which had more would positively fall in price when wages rose. On the contrary, if wages fell, those commodities only would fall which had a less proportion of fixed capital employed on them than the medium in which price was estimated; all those which had more would positively rise in price" (p. 29).

This seems to be wrong as far as the money price is concerned. If gold rises or falls in value, for any reason whatsoever, it does so in equal measure for all the commodities which are reckoned in gold. While it thus represents a relatively unchangeable medium in spite of its changeability, we must absolutely not overlook the fact that any relative combination of fixed and circulating capital in gold, compared with commodities, can bring about a difference. But here Ricardo's false assumption that money, in so far as it serves as means of circulation, exchanges as a commodity against commodities, has a disturbing effect. Commodities are reckoned in it before it circulates them. Suppose that wheat is the medium instead of gold. If for example, as a result of a rise in wages, wheat—as a commodity into which more than the average variable capital enters—were to rise relatively in its price of production, then all commodities would be valued in wheat of a higher "relative value". Commodities into which more fixed capital entered would be expressed in less wheat than before, not because their specific price compared with wheat had fallen, but because their price had fallen in general. A commodity which contained exactly as much living labour—as opposed to accumulated labour—as wheat, would express its rise in

[1] This is in conformity with the second explanation of value given by Adam Smith, according to which value is equal to the quantity of labour which can be bought by a commodity.

[2] Here the relative value is equivalent to the value expressed in money.

price by the fact that it was expressed in more wheat than a commodity whose price had fallen as compared with wheat. If the same causes which led to a rise in the price of wheat bring about a rise for example in the price of clothes, then clothes would not be expressed in more wheat than before; but those commodities whose price as compared with wheat had fallen, for example cotton, would be expressed in less. Cotton and clothes would express the difference between their prices in wheat as their medium.

But what Ricardo means is something different. He means that wheat, as a result of a rise in wages, would have risen as compared with cotton, but not as compared with clothes. Clothes would therefore exchange for wheat at the former price, but cotton for wheat at the increased price. The assumption that changes in the price of wages in England will change for example the production price of gold in California, where wages have not risen, is in itself quite absurd. The levelling out of values by labour time, and much less still the levelling out of production prices through a general rate of profit, does not exist in this direct form as between different countries. Take however even wheat, a home product. Say wheat has risen from 40 to fifty shillings the quarter, that is, by 25 per cent. If a dress has also risen by 25 per cent., then it is worth a quarter of wheat as before. If cotton has fallen by 25 per cent., then the same quantity of cotton which was previously worth one quarter of wheat is now worth only 6 bushels. And the expression of their values in wheat represents exactly the ratio between the prices of cotton and of clothing, because they are measured in the same quantity of wheat, one quarter.

Ricardo's notion is moreover absurd in another way. The *price* of the commodity which serves as the measure of values and therefore as money has absolutely no existence; for otherwise I should have to have, besides the commodity which serves as money, a second commodity which serves as money— a twofold measure of values. The relative value of money is expressed in the innumerable prices of all commodities; for in each of these prices which express the exchange value of the commodities in money, the exchange value of money is expressed in the use value of the commodities. There can therefore be no talk of a rise or fall in *the* price of money. I can say: the price of money in wheat, or its price in clothes, has remained the same; its price in cotton has risen—which is the same as saying that the money price of cotton has fallen. But I cannot say that *the price* of money has risen or fallen. Ricardo however in reality means for example that the price of money in cotton has risen, or the price of cotton in money has fallen, because money has risen in relative value as against cotton, while it has retained the same value as against clothing or wheat. The two are therefore measured with an *unequal measure*.

This Section VI "On an invariable measure of value" deals with the *"measure of value"* without saying anything of importance. The connection between value—its immanent measure in labour time—and the necessity for an external measure of the values of commodities is not understood; it is not even raised as a problem. The very opening of the Section shows the superficial way it is handled:

"When commodities varied in relative value it would be desirable to have the means of ascertaining which of them fell and which rose in real value, and this could be effected only by comparing them one after another with some invariable standard measure of value, which should itself be subject to none of the fluctuations to which other commodities are exposed." But "there is no commodity which is not itself exposed to the same variations . . . that is, there is none which is not subject to require more or less labour for its production" (p. 27).

Even if there were such a commodity, the influence partly of the rise or fall in wages and of the various combinations of fixed and circulating capital, of the different degrees of durability of the fixed capital, or of the different periods of time which must elapse before the product can be brought to market, etc., would prevent it from being "a perfect measure of value, by which we could accurately ascertain the variations in all other things. . . ." "It would be a perfect measure of value for all things produced under the same circumstances precisely as itself, but for no others" (p. 28). That is to say, if "these other things" varied, we could say—if the value of money neither rose nor fell—that the variation was due to a rise or fall in their values, in the labour time necessary for their production. In regard to other things we could not know whether the variations in their money prices were due to the other causes, etc. Later (in an examination of the theory of money) we shall have to come back to this viewpoint, which is unsatisfactory in all respects.

In Section VII of Chapter I, except for the important doctrine on *"relative"* wages, profits and rents, to which we return later, there is nothing but the proof that if money falls or rises in value, a corresponding rise or fall in wages, etc., does not change the relations between these but only their expression in money. If the same commodity is expressed in double the number of pounds sterling, so also is that part of it which is resolved into profit, wages or rent. But the ratio of these three to each other and the real values that they represent remain the same. Ditto, if the profit works out at twice as many pounds sterling, £100 is now expressed in £200, so that the relation between profit and capital, the rate of profit, also remains unaltered. The change in the monetary expression affects profit and capital simultaneously; similarly for profit, wages and rent. For the latter this is also true in so far as it is reckoned not on the acre, but on the capital advanced in agriculture, etc. In short, in this case the variation is not in the commodities, etc.:

"A rise of wages from this cause will, indeed, be invariably accompanied by a rise in the price of commodities; but in such cases it will be found that labour and all commodities have not varied in regard to each other, and that the variation has been confined to money" (p. 30).

(c) Prices of Production and Market Prices

(i) Ricardo's Views

In Chapter II, "On Rent", in developing his theory of differential rent Ricardo propounds the following thesis:

"The exchangeable value of all commodities, whether they be manufactured, or the produce of the mines, or the produce of land, is always regulated, not by the less quantity of labour that will suffice for their production under circumstances highly favourable, and exclusively enjoyed by those who have peculiar facilities of production; but by the greater quantity of labour necessarily bestowed on their production by those who have no such facilities; by those who continue to produce them under the most unfavourable circumstances; meaning—by the most unfavourable circumstances, the most unfavourable under which the quantity of produce required renders it necessary to carry on the production" (p. 37).

The last sentence is not quite correct. The "quantity of produce required" is not a fixed magnitude. It should read: "a definite quantity of products required within definite limits of price". If the price rises above these limits, the quantity required falls with the demand.

The thesis set out above can be expressed in general terms as follows. The value of the commodity which is the product of a particular sphere of production is determined by the labour required to produce the whole mass, the aggregate quantity of commodities pertaining to this sphere of production; not by the particular labour time that each individual capitalist or *entrepreneur* in this sphere of production requires. The general conditions of production and the general productivity of labour in this particular sphere of production, for example cotton manufacture, are the average conditions of production and the average productivity in this sphere, cotton manufacture. The quantity of labour by which for example a yard of cotton is determined is therefore not the quantity of labour contained in it, the quantity employed on it by its manufacturer, but the average quantity with which all cotton manufacturers produce a yard of cotton for the market. Now the special conditions under which individual capitalists produce, say in cotton manufacture, necessarily fall into three categories. Some produce under medium conditions; that is to say, the individual conditions of production under which they produce coincide with the general conditions of production for this sphere. The average conditions are their actual conditions. The productivity of their labour is the average level. The *individual* value of their commodities coincides with the *general* value of these commodities. If, for example, they sell cotton at 2s. the yard—the average value—

they sell it at the *value* represented *in natura* by the yards they produce. Another category produces under conditions *better* than the average. The *individual* value of their commodities is *below* their general value. If they sell them at this general value, they sell them *above* their individual value. Finally, a third category produces under conditions that are *below* the average.

Now the "quantity of produce required" from this particular sphere of production has no fixed magnitude. If the value of the commodities rises beyond certain limits above the average value, the quantity of the product required falls, or this quantity is only required at a given price—or at least within certain limits of price. Hence it is that the last-mentioned category may have to sell its commodities below their individual values, just as the best-placed category sells always above their individual value. It will in fact depend on the numerical ratio or the proportional relationship between the sizes of the groups, which of them has decisive effect in determining the average value. If the middle group is numerically greatly preponderant, it will determine the average value. If this group is numerically weak, and the group working under conditions below the average is numerically strong and preponderant, then the latter determines the general value of the product for this sphere. But this by no means implies, and it is even highly improbable, that the particular capitalist in the latter group who in turn is the most unfavourably placed, will decide the issue (*cf.* Corbett).

But let us leave this out of account. The general result is: The normal value which the products of this kind possess is the same for all, whatever its relation to the individual value of each particular commodity. This common value is the *market value* of those commodities, the value at which they appear on the market. Expressed in money, this market value is the *market price*, as in general, value expressed in money is price. The actual market price is now above, now below, this market value, and only by chance coincides with it. Over a certain period however, the fluctuations equal each other out, and it can be said that the *average* of the actual market prices is the market price which represents the market value. Whether or not the actual market price at any given moment corresponds to this market value in magnitude, quantitatively, it has at least the *qualitative* characteristic in common with it, that all commodities of the same sphere of production which are found on the market (equal quality is of course assumed) have the same price, that is, in practice they represent the general value of the commodities of this sphere.

The above proposition laid down by Ricardo for the purpose of his theory of rent has therefore been interpreted by his disciples to ˈmean that two different market prices cannot exist simultaneously on the same market; or that every individual product of the same kind found on the market at the same time has the same price, and since we can here abstract from the accidental features of this price, the same market value. Here therefore competition, partly of the capitalists with one another, partly of the buyers of the commodity both with the capitalists and among themselves, brings it about that the value of the commodity in a particular sphere of production is determined by the *total mass of social labour time which the total mass of commodities of this particular sphere of social production requires*, and not by *the individual values of the separate commodities*, or the labour time which the individual commodity has cost its *particular* producer and seller.

It obviously follows from this, however, that under all circumstances the capitalists who belong to the first category— those whose conditions of production are more favourable than the average—make an excess profit, that is, their profit is above the general rate of profit for this sphere of production. It is therefore not by equalising out the profits within a particular sphere of production that competition brings about the market value or market price.

The difference between market value and market price is for the purpose of this examination immaterial, since the differences in the conditions of production, the consequent different rates of profit for the individual capitalists in the same sphere of production, remain the same, whatever may be the relation between market price and market value.

Conversely, competition here equalises out the various individual values to the same uniform undifferentiated market value while leaving untouched the discrepancy between the individual profits, the profits of the individual capitalists, and their deviations from the average rate of profit for the sphere of production concerned. In fact it does this by establishing the same market value for commodities produced under conditions of production that are not equally favourable, therefore with unequal productivity of labour, so that these individually represent unequally great quantities of labour time. The commodity produced under more favourable conditions contains less labour time than the one produced under less favourable conditions, but it sells at the same price, has the same value, as if it contained the same labour time.

Now Ricardo, to establish his theory of rent, makes use of two propositions which are not only not the same but express the contradictory effect of competition. The first is that the products of the same sphere sell at one and the same market value, that competition therefore forcibly brings about different rates of profit, deviations from the general rate of profit. The second is that the rate of profit must be the same for each capital investment, or that competition creates a general rate of profit. The first law holds good for the various independent capitals invested in the same sphere of production. The second holds good for capitals in so far as they are invested in different spheres of production. By its first action competition creates market value, that is, the same value for commodities of the same sphere of production, although this identical value must result in different profits; that is, the same value in spite of or rather by means of different rates of profit. The second way in which competition acts is different from this, and incidentally it is also brought about in a different way. This is the competition between capitalists in *different* spheres, which throws capital out of one sphere into another; while the first form of competition—in so far as it is not competition between buyers—takes place among the capitals of *the same* sphere. This second form of competition brings about the price of production, that is to say, the same rate of profit in the different spheres of production, even though this identical rate of profit is in contradiction with the inequality of values, and can therefore only be enforced by prices which are different from values.

Since Ricardo needs both of these propositions for his theory of rent—equal value or price with unequal rate of profit, and equal rate of profit and prices with unequal values —it is most curious that he does not sense this twofold determination of value and price, and that even in the section where he deals *ex professo* with *market price*, in Chapter IV, "On Natural and Market Price", he does not deal at all with market price and market value, although in the passage cited above he took this as the basis for the explanation of differential rent, the excess profits being crystallised into rents. He deals here in fact merely with the reduction of prices in the various spheres of production into prices of production, that is to say, with the market values in the different spheres of production and their relation to each other, and not with the way in which the market value is formed in each separate sphere— though unless these are formed no market values at all can exist.

The market values and therefore the market prices in each separate sphere—when the market price corresponds to the "natural price", that is, when it merely represents the value in money—would yield very different rates of profit, since capitals of equal size in different spheres—quite apart from differences arising from their different circulation processes— employ constant and variable capital in very unequal proportions, and therefore yield very unequal surplus values and hence very unequal profits. The levelling out of the various market values, so that the same rate of profit is produced in the various spheres of production and capitals of equal size yield equal average profits, is therefore only possible through the transformation of the market values into prices of production which differ from the actual values.[1] What competition within *the same* sphere of production effects is the determination of the value of the commodity in this sphere by the average labour time required in it, that is, the creation of the market value. What competition between the *different* spheres of production effects is the creation of the same general rate of profit in the various spheres, through the levelling out of the various market

---

[1] It is possible that *the rate of surplus value*, for example, due to working times of unequal length, is not equalised out in the various spheres of production. It is not necessary to investigate this, since the surplus values themselves are equalised out.

values into market prices which constitute the *prices of production*, and which differ from the actual market values. In this second case competition is not at all directed towards the assimilation of the prices of commodities to their values, but on the contrary, its effect is to reduce their values to prices of production different from these values, to nullify the differences between their values and their prices of production. It is only this latter effect which Ricardo considers in Chapter IV and, oddly enough, he regards it as the reduction of commodity prices—through competition—to their values, the reduction of the market price (a price which is different from value) to the natural price (the value expressed in money). This error arises however from the mistake he had already made in Chapter I, "On Value", of identifying prices of production with value. This mistake in turn arose from the fact that at a point when he was only as yet concerned in explaining value, and was therefore as yet only dealing with the *commodity*, he suddenly bursts in with the *general rate of profit* and all the conditions which arise from the higher development of capitalist productive relations.

The line of thought which Ricardo pursues in Chapter IV is also quite superficial. He starts out with the "accidental and temporary deviations of price" (p. 48) of the commodity which are due to the fluctuating relations between demand and supply. "With the rise or fall of price, profits are elevated above, or depressed below, their general level; and capital is either encouraged to enter into, or is warned to depart from, the particular employment in which the variation has taken place" (p. 48). Here the "general level of profits" as between the various spheres of production, the "particular employments", is already assumed. But what should first have been considered was how the average level of prices in the same employment, and the average level of profits between the different employments, was brought about. Ricardo would then have seen that this latter operation presupposes criss-crossing movements of capital—or, in other words, a distribution, determined by competition, of the total social capital among its various spheres of production. Once it is assumed that in the various spheres of production the market values or average market prices are reduced into prices of production which yield the same average rate of profit,[1] a more constant deviation of market price from production price, a rise above it or a fall below it in particular spheres will cause new migrations of capital and a new distribution of the social capital. The first migration occurs in order to establish prices of production that are different from the values. The second in order to equalise the actual market prices with the prices of production, when they rise above or fall below them. The first is a transformation of values into prices of production. The second is the rotation of the actual market prices of the moment in the various spheres, about the price of production, which now appears as the "natural price" although it is different from the value and is only the result of social activity. It is precisely this latter and more superficial movement which Ricardo considers, and which he sometimes unconsciously confuses with the other. It is of course the same principle which brings about both movements, namely the principle that while

"every man is free to employ his capital where he pleases, he will naturally seek for it that employment which is most advantageous; he will naturally be dissatisfied with a profit of 10 per cent., if by removing his capital he can obtain a profit of 15 per cent. This restless desire on the part of all the employers of stock to quit a less profitable for a more advantageous business has a strong tendency to equalise the rate of profits of all, or to fix them in such proportions as may, in the estimation of the parties, compensate for any advantage which one may have, or may appear to have, over the other" (p. 48).

This tendency has the effect of distributing the total quantity of social labour time among the various spheres of production in accordance with the needs of society. In this way the values in the different spheres of production are transformed into prices of production, while also, on the other hand, the variations of actual prices in the different spheres of production from the prices of production are levelled out.

[1] This is, however, only the case in those spheres where landed property does not intervene.

All this had already been explained by Adam Smith. Ricardo himself says:

"No writer has more satisfactorily and ably shown than Dr. Smith the tendency of capital to move from employments in which the goods produced do not repay by their price the whole expenses, including the ordinary profits,[1] of producing and bringing them to market" (Ch. XXI, p. 194, footnote).

The service rendered by Ricardo—whose mistake on the whole arose from the fact that he was not here more critical of Adam Smith—consists in his more detailed account of this migration of capital from one sphere to the other, or rather of the way in which this operation takes place. He was only able to do this, however, because in his day the credit system was more highly developed than in the time of Adam Smith. Ricardo says:

"It is perhaps very difficult to trace the steps by which this change is effected: it is probably effected by a manufacturer not absolutely changing his employment, but only lessening the quantity of capital that he has in that employment. In all rich countries there is a number of men forming what is called the moneyed class; these men are engaged in no trade, but live on the interest of their money, which is employed in discounting bills, or in loans to the more industrious part of the community. The bankers too employ a large capital on the same objects. The capital so employed forms a circulating capital of a large amount, and is employed, in larger or smaller proportions, by all the different trades of a country. There is perhaps no manufacturer, however rich, who limits his business to the extent that his own funds alone will allow: he has always some portion of this floating capital, increasing or diminishing according to the activity of the demand for his commodities. When the demand for silks increases, and that for cloth diminishes, the clothier does not remove with his capital to the silk trade, but he dismisses some of his workmen, he discontinues his demand for the loan from bankers and moneyed men; while the case of the silk manufacturer is the reverse: he wishes to employ more workmen, and thus his motive for

1 That is to say, the price of production.

borrowing is increased; he borrows more, and thus capital is transferred from one employment to another without the necessity of a manufacturer discontinuing his usual occupation. When we look to the markets of a large town, and observe how regularly they are supplied both with home and foreign commodities, in the quantity in which they are required, under all the circumstances of varying demand, arising from the caprice of taste, or a change in the amount of population, without often producing either the effects of a glut from a too abundant supply, or an enormously high price from the supply being unequal to the demand, we must confess that the principle which apportions capital to each trade in the precise amount that it is required is more active than is generally supposed" (pp. 48–9).

It is therefore *credit* through which the capital of the whole capitalist class is placed at the disposal of each sphere of production, not in proportion to the capital possessed by the capitalists of this sphere, but in proportion to its productive needs—whereas in competition the individual capitals seem to be independent of each other. This is as much the consequence as the condition of capitalist production; and it makes a convenient transition for us from *competition between capitals* to *capital as credit*.

In opening Chapter IV, Ricardo says that by natural price he understands the value of the commodity, that is, its price determined by the comparative labour time in it; and by market price, the accidental and temporary deviations from this natural price or value. Throughout the whole of the rest of the chapter—and he even says so in so many words—he takes natural price as meaning something quite different, namely the price of production which is different from the value. Instead therefore of showing how competition transforms values into prices of production, thus continually bringing about deviations from values, what he shows, following Adam Smith, is how competition between the various trades reduces their market prices into prices of production.

This is how Chapter IV opens:

"In making labour the foundation of the value of commodities, and the comparative quantity of labour which is necessary to their production, the rule which determines the respective quantities of goods which shall be given in exchange for each other, we must not be supposed to deny the accidental and temporary deviations of the actual or market price of commodities from this, their primary and natural price" (p. 48).

Here therefore "natural price" is equivalent to value, and market price is nothing but the deviation of the actual price from the value.

On the other hand he later says:

"Let us suppose that all commodities are at their natural price, and consequently that the profits of capital in all employments are exactly at the same rate, or differ only so much as, in the estimation of the parties, is equivalent to any real or fancied advantage which they possess or forego" (p. 50).

Here therefore *natural price is equivalent to price of production*, that is, the price at which the relation between the profit and the outlays of capital embodied in the commodity is the same, although equal values of commodities supplied by capitals in different branches of production contain very unequal surplus values and therefore unequal profits. If the price is to yield the same profit it must therefore be different from the value of the commodity. On the other hand, capitals of equal size produce commodities of very unequal magnitudes of value, according to whether a larger or smaller portion of the fixed capital enters into the commodity. But on this point we shall have more to say in dealing with the circulation of capitals.

By equalisation through competition Ricardo therefore also understands only the rotation of the actual prices or actual market prices about the price of production—or the natural price in distinction from the value—the levelling out of market prices in different trades to general prices of production, that is, precisely to prices which differ from the real values in the various trades.

"It is then the desire, which every capitalist has, of diverting his funds from a less to a more profitable employment that prevents the market price of commodities from continuing for any length of time either much above or much below their natural price. It is this competition which so adjusts the exchangeable value of commodities that, after paying the wages for the labour necessary to their production, and all other expenses required to put the capital employed in its original state of efficiency, the remaining value or overplus will in each trade be in proportion to the value of the capital employed" (p. 50).

That is absolutely right. Competition levels out prices in the various branches of production in such a way that the remaining value or overplus, the profit, corresponds to the value of the capital employed but not to the real value of the commodity, not to the real overplus of value which it contains after deduction of its costs. In order to bring about this equalisation the price of one commodity must be brought above and that of the other below its real value. It is not the value of the commodities but their price of production about which competition causes the market prices in the various branches of production to rotate.

Ricardo continues: "In the seventh chapter of the *Wealth of Nations*, all that concerns this question is most ably treated" (p. 50). Absolutely right. It is his uncritical faith in the Smithian tradition which here puts Ricardo on the wrong path. Ricardo concludes the chapter by saying that in his subsequent investigation, "we will leave entirely out of our consideration" the accidental deviations of market prices from prices of production; but he overlooks the fact that he has paid no heed at all to the constant deviations of market prices, in so far as these correspond to prices of production, from the real values of commodities, and that he has substituted price of production for value.

Chapter XXX deals with "The Influence of Demand and Supply on Prices". What Ricardo is here defending is the principle that the permanent price is determined by the price of production, not by demand and supply; that therefore the permanent price is determined by the value of the commodities only in so far as this value determines the price of production. If we assume that the prices of the commodities are so levelled out that they all yield 10 per cent. profit, every lasting variation in these prices will be determined by a variation in their values, in the labour time necessary for their

production. As this value continues to determine the general
rate of profit, the changes in it continue to determine the
variations in the prices of production, although naturally the
difference between these prices of production and the values
is not thereby removed. What is effected is only that the
difference between value and actual price shall not be greater
than the difference between prices of production and values
which is brought about by the general rate of profit. With the
changes in the values of commodities their prices of production
also change. A "new natural price" (p. 260) is formed. If, for
example, the workman can produce twenty hats in the same
time in which he previously produced ten hats, and if wages
formed half the cost of a hat, then the costs of production of
the twenty hats, in so far as they consist of wages, have fallen
by half. For the same wages are now paid for the production
of twenty hats as previously for ten. In each hat therefore only
half the outlay in wages is now contained. If the hatter sold
the hat for the same price, he would sell it above the price
of production. If the profit had been 10 per cent., it would
now be $46\frac{2}{3}$ per cent., if we assume that the outlay required
for making a certain quantity of hats was originally 50 for
raw materials, etc., and 50 for labour. It would now be 50 for
raw materials, etc., and 25 for wages. If the commodity is
sold at the old price, the profit is now equal to $46\frac{2}{3}$ per cent.
As a result of the fall in value therefore the new natural price
will fall to such an extent that the price will yield only 10 per
cent. profit. The fall in value or in the labour time necessary
for the production of the commodity reveals itself in the fact
that less labour time is used for the same number of commodities, therefore also less paid labour time, less wages, and that
consequently the costs of production decline, and the wages
paid decline (that is, the amount of wages; this does not assume
any reduction in the rate of wages) proportionately for the
production of each individual commodity. This holds good
when the change in value has taken place in hat making itself.
If it had occurred in the production of the raw material or of
the tools, this would have been similarly expressed in a
reduction in the wages outlay required for the production of
a given quantity of products in this sphere; but for the

hat-manufacturer it would mean that his constant capital would have cost him less. The prices of production or "natural prices"—which have nothing whatever to do with "nature"—can fall (or rise) in two ways as a result of a fall or rise in the values of the commodities.

Firstly, because the wages expended on the production of a given number of commodities fall (or rise), owing to the aggregate absolute amount of labour, both paid and unpaid, expended on this number of commodities having fallen (or risen).

Secondly, if the ratio of the surplus value to the value of the commodity, that is, to the value of the labour contained in it, changes—and therefore the rate of profit rises or falls—as a result of the increased or reduced productivity of labour (both can happen, the one when the variable capital falls in proportion to the constant, the other when wages rise as a result of the means of subsistence becoming dearer).

In this second case, the prices of production would vary only to the extent that they are affected by changes in the value of labour. In the first case, the value of labour remains the same. But in the second case it is not the value of the commodities which change, but only the division between [necessary] labour and surplus labour. However, in this case there would still be a change in productivity and therefore in the value of the individual commodity. The same capital will in the one case produce more, in the other fewer commodities than before. The aggregate of commodities in which it was materialised would have the same value, but the individual commodity would have a different value. It is true that the value of the wages does not determine the value of the commodities, but the value of the commodities which enter into the workers' consumption determines the value of the wages.

Once prices of production of commodities in the various spheres of production are established, these rise or fall in relation to each other with changes in the value of the commodities. If the productivity of labour rises, the labour time necessary for the production of a particular commodity is reduced, and its value therefore falls; irrespective of whether this change in productivity takes place in the labour employed in the final stage or in the constant capital, the price of production of this commodity must also fall to a corresponding extent. The absolute quantity of labour expended on it has been reduced, and therefore also the quantity of paid labour contained in it, and the amount of wages expended on it, even if the rate of wages has remained the same. If the commodity were sold at its former price of production, it would yield a profit higher than the general rate of profit, for previously this profit was equal to 10 per cent. on the higher outlay. The same price would therefore now yield more than 10 per cent. on the reduced outlay. The reverse takes place when the productivity of labour declines and the real values of the commodities rise. If the rate of profit is given, or, which is the same thing, the prices of production are given, a relative rise or fall is dependent on the rise or fall, the variation, in the real values of the commodities. As a result of this variation, new prices of production, or, as Ricardo says, following Adam Smith, "new natural prices", arise in place of the old.

In Chapter XXX, which we have just been quoting, Ricardo identifies, even in so many words, natural price, that is, price of production, with natural value, that is, value determined by labour time.

"Their price [i.e., the price of monopolised commodities] has no necessary connection with their natural value; but the prices of commodities which are subject to competition . . . will ultimately depend . . . on the . . . cost of their production" (p. 262).

In this case also prices of production or natural prices are directly identified with "*natural value*", that is to say, with "*value*". Ricardo knows no other distinction between *value* and *natural price* than that the latter is the monetary expression of value and can therefore be altered by a change in the value of the precious metals without the value itself changing. This alteration however only affects the estimation or expression of the value in money.

He says, for example, the following:

"It [i.e., foreign trade] can only be regulated by altering the natural price, not the natural value, at which commodities can be produced in those countries, and that is effected by altering the distribution of the precious metals" (p. 230).

This confusion explains how it is that a host of later fellows *post Ricardum*, like Say himself, were able to accept "the costs of production" as the ultimate regulator of prices, and had not the slightest inkling of the determination of value by labour time; indeed they directly deny the latter, while accepting the validity of the former.

This whole mistake of Ricardo's and the consequent erroneous conception of rent, etc., as well as the wrong laws governing the rate of profit, etc., arise from the fact that he does not distinguish surplus value from profit; just as, like the other economists, he is crude and lacking in understanding in his handling of determinate forms in general. The following section will show how he allows himself to be ensnared by the views of Adam Smith.

(ii) *Adam Smith's Views*

It must first be noted that in Adam Smith's view "there are always a few commodities of which the price resolves itself into two parts only, the wages of labour and the profits of stock" (*The Wealth of Nations*, Book I, Chapter VI). This difference from Ricardo's standpoint can here be left out of account.

Adam Smith first shows that exchange value resolves itself into quantity of labour; and that after deducting the raw materials, etc., the value contained in exchange value falls into that part of the labour which is paid to the labourer, and that part which is not paid to him—which latter part is resolved into profit and rent, the profit perhaps in turn into profit and interest. Having shown this, he then cheerfully turns right round, and instead of resolving exchange value into wages, profit and rent, he makes these on the contrary into the creators of exchange value; he makes them, as independent exchange values, form the exchange value of the product, and compounds the exchange value of the commodity out of the independent and separately determined values of the wages, the profit and the rent. Instead of having their source in value, they become the source of value. "Wages, profit and rent are the three original sources of all revenue as well as of all exchangeable value" (Book I, Chapter VI).

After he has proclaimed their intrinsic connections, he suddenly again becomes obsessed with their phenomenal form, with the connections between things as they appear in competition—and in competition everything always appears in inverted form, always standing on its head.

These two conceptions are naïvely intertwined in Adam Smith's work, without his becoming aware of the contradiction. Ricardo on the other hand consciously abstracts from the form of competition, from the phenomena of competition, in order to understand *the laws as such*. On the one hand he can be reproached for not having gone far enough, for not being complete enough in his abstraction, and on the other hand, for conceiving the phenomenal form immediately, directly, as an evidence or illustration of the general laws, without in any way *explaining* it. As far as the first point is concerned, his abstraction is too incomplete; and as to the second, the abstraction is a formal one, and is in itself false.

Now it is from the inverted starting point [of competition] that Adam Smith develops the distinction between "the natural prices of commodities" and their "market-price". Ricardo accepts this from him, but forgets that Adam Smith's "natural price" is, according to his premises, nothing but the price of production resulting from competition, and that for Adam Smith himself, this price of production is only identical with the "value" of the commodity in so far as he forgets his more profound standpoint and remains rooted in the false view derived from surface phenomena—that the exchange value of commodities is formed by adding together the independently determined values of wages, profit and rent. While Ricardo altogether contests this view, he accepts Adam Smith's confusion or identification of exchange value with price of production or natural price, which is based on it. In the case of Adam Smith this confusion is justifiable, because his whole examination of natural price starts out from his second, false conception of value. But in Ricardo's case it is wholly unjustifiable, since he nowhere accepts this false theory of Adam Smith's, but contests it *ex professo* as an inconsistency. However, Adam Smith succeeded in catching him again with his "natural price".

After compounding the value of a commodity out of the separate and independently determined values of wages, profit and rent—Adam Smith then asks himself how these primary values are determined. And here he takes as his starting point the phenomena which come to the surface in competition.

Chapter VII of Book I of *The Wealth of Nations* treats "of the Natural and Market Price of Commodities". It says:

"There is in every society or neighbourhood an ordinary or average rate" of wages, profit and rent. "These ordinary or average rates may be called the natural rates of wages, profit, and rent, at the time and place in which they commonly prevail." "When the price of any commodity is neither more nor less than what is sufficient to pay the rent . . . the wages . . . and the profits . . . the commodity is then sold for what may be called its natural price" (p. 48).

This natural price is then the price of production of the commodity, and the price of production coincides with the value of the commodity, since indeed it is presupposed that the value of the latter is compounded of the values of wages, profit and rent.

"The commodity is then sold precisely for what it is worth,[1] or for what it really costs the person who brings it to market;[2] for though in common language what is called the prime cost of any commodity does not comprehend the profit of the person who is to sell it again, yet if he sell it at a price which does not allow him the ordinary rate of profit in his neighbourhood, he is evidently a loser by the trade; since by employing his stock in some other way he might have made that profit" (p. 49).

Here we have the whole story of how natural price arises, and moreover set out in fully appropriate language and logic, since the value of the commodity is built up of the prices of wages, profit and rent; while what in turn constitutes the true value of the latter is in turn their natural rates; thus it is clear that the value of the commodity is identical with its price of production, and the latter with the natural price of the commodity. The rate of profit, as also that of wages, is assumed

---

[1] The commodity is then sold at its value.

[2] At its value, *or* at its price of production.

as given. That fits in with the formation of the price of production—the latter presupposes them. To the individual capitalist also they appear as given. He is not concerned with how, where and when they arise. Adam Smith here adopts the standpoint of the individual capitalist, of the agent of capitalist production, who is deciding the price of production of his commodity—so much for wages, etc., so much for the general rate of profit. *Ergo*. This is how this capitalist sees the operation by which the price of production of the commodity is fixed, or, as it further seems to him, the value of the commodity, its absolute price as distinct from its price fluctuations; in a word, its value—in so far as he has any time to reflect on such matters at all. And because Adam Smith puts himself right in the centre of competition, he at once starts reasoning and arguing with the peculiar logic of the capitalist held captive in this sphere. He interjects: In common language costs do not include the profit which the seller makes, and which necessarily constitutes a surplus over his outlays. Why then do you include profit in the price of production? Adam Smith, like the thoughtful capitalist to whom this question is put, answers in this way:

Why do I include profit in costs? If I sold my commodity at a price which would yield me less than the average profit which the other capitalists in this neighbourhood make, I should be cheated. If I had invested my capital in another trade, I should make the average profit. Thus, in answer to the question, why profit should ever be included in production costs, he replies, "Because I should be cheated if profit at a certain rate did not enter into costs". That is the correct answer from the standpoint of the man who is a mere mouthpiece of competition.

Profit must in general enter into the price of production, because I should be cheated if a profit of only 9 per cent. instead of 10 per cent. were to enter into the price of production. The naïve way in which Adam Smith on the one hand expresses the sentiments of the agent of capitalist production, presenting things just as they appear to and are thought of by the latter, and as they influence him in practice, in fact just as on the surface they seem to happen; while on the other

hand in some passages he reveals their more profound relation-
ships, gives his book its great charm.

We also see here why Adam Smith—in spite of grave inward
qualms on the point—resolves the entire value of the commodity into rent, profit and wages, and leaves out the constant
capital, although of course he admits its existence for each
individual capitalist. For otherwise he would have to say:
The value of a commodity consists of wages, profit and rent,
and that part of the value of the commodity which does not
consist of wages, profit and rent. And so it would be necessary
to determine value independently of wages, profit and rent.

In other respects, however, Adam Smith, having taken his
stand within competition, and having assumed the rate of
profit, etc., as given, correctly expounds the natural price or
price of production; that is to say, the price of production as
distinct from the market price: ". . . the natural price of the
commodity, or the whole value of the rent, labour and profit,
which must be paid in order to bring it" to market.

This price of production of the commodity is different from
its actual or market price. The latter depends on demand and
supply.

The cost of production or the price of production of the
commodity is precisely "the whole value of the rent, labour
and profit, which must be paid in order to bring it" to market.
If demand corresponds with supply, then the market price is
equal to the natural price.

"When the quantity brought to market is just sufficient
to supply the effectual demand, and no more, the market
price naturally comes to be either exactly, or as nearly as
can be judged of, the same with the natural price. . . . The
natural price, therefore, is, as it were, the central price, to
which the prices of all commodities are continually gravitat-
ing. Different accidents may sometimes keep them suspended
a good deal above it, and sometimes force them down even
somewhat below it" (Book I, Chapter VII, p. 50-1).

Adam Smith therefore concludes that in general "The whole
quantity of industry annually employed in order to bring
any commodity to market" will correspond to the needs of
society or the "effectual demand". What Ricardo conceives as

the distribution of the total capital among the various trades here appears in the more naïve form of the "quantity of industry" which is necessary in order to produce "a particular commodity". The levelling out of prices among the sellers of the same commodity to the market price, and the levelling out of the market prices of the various commodities to the price of production, are here still confusedly intertwined.

At this point, Adam Smith, though only quite incidentally, comes to the influence of variations in the real values of commodities on the natural prices or prices of production.

"But in some employments the same quantity of industry will in different years produce very different quantities of commodities; while in others it will produce always the same, or very nearly the same. The same number of labourers in husbandry will, in different years, produce very different quantities of corn, wine, oil, hops, etc. But the same number of spinners and weavers will every year produce the same or very nearly the same quantity of linen and woollen cloth. . . . In the other [non-agricultural] species of industry, the produce of equal quantities of labour being always the same, or very nearly the same,[1] it can be more exactly suited to the effectual demand" (Book I, Chapter VII, pp. 51–2).

In this passage Adam Smith sees that by itself a change in the productivity of equal quantities of labour—therefore in the actual values of commodities—alters the price of production. But then he vulgarises it again by reducing it to the relation between demand and supply. By his own arguments the theory as he presents it is wrong. For though in agriculture, as a result of good or bad seasons, etc., equal quantities of labour yield different quantities of products, he has nevertheless himself shown that as a result of machinery, division of labour, etc., equal quantities of labour can yield very different quantities of product in industry, etc. *This* therefore is not the difference which distinguishes agriculture from the other groups of industry. The distinction is that in the case of the latter the productive power is applied to an extent that is calculated beforehand, while in the other case it depends on

[1] That is to say, so long as the conditions of production remain the same.

accidents of nature. The result however remains the same: the value of the commodities or the quantity of labour which, according to its productivity, has to be expended on a particular commodity, influences its price of production.

In the following passage Adam Smith has shown, too, how the migration of capitals from one branch of production to another brings into being the price of production in the various branches of production. His statement on this point, however, is not as clear as Ricardo's. For if the price of the commodity falls below its natural price, this, according to his argument, is because one of the elements in this price has fallen below the natural rate. It is not therefore due to the withdrawal of capitals alone, or to the migration of capitals, but because labour, capital and land move from one branch to another. In this respect his view is more logical than Ricardo's. But it is wrong.

"Whatever part of it [the natural price] was paid below the natural rate, the persons whose interest it affected would immediately feel the loss, and would immediately withdraw either so much land, or so much labour, or so much stock, from being employed about it, that the quantity brought to market would soon be no more than sufficient to supply the effectual demand. Its market price, therefore, would soon rise to the natural price. This at least would be the case where there was perfect liberty" (Book I, Chapter VII, p. 55).

Here there is an essential difference between Smith's conception of the levelling out to the natural price and Ricardo's. Smith's view is based on his false assumption that the three elements independently determine the value of the commodity, while Ricardo's rests on the correct assumption that it is the average rate of profit (at a given level of wages) which alone determines the prices of production.

"The natural price itself varies with the natural rate of each of its component parts, of wages, profit and rent" (Book I, Chapter VII, p. 56).

In Chapters VIII, IX, X and XI of Book I, Adam Smith then seeks to determine the natural rate of these component parts, wages, rent and profit, and the fluctuations in these rates. Chapter VIII deals with *wages*.

At the start of the chapter on wages, Adam Smith—forsaking the superficial standpoint of competition—shows first the true nature of surplus value, and profit and rent as mere forms of surplus value.

In his treatment of wages his starting point for determining the natural rate is the value of the labour power itself, the necessary wage.

"A man must always live by his work, and his wages must at least be sufficient to maintain him. They must even upon most occasions be somewhat more; otherwise it would be impossible for him to bring up a family, and the race of such workmen could not last beyond the first generation" (Book I, Chapter VIII, p. 60).

This in turn has no meaning, because Adam Smith never asks himself how the value of the necessary means of subsistence, that is, of the commodity, is in any case determined. And here, since he has moved away from his main conception, he would have to say: The price of wages is determined by the price of the means of subsistence, and the price of the means of subsistence is determined by the price of wages. Once it has been assumed that the value of wages is fixed, he then gives an exact account of its fluctuations as they appear in competition and of the circumstances which give rise to these fluctuations. This belongs to the exoteric part of his work, and does not concern us here.[1]

He is trying to derive the value of the commodity from the value of labour as one of its constituent parts. And on the other hand, he says in discussing the level of wages that "the wages of labour do not . . . fluctuate with the price of provisions", and that "the wages of labour vary more from

[1] In fact, he deals with the effect of accumulation on wages. But he does not tell us what it is that determines this accumulation; for it may be rapid, either when the rate of wages is relatively low and the productivity of labour high, and in this case a rise in wages is always only the result of a permanently low level previously; or when the rate of profit is low, but the productivity of labour high. From his standpoint he would have to deduce the rate of accumulation in the first case from the rate of profit, that is, from the rate of wages; in the second case from the amount of profit—which however would in turn necessitate his investigating the value of the commodity.

place to place than the price of provisions" (Book I, Chapter VIII, p. 66). In fact the chapter contains nothing relevant to the question apart from the definition of the minimum of wages, *alias* the value of labour power. Here Adam Smith instinctively comes back again to his more profound approach, and then in turn abandons it, so that even the definition cited above has no significance. For how does he propose to determine the value of the necessary means of subsistence—and therefore of the commodity in general? As to a part of it, by the natural price of labour. And how is this determined? By the value of the means of subsistence or of commodities in general. A wretched merry-go-round. As to the rest, the chapter contains not a word on the issue, on the natural price of labour, but only discussions on rises of wages above the level of the natural rate of labour—showing that these rises occur in the measure that the accumulation of capital is rapid, that there is a progressive accumulation of capital. Then come enquiries into the various conditions of society in which this takes place; and finally he gives a slap in the face to the determination of the value of the commodity by wages—and of wages by the value of the necessary means of subsistence—by showing that in England this does not seem to be the case. In between comes a piece of the Malthusian population theory, based on the fact that wages are determined by the quantity of means of subsistence required for the worker not only to live, but to reproduce the population.

In fact, after trying to prove that wages rose during the eighteenth century, especially in England, Adam Smith poses the question whether this is "to be regarded as an advantage or as an inconveniency to the society". In this connection he then returns for a moment to his more profound standpoint that profit and rent are merely parts of the product of the labourer. The workmen, he says,

"make up the far greater part of every great political society. But what improves the circumstances of the greater part can never be regarded as an inconveniency to the whole. No society can surely be flourishing and happy, of which the far greater part of the members are poor and miserable. It is but equity, besides, that they who feed, clothe, and lodge the whole body of the people, should have such a share of the produce of their own labour as to be themselves tolerably well fed, clothed, and lodged" (Book I, Chapter VIII, p. 70).

In this connection he touches on the theory of population:

"Poverty, though it no doubt discourages, does not always prevent marriage. It seems even to be favourable to generation. . . . Barrenness, so frequent among women of fashion, is very rare among those of inferior station. . . . But poverty, though it does not prevent the generation, is extremely unfavourable to the rearing of children. The tender plant is produced, but in so cold a soil and so severe a climate, soon withers and dies. . . . Every species of animals naturally multiplies in proportion to the means of their subsistence, and no species can ever multiply beyond it. But in civilised society it is only among the inferior ranks of people that the scantiness of subsistence can set limits to the further multiplication of the human species . . . the demand for men, like that for any other commodity, necessarily regulates the production of men; quickens it when it goes on too slowly, and stops it when it advances too fast" (Book I, Chapter VIII, pp. 70–1).

The connection between the wages minimum and the changing conditions of society is as follows:

"The wages paid to journeymen and servants of every kind must be such as may enable them, one with another, to continue the race of journeymen and servants, according as the increasing, diminishing, or stationary demand of the society may happen to require" (p. 72).

"Of the society"—that is to say, of capital!

He then shows that the slave is "dearer" than the free labourer, because the latter himself looks after his wear and tear, while that of the former is managed "by a negligent master or careless overseer". The "fund" for making good the wear and tear is frugally used by the free labourer, while it is prodigally expended, managed in a disorderly way, for the slave.

"The fund destined for replacing or repairing, if I may say so, the wear and tear of the slave, is commonly managed by a negligent master or careless overseer. That destined for performing the same office with regard to the free man, is managed by the free man himself. The disorders which generally prevail in the economy of the rich, naturally introduce themselves into the management of the former: the strict frugality and parsimonious attention of the poor as naturally establish themselves in that of the latter" (Book I, Chapter VIII, p. 72).

It is a characteristic in the determination of the minimum wage or natural price of labour that this price is lower for free wage labourers than for slaves. Here is how Adam Smith puts this point:

". . . the work done by freemen comes cheaper in the end than that performed by slaves. . . . The liberal reward of labour, therefore, as it is the effect of increasing wealth, so it is the cause of increasing population. To complain of it is to lament over the necessary effect and cause of the greatest public prosperity" (p. 72).

He continues his plea for high wages:

"The liberal reward of labour, as it encourages the propagation, so it increases the industry of the common people. The wages of labour are the encouragement of industry, which, like every other human quality, improves in proportion to the encouragement it receives. A plentiful subsistence increases the bodily strength of the labourer, and the comfortable hope of bettering his condition . . . animates him to exert that strength to the utmost. Where wages are high, accordingly, we shall always find the workmen more active, diligent, and expeditious than where they are low" (pp. 72-3).

But higher wages also spur the workmen on to over-exertion and the premature destruction of their labour power:

"Workmen, . . . when they are liberally paid by the piece, are very apt to over-work themselves, and to ruin their health and constitution in a few years. . . . If masters would always listen to the dictates of reason and humanity, they have frequently occasion rather to moderate than to animate the application of many of their workmen" (pp. 73-4).

Further, he argues against the view that "a little more plenty than ordinary may render some workmen idle".

He then investigates whether it is true that workmen are more idle in years of plenty than in years of dearth, and what is the general relation between wages and the price of the means of subsistence. Here again comes the inconsistency:

"The money price of labour is necessarily regulated by two circumstances; the demand for labour, and the price of the necessaries and conveniences of life . . . the money price of labour is determined by what is requisite for purchasing this quantity" (of the necessaries and conveniences of life) (pp. 76–7).

He then examines why—because of the demand for labour—wages can rise in years of plenty and fall in those of scarcity, and shows that the causes of the rise and fall in good and bad years counterbalance one another.

"The scarcity of a dear year, by diminishing the demand for labour, tends to lower its price, as the high price of provisions tends to raise it. The plenty of a cheap year, on the contrary, by increasing the demand, tends to raise the price of labour, as the cheapness of provisions tends to lower it. In the ordinary variations of the price of provisions those two opposite causes seem to counterbalance one another, which is probably in part the reason why the wages of labour are everywhere so much more steady and permanent than the price of provisions" (p. 77).

Finally, after all this beating about the bush, he again puts forward, as against the idea of wages as a source of the value of commodities, his original and more profound theory that the value of commodities is determined by the quantity of labour they contain.

If in good years, or with the growth of capital, the worker obtains more commodities, then also he produces far more commodities; in other words, the individual commodity would contain a less quantity of labour. He can therefore receive a greater quantity of commodities but with less value in them, and so—this is the implied conclusion—profit can increase in spite of a rising absolute wage.

"The increase in the wages of labour necessarily increases the price of many commodities, by increasing that part of it which resolves itself into wages, and so far tends to diminish their consumption both at home and abroad. The same cause, however, which raises the wages of labour, the increase of stock, tends to increase its productive powers, and to make a smaller quantity of labour produce a greater quantity of work." This takes place through the division of labour, the use of machinery, inventions and so on. "There are many commodities, therefore, which, in consequence of these improvements, come to be produced by so much less labour than before that the increase of its price is more than compensated by the diminution of its quantity" (pp. 77-8).

The labour is better paid, but less labour is contained in the individual commodity, so there is less to be paid for each. Thus he makes his false theory, according to which the wage determines the value of the commodity as a constituent element of its value, be negated or rather paralysed, counterbalanced, by his correct theory, which sees the value of the commodity as determined by the quantity of labour it contains.

Chapter IX deals with *profit on capital* ("Of the Profits of Stock"). Here therefore the natural rate of the second element that determines and composes the natural price *or* value of commodities is to be investigated. We shall consider later what Adam Smith says about the cause of the falling rate of profit.

Here Adam Smith finds himself in great difficulties. He says that even the determination of average wages amounts only to determining "the most usual wages", the wages actually paid. "But even this can seldom be done with regard to the profits of stock". Apart from good or bad fortune, the profit "is affected by every variation of price in the commodities"— although it is precisely through the natural rate of profit, as one of the component parts of "value", that we are supposed to determine the natural price of these commodities. It is difficult for an individual capitalist to tell what is this natural rate of profit even in a particular trade. "To ascertain what is the average profit of all the different trades carried on in a great kingdom must be much more difficult". But some notion of "the average profits of stock" may be formed from "the interest of money".

> "It may be laid down as a maxim, that wherever a great deal can be made by the use of money, a great deal will commonly be given for the use of it; and that wherever little can be made by it, less will commonly be given for it" (Book I, Chapter IX, p. 79).

Adam Smith does not say that the rate of interest determines the rate of profit. He expressly states the opposite. But records exist of the rate of interest at different epochs; there are no such records for the rate of profit. The rates of interest are therefore symptoms by which the approximate level of the rate of profit can be judged. The task set, however, was not to compare the level of various actual rates of profit, but to determine the natural level of the rate of profit. Adam Smith takes refuge in a subsidiary investigation into the rate of interest at various periods, which has nothing to do with the problem which he set himself. He considers various periods in England, then compares this with Scotland, France and Holland, and finds that "High wages of labour and high profits of stock . . . are things, perhaps, which scarce ever go together, except in the peculiar circumstances of new colonies" (p. 82).

At this point Adam Smith tries—like Ricardo, but to a certain extent with more success—to give some approximate explanation of high profits:

> "A new colony must always for some time be more under-stocked in proportion to the extent of its territory, and more under-peopled in proportion to the extent of its stock, than the greater part of other countries. They have more land than they have stock to cultivate. What they have, therefore, is applied to the cultivation only of what is most fertile and most favourably situated, the land near the sea shore, and along the banks of navigable rivers. Such land, too, is frequently purchased at a price below the value even of its natural produce.[1] Stock employed in the purchase and

---

[1] In reality, therefore, it costs nothing.

improvement of such lands must yield a very large profit, and consequently afford to pay a very large interest. Its rapid accumulation in so profitable an employment enables the planter to increase the number of his hands faster than he can find them in a new settlement. Those whom he can find, therefore, are very liberally rewarded. As the colony increases, the profits of stock gradually diminish. When the most fertile and best situated lands have been all occupied, less profit can be made by the cultivation of what is inferior both in soil and situation, and less interest can be afforded for the stock which is so employed. In the greater part of our colonies, accordingly, the . . . rate of interest has been considerably reduced during the course of the present century" (pp. 82–3).

This is one of the foundations of Ricardo's explanation of why profits fall, though the way it is presented is different. On the whole Adam Smith here explains everything on the basis of competition between capitals; when they increase, profits fall, and when they decrease, profits rise, as a consequence of which then wages also in turn rise or fall.

"The diminution of the capital stock of the society, or of the funds destined for the maintenance of industry, however, as it lowers the wages of labour, so it raises the profits of stock, and consequently the interest of money. By the wages of labour being lowered, the owners of what stock remains in the society can bring their goods at less expense to market than before, and less stock being employed in supplying the market than before, they can sell them dearer" (p. 84).

Adam Smith then speaks of the highest possible and the lowest possible rates of profit.

"The lowest ordinary rate of profit must always be something more than what is sufficient to compensate the occasional losses to which every employment of stock is exposed. It is this surplus only which is neat or clear profit. . . . The highest ordinary rate of profit may be such as, in the price of the greater part of commodities, eats up the whole of what should go to the rent of the land, and leaves only what is sufficient to pay the labour of preparing and bringing them to market, according to the lowest rate at which labour can anywhere be paid, the bare subsistence of the labourer" (p. 86).

Adam Smith himself characterises what he says about the natural rate of profit:

"Double interest is in Great Britain reckoned what the merchants call a good, moderate, reasonable profit; terms which I apprehend mean no more than a common and usual profit" (p. 87).

And in fact Adam Smith calls this "common profit" neither moderate nor good, but actually names it "the natural rate of profit"—thereby telling us flatly nothing of what it is or how it is determined; although it is through this "natural rate of profit" that we are supposed to determine the "natural price" of commodities.

"In countries which are fast advancing to riches, the low rate of profit may, in the price of many commodities, compensate the high wages of labour, and enable those countries to sell as cheap as their less thriving neighbours, among whom the wages of labour may be lower" (p. 87).

Here low profits and high wages are not cause and effect, but the same cause—the rapid increase or accumulation of capital—produces both. Both enter into, *constitute*, the price. Consequently if one is high while the other is low, the price remains the same, and so on.

Here Adam Smith conceives profit purely as an addition to price, for he continues:

"In reality high profits tend much more to raise the price of work than high wages. If in the linen manufacture, for example, the wages of the different working people . . . should, all of them, be advanced twopence a day; it would be necessary to heighten the price of a piece of linen only by a number of twopences equal to the number of people that had been employed about it, multiplied by the number of days during which they had been so employed. That part of the price of the commodity which resolved itself into wages would, through all the different stages of the manufacture, rise only in arithmetical proportion to this rise of wages. But if the profits of all the different employers of those working people should be raised 5 per cent., that part of the price of the commodity which resolved itself into profit would, through all the different stages of the manufacture, rise in geometrical proportion to this rise of profit. . . . In raising the price of commodities the rise of wages operates in the same manner as simple interest does in the accumulation of debt. The rise of profit operates like compound interest" (pp. 87-8).

At the end of this chapter Adam Smith also tells us the source from which he drew his whole theory that the price of commodities—or their value—is built up out of the values of wages and profits: namely, the *amis du commerce*, the practitioners and disciples of competition:

"Our merchants and master-manufacturers complain much of the bad effects of high wages in raising the price, and thereby lessening the sale of their goods both at home and abroad. They say nothing concerning the bad effects of high profits. They are silent with regard to the pernicious effects of their own gains. They complain only of those of other people" (p. 88).

In Chapter X Adam Smith examines "Wages and Profit in the different employments of Labour and Stock". It is concerned only with detail; it therefore belongs to the chapter which covers competition, and is very good in its way. It is completely exoteric.

In the course of it, he speaks of the uncertainty of success in the liberal professions, for example among lawyers:

"The lottery of the law . . . is very far from being a perfectly fair lottery; and that, as well as many other liberal and honourable professions, are, in point of pecuniary gain, evidently under-recompensed" (pp. 94-5).

Similarly he says of *soldiers*:

"Their pay is less than that of common labourers, and in actual service their fatigues are much greater" (p. 97).

And of sailors in the navy:

"Though their skill and dexterity are much superior to that of almost any artificers, and though their whole life is one continual scene of hardship and danger, . . . their wages are not greater than those of common labourers at the port which regulates the rate of seamen's wages" (p. 98).

He observes ironically:

"It would be indecent, no doubt, to compare either a curate or a chaplain with a journeyman in any common trade. The pay of a curate or chaplain, however, may very properly be considered as of the same nature with the wages of a journeyman" (p. 118).

He specially mentions men of letters as underpaid because of their too great numbers, and he recalls that before the invention of printing "a scholar and a beggar" were synonymous, apparently applying this in a certain sense to men of letters.

The chapter is full of acute observations and important comments.

"In the same society or neighbourhood, the average and ordinary rates of profit in the different employments of stock should be more nearly upon a level than the pecuniary wages of the different sorts of labour" (p. 100).

"The extent of the market, by giving employment to greater stocks, diminishes apparent profit; but by requiring supplies from a greater distance, it increases prime cost. This diminution of the one and increase of the other seem, in most cases, nearly to counterbalance one another" (in the case of articles such as bread, meat, etc.) (p. 101).

"In small towns and country villages, on account of the narrowness of the market, trade cannot always be extended as stock extends. In such places, therefore, though the rate of a particular person's profits may be very high, the sum or amount of them can never be very great, nor consequently that of his annual accumulation. In great towns, on the contrary, trade can be extended as stock increases, and the credit of a frugal and thriving man increases much faster than his stock. His trade is extended in proportion to the amount of both" (p. 102).

Adam Smith is quite correct when, referring to the *false statistical* way of presenting wages, for example in the sixteenth and seventeenth centuries, he says that the wages in these accounts were only for example cotters' wages. These were occupied about their cottages for a part of their time, or they were working for their master, who gave them "a house, a small garden for pot-herbs, as much grass as will feed a cow, and, perhaps, an acre or two of bad arable land", and, when he employed them, very bad wages.

". . . they are said to have been willing to give their spare time for a very small recompense to anybody, and to have wrought for less wages than other labourers. . . . This daily or weekly recompense, however, seems to have been considered as the whole of it, by many writers who have collected the prices of labour and provisions in ancient times, and who have taken pleasure in representing both as wonderfully low" (p. 105).

He makes the absolutely correct general observation that:

"This equality in the whole of the advantages and disadvantages of the different employments of labour and stock can take place only in such as are the sole or principal employments of those who occupy them" (p. 105).

This point, by the way, had already been very well argued by Steuart, especially in relation to agricultural wages when time begins to have a price.

In regard to the accumulation of capital by the towns during the Middle Ages, Adam Smith very correctly observes in this chapter that it was principally due to the exploitation of the country through both trade and manufacture. In addition there are the usurers and *haute finance*—in a word, the money merchants.

"In consequence of such regulations [i.e., regulations made by the guilds], indeed, each class [i.e., within the town corporate] was obliged to buy the goods they had occasion for from every other within the town, somewhat dearer than they otherwise might have done. But in recompense, they were enabled to sell their own just as much dearer; so that so far it was as broad as long, as they say; and in the dealings of the different classes within the town with one another, none of them were losers by these regulations. But in their dealings with the country they were all great gainers; and in these latter dealings consists the whole trade which supports and enriches every town.

"Every town draws its whole subsistence, and all the materials of its industry, from the country. It pays for these chiefly in two ways: first, by sending back to the country a part of these materials wrought up and manufactured; in which case their price is augmented by the wages of the workmen, and the profits of their masters or immediate employers; secondly, by sending to it a part both of the rude and manufactured produce, either of other countries, or of distant parts of the same country, imported into the town; in which case, too, the original price of those goods is augmented by the wages of the carriers or sailors, and by the profits of the merchants who employ them. In what is gained upon the first of those two branches of commerce consists the advantage which the town makes by its manufactures; in what is gained upon the second, the advantages of its inland and foreign trade. The wages of the workmen, and the profits of their different employers, make up the whole of what is gained upon both. Whatever regulations, therefore, tend to increase those wages and profits beyond what they otherwise would be, tend to enable the town to purchase, with a smaller quantity of its labour, the produce of a greater quantity of the labour of the country. They give the traders and artificers in the town an advantage over the landlords, farmers and labourers in the country, and break down that natural equality which would otherwise take place in the commerce which is carried on between them. The whole annual produce of the labour of the society is annually divided between those two different sets of people. By means of those regulations a greater share of it is given to the inhabitants of the town than would otherwise fall to them; and a less to those of the country.

"The price which the town really pays for the provisions and materials annually imported into it is the quantity of manufactures and other goods annually exported from it. The dearer the latter are sold, the cheaper the former are bought. The industry of the town becomes more, and that of the country less advantageous" (pp. 112–13).

When Adam Smith says that the town purchases with a smaller quantity of labour the produce of a greater quantity of the labour of the country, he is thereby returning to the correct determination of value, the determination of value by the quantity of labour. This should be cited as an example in dealing with his theory of surplus value. If the prices of the

commodities which town and country exchange are determined
in such a way that they exchange equal quantities of labour,
then these prices are equal to the values of the commodities.
Profit and wages on both sides of the exchange cannot therefore
determine these values; but the division of these values determines profit and wages. Hence it is that Adam Smith also
finds that the town, which exchanges a smaller quantity of
labour against a greater quantity on the part of the country,
obtains a greater profit and a greater wage in comparison
with the country. This would not be the case if it did not sell
its commodities to the country for more than their value.
If profits and wages are not increased "beyond what they
otherwise would be", if profits and wages therefore are at the
level at which they would stand without artificial interference,
then they do not determine the value of the commodities, but
are determined by it. Profit and wages, then, can only come
through the distribution of the value of the commodity, which
is given and fixed before they appear; and this value cannot
be the result of profits and wages which are fixed before it
itself appears.

Adam Smith continues:

"The inhabitants of a town, being collected into one
place, can easily combine together. The most insignificant
trades carried on in towns have accordingly, in some place
or other, been incorporated. . . . The inhabitants of the
country, dispersed in distant places, cannot easily combine
together. They have not only never been incorporated, but
the corporation spirit never has prevailed among them.
No apprenticeship has ever been thought necessary to
qualify for husbandry, the great trade of the country" (p. 114).

In this connection Adam Smith comes to speak of the
disadvantages of the division of labour. The farmer carries on
a trade requiring more intelligence than that of the manufacturing worker who is subject to the division of labour.

"The direction of operations, besides, which must be
varied with every change of the weather, as well as with
many other accidents, requires much more judgment and
discretion than that of those which are always the same or
very nearly the same" (p. 115).

The division of labour develops the social productive power of labour, or the productive power of social labour, but at the cost of the general productive ability of the labourer. And therefore also this increase in social productive power confronts the labourer as an increased productive power not of his labour, but of the force that controls his labour—capital. If the town labourer is more developed than the country labourer, this is thanks only to the circumstance that his craft causes him to live *in society*, while the craft of the latter makes him live directly *with nature*.

"The superiority which the industry of the towns has everywhere in Europe over that of the country is not altogether owing to corporations and corporation laws. It is supported by many other regulations. The high duties upon foreign manufactures and upon all goods imported by alien merchants, all tend to the same purpose" (p. 116).

These other regulations "secure them" (the towns) against the competition of foreigners. This is an act no longer of the town bourgeoisie, but of the legislating bourgeoisie on a national scale, already acting as the *corps de nation* or as the Third Estate or Lower House of the States Assembly. The specific acts of the town bourgeoisie—directed against the country—are the excise and duties levied at the gates, and in general the indirect taxes, which originate in the towns (see Hüllmann), while the direct taxes are of country origin. It might appear that the excise for example is a tax which the town levied indirectly on itself. The countryman must advance it, but has it repaid to him in the price of the product. In the Middle Ages, however, this was not the case. The demand for his products—in so far as he transformed these at all into commodities and money—was compulsorily restricted to the area under the jurisdiction of the town, so that it was not possible for him to raise the price of his product by the full amount of the town tax.

"In Great Britain the superiority of the industry of the towns over that of the country seems to have been greater formerly than in the present times. The wages of country labour approach nearer to those of manufacturing labour, and the profits of stock employed in agriculture to those of trading and manufacturing stock, than they are said to have done in the last century, or in the beginning of the present [the eighteenth century]. This change may be regarded as the necessary, though very late consequence of the extraordinary encouragement given to the industry of the towns. The stock accumulated in them comes in time to be so great that it can no longer be employed with the ancient profit in that species of industry which is peculiar to them. That industry has its limits like every other; and the increase of stock, by increasing the competition, necessarily reduces the profit. The lowering of profit in the town forces out stock to the country, where, by creating a new demand for country labour, it necessarily raises its wages. It then spreads itself, if I may say so, over the face of the land, and by being employed in agriculture is in part restored to the country, at the expense of which, in a great measure, it had originally been accumulated in the town" (p. 116).

In Chapter XI of Book I Adam Smith then seeks to determine the *natural rate of the rent of land*—the third element that composes the value of the commodity. We reserve this for later, after first returning again to Ricardo.

This much is clear from the foregoing: when Adam Smith identifies the *natural price* or *price of production* of commodities with their *value*, he does so after first abandoning his correct view of *value* and substituting for it the view which the phenomena of competition bring to the surface. In competition the price of production, not the value, appears as the regulator of the market price—so to speak, as the immanent price, as the value of commodities. This price of production, however, in competition, itself in turn appears as given through the given average rates of wages, profit and rent. Consequently, Adam Smith seeks to establish these on their own account, independently of the value of the commodity and rather as elements of the natural price. Ricardo, whose principal task it was to refute this aberration of Adam Smith's, accepts the result of it—necessary in Adam Smith's view, but according to his own theory logically impossible—namely, the identity of values with prices of production.

3. RICARDO'S CONCEPTION OF SURPLUS VALUE

(a) Surplus Value and Profit

RICARDO nowhere considers *surplus value* apart and as distinguished from its particular forms—profit, interest and rent. For this reason his observations on the organic composition of capital, which are of such decisive importance, are limited to those differences in the organic composition which he took over from Adam Smith, actually from the Physiocrats—namely, the differences arising from the process of circulation, fixed capital and circulating capital; while he nowhere touches upon or recognises the differences in the organic composition within the actual process of production. Hence his confusion of value with price of production, his false theory of rent, his erroneous laws relating to the causes of rises and falls in the rate of profit, and so on.

In his observations on profit and wages Ricardo also abstracts from the constant part of the capital, which is not laid out in wages. He treats the subject as if the entire capital were directly expended on wages. *To this extent* therefore he deals with *surplus value* and *not profit*, and hence it is possible to speak of his having a theory of surplus value. On the other hand, however, he thinks he is speaking of profit as such, and in fact his work is everywhere full of views which have their origin in the preconceived idea of profit and not of surplus value. Where he correctly expounds the laws of surplus value, he falsifies them by presenting them as direct laws of profit. Elsewhere, he seeks to present the laws of profit directly, without the intermediate links, as laws of surplus value.

When therefore we speak of his theory of surplus value, we are speaking of his theory of profit, in so far as he confuses the latter with surplus value, that is, profit considered only in relation to the variable capital, the part of capital expended in wages. We shall deal later with what he says of profit as distinct from surplus value.

It is so much in the nature of the case that surplus value can only be treated in relation to the variable capital, the capital directly laid out in wages—and without the recognition of surplus value no theory of profit is possible—that Ricardo treats the entire capital as variable capital and abstracts from the constant capital, although it is occasionally mentioned in the form of loans.

In Chapter XXVI, "On Gross and Net Revenue", Ricardo speaks of:

"Trades where profits are in proportion to the capital, and not in proportion to the quantity of labour employed" (p. 236).

What does his whole doctrine of average profit, on which his theory of rent depends, mean but that profit is "in proportion to the capital, and not in proportion to the quantity of labour employed"? If it were "in proportion to the quantity of labour employed", then equal capitals would yield very unequal profits, inasmuch as their profit would be equal to the surplus value created in their own branch of production, while this surplus value would depend not on the size of the capital as a whole, but on the size of the variable capital, which is equivalent to the quantity of labour employed. What then can it mean to ascribe to a particular use of capital, to particular trades by way of exception, that in them profits are in proportion to the quantity of capital employed and not to the quantity of labour employed? With a given rate of surplus value, the mass of surplus value for a certain capital must always depend not on the absolute size of the capital, but on the quantity of labour employed. On the other hand, if the average rate of profit is given, the amount of profit must always depend on the mass of the capital employed and not on the quantity of labour employed. Ricardo expressly mentions "the carrying trade, the distant foreign trade, and trades where expensive machinery is required" (p. 236). That is to say, he is speaking of trades which employ relatively much constant and little variable capital. These are at the same time trades in which, compared with others, the *total amount* of the capital advanced is large, or which can only be carried on with a large capital. Given the rate of profit, the amount of profit depends entirely on the size of the capitals advanced. This however in no way distinguishes the trades in which large capitals and much constant capital is employed (the two always go together), from the trades in which the capitals employed are small, but is only an application of the principle that capitals of equal size yield profits of equal size, and therefore a larger capital yields more profit than a smaller. This has nothing to do with "the quantity of labour employed". Whether the rate of profit in general is large or small depends however on the total quantity of labour employed by the capital of the whole capitalist class; on the relative quantity of unpaid labour employed; and finally on the relation between the capital employed in labour and the capital that is merely reproduced as means of production.

Ricardo himself, in Chapter VII, argues against the view "that the great profits which are sometimes made by particular merchants in foreign trade will elevate the general rate of profits in the country".

". . . They contend that the equality of profits will be brought about by the general rise of profits; and I am of opinion that the profits of the favoured trade will speedily subside to the general level" (p. 78).

We shall see later how far his view is correct that exceptional profits, when not caused by a rise of the market price above the value, do not raise the general rate of profit in spite of the equalisation of profits; moreover, how far his view is correct that foreign trade and the extension of the market cannot raise the rate of profit. But granted that his view is correct on "the equality of profits" in general, how is it possible for him to distinguish trades "where profits are in proportion to the capital" from others where they are "in proportion to the quantity of labour employed"?

In the same Chapter XXVI, "On Gross and Net Revenue", Ricardo says:

"I admit that, from the nature of rent, a given capital employed in agriculture, on any but the land last cultivated, puts in motion a greater quantity of labour than an equal capital employed in manufactures and trade" (p. 236).

The whole statement is nonsense. In the first place, according to Ricardo, a greater quantity of labour is employed on "the land last cultivated" than on all other land. From this arises, in his view, the rent on the other portions of land. How then does it follow that on all other land *except* that "last cultivated" a given capital sets in motion more labour than in manufactures and trade? That the product of the better portions of land has a market value higher than its individual value, which is conditioned by the quantity of labour that the capital cultivating them employs, is surely not the same thing as that this capital "puts in motion a greater quantity of labour than an equal capital employed in manufactures and trade"? It might well have been correct, however, had Ricardo said that apart from differences in the fertility of land, rent in general springs from the fact that agricultural capital, in proportion to the constant part of the capital, puts in motion a greater quantity of labour than does the average capital in the non-agricultural spheres of production.

Ricardo overlooks the fact that, with a given surplus value, various causes may raise or lower and in general exert an influence on the profit. Because he identifies surplus value with profit, he therefore quite logically tries to show that rises and falls in the rate of profit are dependent only on such circumstances as make the rate of surplus value rise or fall. He further overlooks the fact—apart from the circumstances which, with a given *amount* of surplus value, influence the rate although not the *amount* of profit—that the rate of profit depends on the amount of surplus value and not in any way on the rate of surplus value. The quantity of surplus value depends on the organic composition of the capital, if the rate of surplus value, of the surplus labour, is given—that is to say, on the number of labourers which a capital of given value, say £100, employs. When the organic composition of the capital is given, it depends on the rate of surplus value. It is therefore determined by the two factors—the number of simultaneously employed workers and the rate of surplus labour. If the capital increases, then the amount of the surplus value also increases, whatever its organic composition, if this remains only unchanged. But this does not alter in any way the fact that this amount of surplus value remains the same for a capital of a given size, for example £100. If in this case it is £10, then it is £100 for a capital of £1,000; the proportion however is unchanged.

In another passage, in Chapter XII on "Land-Tax", Ricardo says:

"There cannot be two rates of profit in the same employment, and therefore when the value of produce is in different proportions to capital, it is the rent which will differ, and not the profit" (p. 121).

This applies only to the normal rate of profit "in the same employment". Otherwise it is in direct contradiction to the passage quoted earlier from Chapter II, "On Rent".

In Chapter XII, on "Land-Tax", Ricardo makes the following statement in opposition to Say—and it shows how the Englishman is always keenly aware of the economic distinctions, while the Continental constantly forgets them:

"M. Say supposes, 'A landlord by his assiduity, economy, and skill to increase his annual revenue by 5,000 francs'; but a landlord has no means of employing his assiduity, economy, and skill on his land unless he farms it himself; and then it is in quality of capitalist and farmer that he makes the improvement, and not in quality of landlord. It is not conceivable that he could so augment the produce of his farm by any *peculiar* skill[1] on his part, without first increasing the quantity of capital employed upon it" (p. 119).

In Chapter XIII, "Taxes on Gold", which is important for Ricardo's theory of money, he gives some supplementary or further elucidations in connection with *market price* and *natural price*. They lead to the conclusion that the equalising of the two is effected more or less rapidly according as the particular trade permits of a quick or slow increase or reduction of supply, which in turn is the same thing as a quick or slow bringing in or withdrawal of capital to or from the trade in question.

"The rise in the price of commodities, in consequence of taxation or of difficulty of production, will in all cases ultimately ensue; but the duration of the interval before the market price will conform to the natural price must depend on the nature of the commodity, and on the facility

[1] This is also true of ordinary "skill", which is more or less just a phrase.

with which it can be reduced in quantity. If the quantity of the commodity taxed could not be diminished, if the capital of the farmer or of the hatter, for instance, could not be withdrawn to other employments, it would be of no consequence that their profits were reduced below the general level by means of a tax; unless the demand for their commodities should increase, they would never be able to elevate the market price of corn and of hats up to their increased natural price. Their threats to leave their employments, and remove their capitals to more favoured trades, would be treated as an idle menace which could not be carried into effect; and consequently the price would not be raised by diminished production. Commodities, however, of all descriptions, can be reduced in quantity, and capital can be removed from trades which are less profitable to those which are more so, but with different degrees of rapidity. In proportion as the supply of a particular commodity can be more easily reduced, without inconvenience to the producer, the price of it will more quickly rise after the difficulty of its production has been increased by taxation, or by any other means" (p. 122).

"The agreement of the market and natural prices of all commodities depends at all times on the facility with which the supply can be increased or diminished. In the case of gold, houses, and labour, as well as many other things, this effect cannot, under some circumstances, be speedily produced. But it is different with those commodities which are consumed and reproduced from year to year, such as hats, shoes, corn, and cloth; they may be reduced, if necessary, and the interval cannot be long before the supply is contracted in proportion to the increased charge of producing them" (pp. 125–6).

In the same Chapter XIII, dealing with "Taxes on Gold", Ricardo says: "rent being not a creation, but merely a transfer of wealth" (p. 126).

Is profit a creation of wealth, or is it not rather a transfer of surplus labour from the workman to the capitalist? In reality wages too are not a creation of value; but they are also not a transfer. They are the appropriation of a part of the product of labour by those who produced it.

In the same chapter Ricardo says:

"A tax on raw produce from the surface of the earth will . . . fall on the consumer, and will in no way affect rent; unless by diminishing the funds for the maintenance of labour it lowers wages, reduces the population, and diminishes the demand for corn" (p. 126).

Whether Ricardo is right in saying that "a tax on raw produce from the surface of the earth" falls neither on the landowner nor on the farmer, but on the consumer, does not here concern us. I maintain however that if he is right, such a tax can raise rent; while he holds that it does not affect rent except in so far as it reduces capital, population and the demand for corn, by making the means of subsistence, etc., dearer. Ricardo in fact imagines that a rise in the price of raw produce affects the rate of profit only in so far as it makes the worker's means of subsistence dearer. And it is true that only in this case can a rise in the price of raw produce affect the rate of surplus value and hence the surplus value, and therefore through this the rate of profit. But assuming a given surplus value, a rise in the price of raw produce from the surface of the earth would raise the value of the constant capital in proportion to the variable, increase the proportion of constant capital to variable, and consequently lower the rate of profit and therefore raise the rent. Ricardo starts from the standpoint that in so far as a rise or fall in the price of raw produce does not affect wages, it does not affect profit; for, he argues (except in one passage, to which we shall return later), the rate remains unchanged whether the value of the capital advanced falls or rises. If the capital advanced rises in value, so also does the product rise in value and similarly the part of the product which constitutes the surplus product, that is, the profit. The opposite is true when the capital advanced falls in value. This is only true if—whether as a result of a rise in price of the raw material, taxes, etc.—the values of variable and constant capital change in the same proportion. In this case the rate remains the same, because no change has occurred in the organic composition of the capital. And even then it must be assumed—as is the case with temporary changes—that wages remain the same whether the raw produce rises or falls; that therefore the wage remains the same whether its use value rises or falls with the given, unchanging value. The following cases are possible.

First the two principal subdivisions:

A. Through *a change in the method of production* the *proportion* between the amount of constant and variable capital employed changes. In this case the rate of surplus value remains the same, if it is assumed that the wages remain constant in value. But the surplus value itself is affected, if the number of workmen employed with the same capital—that is, the same variable capital—changes. If the constant capital falls relatively as a result of the change in the method of production, then the surplus value, therefore the rate of profit, increases. In the reverse case, the opposite is true.

It is here throughout assumed that the value *pro tanto*, per 100 for example, of the constant and variable capital remains *the same*.

In this case it is not possible for the change in the method of production to affect the constant and the variable capital in equal degree—for the constant and variable capital, for example—without a change in value—to increase or fall equally. For here the necessity of the rise or fall is always bound up with a change in the productivity of labour. It is the *difference*, not the equality, in the way they are affected, that brings about a change in the method of production; and this has nothing to do with whether, with a given organic composition of capital, a large or small capital has to be employed.

B. *With the method of production remaining unchanged. When there is a change in the proportion of constant and variable capital*, without a change in their relative amounts (so that each constitutes the same aliquot part of the total capital as before), as a result of *a change in the value* of the commodities which enter into either the constant or the variable capital. In this case there are the following possibilities:

(1) The value of the constant capital remains the same; that of the variable rises or falls. This would always affect the surplus value, and through it, the profit.

(2) The value of the variable capital remains the same; that of the constant rises or falls. In the first case the rate of profit

would fall, in the second it would rise. If both fall simultaneously, but in unequal proportions, then one as compared with the other has always risen or fallen.

(3) The value of the constant and of the variable capital are *equally* affected, whether both rise or both fall. If both rise, then the rate of profit falls—not however because the constant capital rises, but because the variable rises and in proportion to it the surplus value falls, inasmuch as only the value of the variable capital rises, although it sets in motion only the same number of workmen as before, perhaps even a smaller number. If both fall, then the rate of profit rises—not however because the constant capital falls, but because the variable falls in value, and therefore the surplus value is increased.

C. *When there is a change in the method of production and a change in the value of the elements which form the constant or variable capital.* In this case one change may paralyse the other—if for example the amount of the constant capital increases while its value falls; or if its amount falls but its value rises in the same proportion. In this case there could be no change in the organic composition. The rate of profit would remain unchanged. Apart from agricultural capital, however, it can never happen that, as compared with the variable capital, its amount *falls* while its value *rises*.

Except for this one case it is therefore only possible for the relative value and amount of the constant capital to rise or fall simultaneously in relation to the variable capital; therefore its value rises or falls absolutely as compared with the variable capital. This case has already been considered. Or it is possible for them to rise or fall simultaneously, but in unequal proportions. This, on the assumption made, always reduces itself to the case when the value of the constant capital rises or falls relatively to the variable. The latter case in fact includes the other. For if its amount rises, then the amount of the variable relatively falls, and *vice versa*. Similarly with the value.

In regard to case C it should also be noted:

It would be possible for the wages to rise but the constant capital to fall, in value, not in amount. If the rise and fall however counterbalanced each other at the two ends, then the rate of profit could remain the same.

Let us take an example:

Constant Capital	Variable Capital	Surplus Value	Value of the Product	Capital Advanced	Rate of Profit
£60	£40	£20	£120	£100	20 per cent.

If the constant capital falls while at the same time the variable rises, the most diverse combinations might arise:

Constant Capital	Variable Capital	Surplus Value	Value of the Product	Capital Advanced	Rate of Profit
£40	£50	£10	£100	£90	$11\frac{1}{9}$ per cent.

The rate of profit would have fallen well below 20 per cent. As against this, take the case:

Constant Capital	Variable Capital	Surplus Value	Value of the Product	Capital Advanced	Rate of Profit
£30	£45	£15	£90	£75	20 per cent.

Thus in this case the two movements cancel each other out entirely.

Or again:

Constant Capital	Variable Capital	Surplus Value	Value of the Product	Capital Advanced	Rate of Profit
£20	£45	£15	£80	£65	$23\frac{1}{13}$ per cent.

Thus in this case even if the surplus value fell the rate of profit could rise, owing to the proportionately greater fall in the value of the constant capital. With the same £100 capital more workers could be employed in spite of the rise in wages and the fall in the rate of surplus value. In spite of the fall in the rate of surplus value, the surplus value itself, and hence the profit, would increase, because the number of workers had increased. The proportion in the above example of 20c and 45v, with a capital outlay of 100, in fact gives us the following:

Constant Capital	Variable Capital	Surplus Value	Value of the Product	Capital Advanced	Rate of Profit
£30$\frac{10}{13}$	£69$\frac{3}{13}$	£23$\frac{1}{13}$	£123$\frac{1}{13}$	£100	$23\frac{1}{13}$ per cent.

The relation between the rate of surplus value and the number of workers is here of great importance. Ricardo never considers it.

It is clear that what has here been considered as a variation within the organic composition of a capital itself can apply equally to the case where there is a difference in organic composition as between different capitals, capitals in different spheres.

First: Instead of a variation in the organic composition of a *single* capital—a difference in the organic composition of different capitals.

Second: A change in organic composition through a change in value of the two parts of a single capital; similarly, a difference in the value of raw materials and machinery employed by different capitals. This does not hold good for the variable capital, as equal wages in the various branches of production are assumed. The difference in the *value* of different working days in the various branches of production has nothing to do with the matter. If the labour of a goldsmith is dearer than that of a day labourer, the surplus labour time of the goldsmith is worth proportionately more than that of the day labourer.

In Chapter XV, "Taxes on Profits", Ricardo says:

> "Taxes on those commodities which are generally deno-
> minated luxuries fall on those only who make use of them. . . .
> But taxes on necessaries do not affect the consumers of
> necessaries in proportion to the quantity that may be
> consumed by them, but often in a much higher proportion.
> A tax on corn, we have observed, not only affects a manufac-
> turer in the proportion that he and his family may consume
> corn, but it alters the rate of profits of stock, and therefore
> also affects his income. Whatever raises the wages of labour,
> lowers the profits of stock; therefore every tax on any com-
> modity consumed by the labourer has a tendency to lower
> the rate of profits" (p. 132).

Taxes on consumers are at the same time taxes on producers, in so far as the object taxed enters not only into individual consumption but also into industrial consumption. This however holds good not only for the means of subsistence consumed by the workman, but for all materials which are industrially consumed by the capitalist. Every such tax reduces the rate of profit, because it raises the value of the constant capital in relation to the variable. For example, a tax levied on flax, or on wool. The flax rises in price. The flax spinner, therefore, can no longer buy the same quantity of flax with a capital of 100. As the method of production has remained the same, he needs the same number of workers to spin the same quantity of flax. But the flax has more value than before, in relation to the capital advanced as wages. Therefore the rate of profit falls. The rise in the price of the linen yarn does not help him over the difficulty. The absolute level of this price is in any case a matter of indifference to him. What matters is only the excess of the price over the price of the capital advanced. If he were now to raise the price of the total product not only by the higher price of the flax, but to such an extent that the same quantity of yarn would yield him the same profit as before, then the demand—which is already falling as a result of the higher price of the raw material of the yarn— would fall still further as a result of the artificial rise in price due to increasing the profit. In spite of the fact that the average rate of profit is given, this increase in price in such cases would not work.

In the same chapter Ricardo says:

"In a former part of this work we discussed the effects of the division of capital into fixed and circulating, or rather into durable and perishable capital, on the prices of commodities. We showed that two manufacturers might employ precisely the same amount of capital, and might derive from it precisely the same amount of profits, but that they would sell their commodities for very different sums of money, according as the capitals they employed were rapidly, or slowly, consumed and reproduced. The one might sell his goods for £4,000, the other for £10,000, and they might both employ £10,000 of capital, and obtain 20 per cent. profit, or £2,000. The capital of one might consist, for example, of £2,000 circulating capital, to be reproduced, and £8,000 fixed, in buildings and machinery; the capital of the other, on the contrary, might consist of £8,000 of circulating, and of only £2,000 fixed capital in machinery and buildings. Now, if each of these persons were to be taxed 10 per cent. on his income, or £200, the one to make his business yield him the general rate of profit must raise his goods from £10,000 to £10,200; the other would also be obliged to raise the price of his goods from £4,000 to £4,200. Before the tax, the goods sold by one of these manufacturers were $2\frac{1}{2}$ times more valuable than the goods of the other; after the tax they will be 2.42 times more valuable: the one kind will have risen two per cent.: the other five per cent.: consequently a tax upon income, whilst money continued unaltered in value, would alter the relative prices and value of commodities" (pp. 133–4).

It is in this final "and"—"prices and value"—that the error lies. This change in price would only show—just as in the case of a different division of capital as between fixed and circulating—that in order to produce *the average rate of profit* the prices which are determined and regulated by it—that is to say, the prices of production—are very different from the *values* of the commodities. This most important aspect of the question simply does not exist for Ricardo.

In the same chapter he says moreover:

"If a country were not taxed, and money should fall in value, its abundance in every market[1] would produce similar effects in each. If meat rose 20 per cent., bread, beer, shoes, labour, and every commodity would also rise 20 per cent.; it is necessary that they should do so, to secure to each trade the same rate of profits. But this is no longer true when any of these commodities is taxed; if, in that case, they should all rise in proportion to the fall in the value of money, profits would be rendered unequal; in the case of the commodities taxed, profits would be raised above the general level, and capital would be removed from one employment to another, till an equilibrium of profits was restored, which could only be after the relative prices were altered" (p. 135).

And so the equilibrium in the general rate of profit is brought about by the relative *values, the actual values* of the commodities, being altered and so levelled out between each other that they are related to each other not on the basis of their actual values but on the basis of the average profit which they must yield.

(b) Quantity of Labour and Value of Labour

Ricardo opens Chapter I, "On Value", with the following superscription at the head of Section I:

[1] Here he has the ridiculous notion that a fall in the value of money must be accompanied by its abundance in every market.

"The value of a commodity, or the quantity of any other commodity for which it will exchange, depends on the relative quantity of labour which is necessary for its production, and not on the greater or less compensation which is paid for that labour" (p. 5).

In this passage Ricardo opens his book—in the style which runs right through his enquiry—with the statement that the determination of the value of commodities by labour time is not inconsistent with wages, that is, the varying compensation paid for that labour time or that quantity of labour. From the very outset he directs his attack against Adam Smith's confusion between the determination of the value of commodities by the relative quantity of labour necessary for their production, and the value of the labour (or the compensation paid for labour).

It is clear that the proportional quantity of labour contained in two commodities A and B is absolutely unaffected by whether the workers who produce A and B receive much or little out of the product of their labour. The value of A and B is determined by the quantity of labour which their production costs, but not by the costs of the labour for the owners of A and B. Quantity of labour and value of labour are two different things. The quantity of labour contained in A and B respectively has nothing to do with how much of the labour contained in A and B has been paid for by the owners of A and B or even performed by the owners of A and B themselves. A and B exchange for each other not in proportion to the paid labour they contain, but in proportion to the total quantity of labour contained in them, paid and unpaid.

"Adam Smith, who so accurately defined the original source of exchangeable value, and who was bound in consistency to maintain that all things became more or less valuable in proportion as more or less labour was bestowed on their production, has himself erected another standard measure of value, and speaks of things being more or less valuable in proportion as they will exchange for more or less of this standard measure . . . as if these were two equivalent expressions, and as if, because a man's labour had become doubly efficient, and he could therefore produce twice the quantity of a commodity, he would necessarily receive twice the former quantity in exchange for it [that is, for his labour]. If this indeed were true, if the reward of the labourer were always in proportion to what he produced, the quantity of labour bestowed on a commodity, and the quantity of labour which that commodity would purchase, would be equal, and either might accurately measure the variations of other things; but they are not equal" (p. 7).

Adam Smith nowhere asserts that the two are "equivalent expressions". On the contrary, he says: Because in capitalist production the workman's wage is *no longer* equal to his product, therefore the quantity of labour that a commodity costs, and the quantity of labour that the workman can buy with this labour, are two different things; *precisely for this reason* the relative quantity of labour contained in commodities ceases to determine their value, which becomes determined rather by the value of the labour, by the quantity of labour which I can buy or command with a definite amount of commodities. For this reason the value of labour, instead of the relative quantity of labour, is the measure of value. Ricardo's reply to Adam Smith is correct—that the relative quantity of labour which is contained in two commodities is in no way affected by how much of this quantity of labour falls to the share of the workmen themselves, by how this labour is rewarded; that therefore, if the relative quantity of labour was the measure of the value of commodities *before* wages came into existence (wages that differed from the value of the product itself), there is absolutely no reason why it should not remain the measure *after* wages came into existence. He rightly contends that Adam Smith could have used the two expressions so long as they were equivalent, but that this is no ground for using the wrong expression instead of the right one when they have ceased to be equivalent.

But Ricardo has thereby in no way solved the problem which is the inner cause of Adam Smith's contradiction. *Value of labour* and *quantity of labour* remain synonymous "expressions" so long as what we are talking of is *materialised labour*. They cease to be so when *materialised labour* and *living labour* are exchanged for each other. Two commodities exchange in proportion to the labour materialised in them. Equal quantities of materialised labour are exchanged against each other. The labour time is their measure of value, but precisely for this reason they are "more or less valuable in proportion as they will exchange for more or less of this standard measure". If one working day is contained in commodity A, it exchanges against any quantity whatsoever of commodities in which similarly one working day is contained; and it is "more or less valuable" in proportion as it will exchange for more or less materialised labour in other commodities, for this exchange relationship expresses, is identical with, the relative quantity of labour which it itself contains.

Now wage labour, however, is a commodity. It is even the basis on which the production of products as commodities takes place. And the law of values does not hold good in relation to it. Therefore this law by no means governs capitalist production. Therein lies a contradiction.

This is the first problem for Adam Smith. The second—which we shall find further amplified by Malthus—lies in the fact that the utilisation of a commodity as capital does not depend on the labour it contains, but on the extent to which it commands the labour of others, gives control over a greater quantity of other labour than it itself contains. This is actually a second latent reason for the assertion that with the emergence of capitalist production the value of commodities is determined, not by the labour they contain, but by the living labour which they command, that is, by the value of labour.

Ricardo answers simply that this is how things are in capitalist production. He not only does not solve the problem. He does not even notice it in Adam Smith's work. In conformity with the whole plan of his investigation, he is content to show that the changing value of labour—in short, wages—does not negate the determination of the value of commodities other than the labour itself by the relative quantity of labour contained in them. "They are not equal"—that is, "the quantity of labour bestowed on a commodity, and the quantity of labour which that commodity would purchase". He contents himself with stating this fact. But what is it that makes the commodity labour different from other commodities? The former is *living labour*, the latter *materialised labour*. They are therefore only two different forms of labour. Since the difference is only one of form, why should a law apply to one that does not apply to the other? Ricardo does not answer this question; he does not even raise it.

Nor does it help at all when he says:

"Is not the value of labour . . . variable; being not only affected, as all other things[1] are, by the proportion between the supply and demand, which uniformly varies with every change in the condition of the community, but also by the varying price of food and other necessaries, on which the wages of labour are expended?" (p. 8).

That the price of labour, like that of other commodities, changes with demand and supply proves nothing, according to Ricardo himself, when what is in question is the *value* of the labour, any more than this change of price with demand and supply proves anything in regard to the value of other commodities. That "wages"—which is only another expression for the value of labour—are influenced by "the varying price of food and other necessaries, on which the wages of labour are expended", proves however just as little why the value of labour is (or appears to be) determined in any other way than the value of other commodities. For these other commodities too are affected by changes in the price of other commodities which enter into their production, and against which they are exchanged. And the *spending* of the wages on food and other necessaries is after all nothing but the *exchange* of the value of the labour against food and other necessaries. The question is just this—why is it that labour does not exchange, for the commodities against which it is exchanged, in accordance with the law of value, on the basis of the relative quantities of labour?

Once the law of value is assumed, the question—put in this way—is in its nature insoluble, and insoluble because in it labour as such is counterposed to commodity, a definite quantity of immediate labour as such to a definite quantity of materialised labour.

This weakness in Ricardo's argument, as we shall see later,

[1] This should read: commodities.

has contributed to the disintegration of his school and has led to the putting forward of absurd hypotheses.

Wakefield is right when he says:

"Treating labour as a commodity, and capital, the produce of labour, as another, then, if the value of these two commodities were regulated by equal quantities of labour, a given amount of labour would, under all circumstances, exchange for that quantity of capital which had been produced by the same amount of labour; antecedent labour . . . would always exchange for the same amount of present labour . . . but the value in relation to other commodities, in so far, at least, as wages depend upon share, is determined, not by equal quantities of labour, but by the proportion between supply and demand" (E. G. Wakefield, Note on p. 231 of Vol. I of his edition of Adam Smith's *Wealth of Nations*, London, 1836).

This is also one of Bailey's hobby-horses, as we shall see later; and also of Say's, who much rejoices in the assertion that here at any rate demand and supply are the decisive factors.

Another point to be noted here is that Section III of Chapter I of Ricardo's book bears the following superscription:

"Not only the labour applied immediately to commodities affect their value, but the labour also which is bestowed on the implements, tools, and buildings, with which such labour is assisted" (p. 13).

Therefore the value of a commodity is to the same extent determined by the quantity of materialised (past) labour and by the quantity of living (immediate) labour necessary to its production. In other words, the quantities of labour are in no way affected by the formal difference—whether the labour is materialised or living, past or present (immediate). If this difference has no significance so far as the determination of the value of commodities is concerned, why does it become of such decisive importance when past labour, capital, is exchanged with living labour? Why in this case should it invalidate the law of value, since the difference in itself, as is clear in the case of commodities, has no significance for the determination of value? Ricardo does not answer this question—he does not even raise it.

(c) Value of Labour Power and Value of Labour

In order to determine market value Ricardo—like the Physiocrats, Adam Smith, etc.—has first to determine *the value of labour power*, or as he puts it, following Adam Smith and his predecessors, the value of labour. How then is the value or natural price of labour determined? In Ricardo's view the natural price is in fact nothing but the expression of value in money. Chapter V, "On Wages", begins with the words:

"Labour, like all other things which are purchased and sold, and which may be increased or diminished in quantity,[1] has its natural and its market price. The natural price of labour is that price which is necessary to enable the labourers, one with another, to subsist and to perpetuate their race, without either increase or diminution."[2]

"The power of the labourer to support himself, and the family which may be necessary to keep up the number of labourers . . . depends on the price of the food, necessaries and conveniences required for the support of the labourer and his family. With a rise in the price of food and necessaries, the natural price of labour will rise; with the fall in their price, the natural price of labour will fall" (p. 52).

"It is not to be understood that the natural price of labour, estimated even in food and necessaries, is absolutely fixed and constant. It varies at different times in the same country, and very materially differs in different countries. It essentially depends on the habits and customs of the people" (pp. 54–5).

Thus the *value of labour* is determined by the means of subsistence for the maintenance and reproduction of the labourers which are traditionally necessary in a given society.

But why? By what law is the value of labour so determined?

Ricardo has in fact no answer except that the law of supply and demand reduces the average price of labour to the means of subsistence necessary to the maintenance of the labourer— physically or socially necessary in a given society. Here, in the groundwork of the whole system, he determines value by

---

[1] That is to say, like all other commodities.

[2] This should read: with that rate of increase which the average progress of production requires.

demand and supply, as Say notes with malicious pleasure. (See Constanzo's translation.)

He should have spoken of labour power instead of speaking of labour. Had he done so, however, capital would also have been revealed as the material conditions of labour confronting the labourer as a power that had become independent of him. And capital would at once have been revealed as *a definite social relationship*. As it is, for Ricardo it is only distinguished as "accumulated labour" from "immediate labour". And it is something purely material, a mere element in the *labour process*—from which the relation between labour and capital, wages and profit, can never be developed.

> "Capital is that part of the wealth of a country which is employed in production, and consists of food, clothing, tools, raw materials, machinery, etc., necessary to give effect to labour " (p. 53).

> "Less capital, which is the same thing as less labour" (p. 44).

> "Labour and capital (that is, accumulated labour)" (p. 280).

The jump which Ricardo makes here is correctly sensed by Bailey.

> "Hence Mr. Ricardo, ingeniously enough, avoids a difficulty, which, on a first view, threatens to encumber his doctrine, that value depends on the quantity of labour employed in production. If this principle is rigidly adhered to, it follows, that the value of labour depends on the quantity of labour employed in producing it—which is evidently absurd. By a dexterous turn, therefore, Mr. Ricardo makes the value of labour depend on the quantity of labour required to produce wages, or, to give him the benefit of his own language, he maintains, that the value of labour is *to be estimated* by the quantity of labour required to produce wages, by which he means, the quantity of labour required to produce the money or commodities given to the labourer. This is similar to saying, that the value of cloth is to be estimated, not by the quantity of labour bestowed on its production, but by the quantity of labour bestowed on the production of the silver, for which the cloth is exchanged" (*A Critical Dissertation on the Nature, Measures, and Causes of Value, etc.*, pp. 50-1).

Literally, the objection here raised is correct. Ricardo distinguishes between *nominal wages* and *real wages*. The nominal wage is the wage expressed in money, the money wage. The nominal wage is "the number of pounds that may be annually paid to the labourer"; but the real wage is "the number of days' work necessary to obtain those pounds" (p. 88).

As the wage is equal to the labourer's necessary means of subsistence, and the value of this wage (the real wage) is equal to the value of these means of subsistence, it is obvious that the value of these means of subsistence is also equal to the real wage—equal to the labour which it can command. If the value of the means of subsistence changes, then the value of the real wage changes. Assume that the labourer's means of subsistence consist only in corn, and that the quantity of means of subsistence he requires is one quarter of corn per month. Then the value of his month's wage is equal to the value of one quarter of corn; if the value of the quarter of corn rises or falls, then the value of the month's labour rises or falls. But however the value of the quarter of corn may rise or fall, however much or little labour may be contained in the quarter of corn, it is always equal to the value of one month's labour. And here we have the hidden ground for Adam Smith's statement that as soon as capital, and consequently wage labour, intervenes, it is not the quantity of labour expended on a product, but the quantity of labour that it can command, that regulates its value. The value of the corn (and other means of subsistence) determined by labour time changes; but so long as the natural price of labour is paid, the quantity of labour that the quarter of corn can command remains the same. It has therefore a permanent relative value as compared with corn. For that reason Adam Smith too treats labour and corn (representing means of subsistence)— see D. Hume—as the measure of value, since a definite quantity of corn, so long as the natural price of labour is paid, commands a definite quantity of labour, whatever may be the quantity of labour expended on a quarter of corn. The same quantity of labour always commands the same use value, or rather the same use value always commands the same quantity of labour. It is through this that Ricardo himself determines the value of labour, its natural price. He says: the quarter of corn has a value that greatly varies, although it always commands or is commanded by the same quantity of labour. Yes, says Adam Smith, however the value, determined by labour time, of a quarter of corn may change, the worker must always pay (sacrifice) the same quantity of labour in order to buy it. Thus the value of corn changes, but the value of labour does not change, for one month's labour is equal to one quarter of corn. Moreover, the value of the corn changes only in so far as we take into account the labour necessary to its production. If on the other hand we consider the quantity of labour against which it exchanges, which it puts in motion, its value does not change. And that is precisely why the quantity of labour for which a quarter of corn is exchanged is the normal measure of value. The values of other commodities, however, have the same relation to labour as they have to corn. A given quantity of corn commands a given amount of labour. A given amount of every other commodity commands a certain amount of corn. Therefore every other commodity, or rather the value of every other commodity, is expressed through the amount of labour that it commands, since it is expressed through the quantity of corn that it commands, and the latter is expressed through the quantity of labour commanded by it.

But how is the relative value of other commodities to corn (necessary means of subsistence) determined? By the quantity of labour which they command. And how is the quantity of labour which they command determined? By the quantity of corn which the labour commands. Here Adam Smith of necessity falls into a vicious circle. Nevertheless, it may be noted in passing, he *never* makes use of this measure of value where he is really developing his theory. But although he and Ricardo say that "labour is the foundation of the value of commodities", while "the comparative quantity of labour which is necessary to their production" is the measure which determines the quantities of goods which shall be given in exchange for each other (Ricardo, p. 48)—in this passage Adam Smith is nevertheless confusing, as Ricardo too often does, labour the *intrinsic* measure with *money* the *external* measure, which already presupposes that the value is determined.

Adam Smith errs by concluding from the fact that a definite quantity of labour is exchangeable for a definite quantity of a use value, that this *definite quantity of labour* is the measure of value, that it always has *the same value*, while the same quantity of a use value can represent widely different exchange values. But Ricardo errs twice over, inasmuch as firstly he does not understand the problem which gave rise to Adam Smith's mistake; secondly, entirely ignoring the law of value of commodities and taking refuge in the law of demand and supply, he even determines the *value of labour*, not by the quantity of labour expended in the production of labour power, but by the quantity of labour expended in the production of the wages falling to the share of the labourer. Thus actually he says: the value of labour is determined by the value of the gold which is paid for it! And what determines this? What determines the amount of gold that is paid? The quantity of use value that a definite quantity of labour commands or the quantity of labour that a definite quantity of use value commands. And thereby he falls into the very *non sequitur* which he condemned in Adam Smith.

At the same time, as we have seen, this prevents him from grasping the specific distinction between *commodity* and *capital*, between the exchange of commodity for commodity and the exchange of capital for commodity, in conformity with the law of exchange of commodities.

(d) Surplus Value

Apart from his confusion between labour and labour power, Ricardo's analysis of the average wage or the value of labour is correct. He says in fact that it is determined neither by the money nor by the means of subsistence which the labourer receives, but by the labour time which it costs for its production—by the quantity of labour materialised in the labourer's means of subsistence. This he calls the real wages. (See later.)

This determination of the value of labour is, incidentally, necessary for his theory. Since the value of labour is determined by the value of the necessary means of subsistence on which this value is to be expended, and the value of the means of subsistence as of all other commodities is determined by the quantity of labour expended on them, it naturally follows that the value of labour is equal to the value of the necessary means of subsistence, which is equal to the quantity of labour expended on them.

However correct this formula is—if we leave out of account the direct opposition between labour and capital—it is nevertheless not adequate. The individual labourer may produce products which do not in any way enter into his consumption; and even when he produces necessary means of subsistence, what he produces, owing to the division of labour, is only one kind of means of subsistence, for example corn, and he gives it only one particular form, for example the form of corn, not of bread. But though he does not directly produce the products by which he lives, he produces in replacement of his wages— reproduces, if we take the continuity of this process into account—commodities of the value of his means of subsistence, or he produces the value of his means of subsistence. This means therefore, if we consider his average daily consumption, that the labour time which is contained in his daily means of subsistence forms one part of his working day. He works one part of the day to reproduce the value of his means of subsistence; the commodities produced during this part of his working day have the same value, or contain a labour time equal to that contained in his daily means of subsistence. It depends on the value of these means of subsistence, and therefore on the social productivity of labour and not on the productivity of the particular branch of industry in which he works, how large a part of his working day is devoted to the reproduction or production of the value, that is, the equivalent, of his means of subsistence. Ricardo of course assumes that the labour time contained in his daily means of subsistence is equal to the labour time which the labourer must work each day in order to reproduce the value of these means of subsistence.

But by not directly showing that one part of the labourer's working day is set aside for the reproduction of the value of his own labour power, Ricardo introduces a difficulty and

obscures the clear comprehension of the relationship. Hence
arises a twofold confusion. The origin of surplus value becomes
unclear—and for this reason Ricardo is reproached by his
successors for having failed to grasp the nature of surplus
value, for having failed to explain it. To this the scholastic
attempts of his successors to explain it are partly due. Moreover, because the origin and nature of surplus value are
not clearly conceived, the surplus labour plus the necessary
labour, in short the total working day, is considered as a
fixed magnitude; the differences in the amount of the surplus
value are overlooked, and the productivity of capital, its
drive for surplus labour—on the one hand for absolute surplus
labour, and then its innate urge to shorten the necessary
labour time—are not recognised, and therefore the historical
justification for capital is left unexplained. Adam Smith, on
the other hand, had already stated the correct formula.
Important as it was to resolve value into labour, it was of
equal importance to resolve surplus value into surplus labour,
and to do so in explicit terms.

Ricardo starts from the actual fact of capitalist production.
The value of labour is smaller than the value of the product
which it creates. The value of the product is therefore greater
than the value of the labour which produces it, or the value of
the wages. The excess of the value of the product over the
value of the wages is equal to the surplus value. Ricardo says
wrongly the profit, but as previously noted he here identifies
profit with surplus value and is in fact speaking of the latter.
For him it is a fact that the value of the product is greater
than the value of the wages. How this fact arises remains
unclear. The total working day is greater than the part of the
working day required for the production of the wage. Why?
That does not emerge. The magnitude of the working day is
therefore wrongly presupposed as fixed, and from this follow
consequences that are directly false. The increase or reduction
of surplus value can therefore be explained *only* from the
growing or diminishing productivity of social labour, which
produces the means of subsistence. That is to say, only relative
surplus value is understood.

It is evident that if the labourer needed his whole day to

produce his own means of subsistence—that is to say, to produce commodities equal to his own means of subsistence—no surplus value would be possible, and therefore no capitalist production and no wage labour. In order for the latter to exist, the productivity of social labour must be sufficiently developed for there to be some excess of the total working day over the labour time necessary for the reproduction of the wages, surplus labour of some amount. But it is equally evident that with a given labour time, a given length of the working day, the productivity of labour may be very different; and on the other hand that with a given productivity of labour the labour time, the length of the working day, may be very different. It is moreover clear that if a certain development of the productivity of labour must be assumed in order for surplus labour to exist, the mere possibility of this surplus labour, that is, the existence of that necessary minimum productivity of labour, does not in itself make it actual. In addition, the labourer must first be compelled to work in excess of that time; and this compulsion is exerted by capital. This is missing in Ricardo, and hence also the whole struggle over the regulation of the normal working day.

At a lower stage in the development of the social productive power of labour, when therefore the surplus labour is relatively small, the class of those who live on the labour of others is in general small in relation to the number of labourers. Proportionately to this number, it can grow to a very significant degree, in the measure that productivity, and therefore relative surplus value, develops.

It is moreover incontestable that the value of labour varies at different times in the same country, and very materially differs in different countries. Nevertheless, it is the temperate zones that are the home of capitalist production. The social productive power of labour may be very undeveloped, and yet this may be counterbalanced in the production of the means of subsistence, on the one hand by the fertility of the natural factors such as the land, and on the other by the limited needs of the inhabitants owing to the climate, etc.—both of which apply in India for example. Where conditions are unfavourable, the minimum of wages may be very small quantitatively in use values owing to the undeveloped state of social needs, although this minimum may cost much labour to produce. But even if the labour necessary for its production were only of average quantity, the surplus value produced— even though high in proportion to the wage, to the necessary labour time, that is, even with a high rate of surplus value— when expressed in use values would be proportionately just as paltry as the wage itself.

Let the necessary labour time be 10, the surplus labour 2; and the total working day 12 hours. If the necessary labour time were 12, the surplus labour $2\frac{2}{5}$, and the total working day $14\frac{2}{5}$ hours, the values produced would be very different. In the first case they would be equal to 12 hours, in the second to $14\frac{2}{5}$ hours. So also would be the absolute size of the surplus values. In the first case the surplus value would be equal to 2 hours, in the second to $2\frac{2}{5}$ hours. Nevertheless the rate of surplus value or of surplus labour would be the same, since $2 : 10$ is equal to $2\frac{2}{5} : 12$. If in the second case the variable capital laid out were larger, so also would be the surplus value or surplus labour appropriated by it. If in the latter case the surplus labour were to increase by $\frac{5}{5}$ of an hour instead of $\frac{2}{5}$, so that it was equal to 3 hours, and the total working day were 15 hours, the rate of surplus value would have risen, although the necessary labour time or the minimum of wages had increased, for $2 : 10$ is equal to $\frac{1}{5}$, but $3 : 12$ is equal to $\frac{1}{4}$. Both could happen, if as a result of corn, etc., becoming dearer the minimum of wages had risen from 10 to 12 hours. Even in this case therefore not only might the rate of surplus value remain the same, but the mass and rate of surplus value might increase.

But suppose that the necessary wage were 10 as before, the surplus labour 2, and all other conditions remained the same— that is to say, no account is taken of lowered production costs for constant capital. Then let the labourer work $2\frac{2}{5}$ hours longer, appropriating for himself 2 hours, while the $\frac{2}{5}$ constitutes surplus labour. In this case wage and surplus value would increase in equal proportion, the former however representing more than the necessary wage or the necessary labour time.

If we take a given magnitude and divide it into two parts,

it is clear that one part can only increase to the extent that the other diminishes, and *vice versa*. But with increasing (fluent) magnitudes this is by no means the case. And the working day is such an increasing magnitude, so long as no normal working day has been won. In the case of such magnitudes both parts may increase, either in equal or in unequal degree. The increase of one is not conditioned by the diminution of the other, and *vice versa*. This then is also the only case in which wages and surplus value can both increase, and even possibly increase in equal proportions measured in exchange value. So far as the use value is concerned, it is self-evident that it may increase even though for example the value of the labour declines. From 1797 to 1815, when in England the price of corn and the nominal wage rose considerably, the number of hours worked daily rose considerably in the principal industries, which were then also in a stage of reckless expansion. I believe that this checked the fall in the rate of profit, through the increased rate of surplus value. In this case, however, whatever the circumstances, the normal working day is lengthened and the labourer's normal span of life, hence the normal duration of his labour power, correspondingly shortened. This applies when such a lengthening of the working day remains constant. If it is only temporary, to compensate for a temporary rise in the cost of wages, its only consequences—except for children and women—may be to prevent the fall in the rate of profit in those enterprises where a prolongation of the labour time is in the nature of the case possible. This is least of all the case in agriculture.

Ricardo paid no attention whatever to this, because he investigated neither the origin of surplus value nor absolute surplus value, and therefore treats the working day as a fixed quantity. For this case, therefore, his law is incorrect: that surplus value (he wrongly says profit) and wages can rise or fall only in inverse proportion, measured in exchange value.

Let us take two examples. In the first let the necessary labour time be 10 hours, the surplus labour 2, the working day 12 hours, the surplus value 2 hours; the rate of surplus value $\frac{1}{5}$. In the second, the necessary labour time is the same, but the surplus value has risen from 2 to 4 hours. Thus we have a working day of 14 hours; the surplus value is equal to 4 hours, the rate of surplus value is $\frac{2}{7}$.

In both cases the necessary labour time is the same; but the surplus value in one case is twice as large as in the other, and the working day in the second example is $\frac{1}{6}$ longer than in the first. Moreover, although the wage is the same, the values produced, corresponding to the quantities of labour, would be very different; in the first case they would be equal to 12 hours, in the second to 14 hours. It is therefore not true that, assuming the wage to be the same (measured in value, in necessary labour time), the surplus value contained in two commodities is in the same proportion as the quantities of labour contained in them. This is only true when the *normal working day* is the same.

Let us further assume that as a result of the rise of labour productivity the necessary wage falls from 10 to 9 hours, although it remains constant expressed in use values, and that the surplus labour time falls from 2 to $1\frac{4}{5}$ hours. In this case 10 : 9 is equal to $\frac{10}{5} : \frac{9}{5}$. Thus the surplus labour time would fall in the same proportion as the necessary. The rate of surplus value would remain the same in both cases, for $\frac{10}{5} : 10$ is equal to $\frac{9}{5} : 9$. The quantity of use values that could be bought with the surplus value would also, on the assumption made, remain the same; but this would only hold good for those use values which are necessary means of subsistence. The working day would fall from 12 to $10\frac{4}{5}$ hours. The amount of value produced in the second case would be smaller than in the first. And in spite of these unequal quantities of labour the rate of surplus value would be the same in both cases.

In discussing surplus value we have distinguished between surplus value and rate of surplus value. Considered in relation to one working day, the surplus value is equal to the absolute number of hours which it represents—2, 3, and so on. The rate is equal to the proportion of this number of hours to the number of hours constituting the necessary labour time. This distinction is very important, because it brings out the varying length of the working day. If the surplus value is 2 hours, the rate is equal to $\frac{1}{5}$ when the necessary labour time is 10, and $\frac{1}{6}$ when the necessary labour time is 12. In the first case the working day is 12 hours; in the second, 14. In the first case the rate of surplus value is higher while at the same time the labourer works a smaller number of hours in the day. In the second case the rate of surplus value is lower, the value of the labour power greater, while at the same time the labourer works a greater number of hours in the day. From this we see how with the surplus value remaining unchanged but with a working day of unequal length, the rate of surplus value may be different. In the earlier case $10 : \frac{10}{5}$ and $9 : \frac{9}{5}$ we see how, with the rate of surplus value remaining unchanged but with a working day of unequal length, the surplus value itself may be different—in one case 2, in the other $1\frac{4}{5}$.

I have previously shown that if the length of the working day, the necessary labour time, and therefore the rate of surplus value, are given, then the amount of the surplus value depends on the number of labourers simultaneously employed by the same capital. This was a tautological statement. For if one working day gives me two hours of surplus labour, then twelve working days give me twenty-four such hours, or two days of surplus labour. The statement is however of great importance in determining profit, which is equal to the proportion which the surplus value bears to the capital advanced and therefore depends on the absolute size of the surplus value. This is important for the reason that capitals of equal size but of different organic composition employ an unequal number of workers, and must therefore produce unequal surplus values and hence an unequal profit. With a falling rate of surplus value profit can rise, and with a rising rate of surplus value profit can fall; or profit can remain the same, if the rise or fall in the rate of surplus value is compensated by an opposite change in the number of workers employed. From this we can at once see how completely wrong it is to identify the laws relating to the rise and fall of surplus value with the laws relating to the rise and fall of profit. If the simple law of surplus value is considered just by itself, the statement seems tautological—that with a given rate of surplus value and a given length of working day the absolute amount of surplus value depends on the amount of capital employed. For the increase in this amount of capital and the increase in the number of simultaneously employed workers are, on the assumption made, identical, or only different expressions for the same factor. But if we come to consider profit, where the amount of the total capital employed and the number of workers employed vary greatly for capitals of equal size, then the importance of the law can be understood.

Ricardo starts with considering commodities of given value, that is, commodities which represent a given quantity of labour. And from this starting point absolute surplus value and relative surplus value seem always to be identical. This at any rate explains his one-sided approach and is in keeping with his whole method of enquiry—to start from the value of commodities as determined by the definite labour time in them, and then to investigate to what extent this is affected by wages, profit, etc. This apparent identity is, however, false, as what is being considered is not the commodity, but capitalist production, commodities as products of capital.

Assume that a given capital employs a definite number of workers, for example 20, and that the wages amount to £20. To simplify the example we will put the fixed capital at 0, that is, leave it out of account. Let us also assume that these twenty workers spin 1,600 lb. of cotton into yarn, working twelve hours a day. If the cotton costs 1s. a lb., 20 lb. cost £1 and 1,600 lb. £80. If 20 workers spin 1,600 lb. in 12 hours, in 1 hour they spin $\frac{1600}{12}$ lb., that is, $133\frac{1}{3}$ lb. If the necessary labour time is equal to 10 hours, the surplus labour time is 2 hours, and this is equal to $266\frac{2}{3}$ lb. yarn. The value of 1,600 lb. yarn would be £104. For if 10 hours of work produce a value of £20, 1 hour produces £2 and 12 hours £24, to which must be added £80 worth of raw material.

But if the workers worked 4 hours of surplus labour time, the product of these 4 hours would amount to £8, and the value of the total product would be £$121\frac{1}{3}$. And this £$121\frac{1}{3}$ is equivalent of $1,866\frac{2}{3}$ lb. of yarn. As before, since the conditions of production had remained the same, 1 lb. of yarn would have the same value, $1\frac{3}{10}$ of a shilling; it would contain the same amount of labour time. So also, in accordance with the assumption, the necessary wages, that is, their value, the labour time contained in them, would have remained constant.

Nevertheless, under the conditions assumed, the relation between value and surplus value in each pound of yarn would be quite different. In the first case, since the necessary labour was equal to £20, the surplus labour to £4, or 10 hours and 2 hours, the ratio of the surplus labour to the necessary labour would be 2 : 10. In the $\frac{3}{10}$ of a shilling newly added labour in a pound of yarn there would in this case be $\frac{1}{6}$ unpaid labour, that is, $\frac{3}{50}$ of a shilling. In the second case, on the other hand, the necessary labour would be equal to £20, the surplus labour to £8. The ratio of the surplus labour to the necessary labour would be 8 : 20. Therefore in the $\frac{3}{10}$ of a shilling of newly added labour in 1 lb. of yarn, there would be $\frac{2}{8}$ unpaid labour, that is, $\frac{6}{50}$ of a shilling. The surplus value in the pound of yarn, although in both cases the yarn has the same value and in both cases the same wages are paid, is in one case twice as large as in the other.

Ricardo, then, deals only with what I have called relative surplus value. He takes as his starting point, as Adam Smith and his predecessors did, that there is a fixed length of the working day. Adam Smith mentions at the most differences in the length of the working day in different industries, which are levelled out or compensated by relatively greater intensity of labour, difficulty, unpleasantness, etc. On the basis of this assumption Ricardo in general correctly explains relative surplus value. Before we give the principal points of his theory, we will cite a few more passages showing his conception of it.

"The labour of a million of men in manufactures will always produce the same value, but will not always produce the same riches" (p. 182).

This means that the product of their day's labour will always be the product of a million days of labour, will contain the same labour time; which is untrue, or is only true when the same normal working day, taking into account the various hardships, etc., of different trades, has been generally established. Even then, however, the statement is wrong in the general form in which it is here expressed. If the normal working day is 12 hours, and one man's annual product, measured in money, is £50, and the value of money remains unchanged, then in this case the product of a million men would always amount to £50 million annually. If the necessary labour is 6 hours, the variable capital expended for these million men would be £25 million a year. The surplus value would also amount to £25 million. The product would always be £50 million, whether the workers received £25 million, or £30 or £40 million. But the surplus value would be in the first case £25 million, in the second £20 million, and in the third £10 million. If the capital advanced consisted only of variable capital, that is, only of capital advanced as wages for these million men, Ricardo would be right. And he would be right only in that one case, when the total capital is equal to the variable capital—an assumption which runs through his work, as also the work of Adam Smith, when he is speaking of the capital of society as a whole, but which does not hold good in capitalist production for any single branch of production, and still less for the production of society as a whole.

That part of the constant capital which enters into the labour process but not into the process of the creation of value, does not enter into the product, into the value of the product, and therefore does not concern us here, where we are considering the value of the annual product, important as it is to take that part of the constant capital into account in determining the general rate of profit. But the position is not the same with that part of the constant capital which enters into the annual product. We have seen that one portion of this part of the constant capital, or what appears in the form of constant capital in one sphere of production, in another sphere appears as the immediate product of labour during the same production period of one year; that therefore a considerable part of the capital advanced each year, which appears as constant capital from the standpoint of the individual capitalist or the particular sphere of production, resolves itself into variable capital from the standpoint of society or of the capitalist class. This part is therefore included in the £50 million; in that part of the £50 million which forms the variable capital or is advanced as wages. But the position is different with the part of the constant capital which is used up to replace the constant capital consumed in industry and agriculture—with the consumed part of the constant capital employed in those branches of production which produce constant capital, raw materials in their first form, fixed capital and auxiliary materials. The value of this part reappears, is reproduced in the product. And it entirely depends on its actual size (assuming that the productivity of labour does not change; but however much it changes, this part of the constant capital is of a definite size) in what proportions it enters into the value of the total product. (On the average, apart from certain exceptions in agriculture, the amount of the product, that is, of the *riches* produced by the million men—which Ricardo distinguishes from the *value*, will in any case also depend on the size of the constant capital which is the pre-requisite of production.) This part of the value of the product would not exist but for the new labour of the million men during the year. On the other hand, the labour of the million men would not have yielded the same amount of products but for this constant capital existing independently of their labour during the year. It enters into the labour process as means of production, but not a single additional hour is worked to reproduce the value of this part. As value, therefore, it is not the result of the year's labour, although its value would not have been reproduced without this year's labour. If the amount of the constant capital which enters into the product were £25 million, the value of the million men's product would be £75 million; if it were £10 million, then the value of the million men's product would amount to only £60 million, and so on. And since the proportion which the constant capital bears to the variable increases in the course of capitalist development, the value of the annual product of a million men will have a tendency to rise continuously, in proportion to the growth of the past labour which plays a part in their annual production. This in itself shows that Ricardo was unable to understand either the essence of accumulation or the nature of profit. With the growth in the proportion of constant capital to variable grow also the productivity of labour, and the productive forces which social labour creates and with which it operates. It is true that as a result of this very increase in the productivity of labour a part of the constant capital is continuously depreciated in value, inasmuch as its value depends not on the labour time which it had originally cost, but on the labour time with which it can be reproduced, and this latter is continuously reduced as the productivity of labour increases. But although because of this its value does not grow in proportion to its amount, nevertheless it does grow, because its amount grows even faster than its value diminishes. However, we shall return later to Ricardo's views on accumulation. This much is at least clear at this stage—that assuming a given working day, the value of the annual product of the labour of the million men will vary very considerably, in accordance with the difference in the amount of the constant capital which enters into the product, and that in spite of the growing productivity of labour it will be greater where the constant capital forms a considerable part of the total capital than in social conditions in which it forms a relatively small part. With the advance in the productivity of social labour, accompanied as it is by the growth of the constant capital, there will consequently also be a constant increase in the part of the annual product of labour which falls to the share of capital as such, and therefore property in the form of capital (let alone revenue) will continuously increase, and the proportion of that part of value which is created by the individual worker and even by the working class will fall more and more, as compared with the product of their past labour confronting them as capital. The alienation and the antagonism between labour power and the objective conditions of labour which have made themselves independent as capital therefore grows continuously. And this is without taking into account the variable capital, that part of the product of the annual labour which is required for the reproduction of the working class but which confronts it as capital.

Ricardo's view that the working day is given, determined, a fixed magnitude, is also expressed by him in other forms—for example, "wages and profits taken together will continue always of the same value" (Chapter XXXII, p. 276); which in other words only means that the daily labour time, the product of which is *divided* between wages and profit, is always the same, is constant.

It is hardly necessary for me to repeat here that in these passages it is necessary to read "surplus value" instead of "profit".

"Wages are to be estimated by their real value, viz., by the quantity of labour and capital employed in producing them, and not by their nominal value either in coats, hats, money, or corn" (Chapter I, Section VII, p. 32).

The value of the means of subsistence which the worker receives, which he buys with his wages—corn, clothing, etc.— is determined by the total labour time necessary for their production: both the quantity of immediate labour and the quantity of materialised labour. But Ricardo confuses the issue by not expressing it in an exact way, by not saying: "their real value, viz., that part of the working day which is required to reproduce the value of the necessary means of subsistence, the equivalent of these means of subsistence that is paid to him in exchange for his labour". Real wages are determined by the average time which the worker must work each day in order to produce or reproduce his own wage.

"The labourer is only paid a really high price for his labour when his wages will purchase the produce of a great deal of labour "(Chapter XX, p. 183, footnote).

(e) Relative Surplus Value

This is in fact the only form of surplus value which Ricardo analyses, under the name of profit. His theory is as follows.

The quantity of labour necessary for the production of a commodity and contained in it determines its value, which is therefore a given, definite amount. This amount is divided between wage worker and capitalist. Ricardo, like Adam Smith, does not here take into account constant capital. It is clear that the share of one can only rise or fall in proportion as that of the other falls or rises. As the value of commodities is due to the labour of the workers, the presupposition of value is in all circumstances labour itself; but labour is impossible unless the worker lives and maintains himself, that is, unless he receives the necessary wages, the minimum wages equivalent to the value of his labour power. Wages and surplus value— these two categories into which the value of the commodity or the product itself is divided—are therefore not only in inverse proportion to each other, but the prior determinant is the movement of wages. Their rise or fall causes the inverse movement on the part of profit (surplus value). Wages do not rise or fall because profit (surplus value) falls or rises, but on the contrary, because wages rise or fall, surplus value (profit) falls or rises. The surplus product—strictly speaking, the surplus value—which remains over after the working class receive their share of their own annual production, forms the substance on which the capitalist class lives.

As the value of commodities is determined by the quantity of labour contained in them, and wages and surplus value (profit) are only shares, proportions, in which two classes of producers divide the value of the commodity between them, it is clear that a rise or fall in wages, although it determines the rate of surplus value (profit), leaves the value of the commodity—or its price as the money expression of the value of the commodity—unaffected. The proportion in which a whole is divided between two participants makes the whole itself neither larger nor smaller. The preconceived notion that a rise in wages increases the price of commodities is therefore false; it only makes the profit (surplus value) fall. Even the exceptions cited by Ricardo, in which a rise in wages is supposed to make the exchange value of some commodities fall and that of others rise, are not true so far as *value* is concerned, and they are only true for *prices of production*.

Since then the rate of surplus value (profit) is determined by the relative height of wages, how is the latter determined? Apart from competition, by the price of the necessary means of subsistence. This in turn depends on the productivity of labour, which is all the greater in proportion to the fertility of the soil—Ricardo here assuming capitalist production. Every technical improvement reduces the price of commodities, of the means of subsistence. Wages or the value of labour therefore rise and fall in inverse ratio to the development of the productive power of labour—in so far as the latter produces the necessary means of subsistence which enter into the average consumption of the working class. The rate of surplus value (profit) therefore falls or rises in direct proportion to the development of the productive power of labour, because this development reduces or increases wages.

The rate of profit (surplus value) cannot fall unless wages rise, and it cannot rise unless wages fall.

The value of wages has to be reckoned not on the basis of the quantity of necessaries which the worker receives, but on the basis of the quantity of labour which these necessaries cost—actually the proportion of the working day which he appropriates for himself; the proportionate share of the total product, or rather of the total value of this product, which the worker receives. It is possible that, reckoned in use values (quantity of commodities or money), his wages may rise as productivity increases, and yet reckoned in value they may fall, and *vice versa*. It is one of Ricardo's greatest merits that he made an examination of relative wages and established them as a definite category. Previously wages had always been looked upon as a simple element, and consequently the worker had been regarded as an animal. In Ricardo, however, he is considered in his social relationship. The position of the classes in relation to each other depends to a greater extent on the proportion which the wage forms than on the absolute amount of the wage.

What has been said above must now be substantiated by quotations from Ricardo.

". . . the value of the deer, the produce of the hunter's day's labour, would be exactly equal to the value of the fish, the produce of the fisherman's day's labour. The comparative value of the fish and the game would be entirely regulated by the quantity of labour realised in each, whatever might be the quantity of production or however high or low general wages or profits might be. If . . . the fisherman . . . employed ten men, whose annual labour cost £100, and who in one day obtained by their labour twenty salmon: If . . . the hunter . . . also employed ten men, whose annual labour cost £100, and who in one day procured him ten deer; then the natural price of a deer would be two salmon, whether the proportion of the whole produce bestowed on the men who obtained it were large or small. The proportion which might be paid for wages is of the utmost importance in the question of profits; for it must at once be seen that profits would be high or low exactly in proportion as wages were low or high; but it could not in the least affect the relative value of fish and game, as wages would be high or low at the same time in both occupations" (Chapter I, Section III, pp. 15–16).

It can be seen that Ricardo derives the whole value of the commodity from the *labour* of the men employed. It is their own work, that is, the product of their work, or the value of this product, which is divided between them and capital.

"No alteration in the wages of labour could produce any alteration in the relative value of these commodities; for suppose them to rise, no greater quantity of labour would be required in any of these occupations but it would be paid for at a higher price. . . . Wages might rise 20 per cent., and profits consequently fall in a greater or less proportion, without occasioning the least alteration in the relative value of these commodities" (p. 17).

"There can be no rise in the value of labour without a fall of profits. If the corn is to be divided between the farmer and the labourer, the larger the proportion that is given to the latter the less will remain for the former. So, if cloth or cotton goods be divided between the workman and his employer, the larger the proportion given to the former the less remains for the latter" (Chapter I, Section IV, p. 21).

"Adam Smith, and all the writers who have followed him, have, without one exception that I know of, maintained that a rise in the price of labour would be uniformly followed by a rise in the price of all commodities. I hope I have succeeded in showing that there are no grounds for such an opinion" (Chapter I, Section VI, p. 29).

". . . a rise of wages, from the circumstance of the labourer being more liberally rewarded, or from a difficulty of procuring the necessaries on which wages are expended, does not, except in some instances, produce the effect of raising price, but has a great effect in lowering profits" (Chapter I, Section VII, p. 31).

The position is different however when the rise in wages is due to "an alteration in the value of money".

"In the one case [i.e., the one just mentioned] no greater proportion of the annual labour of the country is devoted to the support of the labourers; in the other case, a larger portion is so devoted" (p. 31).

That Ricardo consciously identifies value with production costs is shown by the following passages.

"Mr. Malthus appears to think that it is a part of my doctrine that the cost and value of a thing should be the same; it is, if he means by cost, 'cost of production' including profits" (Chapter I, Section VI, p. 30, footnote).

"With a rise in the price of food and necessaries, the natural price of labour will rise; with the fall in their price, the natural price of labour will fall" (Chapter V, p. 52).

". . . the surplus produce remaining, after satisfying the wants of the existing population, must necessarily be in proportion to the facility of production, viz., to the smaller number of persons employed in production" (Chapter V, p. 56).

"Neither the farmer who cultivates that quantity of land which regulates price, nor the manufacturer who manufactures goods, sacrifice any portion of the produce for rent. The whole value of their commodities is divided into two portions only: one constitutes the profits of stock, the other the wages of labour" (Chapter VI, p. 64).

"Suppose the price of silks, velvets, furniture, and any other commodities, not required by the labourer, to rise in consequence of more labour being expended on them, would not that affect profits? Certainly not: for nothing can affect profits but a rise in wages; silks and velvets are not consumed by the labourer, and therefore cannot raise wages" (Chapter VI, p. 70).

"If the labour of ten men will, on land of a certain quality, obtain 180 quarters of wheat, and its value be £4 per quarter, or £720; . . . in all cases, the same sum of £720 must be divided between wages and profits. . . . Whether wages or profits rise or fall, it is this sum of £720 from which they must both be provided. On the one hand, profits can never rise so high as to absorb so much of this £720 that enough will not be left to furnish the labourers with absolute necessaries; on the other hand, wages can never rise so high as to leave no portion of this sum for profits" (Chapter VI, pp. 66–7).

". . . profits depend on high or low wages, wages on the

price of necessaries, and the price of necessaries chiefly on the price of food, because all other requisites may be increased almost without limit" (Chapter VI, p. 71).

"Although a greater value is produced,[1] a greater proportion of what remains of that value, after paying rent, is consumed by the producers,[2] and it is this, and this alone, which regulates profits" (Chapter VI, p. 75).

"It is the essential quality of an improvement to diminish the quantity of labour before required to produce a commodity; and this diminution cannot take place without a fall of its price or relative value" (Chapter II, p. 42).

"Diminish the cost of production of hats, and their price will ultimately fall to their new natural price, although the demand should be doubled, trebled or quadrupled. Diminish the cost of subsistence of men, by diminishing the natural price of the food and clothing by which life is sustained, and wages will ultimately fall, notwithstanding that the demand for labourers may very greatly increase" (Chapter XXX, p. 260).

"In proportion as less is appropriated for wages, more will be appropriated for profits, and *vice versa*" (Chapter XXXII, p. 281).

"It has been one of the objects of this work to show that, with every fall in the real value of necessaries, the wages of labour would fall, and that the profits of stock would rise; in other words, that of any given annual value a less portion would be paid to the labouring class, and a larger portion to those whose funds employed this class.[3] Suppose the value of the commodities produced in a particular manufacture to be £1,000, and to be divided between the master and his labourers, in the proportion of £800 to labourers and £200 to the master; if the value of these commodities should fall to £900, and £100 be saved from the wages of labour, in consequence of the fall of necessaries, the net income of the master would be in no degree impaired" (Chapter XXXII, p. 287).

---

[1] When poorer lands are taken into cultivation.

[2] Here he identifies workers with producers.

[3] It is only in this statement, which has now become quite a commonplace, that Ricardo proclaims the nature of capital, even though he does not suspect it himself. It is not accumulated capital employed by the working-class, by the workers themselves, but a fund by which this class is employed, accumulated labour which employs living, immediate labour.

"If the shoes and clothing of the labourer could, by improvements in machinery, be produced by one-fourth of the labour now necessary to their production, they would probably fall 75 per cent.; but so far is it from being true that the labourer would thereby be enabled permanently to consume four coats, or four pair of shoes, instead of one, that it is probable his wages would in no long time be adjusted by the effects of competition, and the stimulus to population, to the new value of the necessaries on which they were expended. If these improvements extended to all the objects of the labourer's consumption, we should find him probably, at the end of a very few years, in possession of only a small, if any, addition to his enjoyments, although the exchangeable value of those commodities, compared with any other commodity, in the manufacture of which no such improvement were made, had sustained a very considerable reduction; and though they were the produce of a very considerably diminished quantity of labour" (Chapter I, Section 1, p. 9).

"When wages rise, it is always at the expense of profits, and when they fall, profits always rise" (Chapter XXXII, p. 276, footnote).

"It has been my endeavour to show throughout this work that the rate of profits can never be increased but by a fall in wages, and that there can be no permanent fall of wages but in consequence of a fall of the necessaries on which wages are expended. If, therefore, by the extension of foreign trade, or by improvements in machinery, the food and necessaries of the labourer can be brought to market, at a reduced price, profits will rise. If, instead of growing our own corn, or manufacturing the clothing and other necessaries of the labourer, we discover a new market from which we can supply ourselves with these commodities at a cheaper price, wages will fall and profits rise; but if the commodities obtained at a cheaper rate, by the extension of foreign commerce, or by the improvement of machinery, be exclusively the commodities consumed by the rich, no alteration will take place in the rate of profits. The rate of wages would not be affected, although wine, velvets, silks, and other expensive commodities should fall 50 per cent., and consequently profits would continue unaltered.

"Foreign trade, then, though highly beneficial to a

country, as it increases the amount and variety of the objects on which revenue may be expended, and affords, by the abundance and cheapness of commodities, incentives to saving,[1] and to the accumulation of capital, has no tendency to raise the profits of stock unless the commodities imported be of that description on which the wages of labour are expended.

"The remarks which have been made respecting foreign trade, apply equally to home trade. The rate of profits is never increased by a better distribution of labour, by the invention of machinery, by the establishment of roads and canals, or by any means of abridging labour either in the manufacture or in the conveyance of goods.[2] These are causes which operate on price, and never fail to be highly beneficial to consumers; since they enable them, with the same labour, or with the value of the produce of the same labour, to obtain in exchange a greater quantity of the commodity to which the improvement is applied; but they have no effect whatever on profit. On the other hand, every diminution in the wages of labour raises profits, but produces no effect on the price of commodities. One is advantageous to all classes, for all classes are consumers;[3] the other is beneficial only to producers; they gain more, but everything remains at its former price.[4] In the first case they get the same as before; but everything[5] on which their gains are expended is diminished in exchangeable value" (Chapter VII, pp. 80–1).

It is evident that this passage is very carelessly worded. But apart from this formal point, all that is said is only true if—as in this whole investigation of relative surplus value—

---

[1] And why not incentives to spending?

[2] He has just said the exact opposite. He means, apparently, never except when the value of labour is reduced by the improvements mentioned.

[3] But how is it advantageous to the working-class, since Ricardo's assumption is that either these commodities enter into consumption through wages, in which case they reduce wages; or if their becoming cheaper does not reduce wages, then they are not commodities on which wages are expended?

[4] Again, how is this possible, since Ricardo assumes that the reduction of wages which raises profits takes place precisely because the price of the necessary means of subsistence has fallen? Therefore it is not at all true that "everything remains at its former price".

[5] This also is wrong. He means in fact everything except the necessary means of subsistence.

"rate of surplus value" is read instead of rate of profit. Even in the case of luxury commodities such technical improvements can raise the general rate of profit, since the rate of profit in these spheres of production, as in all other spheres, plays a part in the levelling out of all particular rates of profit into the average rate of profit. The rate of profit will also rise in such cases if, owing to the causes mentioned, the value of the constant capital falls in proportion to the variable, or the period of turnover is reduced and a change takes place in the process of circulation. Moreover, the influence of foreign trade is conceived in a completely one-sided way. The essential characteristic of capitalist production is that product develops into commodity, which is in essence bound up with the extension of the market, the creation of the world market, and hence foreign trade.

Apart from this, Ricardo is right in advancing the proposition that all technical improvements, whether through division of labour, improvement of machinery, progress in the means of communication—in a word, everything that serves to reduce the necessary labour time in industry or in the transport of commodities—increase surplus value (and profit), and therefore enrich the capitalist class, because and in so far as these "improvements" reduce the value of labour.

Before concluding this section we have still to quote a few passages in which Ricardo analyses the nature of relative wages.

"If I have to hire a labourer for a week, and instead of ten shillings I pay him eight, no variation having taken place in the value of money, the labourer can probably obtain more food and necessaries with his eight shillings than he before obtained for ten: but this is owing, not to a rise in the real value of his wages, as stated by Adam Smith, and more recently by Mr. Malthus, but to a fall in the value of the things on which his wages are expended, things perfectly distinct; and yet for calling this a fall in the real value of wages, I am told that I adopt new and unusual language, not reconcilable with the true principles of the science" (Chapter I, Section I, p. 11).

"It is not by the absolute quantity of produce obtained

by either class that we can correctly judge of the rate of profit, rent, and wages, but by the quantity of labour required to obtain that produce. By improvements in machinery and agriculture the whole produce may be doubled; but if wages, rent and profit be also doubled, these three will bear the same proportions to one another as before, and neither could be said to have relatively varied. But if wages partook not of the whole of this increase; if they, instead of being doubled, were only increased one-half . . . it would, I apprehend, be correct for me to say . . . that wages had fallen while profits had risen; for if we had an invariable standard by which to measure the value of this produce we should find that a less value had fallen to the class of labourers . . . and a greater to the class of capitalists, than had been given before" (Chapter I, Section VII, p. 31).

"[The fall in wages] will not the less be a real fall because they might furnish him with a greater quantity of cheap commodities than his former wages" (p 32).

De Quincey emphasises some of the arguments which Ricardo developed in opposition to those of other economists.

"When all the economists before Ricardo asked what determined the value of all commodities; it was answered that this value was chiefly determined by wages. When again it was asked—what determined wages? it was recollected that wages must obviously be adjusted to the value of the commodities upon which they were spent; and the answer was in effect that wages were determined by the value of commodities" ("Dialogues of Three Templars on Political Economy Chiefly in Relation to the Principles of Mr. Ricardo", *London Magazine*, 1824, Vol. IX, p. 560).

In the same Dialogues occurs the following passage on the law governing the measurement of value by the quantity of labour and the value of labour.

"In fact so far are the two formulae from presenting merely two different expressions of the same law, that the very best way of expressing negatively Mr. Ricardo's law[1] would

1 That is, that the value of A is to the value of B as the quantities of the labour that produces them.

be to say—A is not to B in value as the values of the producing labour"[1] (p. 348).

The following passages are from Th. de Quincey's *The Logic of Political Economy*, Edinburgh, 1844:

"If the price is ten shillings, then . . . wages and profits, taken as a whole, cannot exceed ten shillings. . . . But do not the wages and profits as a whole themselves, on the contrary, predetermine the price? No; that is the old superannuated doctrine" (p. 204).

"The new economy has shown that all price is governed by proportional quantity of the producing labour, and by that only. Being itself once settled, then, *ipso facto*, price settles the fund out of which both wages and profits must draw their separate dividends" (p. 204). "Any change that can disturb the existing relations between wages and profits must originate in wages" (p. 205).

"Ricardo . . . has endeavoured to bring the question of rent into immediate relation with value, by putting the question upon it in this shape—'Whether the appropriation of land, and the consequent creation of rent, will occasion any variation in the relative value of commodities, independently of the quantity of labour necessary to production?' " (p. 158).

[1] If the organic composition of the capital in A and B were the same, then we could in fact say that they are related to each other in the same proportion as the values of the labour which produced them. For the accumulated labour in each as well as the immediate labour in each would be in the same proportion. The quantities of labour paid in each, however, would be related to each other in the same proportions as the total quantities of immediate labour expended on them. If the organic composition of both capitals is $80c + 20v$ and the rate of surplus value is 50 per cent., and if the first capital is 500 and the other 300, then the product in the first case would be 550 and in the second 330. This relation to each other would then also be in the same proportion as the wages, namely, 100 : 60 or 5 : 3. But even then we should only know the proportion between the values, and not the actual values, since there are very many quantities of value which correspond to proportion 5 : 3.

4. THE RATE OF PROFIT

(a) Amount of Profit and Rate of Profit

IT has already been shown in some detail that, with the working day assumed as fixed, the laws of surplus value—or rather, of the rate of surplus value—are not so directly and simply coincident with or applicable to the laws of profit as Ricardo makes them out to be; that he wrongly identifies surplus value with profit; that these are only identical in so far as the total capital consists of variable capital, or is directly expended in wages; that therefore what Ricardo deals with under the name of "profit" is generally speaking only surplus value; and that it is only in this case too that the total product resolves itself simply into wages and surplus value. Ricardo evidently shares Adam Smith's view that the total annual product resolves itself into revenues. Hence also his confusion between value and price of production.

It is not necessary to repeat here that the rate of profit is not directly governed by the same laws as the rate of surplus value.

First, the rate of profit may rise or fall as a result of a fall or rise in rent, independently of any change in the value of labour.

Secondly, the absolute amount of profit is equal to the absolute amount of surplus value. But the latter is determined not only by the rate of surplus value, but just as much by the number of workers employed. The same amount of profit is therefore possible with a falling rate of surplus value and a rising number of workers, and *vice versa*, etc.

Thirdly, with a given rate of surplus value, the rate of profit depends on the organic composition of capital.

Fourthly, with a given surplus value and the organic composition of capital per 100 also assumed as given, the rate of profit depends on the relative value of the different parts of the capital, which may be affected in different ways, partly by economy of power, etc., in the use of the means of production, partly by changes in value which may affect one part of the capital while leaving the other parts unaffected.

Finally, it would be necessary also to take into account differences in the composition of capital arising from the process of circulation.

Some of the incidental reflections which Ricardo himself makes should have led him to the distinction between surplus value and profit. Because he does not make this distinction, he seems—as has been shown in the analysis of Chapter I "On Value"—to have fallen here and there into the vulgar view that profit is a mere addition over and above the value of the commodity; as for example when he discusses the determination of profit on capital in which fixed capital predominates, etc. This is the source of much nonsense among his disciples. The vulgar view is bound to insinuate itself unless the statement (which for practical purposes is correct) that on the average capitals of equal size yield equal profits, or that the profit depends on the size of the capital employed, is linked by a series of intermediate propositions with the general laws of value, etc.; in a word, when profit and surplus value are treated as identical, which is only correct for the total capital. Hence it is that for Ricardo there are also no ways or means for the determination of a general rate of profit.

Ricardo sees that the rate of profit is not affected by such changes in the value (or price) of commodities as take effect on all parts of the capital in equal degrees, as for example changes in the value of money. He should therefore have reached the conclusion that it *is* affected by such changes as do not take effect on all parts of the capital in equal degree; that therefore changes in the rate of profit are possible with the value of labour remaining unchanged, and even in the opposite direction to changes in the value of labour. Above all, however, he should have clung firmly to the point that he is here calculating the surplus product—or what for him is the same thing, the surplus value, or what is again the same thing, the surplus labour—when he is considering it *sub specie* profit, not in proportion to the variable capital only, but in proportion to the whole capital advanced. With reference to a change in the value of money, he says:

"The variation in the value of money, however great, makes no difference in the *rate* of profits; for suppose the goods of the manufacturer to rise from £1,000 to £2,000, or 100 per cent., if his capital, on which the variations of money have as much effect as on the value of produce, if his machinery, buildings, and stock in trade rise also a 100 per cent., his rate of profits will be the same. . . . If, with a capital of a given value, he can, by economy in labour, double the quantity of produce, and it fall to half its former price, it will bear the same proportion to the capital that produced it which it did before, and consequently profits will still be at the same rate. If, at the same time that he doubles the quantity of produce by the employment of the same capital, the value of money is by any accident lowered one half, the produce will sell for twice the money value that it did before; but the capital employed to produce it will also be of twice its former money value; and therefore in this case, too, the value of the produce will bear the same proportion to the value of the capital as it did before" (Chapter I, Section VII, p. 32).

If in the last sentence Ricardo means surplus product where he says produce, the statement is correct. For the rate of profit is equal to the surplus product (surplus value) divided by the capital employed. But if he means the total product, then the facts are not correctly expressed. In this case, by the proportion of the value of the produce to the value of the capital he would evidently mean nothing more than the excess of the value of the commodity over the value of the capital advanced. In any case it can be seen that *here* he is not identifying profit with surplus value or the rate of profit with the rate of surplus value—the latter being equal to the surplus value divided by the value of labour or the variable capital.

In Chapter XXXII Ricardo says:

". . . the raw produce of which commodities are made is supposed to have fallen in price, and, therefore, commodities will fall on that account. True, they will fall, but their fall will not be attended with any diminution in the money income of the producer. If he sell his commodity for less money, it is only because one of the materials from which it is made has fallen in value. If the clothier sell his cloth for

£900 instead of £1,000, his income will not be less, if the wool from which it is made has declined £100 in value" (p. 290).

The effect in a practical case, which is the point with which Ricardo is here actually dealing, does not concern us. But a sudden fall in the value of wool would certainly affect adversely the money income of such clothiers, who would have in stock a large supply of finished cloth, manufactured at a time when wool was dearer but which has to be sold after wool has fallen in value.

If, as Ricardo here assumes, the clothiers set in motion the same quantity of labour as before (they could even set more in motion, since a part of the capital previously expended only on raw material is set free, and can now be expended on raw material and labour), it is clear that their "money income", taken in absolute terms, will not be smaller, but their rate of profit will be higher than previously; for the same amount, say £100, would now be calculated on £900 instead of £1,000. In the first case the rate of profit is 10 per cent. In the second it is 11⅑ per cent. Now since Ricardo's supposition is that the raw produce of which commodities are made has fallen generally, the general rate of profit would rise and not only the rate of profit in a single branch of production. That Ricardo does not see this is all the more strange because he sees the opposite case.

In Chapter VI in fact, "On Profits", Ricardo deals with the case when, as a result of the necessary means of subsistence becoming dearer owing to the cultivation of inferior land and consequently increasing differential rents, firstly wages, and secondly all raw produce won from the surface of the earth, would rise—an assumption that is by no means necessary, since cotton may very well fall in price, as also silk, wool and linen, although corn rises in price.

In the first place, he says that the surplus value (the word he uses is profit) of the farmer will fall, because the value of the product of the ten men whom he employs amounts to £720 as before, and he has to pay out of this fund of £720 more than before. And he continues:

"But the *rate* of profits will fall still more, because the capital of the farmer . . . consists in a great measure of raw produce, such as his corn and hay-ricks, his unthreshed wheat and barley, his horses and cows, which would all rise in price in consequence of the rise of produce. His absolute profits would fall from £480 to £445 15s.; but if, from the cause which I have just stated, his capital should rise from £3,000 to £3,200, the rate of his profits would, when corn was at £5 2s. 10d., be under 14 per cent.

"If a manufacturer had also employed £3,000 in his business, he would be obliged, in consequence of the rise of wages, to increase his capital, in order to be enabled to carry on the same business. If his commodities sold before for £720 they would continue to sell at the same price; but the wages of labour, which were before £240, would rise, when corn was at £5 2s. 10d., to £274 5s. In the first case he would have a balance of £480 as profit on £3,000, in the second he would have a profit only of £445 15s., on an increased capital, and therefore his profits would conform to the altered rate of those of the farmer" (Chapter VI, p. 69).

Thus in this passage Ricardo makes a distinction between *absolute profit (surplus value)* and *the rate of profit*, and also shows that as a result of the change in value of the capital advanced the rate of profit falls more than the absolute profit (surplus value) falls as a result of the rise in the value of labour. In this case the rate of profit would similarly have fallen, if the value of labour had remained the same, because the same absolute profit would have to be calculated on a larger capital. The opposite result—a rise in the rate of profit (as distinct from an increase in the surplus value or absolute profit)— would follow in the case mentioned earlier, when the value of the raw produce falls. It is evident therefore that rises and falls in the rate of profit can be brought about by other causes than rises and falls in the absolute profit and rises and falls in the rate of absolute profit calculated on the basis of the capital expended in wages.

Ricardo continues after the last quoted passage with the following:

"Articles of jewellery, of iron, of plate, and of copper, would not rise, because none of the raw produce from the surface of the earth enters into their composition" (p. 69).

The prices of these commodities will not rise, but the rate of profit in these branches of production would rise above that in the other branches. For in these latter there would be a smaller surplus value, owing to the rise in wages, on an advanced capital whose value had grown greater for two reasons: first, because the outlay on wages was greater, secondly, because the outlay on raw material was greater. In the second case there is a smaller surplus value on an advanced capital only the variable part of which has grown owing to the rise in wages. In these passages Ricardo himself throws overboard his whole theory of profit, which rests on wrongly identifying rate of surplus value with rate of profit.

"In every case, agricultural as well as manufacturing profits are lowered by a rise in the price of raw produce, if it be accompanied by a rise of wages" (p. 67).

From what Ricardo himself has said it follows that even when the rise in the price of raw produce is not accompanied by a rise of wages, the *rate of profit* would be lowered by a rise in the price of that part of the capital advanced which consists of raw produce.

"Suppose the price of silks, velvets, furniture, and any other commodities, not required by the labourer, to rise in consequence of more labour being expended on them, would not that affect profits? Certainly not: for nothing can affect profits but a rise in wages; silks and velvets are not consumed by the labourer, and therefore cannot raise wages" (p. 70).

There can be no doubt that *the rate of profit* in those particular branches of production would fall, although the value of labour, wages, remained the same. The raw material used by manufacturers of silks, pianos, furniture, etc., would have risen in price, and therefore the proportion which the same surplus value bore to the capital advanced, and hence the rate of profit, would have fallen. And the general rate of profit is the average of the particular rates of profit in all trades. Alternatively, in order to make the average rate of profit as before, those manufacturers would raise the price of their commodities. Such a nominal price increase does not directly affect the rate of profit, but only the way in which profit is distributed.

Ricardo returns once more to the case considered above, where the surplus value (absolute profit) falls because the price of the necessary means of subsistence (and along with these also rent) rises.

"I must again observe that the rate of profits would fall much more rapidly than I have estimated in my calculation; for the value of the produce being what I have stated it under the circumstances supposed, the value of the farmer's stock would be greatly increased from its necessarily consisting of many of the commodities which had risen in value. Before corn could rise from £4 to £12, his capital would probably be doubled in exchangeable value, and be worth £6,000 instead of £3,000. If then his profit were £180, or 6 per cent. on his original capital, profits would not at that time be really at a higher *rate* than 3 per cent.; for £6,000 at 3 per cent. gives £180; and on those terms only could a new farmer with £6,000 money in his pocket enter into the farming business.

"Many trades would derive some advantage, more or less, from the same source. The brewer, the distiller, the clothier, the linen manufacturer, would be partly compensated for the diminution of their profits by the rise in the value of their stock of raw and finished materials; but a manufacturer of hardware, of jewellery, and of many other commodities . . . would be subject to the whole fall in the rate of profits, without any compensation whatever" (p. 73).

What is important here is only what Ricardo does not notice —namely that he is completely throwing overboard his identification of profit with surplus value, and that, independently of the value of labour, the rate of profit can be affected by a change in the value of the constant capital. For the rest his illustration is only partly correct. The profit which farmers, clothiers, etc., would make as a result of the rise in price of the stocks of their commodities which they have on hand and at the market, would naturally come to an end as soon as they have got rid of these commodities. The rise in value of their capital would similarly be no longer a profit for them when this capital is consumed and would have to be replaced. They then all find themselves in the position of the new farmer cited by Ricardo himself, who would have to advance a capital of £6,000 in order to make a profit of 3 per cent. On the other hand jewellers, manufacturers of ironware, money capitalists, etc., although at first they would receive no compensation for their loss, would realise a rate of profit of more than 3 per cent., since only that part of their capital which was laid out in wages would have risen in value.

Another important point in connection with the compensation mentioned by Ricardo of falling profit by rises in the value of capital, is that for the capitalists—and generally in the division of the product of the annual labour—it is not only a question of the division of the product among the various participants in revenue, but also of the division of this product between capital and revenue.

(b) Formation of the General Rate of Profit

On this point Ricardo is by no means theoretically clear:

"I have already remarked that the market price of a commodity may exceed its natural or necessary price, as it may be produced in less abundance than the new demand for it requires. This, however, is but a temporary effect. The high profits on capital employed in producing that commodity will naturally attract capital to that trade; and as soon as the requisite funds are supplied, and the quantity of the commodity is duly increased, its price will fall, and the profits of the trade will conform to the general level. A fall in the general rate of profits is by no means incompatible with a partial rise of profits in particular employments. It is through the inequality of profits that capital is moved from one employment to another. Whilst, then, general profits are falling, and gradually settling at a lower level in consequence of the rise of wages, and the increasing difficulty of supplying the increasing population with necessaries, the profits of the farmer may, for an interval of some little duration, be above the former level. An extraordinary stimulus may be also given for a certain time to a particular branch of foreign and colonial trade" (Chapter VI, p. 70).

"It should be recollected that prices always vary in the market, and in the first instance, through the comparative state of demand and supply. Although cloth could be furnished at 40s. per yard, and give the usual profits of stock, it may rise to 60s. or 80s. from a general change of fashion. . . . The makers of cloth will for a time have unusual profits, but capital will naturally flow to that manufacture, till the supply and demand are again at their fair level, when the price of cloth will again sink to 40s., its natural or necessary price. In the same manner, with every increased demand for corn, it may rise so high as to afford more than the general profits to the farmer. If there be plenty of fertile land, the price of corn will again fall to its former standard, after the requisite quantity of capital has been employed in producing it, and profits will be as before; but if there be not plenty of fertile land, if, to produce this additional quantity, more than the usual quantity of capital and labour be required, corn will not fall to its former level. Its natural price will be raised, and the farmer, instead of obtaining permanently larger profits, will find himself obliged to be satisfied with the diminished rate which is the inevitable consequence of the rise of wages, produced by the rise of necessaries" (p. 71).

With a given *working day* (or if there are only such differences in the working day in the various branches of production as are compensated by the special conditions of the different types of labour), the general rate of surplus value, or surplus labour, is also given, since wages are, on the average, the same. Ricardo has this always in mind, and he confuses this general rate of surplus value with the general rate of profit. I have shown that with the same general rate of surplus value the rates of profit would necessarily be very different in the various branches of production if the commodities were sold at their respective values.

The general rate of profit arises through the total surplus value produced being calculated on the total capital of the community (the class of capitalists). Each capital in each particular branch of production presents itself therefore as an *aliquot* part of a total capital of the same *organic composition*, both as regards constant and variable capital and as regards

338 THEORIES OF SURPLUS VALUE

338 THEORIES OF SURPLUS VALUE

circulating and fixed capital. As such an aliquot part it draws its dividends from the surplus value created by the aggregate capital, in proportion to its size. The portion of surplus value which, during a certain period of time, for example one year, falls to the share of a block of capital of a certain size, for example 100, constitutes the *average profit* or the *general rate of profit*, in which form it enters into the production costs of each branch of production. If this portion for each 100 is equal to 15, then the normal profit is 15 per cent., and the price of production is 115. It may be less, if for example only a part of the capital advanced enters into the process of the formation of value as depreciation. But it is always equal to the capital consumed *plus* 15, the average profit on the capital advanced. If in one case 100 enters into the product, and in another case only 50, then in the first case the price of production is 100 plus 15, that is, 115, and in the second 50 plus 15, that is, 65. At these prices both capitals would have sold their commodities at *the same price of production*, that is to say, at a price which yielded both the same rate of profit. It is clear that the emergence, realisation, formation of the general rate of profit necessitates the transformation of values into prices of production different from these values. Ricardo, on the contrary, assumes the identity of values with prices of production, because he confuses the rate of profit with the rate of surplus value. Consequently he has not the faintest inkling of the universal change which takes place in the prices of commodities through the formation of a general rate of profit before there can be any talk of such a thing. He takes this rate of profit as a premise, which therefore, according to him, even enters into the determination of value. (See Chapter I, "On Value".) With the general rate of profit taken for granted, he considers merely those exceptional modifications in prices which are necessary in order to maintain this general rate, to keep this general rate of profit in existence. He has not the least idea of the fact that a transformation of values into prices of production must first take place in order to *create* the general rate of profit; and that therefore, by taking a general rate of profit as his basis, he is no longer dealing directly with the values of commodities.

Moreover, what is dominant in the preceding passage is *only* Adam Smith's standpoint, and even this in a one-sided way, because Ricardo clings firmly to the reservation in his mind about the general rate of surplus value. According to him, the rate of profit rises above the average level only in particular branches of production, because the market price rises above the natural price as a result of the relation between supply and demand, underproduction or overproduction in particular branches of production. Competition, the influx of new capital to one branch of production, or withdrawal of old capital from another branch, then equalises out market price and natural price with each other and reduces the profit of that particular branch of production to the general level. Here the actual level of profit is assumed as constant and given, and what is in question is only the reduction to this level of the profit in particular branches of production where it has risen above or fallen below the level as a result of demand and supply. In this connection, it is even always assumed by Ricardo that the commodities whose prices yield more than the average profit stand above their value, and those whose prices yield less stand below their value. If competition brings their market value into conformity with their value, then the average level is restored.

The level itself, according to Ricardo, can only rise or fall when wages fall or rise (with a relative degree of permanence), that is to say, when the rate of relative surplus value falls or rises; and this takes place without any change in prices, although Ricardo in this connection himself admits a very significant variation in prices in different branches of production, according to the composition of their capital as between circulating and fixed.

But even when a general rate of profit is established, and consequently prices of production, the rate of profit in particular branches of production may rise because in these branches the time worked is longer and the rate of absolute surplus value rises. That competition between the workers is unable to level this out is proved by the intervention of the State. In such a case the rate of profit in this particular branch of production will rise without any rise of the market price above the natural price. Competition between capitals can and in the long run certainly will ensure that this excess of profit will not fall entirely to the share of the capitalists in these particular branches of production. They will have to lower their commodities below their "natural prices", or the other branches of production will raise their prices somewhat; in any case, even if they do not actually raise them—such a rise might be counteracted by a fall in the value of these commodities—they would not lower them to the full extent demanded by the development of the productive power of labour in their own branches of production. The general level of the rate of profit will rise, and the prices of production will be altered.

Moreover: if a new branch of production becomes established in which a disproportionately large quantity of living labour in relation to accumulated labour is employed, in which therefore the composition of capital is far below the average composition which determines the average profit, it is possible that the relations of supply and demand for such a new branch of production may allow it to sell its product for more than its price of production, at a price that approximates more closely to its actual value. If competition levels this out, this is only possible through the raising of the general level of the rate of profit, because capital as a whole realises, sets in motion, a greater quantity of unpaid surplus labour. The relations of supply and demand do not in the first instance, as Ricardo thinks, cause the commodity to be sold above its value, but only to be sold at a price approximating to its value, above its price of production. The process of equalisation of the rate of profit cannot therefore have the result of reducing it to the old level, but of establishing a new level.

It is the same for example with trade with the colonies, where as a result of slavery and the bounty of nature the value of labour is lower than in the old country; or this may also be due to the fact that, in practice or in law, private ownership of the land has not developed there. If capitals from the motherland can be transferred at will into this new trade, it is true that they will lower the specific extra profit in this branch of business, but they will raise the general rate of profit, as Adam Smith quite correctly observes.

On this issue Ricardo always helps himself out with the phrase: But in the old trades the quantity of labour employed has nevertheless remained the same, and so have wages. The general rate of profit, however, is determined by the ratio of the unpaid labour to the paid labour and to the capital advanced, not in one or other particular trade but in all trades into which capital can be freely transferred. In nine-tenths of these trades the ratio may remain the same; but if in one-tenth there is a change, then the general rate of profit in the ten-tenths must change. However often there is an increase in the amount of unpaid labour set in motion by a capital of a certain size, the result of competition can nevertheless only be that capitals of equal size once again draw equal dividends, equal shares of this increased surplus labour; it cannot be that, in spite of the greater amount of surplus labour in proportion to the aggregate advanced capital, the dividend drawn by each individual capital remains the same, is reduced to its former share of surplus value. If Ricardo makes this assumption, he has absolutely no ground for contesting Adam Smith's view that the mere increasing competition of capitals, resulting from their accumulation, reduces the rate of profit. For here he himself assumes that the rate of profit is lowered simply by competition, although the rate of surplus value is rising. This is certainly connected with his second false assumption that the rate of profit, apart from the lowering or raising of wages, can never rise or fall except for temporary deviations of the market price from the natural price. And what is the natural price? That price which is equal to the capital advanced plus the average profit. This therefore leads us back again to the presupposition that the average profit can never fall or rise except when the relative surplus value changes. Ricardo is therefore wrong when, in opposition to Adam Smith, he says:

"Any change from one foreign trade to another, or from home to foreign trade, cannot, in my opinion, affect the rate of profits" (Chapter XXV, p. 232).

He is equally wrong in thinking that the rate of profit does not affect prices of production because it does not affect values.

Ricardo errs in the assumption that [when a trade which is favourably placed rises above the general level of the rate of profit] this general level is always re-established by a reduction of the rate of profit to the former level and not by raising it.

"They contend that the equality of profits will be brought about by the general rise of profits; and I am of opinion that the profits of the favoured trade will speedily subside to the general level" (Chapter VII, p. 78).

Because of his completely wrong conception of the rate of profit, Ricardo misunderstands entirely the influence of foreign trade, when it does not directly lower the price of the workers' means of subsistence. He does not see of what enormous importance it is for England, for example, to secure cheaper raw materials for industry; and that in this case, though prices fall, the rate of profit rises, while in the opposite case, with rising prices, the rate of profit can fall, even if in both cases wages remain the same.

"It is not, therefore, in consequence of the extension of the market that the rate of profit is raised" (Chapter VII, p. 80).

The rate of profit does not depend on the price of the individual commodity but on the quantity of surplus labour that can be realised with a given capital. In other connections, too, Ricardo fails to recognise the importance of the market, because he does not understand the nature of money.

In addition to this, a further point to be noted is that Ricardo commits all these errors because he tries, by means of high-handed abstractions, to establish the identity of the rate of surplus value with the rate of profit. Hence it is that the vulgar mob has drawn the conclusion that theoretical truths are abstractions which contradict the actual state of things—instead of seeing on the contrary that Ricardo does not carry his correct abstraction far enough and is therefore driven into false abstraction.

II. *ACCUMULATION OF CAPITAL AND CRISES*

1. SIMPLE REPRODUCTION

We first examine the propositions widely scattered through the whole of Ricardo's work:

". . . all the productions of a country are consumed; but it makes the greatest difference imaginable whether they are consumed by those who reproduce or by those who do not reproduce another value. When we say that revenue is saved and added to capital, what we mean is, that the portion of revenue, so said to be added to capital, is consumed by productive instead of unproductive labourers.[1] There can be no greater error than in supposing that capital is increased by non-consumption. If the price of labour should rise so high that, notwithstanding the increase of capital, no more could be employed, I should say that such increase of capital would be still unproductively consumed" (Chapter VIII, Footnote, p. 94).

Here, therefore—as with Adam Smith and others—the only [question raised is whether the revenue saved] is consumed by workers or not. But the issue concerns also the industrial consumption of commodities which form constant capital, and are consumed as instruments of labour or materials of labour, or are consumed in such a way that through this consumption they are transformed into instruments or materials of labour. The conception that the accumulation of capital is the transformation of revenue into wages, that it is equivalent to the accumulation of variable capital, is quite incorrect, that is, one-sided. It leads to a wrong treatment of the whole question of accumulation.

Above all it is essential to have a clear conception of the *reproduction of constant capital.* Here we consider the *annual* reproduction, taking the year as the time measure of the process of reproduction.

[1] Here we find the same distinction as in Adam Smith.

A great part of the constant capital—the fixed capital—enters into the annual labour process, but does not enter [as a whole] into the annual process of the formation of value. [A considerable part of it] is not consumed, and therefore does not require to be reproduced. It is maintained in being—and, along with its use value, also its exchange value—by the fact that it does enter into the process of reproduction and remains in contact with living labour. The greater this part of a country's capital is in one year, the greater, relatively, is the purely formal reproduction (maintenance) of it in the following year—on the assumption that the production process is renewed, continued and kept in flow even if only at the same level. Repairs and other outgoings necessary for the maintenance of the fixed capital are added to its original labour costs. This has nothing in common with its maintenance in the sense used above.

A second part of the constant capital is consumed annually in the production of commodities and must therefore also be reproduced. This includes all that part of the fixed capital which enters each year into the process of formation of value, and that whole part of the constant capital which consists of circulating capital, raw materials and auxiliary materials.

As for this second portion of the constant capital, it is necessary to make the following distinctions.

A certain portion of what *appears* in one sphere of production as constant capital—instruments and materials of labour—is *simultaneously*, in another, parallel sphere of production, the product. For example, yarn forms part of the constant capital of the weaver; it is the product of the spinner, and may have been still in the process of becoming yarn the day before. In using the term *simultaneously*, we mean produced during *the same* year. The same commodities, in different phases, pass through various spheres of production in the course of the same year. They emerge from one sphere as a product, and enter another as commodities forming constant capital. And, as constant capital, they are all consumed during the year; whether, as with fixed capital, only their value enters into the commodity, or also their use value, as in the case of circulating capital. The commodity produced in one sphere of production passes into another sphere of production, to be there consumed as constant capital; while alongside this series of production spheres into which the same commodity enters, the various elements or various phases of this commodity are simultaneously being produced alongside each other. In the course of the same year it is continually consumed in one sphere as constant capital, and in another parallel sphere produced as a commodity. The same commodities which are in this way consumed as constant capital during the year, are also similarly being continuously produced during the same year. A machine is wearing out in sphere A. Simultaneously, it is being produced in sphere B. The constant capital which is consumed during the year in the spheres of production which produce the means of subsistence is at the same time produced in other spheres of production, so that in the course of the year or at the end of the year it is replaced *in natura*.[1] Both of them—the means of subsistence and this part of the constant capital—are products of new labour, active during the year. A portion of the value of the product of spheres producing the means of subsistence replaces the constant capital of these spheres of production; this portion of value, as I showed earlier, forms the revenue of the producers of this constant capital.

But there is also a further portion of the constant capital which is *consumed annually*, without entering as a component into the spheres of production which produce the means of subsistence (consumption goods). It therefore also cannot be replaced from these spheres. We mean the portion of the constant capital—instruments of labour, raw materials and auxiliary materials—which are themselves industrially consumed in the production of the constant capital—machinery, raw materials and auxiliary materials. This part, as we have seen, is replaced *in natura*, either directly from the product of this sphere of production itself (as in the case of seed, livestock, and in part coal), or through the exchange of a portion of the product of the various spheres of production which produce constant capital. In such cases there is an exchange of capital against capital. Through the existence and the consumption

[1] In kind.

of this portion of constant capital not only is the *mass* of products increased, but also the *value* of the annual product. The *portion of value* of the *annual* product which is equal to the value of this portion of the consumed constant capital, buys back *in natura*, or withdraws from the annual product, that part of it which is destined to replace *in natura* the constant capital that is consumed. For example, the value of the seed sown determines the part of the value of the harvest (and thus the quantity of corn) which must be returned to the land, to production, as seed, as constant capital. Without the labour newly applied in the course of the year this portion would not be reproduced; but it is in fact *produced* by the labour of the last or previous years and—in so far as labour productivity remains the same—the *value* which it adds to the annual product is the result not of this year's labour, but of the labour of a previous year. The greater, *proportionately*, is the constant capital in use in a country, the greater will also be this part of the constant capital which is consumed in the production of the constant capital, and which is not only expressed in a greater quantity of products, but also raises the value of this quantity of products. This *value* is therefore not only the result of the current year's labour, but equally the result of the past labour of a previous year, although *but for* the immediate, current year's labour it would not reappear, any more than would the product in which it is embodied. If this portion grows, not only the mass of the annual products grows, but also their *value*, even if the annual labour remains the same. This growth is one form of the *accumulation of capital*, which it is essential to understand. And nothing can be further from this understanding than Ricardo's statement:

"The labour of a million of men in manufactures will always produce the same value, but will not always produce the same riches" (Chapter XX, p. 182).

These million men—with a given working day—will not only produce very different quantities of commodities in accordance with the productivity of labour, but the value of these quantities will be very different, according as they are produced with much or little constant capital, as therefore much or little value originating in the past labour of previous years is added to them.

For the sake of simplicity, when we speak of the reproduction of the constant capital we always make the preliminary assumption that the productivity of labour and consequently the methods of production remain the same. That which, at a given level of production, has to be replaced as constant capital is a definite quantity *in natura*. If productivity remains the same, then also the value of this quantity remains constant. If changes occur in the productivity of labour, as a result of which the same quantity can be newly reproduced at greater or less cost, with more or less labour, then similarly changes occur in the value of the constant capital, and these affect the surplus product after deduction of the constant capital.

For example, let us assume that 20 quarters at £3, or £60, are required for sowing. If each quarter is reproduced with one-third less labour, then a quarter now only costs £2. Now, as previously, 20 quarters have to be deducted from the product for sowing, but the portion of value which they constitute in the total product is now only £40. For the replacement of the same constant capital in such a case, a smaller portion of value and a smaller part in kind of the total product would be required, although 20 quarters have to be returned to the land as seed, just as before.

If the constant capital consumed annually (in the labour of a million men) were £10,000,000 in the case of one nation, and in another nation only £1,000,000, and the annual labour of a million men were £100,000,000, the value of the product of this million men would be 110 million for the first nation, and only 101 million for the other. At the same time it would be not only possible, but certain, that in nation I the individual commodities would be cheaper than in nation II, because the latter would produce a much smaller quantity of commodities with the same labour, much smaller than the difference between 10 and 1. It is true that a greater portion of the value of the product goes to replace the (constant) capital in nation I as compared with II, and therefore also a greater portion of the total product. But the total product is also much greater.

In the case of factory-made goods it is known that a million men in England produce not only a much greater product, but also a product of much greater value, than in Russia for example, although the individual commodity is much cheaper. In agriculture, however, the same relation between capitalistically developed and relatively undeveloped nations does not seem to exist. The product of the backward nation is cheaper than that of the capitalistically developed nation, as measured in its *money price*. And nevertheless the product of the developed nation appears to be the product of much less labour (in the course of a year) than that of the backward one. In England for example less than a third [of the workers] are engaged in agriculture; in Russia $\frac{4}{5}$; in the former $\frac{5}{15}$, in the later $\frac{12}{15}$. These figures are not to be taken literally. In England for example a large number of persons in *industry*—in machine-construction, trade, transport, and so on—are engaged in the production and delivery of elements of agricultural production, while in Russia this is not the case. The proportion of persons engaged in agriculture cannot therefore be directly determined by the number of individuals immediately employed in agriculture. In countries of capitalist production many people participate *indirectly* in this agricultural production, who in undeveloped countries are directly included in it. The difference [therefore] appears to be greater than it is. This difference however is extremely important for the civilisation of the country as a whole, even in so far as it consists merely in the fact that a greater part of the producers engaged in agriculture do not directly participate in it and are saved from the narrow parochialism of country life, belonging as they do to the industrial population. But for the moment we will leave this point. We will also leave aside the fact that most agricultural peoples are compelled to sell their product *below* its value, while in countries of developed capitalist production the agricultural product rises to its value.

In any case, a portion of the value of the constant capital enters into the value of the English agricultural product which does not enter into the value of the product of Russian agriculture. Let us assume that this portion of the value is equal to a day's labour of ten men, and that one English labourer sets this constant capital in motion. I am speaking of that part of the constant capital of the agricultural product which is not replaced by new labour, as is the case, for example, with agricultural implements. If five Russian labourers are required to produce the same product as one Englishman produces through the agency of the constant capital of 10, and if the constant capital used by the Russian is equal to one day's labour, then the English product $= 10c + 1v = 11$ days' labour, and the product of the Russians $= 1c + 5v = 6$. If the Russian land is so much more fertile than the English, that without the use of constant capital or with a constant capital one-tenth the size [but using five times as many labourers] it produces as much grain as one Englishman with ten times the constant capital, then the relation between the values of the same quantities of English and Russian grain is as $11 : 6$. If the quarter of Russian grain is sold at £2, the English quarter is sold at £$3\frac{2}{3}$, for $2 : 3\frac{2}{3} = 6 : 11$. The money price and the value of the English grain would therefore be much higher than that of the Russian, but nevertheless the English grain would be produced with much less [immediate] labour, inasmuch as the *dead* labour, which reappears both in the quantity and in the value of the product, costs no additional new labour. This [the higher price and value of English grain] would be always the case, if the Englishman used less immediate labour than the Russian, but the higher constant capital that he uses—and that costs him *nothing*, although it has cost something and must be paid for—does not raise the productivity of labour to such an extent that it compensates for the natural fertility of the Russian soil. The money price of agricultural products can therefore be higher in countries of capitalist production than in less developed countries, although in fact they cost less labour. The product contains [a greater total] of immediate and past labour, but this past labour costs nothing. The product would be cheaper, but for the difference in natural fertility. This would also explain the higher money price of the labourer's wage.

Up to this point we have been speaking only of the reproduction of the capital involved. The labourer replaces his wages, with a surplus product or surplus value, which forms the profit (including rent) of the capitalist. He replaces that part of the annual product which serves him anew as wages. The capitalist has consumed his profit in the course of the year, but the labourer has created a portion of the product which can again be consumed as profit. The portion of the constant capital which is consumed in the production of means of subsistence is replaced by constant capital which during the year is produced by new labour. The producers of this new portion of the constant capital realise their revenue (profit and wages) in that part of the means of subsistence which is equal to the portion of the value of the constant capital consumed in their production. Finally, the constant capital which is consumed in the production of the constant capital —in the production of machines, raw material and auxiliary materials— is replaced *in natura* or through the exchange of capital from the total product of the various spheres of production which produce constant capital.

2. TRANSFORMATION OF REVENUE INTO CAPITAL

WHAT then is the position with regard to the *increase* of capital, its *accumulation* as distinguished from reproduction, the *transformation of revenue* into capital?

To make the question simpler, let us assume that the productivity of labour remains the same, there is no change in the method of production, that is, the same quantity of labour is required to produce the same quantity of commodities; that therefore the *increase* of capital costs the same labour as the previous year's production of capital of the same size. A portion of the surplus value must be transformed into capital, instead of being consumed as revenue. It must be transformed partly into constant, partly into variable capital. And the proportions in which it is divided into these two different parts of capital depend on the organic composition of capital which we have assumed—since the method of production remains unchanged and also the proportionate value of the two parts. The higher the development of production, the greater will be the portion of the surplus value which is transformed into constant capital, compared with the portion of the surplus value which is transformed into variable capital.

First, therefore, one portion of the surplus value, and of the corresponding surplus product in the form of means of subsistence, has to be transformed into variable capital; that is to say, new labour has to be bought with it. This is only possible if there is an increase in the number of workers, or if the labour time during which they work is lengthened. The latter takes place when for example a part of the labouring population has been only half or two-thirds employed, or also, for longer or shorter periods, through an absolute prolongation of the working day, which then however must be paid for. But this cannot be considered a constant method of accumulation. The labouring population can increase when previously unproductive workers are transformed into productive, or sections of the population who previously did not work—such as women and children, or paupers—are drawn into the productive process. Here we do not deal with this latter point. Finally, it can come about through the absolute growth of the labouring population along with the growth of the population in general. If accumulation is to be a constant, continuous process, a necessary condition is this absolute growth of the population, although it may decline relatively to the capital employed. *Increase of the population* is the basis of accumulation as a constant process. But this presupposes an average wage which permits of the constant growth of the labouring population and not merely its reproduction. Capitalist production makes provision for sudden needs by the very fact that it overworks a part of the labouring population and keeps the other part as a reserve army, half or entirely pauperised.

How then does it stand with the other portion of the surplus value that has to be transformed into constant capital? To simplify the question, let us exclude foreign trade and consider an isolated nation. Let us take an example. Let the surplus value that a linen-weaver has produced be equivalent to £10,000, of which he wants to transform one-half, that is £5,000, into capital. Let us assume that, on the basis of the organic composition of machine weaving, one-fifth of this amount has to be laid out in wages. We are leaving out of account here the turnover of capital as a result of which perhaps an amount of five weeks' wages would suffice, after which he would sell his product and so receive back from circulation the capital for wages. We assume that he must hold in reserve at his banker's £1,000 for wages (for 20 men) and gradually, in the course of the year, lay it out in wages. Then £4,000 is to be transformed into constant capital. He must first buy yarn —as much as twenty men can spin in the course of the year. (We are abstracting throughout from the turnover of the circulating part of the capital.) Further, he must increase the number of looms in his mill, perhaps add a steam-engine or enlarge the old one, and so on. But in order to buy all this, he must find yarn, looms, etc., on the market. He must transform his £4,000 into yarn, looms, coal, etc., that is, he must buy these products. But in order that he can buy them, they must be there. As we assumed that the reproduction of the old capital has taken place under the old conditions, the yarn spinner has laid out his whole capital in order to provide the quantity of yarn required by the weaver in the previous year. How then is he to satisfy the increased demand by an increased supply of yarn? It is just the same with the machinery manufacturer who supplies the looms, etc. He has produced only enough new looms to cover the average consumption of looms in weaving. But the weaver who is eager to accumulate places orders for £3,000 of yarn and £1,000 of looms, coal (the coal producer is in the same position), and so forth. Or he gives the spinner £3,000, the machinery manufacturer and the coal merchant, etc., £1,000, so that they can transform this money into yarn, looms and coal for him. He would therefore have to wait until this process is completed before he could make a start with his accumulation, his production of new linen. This would be the first interruption. But now the spinner finds himself in the same position with the £3,000 as the weaver did with the £4,000, except that he can at once deduct his profit. He can find an additional number of spinners, but he needs flax, spindles, coal, etc. In the same way the coal supplier, apart from new workers, needs new machinery or implements. And the maker of machinery, who is to supply the new looms, spindles, etc., needs—besides the additional workers—iron and so on. Worst of all, however, is the position with the flax grower, who can supply the additional quantity of flax only the following year.

In order therefore that the weaver can, without complications and interruptions, transform a portion of his profit each year into constant capital—and in order that accumulation can be a continuous process—he must find an additional quantity of yarn, looms, etc., on the market. He, the spinner, the coal supplier, etc., [can] only make use of more workers if they find [more] flax, spindles and machines on the market.

A portion of the constant capital which is calculated to be used up each year, and enters as wear and tear into the value of the product, is in fact *not* used up. Take for example a machine which lasts twelve years and costs £12,000, which makes the average depreciation to be written off each year £1,000. At the end of the twelve years, as £1,000 has entered each year into the product, the value of £12,000 has been reproduced, and a new machine of the same kind can be bought for this price. The repairs and patching up needed in the course of the twelve years are counted as part of the production costs of the machine; they have nothing to do with the question we are discussing. Reality, however, is in fact different from that method of average accounting. In the second year the machine may run better than in the first. And yet after twelve years it is no longer usable. It is the same as with a cow, whose average life is ten years, but which does not for that reason die by a tenth each year, although at the end of the ten years it must be replaced by a new individual. However, in the course of a *given* year a definite quantity of machinery, etc., is always reaching this stage, when it must actually be replaced by new machines. Each year, therefore, a definite quantity of the old machinery, etc., must actually, *in natura*, be replaced by new. And the average annual production of machinery, etc., corresponds with this. The value with which they are to be paid for is lying ready, from the proceeds of the commodities, according to the reproduction period of each machine. But the fact remains that a considerable part of the value of the annual product, of the value which is paid for it each year, though in fact necessary, in order for example to replace the old machinery at the end of twelve years, is certainly not actually required to replace one-twelfth each year *in natura*, which, in reality, could not even be done. This fund may in part be used for wages or to buy raw materials, before the commodity is sold or paid for, being constantly thrown into circulation but not immediately returning from circulation. This cannot however be the case throughout the whole year, as the commodities which complete their turnover in the year realise their value in full, and must therefore pay for, realise, both the wages, raw materials and worn out machinery contained in them, as well as the surplus value. Where therefore much constant capital, consequently also much fixed capital, is employed, there exists in that part of the value of the product which provides the depreciation of the fixed capital, an *accumulation fund*, which from the standpoint of the person who benefits from it can be used for the provision of new fixed capital (or also circulating capital), without any deduction from the surplus value being made for this part of the accumulation (see MacCulloch). This accumulation fund is not found at levels of production and in nations where there is no considerable amount of fixed capital. This is an important point. It is a fund for the constant introduction of improvements, extensions, and so forth.

But the point we want to come to here is the following. If the total capital employed in the machine-building industry were even only large enough to replace the annual wear and tear of machinery, it would produce much more machinery than is required each year, since in part the wear and tear is conventional and in reality only has to be replaced *in natura* after a certain period of years. The capital so employed therefore produces annually a mass of machinery which is available for new capital investments and anticipates these new capital investments. For example, in a certain year the machine builder starts his production. He supplies machinery to the value of £12,000 during the year. Then in each of the eleven following years, for the simple reproduction of the machinery produced by him he would only have to produce to the value of £1,000; and even this annual production would not be annually consumed. Even less would his production be consumed if he employs his whole capital. In order that this capital should continue in motion and merely reproduce itself continuously each year, a continuous new extension of the industry which uses these machines is required. Even more is required, if he himself accumulates. Here therefore, even *if in this sphere of production the capital invested in it is only reproduced,* continuous accumulation in the other spheres of production is necessary. In this way, however, this continuous accumulation also finds one of its elements continuously in supply on the market. Here in one sphere of production is a constant supply of commodities for accumulation, for new, additional industrial consumption in other spheres, even if in this sphere the existing capital is merely reproduced.

With the £5,000 profit or surplus value which is transformed into capital, for example by the weaver, there are two possible cases—always on the assumption that he *finds on the market the labour* which he has to buy with £1,000 of this £5,000 in order, in conformity with the conditions of his sphere of production, to transform the capital of £5,000 into capital. This portion is transformed into variable capital and is laid out in wages. But in order to make use of this labour he needs yarn, auxiliary materials and more machines—except in the case of the prolongation of the working day. In this latter case there is no *new* capital to be laid out directly for the machinery itself—it is only necessary to replace the value of the machinery at a somewhat more rapid rate. In this case only auxiliary materials require an advance of additional capital.

The weaver may find these, his conditions of production, on the market. Then the purchase of these commodities is distinguished from that of other commodities only by the fact that he buys commodities for *industrial consumption* instead of for *individual* consumption. Or he may not find them on the market; then he must order them—as for example machines which are to be newly constructed—just as he must order articles for his private consumption if he does not find them on the market. If the raw material (flax) will only be produced to order—somewhat as indigo, jute, etc., is produced by the Indian ryots on orders and advances made by English merchants—the linen weaver's accumulation would be impossible for the current year in his own business. On the other hand if we assume that the spinner transforms £3,000 into [yarn] and the weaver does not accumulate, then the spun yarn—although all the conditions for its production were in supply on the market—will be unsaleable, and the £3,000, while transformed into yarn, has not been transformed into capital.

Credit, which we do not need to treat further here, is the means whereby accumulated capital is not used directly in the sphere where it is produced, but where it has the most chance of being turned to good account. Every capitalist, however, will prefer to use his accumulation as far as possible in his own enterprise. If he invests it in someone else's, he becomes a money capitalist and draws only interest instead of profit—or he would have to take to speculation. We are speaking here, however, of accumulation by and large, and only for the sake of illustration assume that it is invested in a special branch of production.

If on the other hand the flax-grower had extended his production, that is to say accumulated, and the spinner and weaver and machinery manufacturer, etc., had not, then he would have superfluous flax in store and would probably produce less in the following year.

For the time being we are leaving individual consumption altogether out of account, and are considering merely the mutual relations between the producers. If these relations exist, then the producers constitute in the first place a mutual market for the capitals which they must mutually replace; the newly employed or more fully employed workers constitute a market for a portion of the means of subsistence produced; and as the surplus value is greater in the following year, the capitalists can consume a growing portion of their revenue, and thus also to a certain extent constitute a market for each other. But even so a considerable portion of the annual product may remain unsaleable.

The question has now to be formulated in this way: *assuming general accumulation*, that is, assuming that capital is accumulated to a greater or less extent in all branches of production—which in reality is a condition of capitalist production, and is just as much the urge of the capitalist as a capitalist as it is the urge of the miser to pile up money (while it is also necessary in order that capitalist production should continue)—what are the *conditions* for this general accumulation, how does it come about? Or, as the linen weaver can represent for us the capitalists as a whole, what are the *conditions* in which he can uninterruptedly retransform the £5,000 into capital and year in, year out, continuously carry on the process of accumulation? To accumulate the £5,000 means nothing else than to transform this money, this sum of values, into capital. *The conditions for the accumulation of capital are therefore entirely the same as those in which it is reproduced or originally produced at all.* These conditions, however, were: that with one part of the money labour is bought, and with the other part commodities (raw materials and machinery, etc.) which can be *industrially consumed* by this labour. Many commodities can only be industrially consumed, such as machinery, raw materials, semi-manufactured goods, and so on. Others, such as houses, horses, wheat, corn (from which brandy or spirit, etc., is made), and so on, can be consumed industrially or individually. In order that these commodities can be bought they must be found as commodities on the *market*—in the intermediate stage between the completion of production and the consumption that has not yet begun, in the hands of the seller, in the stage of circulation—or they must be procurable to order (capable of being produced, as with the construction of new factories, etc.). They were so found—this was presupposed in the production and reproduction of capital—through the division of labour carried out in capitalist production on a social scale (distribution of labour and capital among the various spheres of production); through the *simultaneous* process over the whole field of *parallel* production and reproduction. This was the condition of the *market*, of the production and reproduction of capital. The greater the capital, the more developed the productivity of labour and in general the stage of capitalist production, so much the greater is also the mass of commodities found in circulation on the market, in transition from production to consumption (individual and industrial), and so much the greater is the certainty for each particular capital that it will find the conditions for its reproduction ready on the market. This is all the more the case because by the nature of capitalist production each separate capital, in the first place, works on a scale that is not determined by individual demand (orders and the like, private needs), but by the striving to use as much labour and therefore to realise as much surplus value as possible and to produce the greatest possible mass of commodities with a given capital; and in the second place, each individual capital strives to take for itself the greatest possible place on the market and to push aside and exclude its competitors.

This is the *competition of capitals*. The greater the development of the means of communication, the more can the supply on the market be reduced.

"There will, indeed, where production and consumption are comparatively great, naturally be, at any given moment, a comparatively great surplus in the intermediate state, in the market, on its way from having been produced to the hands of the consumer; unless indeed the quickness with which things are sold off should have increased so as to counteract what would also have been the consequence of the increased production" (*An Inquiry into those Principles respecting the Nature of Demand and the Necessity of Consumption, lately advocated by Mr. Malthus, etc.*, London, 1821, pp. 6–7).

The accumulation of new capital can therefore proceed only under the same conditions as the reproduction of already existing capital.

We take no account here of the case in which more capital is accumulated than can be invested in production, and for example lies fallow in the form of money at the bank; hence comes lending abroad and so on—in a word, speculative investments. Nor do we consider the case where it is impossible to sell the mass of goods produced, crises, etc. This belongs to the section on competition. Here we are examining only the forms of capital in the various phases of its process, it being throughout assumed that commodities are sold at their value.

The weaver can retransform his £5,000 surplus value into capital if, in addition to labour for £1,000, he finds yarn, etc., in finished form on the market or can obtain them to order. This requires, therefore, the production of a *surplus product* in the form of commodities which enter into his constant capital, especially of those which require a somewhat lengthy period for production and cannot be increased in quantity quickly, or cannot be increased at all within the year—such as raw material, for example flax.

This is where merchant's capital comes into play, keeping available in warehouses supplies for growing consumption, individual and industrial; this, however, is only a form of intermediary agency that is not relevant here, but belongs to an examination of the competition of capitals.

As the production and reproduction of the existing capital in one sphere presupposes parallel production and reproduction in other spheres, so accumulation, or the formation of additional capital in one branch of production, presupposes the simultaneous or parallel production of additional products in the other branches of production. Consequently the level of production in all spheres which supply constant capital must grow simultaneously, in conformity with the average share, determined by demand, which each particular sphere takes in the general growth of production; and all spheres supply constant capital which do not produce finished products for individual consumption. Of the greatest importance in this growth is the increase in machinery (working tools), raw materials and auxiliary materials, since all other industries into which they pass, whether producing semi- or fully-manufactured articles—if these conditions are present—have only to set more labour in motion.

It seems therefore that a continuous surplus production is necessary in all spheres in order that accumulation may be possible.

This has still to be somewhat more closely defined.

Then there is the second essential question:

[This refers to the portion of the] surplus value which is transformed back again into capital: [or the] portion of the profit, including rent; if the landowner wishes to accumulate, to transform rent into capital, it is always the industrial capitalist who gets the surplus value in his hands; this is also the case when the worker transforms a part of his revenue into capital. This part of the profit which is transformed back again into capital consists entirely of labour added during the previous year. The question arises whether this new capital is all laid out in wages, exchanged only against new labour?

An argument for this is: all value comes originally from labour. All constant capital is originally as much the product of labour as is the variable capital. And here we seem again to come up against the direct genesis of capital from labour.

An argument against it is: is the formation of additional capital to take place under worse conditions of production than the reproduction of the old capital? Must it go back to a lower level of the method of production? But this would have to be the case if the new value were laid out entirely on direct labour, which would thus also have itself, without fixed capital, etc., to produce this fixed capital, just as originally labour had first itself to produce its constant capital. This is pure nonsense. But it is the presupposition made by Ricardo and others. This must be gone into more closely.

3. TRANSFORMATION OF ACCUMULATED SURPLUS VALUE INTO VARIABLE AND CONSTANT CAPITAL

THE question is this:

Can a part of the surplus value be transformed into capital, by the capitalist, instead of *selling* it—or more precisely, the surplus product in which it is expressed—putting it rather to *direct* use as capital? An affirmative answer to this question would already imply that the whole sum of the surplus value to be transformed into capital is *not* transformed into variable capital or is not laid out in wages.

With that part of the products of agriculture which consists of grain or cattle, this is clear from the outset. A part of the grain which belongs to that portion of the harvest representing the surplus product or surplus value for the farmer, and similarly a part of the cattle, can at once serve again as means of production—as seed or beasts of burden—instead of being sold. It is the same with the part of the materials for manuring produced on the land itself, which materials at the same time circulate as commodities in trade, that is, can be sold. The farmer can immediately transform this part of the surplus product [accruing] to him as surplus value, as profit, back again into means of production within his own sphere of production, thus transforming it *directly* into capital. This part is not paid out in wages, is not transformed into variable capital. It is withdrawn from individual consumption, without being *productively* consumed in the sense used by Adam Smith and Ricardo. It is *industrially* consumed, but as raw material, not as means of subsistence of either productive or of unproductive workers. Grain however serves not only as a means of subsistence for productive workers and others, but also as auxiliary material for cattle, as raw material for spirits, starch and so on. Cattle for their part (for fattening, or draught animals) serve not only as means of subsistence but also provide raw materials for a mass of industries—skins, hides, fat, bones, horns, etc.—and motive power, partly for agriculture itself and partly for the transport industry.

In all [branches of production] in which the *time of reproduction* extends over [more than] a year, as is the case with a considerable part of the production of livestock, timber, etc., but which products at the same time have to be continuously reproduced—that is, require the application of a definite quantity of labour—accumulation and reproduction coincide in so far as the newly applied labour, which represents not only the paid but also the unpaid labour, has to be accumulated *in natura* until the product is ready for sale.

We are not referring here to the laying aside of the profit added annually [to the capital] on the basis of the general rate of profit; this is not real accumulation, but only a method of accounting. Here we are dealing with the accumulation of the total labour which is repeatedly applied over the course of several years, in which therefore not only paid but also unpaid labour is accumulated *in natura* and immediately again transformed into capital. In such cases on the other hand the accumulation of the profit is independent of the quantity of newly added labour.

The position is the same with commercial crops (whether they provide raw materials or auxiliary materials). Their seed, and that part of them that can be used again for manure, etc., represents a portion of the total product. Even if it were unsaleable this would not alter the fact that as soon as it enters again into the means of production it forms a part of the total value and as such forms constant capital for new production.

This already settles one important question—relating to raw materials and means of subsistence, in so far as these are actually agricultural products. In this sphere therefore accumulation directly coincides with reproduction on an enlarged scale, in such a way that a part of the surplus product serves again, directly in its own sphere of production, as means of production without being exchanged for wages or other commodities.

The second important question relates to *machinery*. Not the machine that produces commodities, but the machinery-producing machine, the constant capital of the machinery-producing industry. Given this, nothing besides labour is required in order to provide the raw materials of the extractive industries, iron, etc., for the production of containers and machines. And with the latter are produced the machines for working up the raw material itself. The difficulty we are confronted with here is: not to fall into a *cercle vicieux* of presuppositions. That is to say, in order to produce more machinery, more material (iron, etc., coal, etc.) is necessary, and in order to produce this, more machinery is necessary. Whether we assume that industrialists building machines and industrialists producing machines (with the machine-building machines) are in the same group or not, makes no difference. This much is clear: a part of the surplus product is represented in machine-building machines (at least it is the business of the machine manufacturer to see that it is so represented). These do not need to be sold, but can enter again, *in natura*, into new production as constant capital. Here therefore we have a second category of the surplus product which enters directly (or indirectly through exchange in the same sphere of production) into new production (accumulation) as constant capital, without having gone through the process of a prior transformation into variable capital.

The question whether a part of the surplus value can be directly transformed into constant capital immediately resolves itself into the question whether a part of the surplus product, in which the surplus value is represented, can again enter its own sphere of production as means of production directly, without being previously alienated.

The general law is as follows:

Where a part of the product, and therefore also of the surplus product (that is, the use value in which the surplus value is represented), can again enter directly, without an intermediary phase, as constant capital into the sphere of production from which it emerged—as means of labour or material for labour—accumulation within this sphere of production can and must take such a form that a part of the surplus product, instead of being sold, is again incorporated as [means of production] for reproduction, directly (or through exchange with other specialists in the same sphere of production, who accumulate in the same way), so that accumulation and reproduction on an enlarged scale here directly coincide. They must everywhere coincide, but not in this direct way.

This is also the case with a part of the auxiliary materials. For example, with the coal produced in a year. A part of the surplus product can itself be used in the further production of coal, and can therefore be used by its producers directly, without any intermediary phase, as constant capital for production on an expanded scale.

Among industrialists there are machine builders who construct whole factories for manufacturers. Let us assume that one-tenth of their product is surplus product or unpaid labour. It is clear that it makes no difference whether this tenth, the surplus product, consists in factories built for third persons and sold to them, or in a factory which the producer builds for himself, sells to himself. What we are considering here is only the form of the use value in which the surplus labour is represented—whether it can enter again as means of production into the sphere of production of the capitalist to whom the surplus product belongs. Here we have yet another example of how important is the determination of *the use value in the analysis of economic forms*.

Here, therefore, we already have a special part of the surplus product in which surplus value [is incorporated], which can and must be directly transformed into constant capital in order to be *accumulated as capital*; without this, no accumulation of capital can take place at all.

Secondly, we have seen that where capitalist production is developed—that is, the productivity of labour; that is, the constant capital; that is, especially the portion of the constant capital which consists in fixed capital—the mere reproduction of the fixed capital in all spheres, and the parallel reproduction of the existing capital which reproduces fixed capital, forms an accumulation fund—that is, supplies machinery which is constant capital for production on an enlarged scale.

Thirdly, there is still the question: can a part of the surplus product be re-transformed into constant capital through an intermediary exchange between the producers for example of machinery, agricultural implements and so on, and those of raw materials, iron, coal, metals, timber, etc.—that is to say, by the exchange of various constituents of constant capital? For example, if the producer of iron, coal, timber, etc., buys machinery or tools from a machine builder, and the machine builder buys metals, timber and coal from the primary producers, they replace through this exchange the reciprocal components of their constant capital. Hence arises the question: to what extent does this take place with the surplus product?

We saw earlier that, in the simple reproduction of the advanced capital, the portion of the constant capital used up in the reproduction of the constant capital is replaced either directly *in natura* or by exchange between the producers of constant capital—an exchange of capital against capital, and not either of revenue against revenue or of revenue against capital. Moreover, the constant capital that is used up or industrially consumed in the production of consumable goods—articles which enter into individual consumption—is replaced by new products of the same kind, which are the result of newly added labour, and can consequently be resolved into revenue (wages and profit). In the spheres which produce consumable goods, that part of the mass of products which is equal to the portion of their value which replaces their constant capital represents therefore the revenue of the producers of constant capital; while on the other hand, in the spheres producing constant capital, that part of the mass of products which represents newly added labour—and therefore forms the revenue of the producers of this constant capital—represents constant capital (replacement capital) for the producers of means of subsistence. This assumes, therefore, that the producers of constant capital exchange their surplus product (which means here the excess of their product over that portion of it which is equal to *their* constant capital) for means of subsistence, and individually consume its value. This surplus product, however, forms:

(1) Wages (or the reproduced fund for wages), and this portion must remain allocated by the capitalists for paying out in wages, therefore for individual consumption. And assuming a minimum level of wages, the worker too can only realise the wages he receives in means of subsistence.

(2) The capitalist's profit (including rent). If this portion is large enough, it can be consumed partly individually, partly industrially. And in this latter case an exchange of this product takes place between the producers of constant capital; but this is no longer an exchange of the part of the product representing the constant capital which has to be mutually replaced between them—it is a part of the surplus product, revenue (*newly added* labour), which is transformed directly into constant capital; in this way the amount of the constant capital is increased, and the scale on which it is reproduced is expanded. Therefore also in this case a part of the existing surplus product, of the labour newly added during the year, is transformed directly into constant capital, without being first transformed into variable capital. Here also, therefore, we see once again that the industrial consumption of the surplus product—or accumulation—is not at all the same thing as the whole surplus product being paid out in wages to productive workers.

We can look at it in this way: the maker of machines sells [a part] of his commodities to the producer, for example, of cloth. The latter pays him money. With this money he buys iron, coal, etc., instead of means of subsistence. If we consider the aggregate of profits, it is clear that the producers of means of subsistence are unable to buy any replacement machinery or any replacement raw materials, unless the producers of replacements for constant capital buy their means of subsistence from them—that is to say, unless this circulation is in essence an exchange between means of subsistence and constant capital. Because of the separation of the acts of purchase and sale there can naturally arise very important interruptions and complications in this compensatory process.

If a country is unable itself to produce the quantity of machinery which its accumulation of capital allows, it buys it from abroad. It does the same if it is itself unable to produce the necessary quantity of means of subsistence (for wages) and raw materials. Here, as soon as international trade comes into the picture, it is as clear as daylight that a portion of the surplus product of the country—in so far as it is destined for accumulation—is not transformed into wages, but directly into constant capital. But then it may still be thought that over there, in another country, the money that has been thus expended is paid out entirely in wages. We have seen that, even leaving foreign trade out of account, this is not so and cannot be so.

The proportion in which the surplus product is divided between variable and constant capital depends on the average composition of capital, and the more developed is capitalist production the smaller *relatively* will be the part directly expended as wages. The idea that, because the surplus product is only the product of the labour newly added during the year, therefore also it is transformed into variable capital only, is only expended in wages—this idea is absolutely in line with the false conception that because the product is only the result, or the materialisation, of labour, its value is resolved into revenue only—wages, profit and rent. This is the false conception put forward by Adam Smith and Ricardo.

A large part of the constant capital, namely the fixed capital, can consist of such things as enter directly into the production process for the production of means of subsistence, raw materials, etc., or serve either to shorten the circulation process, like railways, roads, canals, telegraphs, etc., or for the maintenance and building up of stocks of commodities, like docks, warehouses, etc.; or increase the yield only after a somewhat long period of reproduction, like levelling work, drainage, etc. In accordance with the larger or smaller part of the surplus product that is transformed into one of these kinds of fixed capital, the direct, immediate consequences for the reproduction of means of subsistence, etc., will be very different.

4. CRISES

(a) Causes of Crises

ONCE the expanded production of constant capital is assumed
—that is to say, production beyond what is needed to replace
the former capital, therefore also what is needed to produce
the former quantity of means of subsistence—the expansion of
production, or accumulation, presents no further difficulty in
the spheres producing machinery, raw materials and so on.
If the additional labour required is available, then they find
on the market all the requirements for the formation of new
capital, for the transformation of their additional money into
new capital.

But the whole process of accumulation resolves itself above
all into *expanded production*, which on the one hand corresponds
to the natural increase of the population, and on the other
forms an immanent basis for the phenomena which become
manifest in *crises*. The measure of this expanded production
is *capital* itself—the actual level of the conditions of production
and the boundless urge of the capitalists to enrich themselves
and increase their capital—and not in any way *consumption*.
The latter is limited from the outset, as the greater part of
the population, the working population, can only increase its
consumption within very narrow limits, while to the same
degree as capitalism develops, the demand for labour decreases
relatively, although it increases *absolutely*. Moreover, all equalisa-
tions are *accidental*, and although the proportionate use of
capitals in the various spheres is equalised by a continuous
process, nevertheless the continuity of this process itself equally
presupposes the constant disproportion, which it has continuously, often violently, to even out.

Here we have only to consider the forms which capital
passes through in the various stages of its development.
Hence we do not go into the real relations within which the
actual process of production takes place. It is throughout
assumed that commodities are sold at their value. We do not
consider the competition of capitals, nor the credit system,

nor the actual composition of society, which certainly does not consist merely of the two classes, workers and industrial capitalists—and in which therefore consumers and producers are not identical. The first category [consumers], (whose revenues are in part not primary but secondary, derived from profits and wages), is much wider than the second [producers], and hence the way in which they spend their revenues, and the size of their revenues, brings about very considerable modifications in the economic structure and particularly in the process of circulation and reproduction of capital. It may be added that, while in dealing with money—both in so far as it represents a form different from the natural form of commodities, and in its form as means of payment—we found that it contained the possibility of crises, this emerges even more clearly when we consider the general nature of capital, even without taking into account the further actual relations which constitute the total prerequisites for the real process of production.

The view adopted by Ricardo from the inane Say, but which was really Mill's (which we shall come back to when we deal with that miserable fellow Say), that no *over-production*, or at any rate *no general glut of the market* is possible, rests on the principle that exchange is of *products against products*. Or, as [James] Mill put it, on the "metaphysical equilibrium of sellers and buyers", [which was] further developed [to the principle of] demand being determined only by production itself, or even of the identity of demand and supply. The same principle is expressed also in the form of which Ricardo was particularly fond, that any quantity of capital can be productively employed in any country. In Chapter XXI, on the Effects of Accumulation on Profits and Interest, Ricardo says:

> "M. Say has, however, most satisfactorily shown that there is no amount of capital which may not be employed in a country, because a demand is only limited by production. No man produces but with a view to consume or sell, and he never sells but with an intention to purchase some other commodity, which may be immediately useful to him, or which may contribute to future production. By producing, then, he necessarily becomes either the consumer of his

own goods, or the purchaser and consumer of the goods of some other person. It is not to be supposed that he should, for any length of time, be ill-informed of the commodities which he can most advantageously produce, to attain the object which he has in view, namely, the possession of other goods; and, therefore, it is not probable that he will continually produce a commodity for which there is no demand" (pp. 192–3).

Ricardo, who always tries to be consistent, discovers that his authority Say has put something across him here. In a footnote to this passage he says:

"Is the following quite consistent with M. Say's principle? 'The more disposable capitals are abundant in proportion to the extent of employment for them, the more will the rate of interest on loans of capital fall' (Vol. II, p. 108). If capital to any extent can be employed by a country, how can it be said to be abundant, compared with the extent of employment for it?"

As Ricardo cites Say, we shall criticise Say's theories later, when we deal with this humbug himself.

Meanwhile we note here only the following: In reproduction, just as in the accumulation of capital, the point is not only the replacement of *the same* mass of use value as the capital consists of, on the old scale or (in accumulation) on an enlarged scale, but the replacement of the *value* of the capital advanced along with the usual rate of profit. If therefore through any circumstance whatever or a combination of circumstances the market price of the commodities (of all or of the majority—it makes no difference) falls far below their price of production, then, in the first place, the reproduction of the capital will be considerably curtailed. Even more, however, will accumulation be held back. The transformation into capital of surplus value piled up in the form of money (gold or notes) would only bring loss. It therefore lies idle as a hoard in the banks, or even in the form of credit money, which in essence makes no difference. This stagnation could occur as a result of the opposite causes, when the *real preconditions* for reproduction were lacking (as for example if grain became dear, or because not enough constant capital *in natura* had been accumulated). There is a check in reproduction, and therefore in the flow of circulation. Purchase and sale come into sharp conflict, and unemployed capital appears in the form of money lying idle. The same phenomenon (and this as a rule precedes crises) can occur if the production of surplus capital takes place at a very rapid rate, and its re-transformation into productive capital so increases the demand for all the elements of the latter that real production cannot keep pace, and consequently there is a rise in the prices of all commodities which enter into the formation of capital. In this case the rate of interest falls sharply, however much profits may rise, and this reduction in the rate of interest leads then to the most risky speculative ventures. The check in reproduction leads to the decrease of the variable capital, to a fall in wages and a fall in the amount of labour employed. This in turn reacts anew on prices and brings about a new fall in prices.

It must never be lost sight of that in capitalist production what matters is not direct use value, but exchange value, and in particular the expansion of surplus value. This is the driving motive of capitalist production, and it is a pretty conception that—in order to reason away the contradictions of capitalist production—abstracts from the basis of the latter and presents it as production whose aim is to meet the direct consumption of the producers.

Further: as the circulation process of capital is not a one-day affair, but extends over fairly long periods before the return of the capital to its original form; as these periods however coincide with the periods within which market prices equalise with prices of production; as in the course of these periods great upheavals and changes in markets take place, since great changes in the productivity of labour and therefore in the *real value* of commodities take place—it is therefore very evident that from the starting point—the advance of the capital—until its return at the end of one of these periods, great catastrophes must occur and elements of crises must accumulate and develop—and these cannot in any way be got rid of by the pitiful claptrap that products exchange against products. The equalisation of value in one period with the value of the same commodity in a later period, which Mr.

Bailey considers a scholastic fantasy, forms on the contrary the basic principle of the process of circulation of capital.

When we speak of the *destruction of capital* through crises, two different kinds of things must be distinguished.

In so far as the process of reproduction is checked and the labour process is restricted or here and there is altogether stopped, *real* capital is destroyed. Machinery which is not used is not capital. Labour which is not exploited is equivalent to lost production. Raw material that lies unused is not capital. Use values (also newly constructed machinery) which are either unused or remain unfinished, commodities which rot in warehouses—all this is destruction of capital. All this is nothing but a check in the process of reproduction, so that the *actually existing* means of production do not in fact serve as means of production, are not set in operation. Hence their use value, and their exchange value, go to the devil.

But in the second place the *destruction of capital* resulting from crises means the depreciation of sums of value, preventing them from later on renewing their process of reproduction as capital on the same scale. This is the ruinous effect of the fall in the price of commodities. No use value is destroyed by this. What one loses, the other gains. [But] sums of value in operation as capitals are prevented from renewing themselves as *capital* in the hands of the same persons. The old capitalists go bankrupt. If the value of their commodities, through the sale of which they reproduce their capital, equals £12,000, of which perhaps £2,000 is profit, and these fall to £6,000, then such a capitalist can neither pay the debts he has contracted, nor, even if he had no debts, can he with the £6,000 start his business up again on the former scale, when commodity prices rise once more to their prices of production. Capital to the value of £6,000 is therefore destroyed, although the buyer of these commodities—since he has bought them in at half their price of production—can do very well out of it and even make a profit when trade revives. A considerable part of the nominal capital of society—that is of the *exchange value* of the existing capital—is once for all destroyed, although it is precisely this destruction, since it does not affect the use value, which may very much facilitate the new reproduction. This is at the same time a period when the money capitalist enriches himself at the cost of the industrial capitalist. As for the fall in the purely fictitious capital, State bonds, shares, etc.—provided that it does not lead to the bankruptcy of the State or of the share company, or to the complete stoppage of reproduction through impairing the credit of industrial capitalists who hold such securities—this is merely a transference of wealth from one hand to another, and its effect on reproduction will on the whole be favourable, in so far as the parvenus who get hold of these shares or bonds at cheap prices are for the most part more enterprising than the former holders.

(b) Overproduction of Commodities and Overabundance of Capital

Ricardo is always, to the best of his knowledge, consistent. Therefore for him the statement that no *overproduction* (of commodities) is possible is identical with the statement that no plethora or overabundance of capital is possible.[1]

"There cannot, then, be accumulated in a country any amount of capital which cannot be employed productively until wages rise so high in consequence of the rise of necessaries, and so little consequently remains for the profits of stock, that the motive for accumulation ceases" (Chapter XXI, p. 193).

"It follows, then, from these admissions, that there is no limit to demand—no limit to the employment of capital while it yields any profit, and that, however abundant capital may become, there is no other adequate reason for a fall of profit but a rise of wages, and further, it may be added that the only adequate and permanent cause for the rise of wages is the increasing difficulty of providing food and necessaries for the increasing number of workmen" (Chapter XXI, p. 197).

What then would Ricardo have said to the stupidity of his successors, who deny overproduction in one form (general overabundance of commodities on the market), and in another form, as overproduction of capital, plethora of capital,

---

[1] Here a distinction must be made. When Adam Smith explains the fall in the rate of profit as due to the overabundance of capital, the accumulation of capital, he is speaking of a *permanent* effect, and this is wrong. On the other hand, a transitory overabundance of capital, overproduction, crisis, is something different. There are no permanent crises.

over-abundance of capital, not only admit it, but even make of it a cardinal point in their doctrine?

Not a single responsible economist of the post-Ricardo period denies the [possibility of] overabundance of capital. On the contrary, they all explain crises by it (in so far as they do not trace their causes to phenomena arising from credit). Therefore they all admit overproduction in one form, but deny it in the other. So the only question that remains is: what are the relations between these two forms of overproduction—the form in which it is denied and the form in which it is asserted?

Ricardo himself actually had no knowledge of crises, of general crises on the world market arising out of the process of production itself. He could explain the crises of 1800 to 1815 by the increase in the price of wheat resulting from harvest failures, by the devaluation of paper currency, the depreciation of colonial commodities, and so forth, because as a result of the continental blockade the market was forcibly contracted, from political, not economic, reasons. He could similarly explain the crises after 1815, partly by a bad year and shortage of grain, partly by the fall in the price of corn due to the causes which, by his own theory, necessarily drove up grain prices during the war and the blockade of England from the Continent, having ceased to operate; partly by the transition from war to peace and the consequent "sudden changes in the channels of trade" (see Chapter XIX of his *Principles*, which deals with this). Later historical phenomena, especially the almost regular periodicity of crises on the world market, made it no longer possible for Ricardo's successors to deny the facts or to interpret them as accidental. Instead, they invented—apart from those who explain everything by credit, but then [admit] that they themselves have to presuppose in turn the overabundance of capital—the pretty distinction between *overabundance of capital* and *overproduction*. They keep to the phrases and good reasons used by Ricardo and Adam Smith in arguing against the latter, while from the former they seek to deduce phenomena otherwise inexplicable to them. Wilson for example explains certain crises by the overabundance of fixed capital, others by the overabundance of circulating capital. The overabundance of capital itself is affirmed by the best economists (like Fullarton) and has already become such a fixed prejudice that the phrase even occurs in the learned Roscher's *Compendium* as something that is self-evident.[1]

The question therefore arises: what is overabundance of capital, and what distinguishes this thing from overproduction? According to the same economists capital is equivalent to money or commodities. Overproduction of capital is therefore overproduction of money or of commodities. And yet these two phenomena are supposed to have nothing in common with each other. Nor does even overproduction of money help, since for them money is a commodity, so that the whole phenomenon resolves itself into overproduction of commodities, which they admit under one name and deny under another. If moreover it is said that the overproduction is of fixed capital or of circulating capital, the basis of this statement is that commodities are here no longer considered simply as commodities, but in their designation as capital. However, this statement on the other hand is an admission that in capitalist production and its phenomena—for example, overproduction— we are dealing not only with the simple relation in which the product appears as *commodity*, but with its social determinants, through which it is *more than* and even something different from a commodity.

In general, the phrase *overabundance of capital* as against *overproduction of commodities* is often merely a prevaricating expression, or [that kind of] thoughtlessness that admits the same phenomenon as present and necessary when it is called A, but denies it when it is called B; that therefore in fact has scruples and doubts only about the *name to be given* to the phenomenon, but not about the phenomenon itself. Or [the phrase springs from the striving] to overcome the difficulty in explaining the phenomenon by denying it in a form in which it comes up against prejudices, and admitting it only in a form in which no one bothers about it. But apart from these aspects of it, the transition from the phrase "*overproduction of commodities*" to the phrase "*overabundance of capital*" represents

[1] To do them justice, however, it must be noted that other economists, such as Ure, Corbett, etc., explain overproduction as the *regular condition of large-scale industry* so far as the home country is considered, so that overproduction leads to crises only under certain conditions when the foreign market also contracts.

in fact a *step forward*. In what does this consist? [In the recognition] that the producers confront one another not as mere owners of commodities, but as capitalists.

(c) *Unity of Purchase and Sale, of the Process of Production and the Process of Circulation*

A few more passages from Ricardo:

"One would be led to think . . . that Adam Smith concluded we were under some necessity of producing a surplus of corn, woollen goods, and hardware, and that the capital which produced them could not be otherwise employed. It is, however, always a matter of choice in what way a capital shall be employed, and therefore there can never for any length of time be a surplus of any commodity; for if there were, it would fall below its natural price, and capital would be removed to some more profitable employment" (Chapter XXI, p. 194, footnote).

"Productions are always bought by productions, or by services; money is only the medium by which the exchange is effected. Too much of a particular commodity may be produced, of which there may be such a glut in the market as not to repay the capital expended on it; but this cannot be the case with respect to all commodities" (Chapter XXI, p. 194).

"Whether these increased productions and the consequent demand which they occasion shall or shall not lower profits, depends solely on the rise of wages; and the rise of wages, excepting for a limited period, on the facility of producing the food and necessaries of the labourer" (Chapter XXI, p. 194).

"When merchants engage their capitals in foreign trade, or in the carrying trade, it is always from choice and never from necessity: it is because in that trade their profits will be somewhat greater than in the home trade" (Chapter XXI, p. 195).

In relation to crises, all authors who portray the actual movement of prices, or all practical people writing at particular stages of a crisis, have correctly ignored the allegedly theoretical twaddle and have been content to take it for granted that the doctrine of the impossibility of a market plethora, though it might be true in abstract theory, is in practice false. The regular repetition of crises has in fact reduced the rigmaroles of Say and others to a phraseology which is only used in times of prosperity, but in times of crisis is discarded.

In world market crises the contradictions and antagonisms of bourgeois production break through to the surface. But instead of investigating the nature of the conflicting elements which force their way through in the catastrophe, the apologists content themselves with denying the catastrophe itself; and, faced with its regular recurrence, with insisting that production would never lead to crises if it were carried on according to the textbooks. The apologetics consist, then, in falsifying the simplest economic relations, and especially in stubbornly maintaining the unity in face of the contradiction.

If for example purchase and sale, or the movement of metamorphosis of commodities, represent the unity of two processes—or rather the course of a single process through two opposite phases, and thus in essence the unity of the two phases— this movement is nevertheless, equally in essence, the separation of the two phases, making them independent of each other. Since in fact they belong together, the independence of the two linked phases can only show itself forcibly, as a destructive process. It is precisely the *crisis* in which their unity asserts itself—the unity of different things. The independence in relation to each other, which is assumed by these mutually dependent and complementary phases, is forcibly destroyed. The crisis therefore makes manifest the unity of the phases which have become independent of each other. No crisis would take place, were it not for this inner unity of what on the surface are phases unrelated to each other. But No!—says the apologist economist. Because there is unity, there can be *no* crisis. Which in turn is nothing but to say that the unity of opposite [factors] excludes their antagonism.

In order to prove that capitalist production cannot lead to general crises, all its conditions and definite forms, all its principles and *differentiae specificae* (specific differences) are denied; in short, capitalist production itself is denied. And in fact what is demonstrated is that if the capitalist mode of production— instead of being a specifically developed, unique form of social production—were a mode of production dating back to the crudest beginnings of social production, the antagonisms and contradictions peculiar to it, and therefore also their explosion in crises, would not exist.

"Productions", Ricardo, following Say, observes, "are always bought by productions, or by services; money is only the medium by which the exchange is effected."

Here therefore, in the first place, the *commodity*, in which the antagonism between exchange value and use value exists, is transformed into a simple product (use value), and consequently the exchange of commodities is transformed into a mere bartering of products, of simple use values. This is to go back not only to before capitalist production, but to before simple commodity production; and the most developed phenomenon of capitalist production—world market crisis—is flatly denied by the flat denial of the first condition of capitalist production, namely, that the product is a commodity and must therefore take the form of money and pass through the process of metamorphosis. Instead of speaking of wage labour, the term used is "services", a word in which the specific characteristic of wage labour and of its use—namely, that it increases the value of the commodities for which it is exchanged, that it produces surplus value—is again disregarded, and with it also the specific relation whereby money and commodities are transformed into capital. "Service" is labour considered only as *use value* (a secondary matter in capitalist production), just in the same way as in the word "*productions*" the essence of the *commodity* and of the contradiction contained in it is suppressed. Then, quite consistently, *money* is conceived as merely the intermediary in the exchange of products, not as an essential and necessary form of existence of the commodity, which must present itself as exchange value—general social labour. Inasmuch as, through the transformation of the commodity into mere use value (product), the essence of exchange value is expunged, it is then easy to deny—or rather it is then necessary to deny—*money* as an essential and independent form of the commodity in the process of the metamorphosis from its original form. In this way, therefore, crises are reasoned out of existence through losing sight of or denying the first preconditions of capitalist production: the nature of the product as a commodity, the duplication of the commodity in commodity and money, the consequent separate phases in the exchange of commodities, and finally the relation of money or commodities to wage labour.

Those economists, however, are no better, who (like John Stuart Mill, for example) seek to explain crises by these simple *possibilities* of crisis contained in the metamorphosis of commodities—such as the separation between purchase and sale. These characteristics, which explain the possibility of crisis, are very far from explaining their actuality, and still less, *why* the phases of the process come into such conflict that their inner unity can only assert itself through a crisis, through a violent process. This *separation* appears in the crisis; it is the elementary form of crisis. To *explain* the crisis by its elementary form is to explain the existence of the crisis by expressing its presence in its abstract form, that is, to explain the crisis by the crisis.

Ricardo says:

"No man produces but with a view to consume or sell, and he never sells but with an intention to purchase some other commodity, which may be immediately useful to him, or which may contribute to future production. By producing, then, he necessarily becomes either the consumer of his own goods, or the purchaser and consumer of the goods of some other person. It is not to be supposed that he should, for any length of time, be ill-informed of the commodities which he can most advantageously produce, to attain the object which he has in view, namely, the possession of other goods; and, therefore, it is not probable that he will continually produce a commodity for which there is no demand" (Chapter XXI, pp. 192–3).

This is the childish babble of a Say, but it is not worthy of Ricardo. In the first place no capitalist produces in order to consume his product. And when we are speaking of capitalist production, then it is correct to say "No man produces with a view to consume his own product", even if he uses portions of his product for industrial consumption. But here it is private consumption that is in question. In the earlier passage, it was forgotten that the product is a commodity. Now even the social division of labour is forgotten. In conditions in which men produce for themselves, there are in fact no crises, but also no capitalist production. Nor have we ever heard that the ancients, with their slave production, at any time experienced crises, although among the ancients too individual producers went bankrupt. The first part of the alternative is nonsense. So is the second. A man who has produced has not the choice whether he will sell or not. He *must* sell. And in crises appears precisely the circumstance that he cannot sell, or only below the price of production, or even that he must sell at a positive loss. What does it avail him or us, therefore, that he has produced in order to sell? What concerns us is precisely to discover what has cut across this good intention of his.

Further: "No man sells but with a view to purchase some other commodity, which may be immediately useful to him, or which may contribute to future production". What a pleasant portrayal of bourgeois relations! Ricardo even forgets that a man may sell in order to pay, and that these compulsory sales play a very significant role in crises. The immediate purpose of the capitalist when he sells is to transform his commodities or rather his commodity capital back again into money capital, and thereby to realise his profit. Consumption —revenue—is consequently not the determining motive of this process, which it is, however, for the man who only sells commodities in order to transform them into means of subsistence. But this is not capitalist production, in which revenue appears as a result but not as the determining purpose. Everyone sells with the immediate aim of selling; that is, in order to transform commodities into money.

During the crisis the man may be very pleased when he has made a sale, without any immediate thought of a purchase. However, if the value that has been realised is now again to function as capital it must pass through the process of reproduction, that is, be exchanged once more for labour and commodities. But crisis is precisely the moment of disturbance and interruption in the process of reproduction. And this disturbance cannot be explained by the fact that it does not take place in periods when there is no crisis. There can be no doubt that nobody "will continually produce a commodity for which there is no demand", but no one is talking about such an absurd hypothesis. Also, it has nothing whatever to do with the matter. "The possession of other goods" is not the immediate aim of capitalist production, but the appropriation of value, of money, of abstract wealth.

The basis of Ricardo's approach is here also James Mill's principle of the "metaphysical equation of purchases and sales", which I have already examined—an equation that sees *only* the unity but not the separation in the process of purchase and sale. This is also the basis of Ricardo's statement (following James Mill).

Money is not only "the medium by which the exchange is effected", but equally it is the medium through which the exchange of product for product falls into two acts which are independent of each other and separate in space and time. With Ricardo this false conception of money comes however from the fact that he is always looking at the *quantitative determination* of exchange value, that is, that it is equal to a definite quantity of labour time, but on the other hand forgets the *qualitative* characteristic that the individual labour, through its alienation, must present itself as *abstract, general, social labour*.[1]

Before we advance one further step, this must be said:

Through the disjunction between the direct production process and the circulation process, the *possibility* of crisis, which became apparent in the simple metamorphosis of the commodity, is once more and further developed. When these two processes do not pass from one to the other in a continuous stream, but become independent of each other, the crisis is there.

In the metamorphosis of commodities the possibility of crisis shows itself in this way:

First, the commodity, which exists in its real form as a use value, and in its notional form, in its price, as an exchange value, must be transformed into money: C–M. Once this difficulty, the sale, is solved, then the purchase, M–C, presents

---

[1] That for Ricardo money is merely *means of circulation* is linked with the fact that he [regards] *exchange value* as merely a transient form, in general as something purely formal in bourgeois or capitalist production; for which reason capitalist production is for him not a specifically determined mode of production, but *the* mode of production in general.

no difficulty, as money is immediately exchangeable for everything else. The use value of the commodity, the usefulness of the labour contained in it, must be assumed from the start—otherwise it is not in any sense a commodity. It is further assumed that the individual value of the commodity is equal to its social value, that is, that the labour time materialised in it is equal to the labour time socially necessary for the production of this commodity. The possibility of crisis, in so far as it shows itself in the simple form of the metamorphosis, therefore comes from the mere fact that the differences in form—the phases—which in its movement it passes through, in the first place, are necessary complementary forms and phases; and secondly, in spite of this inner necessary connection with each other, are independent parts and forms of the process, existing independently of each other, separate in time and space, cut off and divided from each other. It lies therefore in the very separation between sale and purchase. It is only in the form of commodity that the commodity has this difficulty to overcome. As soon as it has the form of money it has got over the difficulty. But moreover, this too is due to the separation between purchase and sale. If the commodity could not be withdrawn from circulation in the form of money, or its retransformation into a commodity could not be deferred; if—as in direct barter—purchase and sale were one, the *possibility* of crisis, on the assumptions made, would disappear. For it is assumed that the commodity is a *use value* for other possessors of commodities. In the direct barter form, the commodity is only not exchangeable if it has no use value, or if there are no other use values on the other side to be exchanged for it. Therefore only under these two conditions: if either there has been useless production on the one side or there is nothing useful on the other side to exchange as an equivalent for the first use value. In both cases, however, no exchange whatever would take place. But in so far as exchange did take place, its two phases would not be separated. The buyer would be seller, the seller buyer. The *critical* moment which results from the form of exchange—in so far as it is circulation—would therefore not be present, and when we say that the simple form of metamorphosis contains the possibility of crisis, we are only saying that in this form lies the very possibility of the tearing apart and division of essentially complementary phases. But this affects also the content. In direct barter the bulk of production, on the part of the producer, is directed to the satisfaction of his own needs, or, at a somewhat further developed stage of the division of labour, to the satisfaction of the needs of his fellow-producers which are known to him. What is to be exchanged as a commodity is his surplus, and it is unimportant whether this surplus is exchanged or not. In commodity production the transformation of the product into money, its sale, is a *conditio sine qua non*. Direct production for one's own needs does not take place. In this case, if there is no sale, there is crisis. The difficulty in transforming the *commodities*—the particular product of individual labour—into *money*, their opposite, into abstract general, social labour, consists in the fact that *money* is not the particular product of individual labour; that the man who has sold, that is, holds the commodity in the form of money, is not compelled immediately to purchase again, to transform the money back again into a particular product of individual labour. In barter, this contradiction does not exist. In the barter form no one can be a seller without being a buyer, or a buyer without being a seller. The difficulty in selling—on the assumption that the commodity to be sold has use value—arises simply from the ease with which the buyer can postpone the re-transformation of the money into commodity. The difficulty in transforming the commodity into money, in selling, arises simply from the fact that the commodity must be transformed into money, but there is no need for the money to be immediately transformed into commodity, and therefore sale and purchase may fall asunder. We have said that this form contains the possibility of crisis, that is to say, the possibility that phases which are linked together, which are inseparable, become separated and consequently are forcibly reunited, their intimate connection realised by violence, which overcomes their subjective independence. And crisis is nothing but the forcible assertion of the unity of phases of the production process which have become independent of each other.

The general, abstract possibility of crisis is nothing more

than the *most abstract form* of crisis, without content, without its pregnant motivating factor. Sale and purchase may be sundered. They represent, therefore, crisis *in potentia*, and their coincidence always remains a critical factor for the commodity. They may, however, pass smoothly over from one to the other.

The most abstract form of crisis and consequently the formal possibility of crisis is therefore the metamorphosis of the commodity itself; in which it is only as a developed movement that the contradiction between exchange value and use value, and between money and commodity, which the unity of the commodity comprises, is involved. But this form does not in itself contain that which transforms this possibility of crisis into a crisis; all it implies is that *the* form for a crisis exists.

And in the investigation of bourgeois economy this is the important thing. World market crises must be conceived as the real gathering together and forcible smoothing out of all the contradictions of bourgeois economy. The separate factors which converge in these crises must therefore emerge and develop in each sphere of bourgeois economy, and the further we delve into it, the more there will be on the one hand the development of new definite features of this contradiction, while on the other hand its more abstract forms must prove to be recurrent and contained in more concrete forms.

We can therefore say: Crisis in its first form is the metamorphosis of the commodity itself, the falling asunder of purchase and sale.

Crisis in its second form [arises from the] function of money as means of payment, in which money figures in two different phases divided from each other in time, in two different functions. Both of these two forms are still quite abstract, although the second is more concrete than the first.

First, therefore, in considering the *process of reproduction* of capital, which coincides with its circulation, it is necessary to show that these above-mentioned forms are simply repeated over and over again, or rather here first receive a content, a foundation on which they can manifest themselves.

Let us examine the movement which capital passes through from the moment when it leaves the production process as commodity in order once again to come out of it as commodity.

If we here abstract from everything else that determines its content, then the total commodity capital, and each individual commodity of which it consists, has to pass through the process C–M–C, the metamorphosis of the commodity. The general possibility of crisis which is contained in this form—the separation of purchase and sale—is therefore implicit in the movement of the capital, in so far as this capital is *also* commodity and nothing but commodity. The connection between the metamorphoses of commodities with each other results moreover in one commodity transforming itself into money, because the other is re-transforming itself from the form of money into commodity. Consequently, the separation of purchase from sale appears here also in such a way that the transformation of the one capital from the form commodity into the form money must correspond to the re-transformation of the other capital from the form money into the form commodity, the first metamorphosis of the one capital to the second of the other, the one capital leaving the production process and the other returning into the production process. This mutual confluence and intertwining of the reproduction or circulation processes of different capitals is on the one hand necessitated by the division of labour, and on the other is accidental; and thus the determination of the content of crisis is already a stage further.

Secondly, however, as concerns the possibility of crisis arising from the form of money as *means of payment*, there are already in capital a number of more concrete causes for this possibility being realised. For example, the weaver has to pay for his whole constant capital, the elements of which are supplied by spinner, flax grower, machinery manufacturer, iron manufacturer, timber merchant, coal producer, and so on. In so far as these latter produce constant capital which only enters into [the process of production] without entering into the final commodity, the cloth, they replace each other's means of production by means of an exchange of capital. Let us suppose that the weaver then sells his cloth to the *merchant* for £1,000, but in return for a bill of exchange, so that money figures as *means of payment*. Similarly, the flax grower has sold to the spinner in return for a bill of exchange, and the spinner to the weaver, ditto the machinery manufacturer to the weaver, ditto the iron manufacturer and timber merchant to the machinery manufacturer, ditto the coal producer to the spinner, weaver, machinery manufacturer, and iron and timber suppliers. In addition, the iron, coal, timber and flax producers have paid each other with bills of exchange. Then if the merchant does not receive money for his commodity, he cannot pay his bill of exchange to the weaver. The flax grower has drawn on the spinner, the machinery manufacturer on the weaver and the spinner. The spinner cannot pay, because the weaver cannot pay; neither of them pays the machinery manufacturer, and the latter does not pay the suppliers of iron, timber, and coal. And all of them in turn, because they do not realise the value of their commodities, cannot replace the portion of the value which is to replace their constant capital. In this way a general crisis arises. This is nothing other than the developed *possibility of crisis* arising from money as means of payment; but we see here, in capitalist production, that very connection between mutual claims and obligations, between purchases and sales, through which the possibility can develop into actuality.

In any case: if purchase and sale do not get held up reciprocally, and therefore do not require forcible adjustment—or if money so functions as means of payment that claims are settled, and the contradiction inherent in money as means of payment is not realised—if therefore these two abstract forms of crisis do not in actuality make their appearance as such, no crisis exists. No crisis can exist unless sale and purchase become separated from each other and come into conflict, or the contradictions inherent in money as means of payment come to the surface; unless therefore crisis at the same time emerges in the simple form—as the contradiction between purchase and sale, or the contradiction inherent in money as means of payment. But these also are mere *forms*, general possibilities of crises; and consequently also forms, abstract forms, of actual crisis. In them the nature of crisis appears in its simplest forms, and, in so far as this form is itself its simplest content, in its simplest content. But it is not as yet a content which has *a determinate cause*. The simple circulation of money and even the circulation of money as means of payment—and both make their appearance long *before* capitalist production, without crises occurring—are possible and in fact take place without crises. On the basis of these forms alone, therefore, it is not possible to explain why they show their critical side, why the contradiction contained in them as a possibility emerges as a real contradiction.

From this we can see how great is the stupidity of economists who, when they are no longer able to reason out of existence the phenomenon of overproduction and crisis, soothe themselves by saying that only the possibility of crises is given in those forms, and that therefore their emergence is *accidental*, and so the advent of crisis is itself a mere *accident*.

The contradictions developed in the circulation of commodities, and further developed in the circulation of money—and the consequent possibilities of crisis—reproduce themselves spontaneously in capital, inasmuch as the developed circulation of commodities and circulation of money in fact arise only on the basis of capital.

What has to be done, however, is to follow through the further development of the potential crisis—the real crisis can only be presented on the basis of the real movement of capitalist production, competition and credit—in so far as crisis arises from the forms characteristic of capital, its *properties* as capital, and not from its mere existence as commodity and as money. The mere direct *process of production* of capital cannot by itself add anything new in this connection. In order to exist at all, the conditions for it are assumed. For that reason, in the first section dealing with capital—the immediate process of production—no new element of crisis has to be added. *By its nature* crisis is present in it. For the process of production is appropriation and therefore production of surplus value. But this cannot appear in the process of production itself, because the latter is not concerned with the realisation of both the reproduced value, and the surplus value. Crisis can only appear in the process of circulation, which in essence is at the same time the process of reproduction.

Here it must further be noted that we must examine the process of circulation or process of reproduction *before* examining

already existing capital—capital and profit—as we have to
show not only how capital produces, but how capital is produced. The actual movement, however, starts from the capital
in hand—that is, the actual movement that is based on
developed capitalist production, beginning out of itself and
presupposing itself. The reproduction process and the occasions
of crises which are further developed in it are therefore not
fully handled under this heading, and require further elaboration in the chapter on "Capital and Profit".

The circulation process as a whole or the whole process of
reproduction of capital is the unity of its production phase
with its circulation phase, a process which runs through both
those processes as its phases. Therein lies a further developed
possibility or abstract form of crisis. The economists who deny
crises therefore insist only on the unity of these two phases.
If they were only separate without being a unity, then no
forcible restoration of their unity would be possible, no crisis.
If they were only a unity without being separate, then no
forcible separation would be possible, which again is crisis.
It is the forcible restoration of unity between independent
phases, and the forcible separation from each other of processes
which in essence are one.

Therefore:

1. The general *possibility* of crises is given in the process of
metamorphosis of capital itself, and in fact in a twofold way: in
so far as money functions as *means of circulation*, through the
separation of purchase and sale; and in so far as it functions
as *means of payment*, where it has two separate aspects, as *measure
of value* and as *realisation of value*. These two aspects become
separated. If in the interval between them the value has
altered, the commodity at the moment of its sale is not worth
what it was worth at the moment when money functioned as
measure of value and therefore of the reciprocal obligations;
then the obligation cannot be met from the proceeds of sale
of the commodities, and therefore the whole series of transactions, which depend in a backward chain on this one transaction, cannot be settled. If even for a certain time the
commodities cannot be sold, although their value has not
changed—in such a case money cannot function as means of

payment, since it has to function as such within a definite term laid down in advance. But as the same sum of money functions here for a series of mutual transactions and obligations, the inability to pay appears not at one point only but at many, and hence crisis.

These are the formal possibilities of crises. The first-mentioned forms are possible without the latter; that is to say, crises are possible without credit, without money functioning as means of payment. But the latter forms are not possible without the former, that is, without the separation between purchase and sale. But in the latter case crisis appears not only because commodities are unsaleable, but also when they cannot be sold within a certain period; and in this case crisis arises and derives its character not only from the fact that commodities cannot be sold, but from the non-fulfilment of a whole series of payments which depend on the sale of these particular commodities within this particular period of time. This is the characteristic form of money crises.

Therefore if a crisis appears because purchase and sale become separated, it develops *as a money crisis* when money has developed as *means of payment*, and this *second form* of crises follows as a matter of course when the first makes its appearance. In investigating why the general possibility of crises becomes *an actual crisis*, in investigating the conditions of crisis, it is therefore quite superfluous to concern ourselves with those crises which arise from the development of money as means of payment. Precisely for this reason the economists like to advance this self-explanatory form as the cause of crises. In so far as the development of money as means of payment is linked with the development of credit and of surplus credit, it is true that the causes of the latter have to be investigated; but this is not yet the place to do it.

2. In so far as crises result from changes and revolutions in prices which do not coincide with changes in the values of commodities, they naturally cannot be investigated when we are considering capital in general, when it is assumed that prices are identical with the values of commodities.

3. The general possibility of crises is the formal metamorphosis of capital itself, the separation in time and space of purchase

and sale. But this is never the cause of crisis. For it is nothing but the most general form of crisis, that is, crisis itself in its most generalised expression. It cannot however be said that the abstract form of crisis is the cause of crisis. If we seek its cause, what we want to know is why its abstract form, the form of its possibility, develops from possibility into actuality.

4. The general conditions of crises, in so far as they are independent of price fluctuations (and whether these are linked with the credit system or not; price fluctuations as distinct from fluctuations of value), must be explicable from the general conditions of capitalist production.

[We find, then, as factors in a crisis:]

The reconversion of money into capital. A definite level of production or reproduction is assumed. The fixed capital can here be considered as given, remaining the same and not entering into the process of realisation. As the reproduction of the raw material is dependent not only on the labour expended on it, but on the productivity of this labour in association with natural conditions, it is possible [even with the method of production remaining the same] for the mass of the product of the same quantity of labour to fall (with bad harvests). The value of the raw material therefore rises, while its mass falls. The proportions in which money has to flow back into the various component parts of the capital, in order to continue production on the former level, are dis-turbed. More must be paid out for raw material, less remains for labour, and the same quantity of labour as before cannot be absorbed. In the first place, this is not physically possible, because there is a deficiency of raw material; secondly, because a greater part of the value of the product has to be transformed into raw material, and consequently a smaller part can be transformed into variable capital. Reproduction can not be repeated at the same level. A part of the fixed capital stays idle, a part of the workers is thrown out on the streets. The rate of profit falls, because the value of the constant capital compared with the variable has risen and less variable capital is employed. The fixed charges—interest, rent—which are based on the anticipation of stable rates of profit and of exploitation of labour, remain the same, and in part cannot be paid. Hence crisis. Crisis of labour and crisis of capital. This is therefore an interruption of the reproduction process resulting from an increased value of the part of the constant capital that has to be replaced out of the value of the product. In this case, although the rate of profit falls, there is a rise in the price of the product. If this product enters into other spheres of production as a means of production, the rise in its price results in the same disturbance of reproduction in these spheres. If it enters into general consumption as a means of subsistence, it either enters also into the consumption of the workers or it does not. In the first case, the effects are the same as that of a disturbance in the variable capital, which is dealt with later. But in so far as it enters generally into consumption, the result may be (unless the consumption of it falls) a fall in the demand for other products. Hence their reconversion into money at their value will be hindered to a corresponding degree, and thus the other side of their reproduction—not the reconversion of money into productive capital, but the reconversion of commodities into money—will be disturbed. In any case the mass of profit and the mass of wages in this branch of industry falls, and this means a fall in part of the necessary returns from the sale of commodities of other branches of production.

This shortage of raw material may however also make its appearance apart from the influence of harvests or of the natural productivity of the labour which supplies the raw material. If for example an undue portion of the [accumulated] surplus value, of the surplus capital, is [expended] on machinery, etc., in a particular branch of production, the raw material, although it would have been adequate for the old level of production, will be inadequate for the new. This therefore results from the disproportionate conversion of the surplus capital into its different elements. It is a case of *overproduction of fixed capital* and produces exactly the same phenomena as in the first case.

(d) General and Partial Overproduction

In Chapter XXI Ricardo says:

"Too much of a *particular* commodity may be produced, of which there may be such a glut in the market as not to repay the capital expended on it; but this cannot be the case with respect to *all* commodities" (p. 194).

That only *particular* but not *all* kinds of commodities can constitute a glut in the market, and that consequently over-production can always only be partial, is a paltry evasion. In the first place, if the mere nature of a commodity is considered, there is nothing in it which would prevent *all* commodities being in over supply on the market and therefore all falling below their price. What is involved here is precisely the moment of crisis. In fact, all commodities [may be in over supply] except *money*. The necessity for *the* commodity to transform itself into money means only that the necessity exists for *all* commodities. And inasmuch as there is a difficulty in a single commodity making this metamorphosis, the difficulty can exist for all commodities. The general nature of the metamorphosis of commodities—which includes the separation of purchase and sale as well as their unity—instead of excluding the *possibility* of a general glut, is rather *the* possibility of a general glut.

Moreover, in the background of Ricardo's arguments and similar arguments put forward by others there is in fact not only the relation of purchase and sale, but also that of demand and supply, which we have to consider only when we investigate the competition of capitals. Just as Mill says that purchase is sale, etc., so is demand supply and supply demand; but they are equally separate, and can assume independence of each other. At a given moment the supply of all commodities may be greater than the demand for all commodities, because the demand for the general commodity, money, exchange value, is greater than the demand for all particular commodities; in other words, because the compulsion for the commodity to take the form of money, to realise its exchange value, is greater than the compulsion for the commodity to be reconverted into use value. If the relation between demand and supply is conceived in a wider and more concrete way, there enters into it the relation between production and consumption. Here again there must be borne in mind the *unity* of these two phases, which exists in their nature and forcibly asserts itself precisely in crisis, against the equally existent, and for bourgeois production even characteristic, separation and opposition of the two.

As for the antithesis between partial and universal over-production—that is, in so far as the former is emphasised only as a means of getting rid of the latter—the following further points may be noted:

First: A general rise of prices in all articles of capitalist production usually precedes a crisis. Consequently they all have a share in the following crash, and all constitute an overloading of the market at the prices which they had before the crash. The market can absorb a mass of commodities at falling prices, prices that have fallen below their prices of production, which it could not absorb at their former market prices. The excess of commodities is always relative, that is, it is an excess at certain prices. The prices at which the commodities are then absorbed are ruinous for the producer or merchant.

Secondly:

For a crisis (and therefore also overproduction) to be general, it is sufficient for it to grip the principal articles of trade.

Let us examine more closely how Ricardo tries to argue away the possibility of a general glut of the market:

"Too much of a particular commodity may be produced, of which there may be such a glut in the market as not to repay the capital expended on it; but this cannot be the case with respect to all commodities; the demand for corn is limited by the mouths which are to eat it, for shoes and coats by the persons who are to wear them; but though a community, or a part of a community, may have as much corn, and as many hats and shoes as it is able, or may wish to consume, the same cannot be said of every commodity produced by nature or by art. Some would consume more wine if they had the ability to procure it. Others, having enough of wine, would wish to increase the quantity or improve the quality of their furniture. Others might wish to ornament their grounds, or to enlarge their houses. The wish to do all or some of these is implanted in every man's breast; nothing is required but the means, and nothing can afford the means but an increase of production" (p. 194).

Can there be a more childish line of reasoning? It runs like this. More may be produced of a particular commodity than can be consumed. But that cannot be true of *all* commodities at the same time. Because the needs which are satisfied through commodities have no limits and all these needs are not satisfied at the same time. On the contrary. The satisfaction of one need makes another so to speak latent. Therefore nothing is required but the means to satisfy these needs, and these means can only be provided through an increase of production. Therefore no general overproduction is possible.

What is the relevance of all this? In times of overproduction a great part of the nation (especially the working class) is less than ever supplied with grain, shoes, etc., to say nothing of wine and furniture. If overproduction could only occur after all members of the nation had satisfied even their most essential needs, in the history of bourgeois society up to the present not only no general overproduction, but even no partial overproduction, could have occurred. If for example the market is over-supplied with shoes or calico or wines or colonial products, does this mean that perhaps even only two-thirds of the nation have over-satisfied their need for shoes, calico, etc.? What in any case has overproduction to do with absolute needs? It is only needs with capacity to pay that count. What is in question is not absolute overproduction— overproduction in itself, in relation to the absolute need or the desire to possess commodities. In this sense neither partial nor general overproduction exists. And [in this sense] they are not in any kind of contradiction with each other.

But, Ricardo may say, when there are numbers of people who need shoes and calico, why do they not acquire the means to buy them by producing something with which they can buy shoes and calico? Would it not be even simpler to say: why do they not produce shoes and calico for themselves? And what is even more strange in overproduction is that the actual producers of the very commodities which overfill the market—the workers—suffer from lack of them. In this case it cannot be said that they should produce the things in order to get them, for they have produced them, and yet they have not got them. Nor can it be said that the particular commodities are in glut on the market because no need for them exists. If therefore even *partial* overproduction is not to be explained by the fact that the commodities in excess on the market exceed the need for them, in the same way *universal* overproduction cannot be explained away by the fact that needs, unsatisfied needs, exist for many of the commodities which are on the market.

Let us keep to the cotton weaver by way of example. So long as reproduction continued without a check—therefore also the phase of this reproduction in which the product, the cotton, existing as a commodity, a saleable commodity, is reconverted into money at its value—for so long also, shall we say, the workers who produce the cotton consumed a portion of it; and with extended reproduction—that is, accumulation—they absorbed progressively more of it, or more workers too were employed in the production of the cotton, who also were in part consumers of it.

So long as the weaver reproduces and accumulates, his workers also buy a part of his product; they expend a part of their wages on cotton. Because he produces, they have the means to buy a part of his product, and thus in part provide him with the means of selling it. The worker can only buy—represent demand for—commodities which enter into individual consumption, as he does not himself make a profit from his labour, and does not himself possess the conditions for setting it to work—the means of labour and material of labour. Where production is developed in capitalist form, this therefore already excludes the greatest part of the producers, the workers themselves, from being consumers, buyers, of means of production. They buy no raw material and no means of labour; they buy only means of subsistence, commodities which enter directly into individual consumption. Consequently there is nothing more ridiculous than to speak of the identity of producers and consumers, since for an extraordinarily great number of branches of production—all those not producing articles for direct consumption—the mass of those engaged in production are absolutely excluded from the purchase of their own products. They are never directly consumers or buyers of this great part of their own products, although they pay a part of the value of these products in the consumption articles which they buy. This also shows the ambiguity of the word consumer and the error of identifying it with the word buyer. Industrially, it is precisely the workers who consume the machinery and raw material, who use it up in the labour process. But they do not use it up for themselves, and consequently they are not buyers of it. For them they are not use values, not commodities, but objective conditions of a process of which they themselves are the subjective conditions.

It may however be said that their employer represents them in the purchase of means of labour and materials of labour. But he represents them under different conditions from those in which they would represent themselves; that is, on the market. He has to sell a mass of commodities embodying surplus value, unpaid labour. They would have to sell only a mass of commodities which reproduced the value advanced in production—the value of the means of labour, the material of labour and the wages. He therefore has need of a wider market than they would require.

They are therefore producers, without being consumers— even when there is no interruption in the process of reproduction—in respect of all the articles which have to be consumed not individually but industrially.

So nothing is more preposterous as a means of denying crises than the assertion that consumers (buyers) and producers (sellers) are identical in capitalist production. They are completely separate. In so far as the reproduction process takes place, this identity can be asserted for only one out of every three thousand producers, that is to say, for the capitalist. It is just as false the other way round—that the consumers are producers. The landowner does not produce rent, and yet he consumes. The position is the same with the whole of money capital.

The apologetic phrases used to deny crises are important from this aspect—that they always prove the opposite of what they set out to prove. In order to deny crises, they assert unity where there is opposition and contradiction. This is important in so far as it can be said: they prove that, if the contradictions which they day-dream out of existence in fact did not exist, then too no crises would exist. But in fact crisis exists, because those contradictions exist. Every reason which they advance against crisis is a contradiction day-dreamed away—therefore a real contradiction, therefore a cause of crisis. The desire to day-dream contradictions out of the way is at the same time the expression of contradictions that are really present, but which they vainly desire *should* not exist.

What the workers in fact produce is surplus value. So long as they produce it, they are able to consume. As soon as [its production] ceases, their consumption ceases, because their production ceases. But it is in no way true that they are able to consume because they produce an equivalent for their consumption. Rather is it the case that the very moment they have produced such an equivalent, their consumption ceases, they have no equivalent to consume. Either their labour is dispensed with or cut down, or in any case their wages lowered. In the latter case—when the level of production remains the same—they do not consume any equivalent for their production. But then they lack the means of subsistence, not because they do not produce enough, but because they get too little of their product for themselves.

If therefore the relations are reduced to that simply of consumer and producer, the fact is lost sight of that the producing wage-labour and the producing capitalist are two producers of a very different kind, even if we leave out of account the consumers who produce nothing at all. Once again the antagonism is denied by abstracting from an antagonism that is actually present in production. The mere relationship between wage-labourer and capitalist involves:

(1) That the greatest part of the producers (the workers) are non-consumers (non-buyers) of a very considerable part of their product, namely, of the means of labour and the material of labour.

(2) That the greatest part of the producers, the workers, can only consume an equivalent for their product so long as they produce more than this equivalent—surplus value or surplus product. They must always be *over-producers*, must always produce over and above their needs, in order to be

able to be consumers or buyers within the limits of their needs.

With this class of producers, therefore, the unity between production and consumption is in any case *prima facie* false.

When Ricardo says that the only limit of demand is production itself, and this is limited by capital, this means in fact, when stripped of the false assumptions, nothing more than that capitalist production finds its measure only in capital—the concept of capital including here also the labour power incorporated in the capital (bought by it) as one of its conditions of production. Here the question arises whether capital as such is also the limit for consumption. In any case this is true negatively; that is to say, no more can be consumed than is produced. But the question is whether this is the positive limit, whether as much can and must be consumed—on the basis of capitalist production—as is produced. What Ricardo says, correctly analysed, means the direct opposite of what he is trying to say—namely, that production takes place without regard to the existing limits of consumption, but is limited only by capital itself. And this, to be sure, is characteristic of this mode of production.

So, in accordance with the assumption, the market is over-supplied for example with cotton cloth, so that it is partly unsaleable, or cannot be sold at all, or can be sold only far below its *price*—or, shall we say, its *value*. For the moment we shall say *value*, as in considering circulation or the process of reproduction we are still concerned with the value, not yet with the price of production and even less with the market price. In our whole enquiry it is, of course, taken for granted that it cannot be denied that in individual spheres too much may be produced, and *for that reason* too little may be produced in other spheres; that partial crises therefore may arise from *disproportionate production* (proportionate production is, however, always only the result of disproportionate production on the basis of competition). And a general form of this disproportionate production may be overproduction of fixed capital, or on the other hand overproduction of circulating capital.[1] As it is a condition for the sale of commodities at

[1] When spinning machines were invented, there was an overproduction of yarn in relation to weaving. This disparity was removed when mechanical looms were introduced into weaving.

their value that only the socially necessary labour time is
contained in them, so it is for a whole sphere of production
of capital that only the necessary part of the total labour
time of society is applied to this particular sphere; only the
labour time which is required for the satisfaction of the social
need (the demand). If more is used, even though each
individual commodity may contain only the necessary labour
time, in total they contain more than the socially necessary
labour time—just as the individual commodity has in fact use
value, but the total, in the circumstances assumed, loses a
portion of its use value.

However, we are not dealing here with crisis in so far as it
is due to disproportionate production, that is, a disproportion
in the division of the social labour among the individual
spheres of production. This can only be dealt with in an
examination of the competition between capitals. Here it has
already been said that a rise or fall in market values consequent
on this disproportion results in a withdrawal of capital from
one sphere of production and its transfer to another, the
migration of capital from one branch of production into the
other. Of course this equalisation itself presupposes the opposite
of equalisation and therefore may involve crisis; and the
crisis itself may be a form of equalisation. Ricardo and others
admit this form of crisis.

In the analysis of the production process we saw that the
whole striving of capitalistic production is directed towards
the appropriation of the greatest possible amount of surplus
labour, that is, to materialise the greatest possible amount of
immediate labour time with the given capital. This may be
done through the prolongation of the labour time, or reduction
of the necessary labour time, development of the productive
power of labour, the use of co-operation, division of labour,
machinery, etc., in short, production on a higher level, that is,
mass production. Production without regard to the limits of
the market is therefore in the nature of capitalist production.

In considering reproduction it is for the moment assumed
that the method of production remains the same, and remains
the same for a period while production expands. In this case
the mass of commodities produced is increased, because more

capital is used, not because it is more productively used. But
the merely quantitative increase of capital at the same time
implies that its productive power is increased. If its quantitative
increase is a consequence of the development of productive
power, the latter in turn develops on the assumption of a
wider, extended capitalistic basis. Here reciprocal action takes
place. Reproduction on an extended basis—accumulation—
even if originally appearing only as a quantitative expansion
of production—with more capital under the same conditions
of production—therefore always at a certain point shows itself
also qualitatively, as greater productivity of the conditions
through which reproduction takes place. Hence there is an
increase in the mass of products not only in simple proportion
to the growth of capital in expanded reproduction—accumulation.

Now let us return to our example of cotton cloth.

The stagnation in the market, which is over-supplied with
cottons, disturbs reproduction for the weaver. This disturbance
first affects his workers. The latter therefore are now to a
smaller extent, or not at all, consumers of his commodity—
cotton—and of other commodities which enter into their
consumption. They have, it is true, a need for cottons, but
they cannot buy them because they have not the means to do
so, and they have not the means because they cannot continue
to produce, and they cannot continue to produce because too
much has been produced, too many cotton goods are in store
on the market. Neither Ricardo's advice "to enlarge their
production", nor his alternative, "to produce something else",
can help them. They now constitute a part of the temporary
overproduction, overproduction of workers, in this case of
cotton producers, because there is an overproduction of cotton
goods on the market.

But apart from the workers employed directly by the capital
invested in cotton weaving, numbers of other producers are
affected by this check in the reproduction of cotton: spinners,
cotton growers, producers of spindles and looms, of iron, coal,
and so on. All these would be similarly checked in their
reproduction, as the reproduction of cotton goods is the
condition for their own reproduction. This would take place,

even if they had not overproduced in their own spheres, that is, had not produced beyond the limit set by and justified by the cotton industry when it was going swimmingly. All these industries have only this in common: that they consume their revenue (wages and profit, in so far as the latter is consumed as revenue and not accumulated) not in the form of their own product, but in the product of the spheres which produce articles of consumption, of which cotton is one. So the consumption and the demand for cotton falls, precisely because there is too much of it on the market. But so also does that of all other commodities on which, as articles of consumption, the revenue of these indirect producers of cotton cloth is spent. The means with which they can buy cotton cloth and other articles of consumption become restricted and contract, because there is too much cotton on the market. This affects also other commodities (articles of consumption). They are now suddenly in *relative* overproduction, because the means to buy them, and therewith the demand for them, have contracted. Even if there has been no overproduction in these spheres, now they are overproducing.

But if it is not only cotton, but also linen, silk and woollen goods in which overproduction has taken place, it can be understood how overproduction in these few but leading articles brings about a more or less general (*relative*) overproduction over the whole market. On the one hand a superfluity of all things needed for reproduction, and a superfluity of all kinds of unsold commodities on the market. On the other hand bankrupt capitalists and hungry workers, destitute of everything.

Nevertheless, this argument has two sides to it. If it is easy to understand how overproduction in a few leading articles of consumption must bring in its train a more or less general overproduction—the manifestation of the former—this in no way explains how overproduction of those articles can arise. For the phenomenon of general overproduction is brought about by the interdependence not only of the worker directly employed in these industries, but of all branches of industry which produce the earlier elements of their products, their constant capital in different phases. For the latter branches of industry, overproduction is an effect. But whence comes it in the former? For the latter go on producing so long as the former continue to produce, and along with this continued production a general growth of revenue, and therefore of their own consumption, seems assured.

(e) Expansion of Production and Expansion of the Market

This question may perhaps be answered by pointing to the constantly expanding production, which expands each year for two reasons: first, because the capital invested in production is constantly growing, and secondly, because it is constantly used more productively; in the course of reproduction and accumulation there is a constant aggregation of small improvements which eventually alter the whole level of production. There is a piling up of improvements, an accumulating development of productive powers. If anyone likes to reply that the constantly expanding production requires a constantly expanding market, and that production expands more rapidly than the market, this is only putting in another way the phenomenon that has to be explained—in its real form, instead of an abstract form. The market expands more slowly than production; or in the cycle through which capital passes in its reproduction—a cycle in which there is not merely reproduction, but reproduction on an extended scale; it describes not a circle, but a spiral—a moment comes when the market manifests itself as too narrow for production. This is at the close of the cycle. This however merely means: the market is overfilled. Overproduction is manifest. Had the extension of the market kept pace with the extension of production, there would be no glut of the market, no overproduction.

However, the mere admission that the market must expand along with production is also from another aspect one more admission of the possibility of overproduction, since the market is limited externally in the geographical sense, the internal market is limited as compared with a market that is both internal and external, the latter again as compared with the world market—which however at each moment of time is in turn limited, [even though] in itself capable of extension.

Consequently the admission that the market must expand if overproduction is not to occur, is also an admission that overproduction can occur. For since market and production are two independent factors, it is therefore possible that the expansion of one may not correspond with the expansion of the other, that the limits of the market may not be extended rapidly enough for production, or that new markets—new extensions of the market—may be rapidly overtaken by production, so that the expanded market now appears just as much a barrier as the narrower one did previously.

Ricardo is therefore consistent in denying the necessity for *an expansion of the market* to correspond with an expansion of production and growth of capital: all capital available in a country can also be advantageously employed in that country. He therefore polemises against Adam Smith, who on the one hand put forward *his* (Ricardo's) view and, with his usual rational instinct, also contradicted it. Adam Smith too does not recognise the phenomenon of overproduction, crises resulting from overproduction. What he sees are mere credit and money crises, which come to the surface of their own accord along with the credit and banking system. In fact he sees in the accumulation of capital an unqualified increase in the total wealth and well-being of the nation. On the other hand he conceives the development of the internal market into the foreign, colonial and world market, as in itself evidence of what can be called a relative overproduction in the internal market. It is worth quoting Ricardo's polemic against him on this point:

"When merchants engage their capitals in foreign trade, or in the carrying trade, it is always from choice and never from necessity; it is because in that trade their profits will be somewhat greater than in the home trade.

"Adam Smith has justly observed 'that the desire of food is limited in every man by the narrow capacity of the human stomach,[1] but the desire of the conveniences and ornaments of building, dress, equipage, and household furniture seems to have no limit or certain boundary'. Nature, then, has necessarily limited the amount of capital

---

[1] Adam Smith is very much mistaken here, as he leaves out of account the luxury articles of agriculture.

which can at any one time be profitably engaged in agriculture,[1] but she has placed no limits to the amount of capital that may be employed in procuring 'the conveniences and ornaments' of life.[2] To procure these gratifications in the greatest abundance is the object in view, and it is only because foreign trade, or the carrying trade, will accomplish it better, that men engage in them in preference to manufacturing the commodities required, or a substitute for them, at home. If, however, from peculiar circumstances, we were precluded from engaging capital in foreign trade, or in the carrying trade, we should, though with less advantage, employ it at home; and while there is no limit to the desire of 'conveniences, ornaments of building, dress, equipage, and household furniture', there can be no limit to the capital that may be employed in procuring them, except that which bounds our power to maintain the workmen who are to produce them.

"Adam Smith, however, speaks of the carrying trade as one not of choice, but of necessity; as if the capital engaged in it would be inert if not so employed, as if the capital in the home trade could overflow if not confined to a limited amount. He says, 'when the capital stock of any country is increased to such a degree *that it cannot be all employed in supplying the consumption, and supporting the productive labour of that particular country*,[3] the surplus part of it naturally disgorges itself into the carrying trade, and is employed in performing the same offices to other countries'.

". . . But could not this portion of the productive labour of Great Britain be employed in preparing some other sort of goods, with which something more in demand at home might be purchased? And if it could not, might we not employ this productive labour, though with less advantage, in making those goods in demand at home, or at least some substitute for them? If we wanted velvets, might we not attempt to make velvets; and if we could not succeed, might we not make more cloth, or some other object desirable to us?

---

[1] Is that why there are nations which export agricultural products? As if, in spite of nature, it would not be possible to sink all possible capital in agriculture, in order to produce in England for example melons, figs, grapes, etc., and flowers, etc., and birds and game, etc. And as if the raw materials of industry are not produced by the capital in agriculture. See for example the capital that the Romans put into the artificial breeding of fish alone.

[2] As if Nature had anything to do with the matter!

[3] This passage is emphasised by Ricardo himself.

"We manufacture commodities, and with them buy goods abroad, because we can obtain a greater quantity[1] than we could make at home. Deprive us of this trade, and we immediately manufacture again for ourselves. But this opinion of Adam Smith is at variance with all his general doctrines on this subject. 'If a foreign country can supply us with a commodity cheaper than we ourselves can make it, better buy it of them with some part of the produce of our own industry, employed in a way in which we have some advantage. *The general industry of the country, being always in proportion to the capital which employs it,*[2] will not thereby be diminished, but only left to find out the way in which it can be employed with the greatest advantage.'

"Again: 'Those, therefore, who have the command of more food than they themselves can consume, are always willing to exchange the surplus, or, what is the same thing, the price of it, for gratifications of another kind. What is over and above satisfying the limited desire is given for the amusement of those desires which cannot be satisfied, but seem to be altogether endless. The poor, in order to obtain food, exert themselves to gratify those fancies of the rich; and to obtain it more certainly, they vie with one another in the cheapness and perfection of their work. The number of workmen increases with the increasing quantity of food, or with the growing improvement and cultivation of the lands; and as the nature of their business admits of the utmost subdivisions of labours, the quantity of materials which they can work up increases in a much greater proportion than their numbers. Hence arises a demand for every sort of material which human invention can employ, either usefully or ornamentally, in building, dress, equipage, or household furniture; for the fossils and minerals contained in the bowels of the earth, the precious metals, and the precious stones.'

"It follows, then, from these admissions, that there is no limit to demand—no limit to the employment of capital while it yields any profit, and that, however abundant capital may become, there is no other adequate reason for a fall of profit but a rise of wages, and further, it may be added that the only adequate and permanent cause for the

[1] The qualitative difference does not exist!
[2] In very different proportion. Ricardo also emphasises this sentence.

rise of wages is the increasing difficulty of providing food and necessaries for the increasing number of workmen" (Chapter XXI, pp. 195–7).

The word *overproduction* in itself leads to error. So long as the most urgent needs of a great part of society are not satisfied, or *only* its most immediate needs, there can naturally be absolutely no talk of an *overproduction of products*—in the sense that the mass of products would be excessive in relation to the need for them. What must be said is the opposite: that in this sense, on the basis of capitalistic production, there is constant *underproduction*. The limit of production is the *capitalist's profit*, and not at all the *need of the producers*. But overproduction of *products* and overproduction of *commodities* are two completely different things. If Ricardo thinks that the form *commodity* makes no difference to the product, and further, that the *circulation of commodities* is only formally different from barter, that in this circulation exchange value is only a form, without significance, of the exchange of things, and that therefore money is a merely formal means of circulation, this is in fact the outcome of his presupposition that the bourgeois mode of production is the absolute mode of production, and consequently is a mode of production without any precise specific character, that what is specific in it is only formal. It is therefore not possible for him to admit that the bourgeois mode of production contains within itself a barrier to the free development of the productive forces, a barrier which comes to the surface in crises, and incidentally in *overproduction*—the basic phenomenon in crises.

Ricardo saw, from the passages of Adam Smith which he quotes, approves and therefore repeats, that the limitless "desire" for all kinds of use values is constantly satisfied, on the basis of a state of things in which the mass of producers remains more or less restricted to necessities, in which this very considerable mass of producers therefore remains more or less excluded from the consumption of wealth—in so far as wealth oversteps the circle of the necessary means of subsistence.

Incidentally, this is also the case, and to a still higher degree, in the ancient form of production based on slavery. But the ancients never even thought of transforming the surplus product into capital. At least, only to a small extent. The widespread occurrence among them of the amassing of treasure in the narrow sense shows how much surplus product lay completely idle. They converted a great part of the surplus product into unproductive expenditure on works of art, religious monuments and public works. Still less was their production directed to the unfettering and development of the material forces of production—division of labour, machinery, use of natural forces and science in private production. Broadly speaking they never got beyond handicraft labour. The wealth which they produced for private consumption was consequently relatively small, and only seems large because it was amassed in the hands of a few people, who, incidentally, did not know what to do with it. If consequently there was no *overproduction* among the ancients, there was nevertheless *overconsumption* on the part of the rich, which in the final periods of Rome and Greece broke out into insane extravagance. The few trading peoples among them lived partly at the expense of all these essentially poor nations. It is the absolute development of the productive forces, and hence mass production, with the mass of producers confined within the circle of the necessary means of subsistence on the one hand, and on the other hand the barrier set by the capitalists' profit, which forms the basis of modern overproduction.

All the difficulties which Ricardo and others raise against overproduction, etc., rest on the fact that they either look on bourgeois production as a mode of production in which no distinction exists between purchase and sale—direct barter— or they regard it as *social* production, of such a kind that society distributes its means of production and productive forces as if according to a plan, in the degree and measure in which they are necessary for the satisfaction of its various needs; so that to each sphere of production falls the quota of social capital required for the satisfaction of the need to which it corresponds. This fiction arises entirely from the inability to grasp the specific form of bourgeois production; and this inability in turn from the obsession that bourgeois production is production pure and simple. Just like a man who believes in a particular religion and sees in it religion pure and simple, with only *false* religions outside it.

On the contrary, it would be much more pertinent to ask: on the basis of capitalist production, in which everyone works for himself, and particular labour must at the same time appear as its opposite, abstract general labour, and in this form as social labour—how can the necessary balance and interdependence of the various spheres of production, their dimensions and the proportions between them, be possible except through the constant neutralisation of a constant disharmony? This moreover is admitted when adjustments through competition are spoken of; for these adjustments always presuppose that there is something to be adjusted, and harmony therefore is always only a result of the movement which neutralises the existing disharmony. For this reason, too, Ricardo admits the glut of the market for particular commodities; and then a general simultaneous glut in the market is said to be *impossible*. Consequently the impossibility of overproduction for any particular sphere of production is not denied. What is said to be [impossible] is the *simultaneity* of this phenomenon for all spheres of production, and hence general overproduction. This last phrase is always to be taken *cum grano salis*, for in times of general overproduction the overproduction in some spheres is always only the *result*, the *consequence*, of overproduction in the leading articles of commerce; [in these it is] always only *relative*, overproduction because overproduction exists in other spheres. Apologetics twists this precisely into its opposite. Overproduction in the leading articles of commerce, in which alone active overproduction manifests itself—these are in general articles which can only be produced in the mass and on a factory scale, also in agriculture—[is supposed only to exist] because overproduction exists in the articles in which relative or passive overproduction appears. According to this idea overproduction only exists because overproduction is not universal. The relativity of overproduction—that actual overproduction in some spheres leads to it in others—is expressed in this way: There is no universal overproduction, because if overproduction were universal, all spheres of production would retain the same relation to one another; therefore universal overproduction is equivalent to proportional production, which excludes overproduction. And this is supposed to be an argument against overproduction. That is to say, on the ground that universal overproduction in the absolute sense would not be overproduction, but only a greater than usual development of productive power in all spheres of production, it is said that actual overproduction, which is precisely not this non-existent, self-abrogating overproduction, does not exist—although it only exists because it is not this. If this miserable sophistry is more closely examined, we get the following result. Overproduction takes place, say, in iron, cotton goods, linen, silk, cloth, etc. It cannot then be said, for example, that too little coal has been produced and that therefore this overproduction has occurred; for the over-production of iron, etc., involves an exactly similar overproduc-tion of coal, just as an overproduction of woven cloth involves that of yarn. (Overproduction of yarn as compared with cloth, iron as against machinery, etc., would be possible. This would always be a relative overproduction of constant capital.) There can therefore be no question of the overproduction of articles whose overproduction is implied because they enter as elements, raw materials, auxiliary materials or means of labour into the articles the positive overproduction of which is precisely the fact to be explained (the "particular commodity of which too much has been produced, of which there may be such a glut in the market as not to repay the capital expended on it"). The discussion concerns other articles which directly belong to other spheres of production, and can neither be subsumed under the leading articles of commerce which, according to the assumption, have been overproduced; nor do they belong to spheres in which, because they form the intermediate product for the leading articles of commerce, production must have advanced at least as much as in the final phases of the product—although there is no reason why they themselves should not have gone still further ahead, and thus have brought about an overproduction within the other overproduction. For example, although sufficient coal must have been produced in order to keep going all the industries into which coal enters as a necessary condition of production, and therefore the overproduction of coal is implied in the overproduction of iron, yarn, etc. (the coal having been produced only in proportion to the production of iron and yarn), it is *also* possible that more coal was produced than even the overproduction in iron, yarn, etc., required. This is not only possible, but very probable. For the production of coal and yarn and of those other spheres of production which produce only the conditions and earlier phases of the product to be completed in another sphere, is not governed by the immediate demand, by the immediate production or reproduction, but by the *degree, measure, proportion* in which these are expanding. And it is self-evident that in this calculation the goal may be overshot. Nevertheless [overproduction is said to originate from the fact that] there has not been enough produced, there has been underproduction, of other articles, such as for example pianofortes, precious stones, and so forth. The absurdity of this statement emerges all the more clearly when it is given an international setting, as Say and others after him have done. Thus, for example, England has not overproduced, but Italy has underproduced. If Italy, firstly, had had capital enough to replace the English capital that had been exported to Italy in the form of commodities; and secondly had so invested this capital that it produced the specific articles which English capital needed (partly to replace itself and partly to replace the revenue flowing from it) there would have been no overproduction. That is, there would not have existed the fact of actual—in relation to the *actual* production in Italy—existing overproduction in England, but only the fact of *imaginary underproduction in Italy*—imaginary, because it presupposes a capital in Italy and a development of the productive forces which did not exist there; and secondly because it makes the same utopian presupposition that this *non*-existing capital in Italy had been applied exactly as required in order that the English supplies and Italian demand, English and Italian production, should be complementary to each other. This means in other words nothing [but]: No overproduction would occur if demand and supply corresponded to each other; if capital were distributed in such proportions in all spheres of production that the production of one article involved the consumption of the other and thus its own consumption. There would be no overproduction, if there were no overproduction. But as capitalistic production is only able to let itself go without restraint in certain spheres, in definite conditions, no capitalistic production at all would be possible if it had to develop in all spheres *simultaneously* and *in equal degree*. Because in these spheres absolute overproduction takes place, relative overproduction takes place also in the spheres where there has not been overproduction. This explanation of overproduction in one direction by underproduction in another means nothing [but]: If production were proportionate, there would be no overproduction. Ditto, if demand and supply corresponded to each other. Ditto, if all spheres comprised equal opportunities of capitalistic production and its expansion—division of labour, machinery, export to distant markets, production on a mass scale, etc. Or in still more abstract form: if all countries which trade with one another possessed an equal capacity for production, and indeed for different and complementary production. That is to say: overproduction takes place, because all these pious wishes are not fulfilled. Or in even more abstract form: there would be no overproduction at one point if overproduction took place at all points in equal degree. But capital is not large enough to overproduce in this universal way, and consequently universal overproduction occurs.

Let us examine this fantasy still more closely:

It is admitted that there can be overproduction in each *particular branch of production*. The one circumstance that might prevent overproduction in *all* at the same time is, so it is alleged, that commodity exchanges against commodity, that is to say, they take refuge in the conditions of barter which they assume. But this way of escape is cut off by the very fact that trade in commodities is not barter, and therefore the seller of a commodity is not necessarily at the same time the purchaser of another. This whole subterfuge therefore rests on abstracting from *money*, and abstracting from the fact that what is in question is not the exchange of products but the circulation of commodities, for which the separation of purchase and sale is essential.

The circulation of capital in itself comprises *possibilities* of interruptions. For example, in the reconversion of money into its conditions of production the point is not only to transform money back again into the same use values (in kind), but it is essential for the repetition of the process of reproduction that these use values are to be had at their old value (lower is naturally still better). The very significant part of these elements of reproduction which consists of raw materials can however rise in price for two reasons: *first* if the instruments of production increase in quicker proportion than the raw materials can be provided within a definite period of time. *Secondly*, as a result of the variable character of harvests. That is why weather conditions, as Tooke rightly observes, play such an important role in modern industry. That is also true of the means of subsistence in relation to wages. The reconversion from money into commodity can therefore come up against difficulties and bring about possibilities of crisis, just as well as the conversion of commodity into money. In so far as simple circulation is considered—not the circulation of capital—this difficulty does not arise.

There are besides a number of other factors, conditions and possibilities of crisis which can only be considered when examining the concrete relations, in particular of the competition of capitals and of credit.

The overproduction of commodities is denied, though the overproduction of capital is admitted. But capital itself consists of commodities, or in so far as it consists of money it must be reconverted into commodities of one kind or another in order to be able to function as capital. What then does overproduction of capital mean? Overproduction of quantities of value destined to produce surplus value, or, if considered in their material content, overproduction of commodities destined for reproduction—that is, reproduction on too large a scale, which is the same thing as overproduction pure and simple. Defined more exactly, this in turn means nothing but that too much has been produced for the purpose of enrichment, or that too large a part of the product has been destined, not for consumption as revenue, but for making more money, for accumulation; not to satisfy the personal requirements of

its possessor, but to secure for him abstract social riches,
money and more power over the labour of others—capital—
or to increase the power in his hands. This is what some say.
Ricardo denies it. How then do the others explain the overproduction of commodities? That production is not sufficiently
widely diversified, that certain articles of consumption have
not been produced in sufficiently great quantities. It is clear
that this cannot refer to industrial consumption; for the
manufacturer who overproduces in linen thereby of necessity
increases his demand for yarn, machinery, labour, etc.
Therefore the reference must be to personal consumption.
Too much linen has been produced, but perhaps too few
oranges. Previously money was denied, for the purpose of
[denying] the separation between purchase and sale. Here,
capital is denied, in order to transform the capitalists into
people who carry out the simple operation C–M–C, and for
individual consumption, not as capitalists with the aim of
getting richer, with the aim of reconverting a part of the
surplus value into capital. But the statement that there is
too much capital in fact means nothing but that too little is
consumed, and in the given conditions can be consumed, as
revenue (Sismondi). Why then does the producer of linen
demand of the producer of corn that he consume more linen,
or the latter demand of the former that he consume more
corn? Why does the man who deals in linen not himself realise
a larger part of his revenue, his surplus value, in linen, and
the farmer in corn? Each of them individually will admit that,
apart from the limit to his requirements, what prevents him
from doing this is his need to capitalise it. But collectively they
will not admit it.

In this treatment we have completely abstracted from that
element of crises which arises from the fact that commodities
are reproduced more cheaply than they have been produced.
Hence depreciation of the commodities on the market.

In the general crises on the world market, all the contradictions of bourgeois production break through collectively; in
particular crises (particular as to content and in extent) they
appear only in a scattered, isolated and one-sided form.

Overproduction is specifically conditioned by the general

law of the production of capital: production is in accordance with the productive forces, that is, with the possibility that the given quantity of capital has of exploiting the maximum quantity of labour, without regard to the actual limits of the market, the needs backed by the ability to pay; and this takes place through the constant expansion of reproduction and accumulation, and therefore the constant reconversion of revenue into capital; while on the other hand the mass of producers remain restricted to the average level of needs, and on the basis of capitalist production must remain so restricted.

5. ACCUMULATION AND CONSUMPTION

In Chapter VIII, "On Taxes", Ricardo says:

"When the annual productions of a country more than replace its annual consumption, it is said to increase its capital; when its annual consumption is not at least replaced by its annual production, it is said to diminish its capital. Capital may therefore be increased by an increased production, or by a diminished unproductive consumption" (p. 94).

By "unproductive consumption" Ricardo here means, as he says in the note to the next paragraph (p. 94), consumption by unproductive labourers, "those who do not reproduce another value". By increase of the annual production is therefore meant increase of the annual industrial consumption. This can be increased by the direct expansion of it, with non-industrial consumption remaining the same or even growing, or by a reduction of the non-industrial consumption. "When we say", the Note referred to states, "that revenue is saved and added to capital, what we mean is, that the portion of revenue, so said to be added to capital, is consumed by productive instead of unproductive labourers".

I have shown that the conversion of revenue into capital is by no means identical with the conversion of revenue into variable capital or with its expenditure as wages. This is however what Ricardo thinks. In the same Note he says:

"If the price of labour should rise so high that, notwithstanding the increase of capital, no more could be employed, I should say that such increase of capital would be still unproductively consumed."

It is therefore not the consumption of revenue by productive workers that makes this consumption "productive", but its consumption by workers who produce surplus value. Hence, capital increases only when it commands *more labour* [than it pays for].

In Chapter VII, "On Foreign Trade", attention must be drawn to the following passages:

"There are two ways in which capital may be accumulated; it may be saved either in consequence of increased revenue or of diminished consumption. If my profits are raised from £1,000 to £1,200, while my expenditure continues the same, I accumulate annually £200 more than I did before. If I save £200 out of my expenditure, while my profits continue the same, the same effect will be produced; £200 per annum will be added to my capital. . . .

"If, by the introduction of machinery, the generality of the commodities on which revenue was expended fell 20 per cent. in value, I should be enabled to save as effectually as if my revenue had been raised 20 per cent.; but in one case the rate of profits is stationary, in the other it is raised 20 per cent.—If, by the introduction of cheap foreign goods, I can save 20 per cent. from my expenditure, the effect will be precisely the same as if machinery had lowered the expense of their production, but profits would not be raised" (pp. 79–80).

That is to say, they would not be raised if the cheaper products entered neither into the variable nor into the constant capital.

Consequently, with *the same expenditure of revenue* [there is expanded] accumulation as a result of the rise in the rate of profit (accumulation however depends not only on the height of the rate of profit, but also on the mass of the profit); with *the same rate of profit* [there is increased] accumulation as a result of reduced expenditure—in regard to which, however, Ricardo here assumes that it takes place as a result of the cheapening, either by machinery or foreign trade, of the "commodities on which revenue is expended".

In Chapter XX, on "Value and Riches, their Distinctive Properties", [the following passages are relevant to our subject]:

". . . the wealth[1] of a country may be increased in two ways: it may be increased by employing a greater portion of revenue in the maintenance of productive labour, which will not only add to the quantity, but to the value of the mass of commodities; or it may be increased, without employing any additional quantity of labour, by making

---

[1] By wealth, Ricardo means use values.

the same quantity more productive, which will add to the abundance, but not to the value of commodities.

"In the first case, a country would not only become rich, but the value of its riches would increase. It would become rich by parsimony—by diminishing its expenditure on objects of luxury and enjoyment, and employing those savings in reproduction.

"In the second case, there will not necessarily be either any diminished expenditure on luxuries and enjoyments, or any increased quantity of productive labour employed, but, with the same labour, more would be produced; wealth would increase, but not value. Of these two modes of increasing wealth, the last must be preferred, since it produces the same effect without the privation and diminution of enjoyments which can never fail to accompany the first mode. Capital is that part of the wealth of a country which is employed with a view to future production, and may be increased in the same manner as wealth. An additional capital will be equally efficacious in the production of future wealth, whether it be obtained from improvements in skill and machinery, or from using more revenue reproductively; for wealth always depends on the quantity of commodities produced, without any regard to the facility with which the instruments employed in production may have been procured. A certain quantity of clothes and provisions will maintain and employ the same number of men, and will therefore procure the same quantity of work to be done, whether they be produced by the labour of 100 or 200 men; but they will be of twice the value if 200 have been employed on their production" (pp. 185–6).

Ricardo's first conception was:

Accumulation increases, if the rate of profit rises, with expenditure remaining the same; or when the rate of profit remains the same, if the expenditure (reckoned in value) diminishes because the commodities on which the revenue is expended become cheaper.

Now he raises another contradictory point:

Accumulation grows, capital is accumulated in quantity and in value, when a greater part of revenue is withdrawn from individual consumption and used for industrial consumption, when more productive labour is set in motion with the part of the revenue so saved. In this case accumulation takes place through parsimony. Or the amount of the expenditure remains the same, and no additional productive labour is employed; but the same labour produces more, its productive power is raised. The elements of which productive capital consists—raw materials, machinery, etc. (previously it was the commodities on which the revenue was expended, now it is the commodities which are used as means of production)—are produced with the same labour in greater quantities, better, and therefore cheaper. In such cases accumulation depends neither on a rise in the rate of profit, nor on a larger part of the revenue, as a result of saving, being converted into capital, nor on a smaller part of the revenue being unproductively expended as a result of the cheapening of the commodities on which revenue is spent. Here it depends on the labour becoming more productive in the spheres of production which produce the elements of capital itself, and therefore the commodities which enter into the process of production, as raw materials, instruments, etc., are cheapened.

If the productive power of labour has been increased through greater production of fixed capital in proportion to the variable capital, in this case not only the *mass* but also the *value* of reproduction will rise, inasmuch as a portion of the value of the fixed capital enters into the annual reproduction. This can take place simultaneously with the growth of the population and an increase in the number of workers employed, although the latter *relatively*, in proportion to the constant capital which it sets in motion, continuously declines. Thus there takes place a growth not only of wealth but of value, and a larger quantity of living labour will be set in motion, although the labour has grown more productive and the quantity of labour, in proportion to the quantity of commodities produced, has fallen. Finally, even with the productivity of labour remaining the same, variable and constant capital may grow in equal degree with the natural increase of population each year. In this case too, capital is accumulated, both in mass and in value. All these latter points are left out of account by Ricardo.

In the same chapter Ricardo says:

"The labour of a million of men in manufactures will always produce the same value, but will not always produce the same riches.[1] By the invention of machinery, by improvements in skill, by a better division of labour, or by the discovery of new markets, where more advantageous exchanges may be made, a million of men may produce double or treble the amount of riches, of 'necessaries, conveniences, and amusements', in one state of society that they could produce in another, but they will not on that account add anything to value;[2] for everything rises or falls in value in proportion to the facility or difficulty of producing it, or, in other words, in proportion to the quantity of labour employed on its production.[3] Suppose, with a given capital, the labour of a certain number of men produced 1,000 pair of stockings, and that by inventions in machinery the same number of men can produce 2,000 pair, or that they can continue to produce 1,000 pair, and can produce besides 500 hats; then the value of the 2,000 pair of stockings, or of the 1,000 pair of stockings and 500 hats, will be neither more nor less than that of the 1,000 pair of stockings before the introduction of machinery; for they will be the produce of the same quantity of labour.[4] But the value of the general mass of commodities will nevertheless be diminished; for, although the value of the increased quantity produced in consequence of the improvement will be the same exactly as the value would have been of the less quantity that would have been produced, had no improvement taken place, an effect is also produced on the portion of goods still unconsumed, which were manufactured previously to the improvement; the value of those goods will be reduced, inasmuch as they must fall to the level, quantity for quantity, of the goods produced under all the advantages of the improvement: and the society will, notwithstanding the increased quantity of commodities, notwithstanding its augmented riches, and its augmented

[1] This is quite wrong. The value of the product of the million men does not depend only on their labour, but also on the value of the capital with which they work; it will therefore vary considerably, according to the amount of already produced productive forces with which they work.

[2] They certainly will, inasmuch as their past labour enters in much greater measure into the new reproduction.

[3] Each individual commodity may be cheapened, but the increased total mass of commodities will rise in value.

[4] N.B.: If the newly introduced machinery costs *nothing*.

means of enjoyment, have a less amount of value. By constantly increasing the facility of production, we constantly diminish the value of some of the commodities before produced, though by the same means we not only add to the national riches, but also to the power of future production" (pp. 182–3).

Here Ricardo speaks of the diminution of value resulting from a progressive development of the productive powers, which affects the commodities produced under less favourable conditions, whether they are then still on the market or functioning as capital in the process of production. It by no means follows from this that "the value of the general mass of commodities will be diminished", although the value of one part of this mass will be diminished. This consequence would follow only when, first, the value of the newly added machinery and commodities resulting from the technical advance was smaller than the loss of value brought about in goods of the same kind already in existence; secondly, if we leave out of account the fact that with the development of the productive powers there goes also a constant increase in the number of spheres of production, and therefore also capital investments are opened up which previously did not exist at all. In the course of the development production is not only cheapened, but also *diversified*.

Let us pass on now to Chapter IX, "Taxes on Raw Produce":

"With respect to the third objection against taxes on raw produce, namely, that the raising wages, and lowering profits, is a discouragement to accumulation, and acts in the same way as a natural poverty of soil; I have endeavoured to show in another part of this work that savings may be as effectually made from expenditure as from production; from a reduction in the value of commodities as from a rise in the rate of profits. By increasing my profits from £1,000 to £1,200, whilst prices continue the same, my power of increasing my capital by savings is increased, but it is not increased so much as it would be if my profits continued as before, whilst commodities were so lowered in price that £800 would procure me as much as £1,000 purchased before" (pp. 105–6).

The whole value of the product (or rather of that part of the product which is divided between the capitalist and the worker) can be depreciated, without the net income falling, as measured by the mass of its value. (In proportion, it *can* even rise). This is discussed in Chapter XXXII, which deals with "Mr. Malthus's Opinions on Rent":

> "The whole argument, however, of Mr. Malthus, is built on an infirm basis: it supposes, because the gross income of the country is diminished, that, therefore, the net income must also be diminished in the same proportion. It has been one of the objects of this work to show that, with every fall in the real value of necessaries, the wages of labour would fall, and that the profits of stock would rise; in other words, that of any given annual value a less portion would be paid to the labouring class, and a larger portion to those whose funds employed this class. Suppose the value of the commodities produced in a particular manufacture to be £1,000, and to be divided between the master and his labourers in the proportion of £800 to labourers and £200 to the master; if the value of these commodities should fall to £900, and £100 be saved from the wages of labour, in consequence of the fall of necessaries, the net income of the master would be in no degree impaired, and, therefore, he could with just as much facility pay the same amount of taxes after as before the reduction of price" (p. 287).

In Chapter V, "On Wages", the following passage is worth noting:

> "Notwithstanding the tendency of wages to conform to their natural rate, their market rate may, in an improving society, for an indefinite period, be constantly above it; for no sooner may the impulse which an increased capital gives to a new demand for labour be obeyed, than another increase of capital may produce the same effect; and thus, if the increase of capital be gradual and constant, the demand for labour may give a continued stimulus to an increase of people" (p. 53).

From the capitalist standpoint everything is seen upside down. The number of the labouring population and the degree of productivity of labour determine both the reproduction of capital and also that of the population. Here it appears the other way up, that the [growth of the] *capital* determines the [growth of the] population.

Chapter IX, "Taxes on Raw Produce":

"An accumulation of capital naturally produces an increased competition among the employers of labour, and a consequent rise in its price" (p. 103).

This depends on the proportion in which, with the accumulation of capital, its different component parts grow. Capital may accumulate and the demand for labour may fall absolutely or relatively.

According to Ricardo's theory of rent, with the accumulation of capital and the growth of the population the rate of profit has the tendency to fall, because the means of subsistence rise in value or agriculture becomes less productive. Accumulation therefore has the tendency to check accumulation, and the *law of the falling rate of profit*—because in proportion as industry develops agriculture grows less productive—hangs like a doom over bourgeois production. Adam Smith, on the other hand, sees the falling rate of profit with satisfaction. Holland is the example he takes. It compels most capitalists, except the largest capitalists, to engage their capital in industry instead of living on interest; in this way it is a spur to production. Among Ricardo's disciples the dread of this baleful tendency assumes tragi-comic forms.

Here we bring together the passages from Ricardo which refer to this subject:

"In different stages of society, the accumulation of capital, or of the means of employing labour, is more or less rapid, and must in all cases depend on the productive powers of labour. The productive powers of labour are generally greatest when there is an abundance of fertile land: at such periods accumulation is often so rapid that labourers cannot be supplied with the same rapidity as capital.

"It has been calculated that under favourable circumstances population may be doubled in twenty-five years; but under the same favourable circumstances the whole capital of a country might possibly be doubled in a shorter period. In that case, wages during the whole period would have a tendency to rise, because the demand for labour would increase still faster than the supply.

"In new settlements, where the arts and knowledge of

countries far advanced in refinement are introduced, it is probable that capital has a tendency to increase faster than mankind; and if the deficiency of labourers were not supplied by more populous countries, this tendency would very much raise the price of labour. In proportion as these countries become populous, and land of a worse quality is taken into cultivation, the tendency to an increase of capital diminishes; for the surplus produce remaining, after satisfying the wants of the existing population, must necessarily be in proportion to the facility of production, viz. to the smaller number of persons employed in production. Although, then, it is probable that, under the most favourable circumstances, the power of production is still greater than that of population, it will not long continue so; for the land being limited in quantity, and differing in quality, with every increased portion of capital employed on it there will be a decreased rate of production, whilst the power of population continues always the same" (Chapter V, pp. 55–6).

This latter statement is a parson's fabrication. The power to increase the population falls with the productive power of labour. Apart from this, it is to be noted here, first, that Ricardo admits that "the accumulation of capital . . . must in all cases depend on the productive powers of labour", so that labour, not capital, is primary.

Further, from what Ricardo says it would be thought that in industrially developed countries with an older civilisation more people are engaged in agriculture than in colonies, while the facts are the other way round. In proportion to the same product, England for example uses fewer agricultural labourers than any other country either new or old. It is true that a larger proportion of the non-agricultural population plays an indirect part in agricultural production. But even so, this is by no means equal to the greater proportion of the population directly engaged in agriculture in less developed countries. Assuming even that in England grain is dearer, and the costs of production are higher. More capital is employed. More past labour, even though less living labour, enters into agricultural production. But because of the production level already attained the reproduction of this capital costs less labour, although its value is replaced in the product.

In Chapter VI, "On Profits", the following is said in regard to the fall in the rate of profit:

"The natural tendency of profits then is to fall; for, in the progress of society and wealth, the additional quantity of food required is obtained by the sacrifice of more and more labour. This tendency, this gravitation as it were of profits, is happily checked at repeated intervals by the improvements in machinery connected with the production of necessaries, as well as by discoveries in the science of agriculture, which enable us to relinquish a portion of labour before required, and therefore to lower the price of the prime necessary of the labourer. The rise in the price of necessaries and in the wages of labour is, however, limited; for as soon as wages should be equal (as in the case formerly stated) to £720, the whole receipts of the farmer, there must be an end of accumulation; for no capital can then yield any profit whatever, and no additional labour can be demanded, and consequently population will have reached its highest point. Long, indeed, before this period, the very low rate of profits will have arrested all accumulation, and almost the whole produce of the country, after paying the labourers, will be the property of the owners of land and the receivers of tithes and taxes" (pp. 71–2).

This is the bourgeois "Twilight of the Gods" as conceived by Ricardo, the Day of Judgment.

". . . Long before this state of prices was become permanent there would be no motive for accumulation; for no one accumulates but with a view to make his accumulation productive, and it is only when so employed that it operates on profits. Without a motive there could be no accumulation, and consequently such a state of prices never could take place. The farmer and manufacturer can no more live without profit than the labourer without wages. Their motive for accumulation will diminish with every diminution of profit, and will cease altogether when their profits are so low as not to afford them an adequate compensation for their trouble, and the risk which they must necessarily encounter in employing their capital productively.

"I must again observe that the rate of profits would fall much more rapidly than I have estimated in my calculation; for the value of the produce being what I have stated it under the circumstances supposed, the value of the farmer's stock would be greatly increased from its necessarily consisting of many of the commodities which had risen in value. Before corn could rise from £4 to £12, his capital would probably be doubled in exchangeable value, and be worth £6,000 instead of £3,000. If then his profit were £180, or 6 per cent. on his original capital, profits would not at that time be really at a higher *rate* than 3 per cent.; for £6,000 at 3 per cent. gives £180; and on those terms only could a new farmer with £6,000 money in his pocket enter into the farming business. . . .

"We should also expect that, however the rate of profits of stock might diminish in consequence of the accumulation of capital on the land, and the rise of wages, yet that the aggregate amount of profits would increase. Thus supposing that, with repeated accumulations of £100,000, the rate of profit should fall from 20 to 19, to 18, to 17 per cent., a constantly diminishing rate, we should expect that the whole amount of profits received by those successive owners of capital would be always progressive; that it would be greater when the capital was £200,000 than when £100,000; still greater when £300,000; and so on, increasing, though at a diminishing rate, with every increase of capital. This progression, however, is only true for a certain time; thus, 19 per cent. on £200,000 is more than 20 on £100,000; again, 18 per cent. on £300,000 is more than 19 per cent. on £200,000; but after capital has accumulated to a large amount, and profits have fallen, the further accumulation diminishes the aggregate of profits. Thus, suppose the accumulation should be £1,000,000, and the profits 7 per cent., the whole amount of profits will be £70,000; now if an addition of £100,000 capital be made to the million, and profits should fall to 6 per cent., £66,000 or a diminution of £4,000 will be received by the owners of stock, although the whole amount of stock will be increased from £1,000,000 to £1,100,000.

"There can, however, be no accumulation of capital so long as stock yields any profit at all, without its yielding not only an increase of produce, but an increase of value. By employing £100,000 additional capital, no part of the former capital will be rendered less productive. The produce of the land and labour of the country must increase, and its value will be raised, not only by the value of the addition which is made to the former quantity of productions, but by the new value which is given to the whole produce of the land, by the increased difficulty of producing the last portion of it. When the accumulation of capital, however, becomes very great, notwithstanding this increased value, it will be so distributed that a less value than before will be appropriated to profits, while that which is devoted to rent and wages will be increased. . . .

"Although a greater value is produced, a greater proportion of what remains of that value, after paying rent, is consumed by the producers, and it is this, and this alone, which regulates profits. Whilst the land yields abundantly, wages may temporarily rise, and the producers may consume more than their accustomed proportion; but the stimulus which will thus be given to population will speedily reduce the labourers to their usual consumption. But when poor lands are taken into cultivation, or when more capital and labour are expended on the old land, with a less return of produce, the effect must be permanent. . . .

"The effects then of accumulation will be different in different countries, and will depend chiefly on the fertility of the land. However extensive a country may be where the land is of a poor quality, and where the importation of food is prohibited, the most moderate accumulations of capital will be attended with great reductions in the rate of profit and a rapid rise in rent; and on the contrary a small but fertile country, particularly if it freely permits the importation of food, may accumulate a large stock of capital without any great diminution in the rate of profits, or any great increase in the rent of land" (Chapter VI, pp. 72-6).

Also as a result of taxation it may come about that "sufficient surplus produce may not be left to stimulate the exertions of those who usually augment by their savings the capital of the State" (Chapter XII, p. 118).

"There is only one case, and that will be temporary, in which the accumulation of capital with a low price of food may be attended with a fall of profits; and that is when the funds for the maintenance of labour increase much more rapidly than population;—wages will then be high and profits low. If every man were to forego the use of luxuries, and be intent only on accumulation, a quantity of necessaries might be produced for which there could not be any immediate consumption. Of commodities so limited in number there might undoubtedly be a universal glut, and consequently there might neither be demand for an additional quantity of such commodities nor profits on the employment of more capital. If men ceased to consume, they would cease to produce" (Chapter XXI, pp. 194–5).

Such are Ricardo's views on accumulation and the law of the falling rate of profit.

INDEX

ARND, KARL
Die naturgemässe Volkswirthschaft gegenüber dem Monopoliengeist und dem Kommunismus, 48

BAILEY, SAMUEL
A critical Dissertation on the Nature, Measures and Causes of Value, etc., 210, 302
A letter to a Polit. Economist, etc., 210

BARTON, JOHN
Observations on the Circumstances which influence the condition of the Labouring Classes of Society, 150-1

BELLERS, JOHN
Essays about the Poor, Manufactures, Trade Plantations, & Immorality, etc., 32, note 1

BLANQUI, JEROME A.
Histoire de l'Economie Politique, 55-6, 57, 172

CANTILLON, RICHARD
Essai sur la nature du commerce, quoted by Adam Smith, 111

CAREY, HENRY CHARLES
The Past, the Present and the Future, 204

CAZENOVE, JOHN
Preface to T. R. Malthus, *Definition in Political Economy,* 112

D'AVENANT, CH.
An essay upon the probable methods of making a people gainers in the balance of trade, etc., 24
Considerations on the East India Trade, 24
Discourses on the Publick Revenues and on the Trade of England, 24
Essay on the East India Trade, 24
Surplus Value, 24
The East India Trade a Most profitable Trade to the Kingdom, etc., 24

DE QUINCEY, THOMAS
Dialogues of Three Templars on Political Economy Chiefly in Relation to the Principals of Mr. Ricardo, 327
The Logic of Political Economy, 328

HODGSKIN, THOMAS
Popular Political Economy, etc., 129

HUME, DAVID
Essays, 34, 35-6
Interest determined by supply of and demand for capital, 34-5
Interest on capital an alternative form of surplus value, 34
Land-rent the original form of surplus value, 34

JONES, RICHARD
An Essay on the Distribution of Wealth, 48

LAUDERDALE, EARL OF
An Inquiry into the Nature and Origin of public Wealth, 134

LOCKE, JOHN
High rate of interest caused by shortage of money, 26
Labour as a determinant of value, 27-8
Of Civil Government, 27, 28
Rent identified with usury, 29
Some considerations of the consequences of the lowering of interest, and raising the value of money, 26, 29, 134, note 1
Surplus value, 26.

MARX, KARL (For Marx's criticisms of Smith's views on productive labour and Ricardo's views on surplus value and accumulation of capital, see under the latter.)
Competition of capitals, 358
Simple reproduction of constant capital, 343-50
Transformation of accumulated surplus value into variable and constant capital, 361-7
Transformation of revenue into variable capital, 351-2
Transformation of revenue into constant capital, 352-60
Crises:
Crises caused by the contradictions and antagonisms of bourgeois production, 377

MARX, KARL: Crises—(cont.)
Destruction of capital through crises, 372
Metamorphosis of commodities and money is the condition which makes crises possible, 381-3
Overproduction of commodities and overabundance of capital, 373-5
Reproduction of capital curtailed when the market price of commodities falls below their price of production, 370
Tendency for the demand for Labour to increase absolutely but decline relatively as capitalism develops, 368
Critique of Political Economy, 108, note 1, 116, note 1, 172, note 1
Expansion of production and expansion of the market:
Overproduction of commodities leads to a search for new markets, 402-7
Production expands firstly because the capital invested in production is constantly growing and secondly because it is constantly used more productively, 402
General and partial overproduction:
Possibility of a general glut of commodities insisted upon, 392
Poverty of Philosophy, 112
Productive labour:
Independent handicraftsmen who employ no workers are neither productive nor unproductive, 191
Labour transforms its own social productive powers into the productive powers of capital, 179
Labour which produces use-values only is not productive, 186-7
Money is the means by which the capitalist appropriates surplus value, 179-85
Only labour which is directly transformed into capital is productive, 178
The productive forces of labour affect only the use-value of a commodity, 178
Surplus value:
Absolute and relative surplus value, 311
Rate of surplus value, 309, 311

MASSIE, JOHN
An Essay on the governing causes of the natural rate of interest, etc., 34, 36-8, 38, 38-9
Interest merely a part of profit, 34

Rate of interest determined by the rate of profit, 34

MILL, JAMES
Metaphysical equation of purchases and sales, 381, 392

MILL, JOHN STUART
Explanation of crises, 379

MIRABEAU THE ELDER
Deceived by the semblance of feudalism given by the Physiocrats to bourgeois society, 50
Surplus value in the form of interest on money regarded as usury, 47

NORTH, SIR DUDLEY
Conception of capital, 26, 32
Conception of interest, 31
Conception of price and money, 31
Discourses upon Trade, 26, 29, 30-2
High rate of interest caused by shortage of capital, 26

PETTY, SIR WILLIAM
Differential rent, 21-2
Distinction between natural and political price, 15
Political anatomy of Ireland, 16, note 1, 23, note 1, 26
Political Arithmetick, 20-1, 21-2, 22
Quantulumcunque concerning money, 26
Rent and interest as alternative forms of surplus value, 17
Surplus value, 15-20, 22
Treatise of Taxes and Contributions, 15, 16, 16-17, 17, 17-18, 18, 18-19, 20, 23, 26
Value of commodities determined by the comparative quantity of labour they contain, 15
Value of labour determined by the necessary means of subsistence, 16

PHYSIOCRATIC SYSTEM, THE (see also under Quesnay and Turgot)
Laissez-faire, laissez-allez, 53
Minimum level of wages the pivotal point of Physiocratic doctrine, 45
Productive and unproductive labour, Influence of the Physiocrats on Smith's theories of this, 159, 160, 167, 171
Produit net, 55

PHYSIOCRATIC SYSTEM, THE—(cont.)
Surplus value:
Agricultural labour alone can create surplus value, 46, 47, 55, 62
Land rent regarded as surplus value to the second power, 48
Only labour which produces surplus value is productive, 46
Origin of surplus value transformed from the sphere of circulation into the sphere of direct production, 45, 50
Surplus value dependent on the productivity of labour, 49
Taxes to be levied entirely on landed property 53

QUESNAY, FRANÇOIS
Analyse du Tableau Economique, 58
Divides nation into three classes of citizens, 58
Maximes Generales, 63
Supports absolute monarchy, 54
Tableau Economique, 67-104

RICARDO, DAVID
Accumulation of capital:
Accumulation of capital leads to a fall in the rate of profit which in turn tends to check accumulation, 422
Accumulation of capital occurs either through a rise in the rate of profit, or through an increase in the productive powers of labour, 417-18
Capital accumulates when revenue is consumed by productive workers. Marx's comments on this, 343
Capital of a country is increased when production exceeds consumption and vice versa, Marx's criticism of this, 415
Denounced by Carey as the father of communism, 204
Labour Theory of Value:
Confusion in his use of the term relative value, 208-9
Definition of exchange value, 208
Differences in value due to the different periods of turnover of the circulating capital employed, 215-17
Differences in value due to the employment of fixed capital of different degrees of durability, 212, 215-17
Differences in value due to the incorporation in the commodities of fixed capital in different proportions, 211, 215-17
Differences in value due to the relative

time during which a commodity remains within the labour process as a whole, 217
Effect of rises and falls in the value of labour on the value of commodities, 218-19
Failure to examine the type or character of labour, 201
Quantity of labour contained in the production of a commodity is not the same thing as the value of that labour, 296-7
Value of constant capital also included in value of a commodity, 211
Value of labour determined by the means of subsistence necessary for the maintenance and reproduction of the labourers, 301
Overproduction and Crises:
Denies the necessity for an expansion of the market, 403
Explanation of the crises of 1800 and 1815, 374
Failure to grasp the significance of the separation in the process of purchase and sale as the condition which makes crises possible, 376-81
General overproduction of commodities is not possible, 369, 373, 391-2, 393
Prices of Production and Market Prices:
Effect of changes in the values of commodities on the prices of production, 258
Existence of a general rate of profit for each sphere of production, 249
Products of the same sphere of production sell at one and the same market price, 249
Rate of Profit:
Formation of the general rate of profit, 336-42
Rate of profit contrasted with rate of surplus value, 329
Surplus Value:
Confusion of surplus value with profit, 283
Effect on the rate of profit of changes in the method of production, changes in the proportion of constant and variable capital and changes in the value of the elements which form the constant and variable capital, 290-2
Failure to consider absolute surplus value or changes in value due to changes in the length of the working day, 314

RICARDO, DAVID: Surplus Value—(*cont.*)
Failure to consider surplus value independently of the special forms it assumes, 283
Theory of Profit:
Confusion between average prices of production and value of commodities, 212-13, 224, 236-41
Effect of rises in wages on profits and prices, Contrast with Smith's views, 241
Value of Labour:
Identified with the value of the labourer's necessary means of subsistence, 295, 306,

RIVIERE, MERCIER DE LA
Ordre naturel et essentiel des sociétés politiques, 54, 56, 63

SAY, JEAN-BAPTISTE
Condensed political economy into a text-book, 202
Criticism of Ricardo, 203
Value of labour determined by supply and demand, 300, 302

SMITH, ADAM
Capital and landed property as sources of value, Smith's confusion over this, 134-9
Conception of the average wage, 107
Confusion between labour as a detriment and labour as a measure of value, 108, 115
Confusion between living and materialised labour, 114
Debt to the Physiocrats, 108
Labour Theory of value, 107-16, 117
Price divided into wages, profit and rent, 140-7
Prices of Production and Market prices:
Connection between rate of profit and rate of interest, 273
Distinguishes between natural price and market price, 264
Identification of prices of production with exchange value or natural price, 262
Wages, are determined by the value of the necessary means of subsistence, 267
Wages, profit and rent are the three sources of exchange value, 260
Productive and unproductive labour:
Criticisms of Smith's views on productive and unproductive labour, 175-7

Mercantilist views on productive and unproductive labour; Comparison with Smith's views, 173-4
Productive labour is labour which produces capital, 148, 152
Productive labour is labour which produces tangible commodities. Confusion between this and Smith's other theory of productive labour, 158-9, 169-71, 174-5
The Physiocrats and their influence on Smith's concepts of productive and unproductive labour, 159, 160, 167, 171
Unproductive labour is labour which is exchanged against revenue, 153
Surplus value:
Confusion of surplus value with profit, 129-33
His advance on the Physiocrats, 124-6
How it arises in capitalist production, 119
Surplus value in the form of land rent, 121-2
Surplus value in the form of interest on capital, 122-4,
Taxes are derived ultimately from some form of surplus value, 124

STEUART, SIR JAMES
Distinction between positive and relative profit, 40
Principles of Political Economy, 40, 41, 41-2, 43
Price divided into the real value of the commodity and the profit upon alienation, 41
Profit regarded as a vibration of the balance of wealth between the parties, 41

STORCH, HEINRICH, FREIDRICH VON
Cours d'economie politique, 192, note 1

TURGOT, ANNE ROBERT JACQUES
Justifies surplus value in the form of interest on money, 47
Reflexions sur la Formation et la Distribution des Richesses, 43, 58-9, 59, 60-1, 61, 62, 64, 65, 65-6
Surplus value:
Realised in circulation, 59
A pure gift of nature, 59-60

WAKEFIELD, EDWARD GIBBON
Edition of Smith's *Wealth of Nations,* 1836, 300